Authors
& Artists
for Young
Adults

ISSN 1040-5682

Authors & Artists for Young Adults

VOLUME 76

 GALE
CENGAGE Learning

Detroit • New York • San Francisco • New Haven, Conn • Waterville, Maine • London

Authors and Artists for Young Adults, Volume 76

Project Editor: Robert James Russell

Editorial: Dana Ferguson, Amy Fuller, Michelle Kazensky, Lisa Kumar, Jennifer Mossman, Joseph Palmisano, Mary Ruby, Amanda Sams, Marie Toft

Rights and Permissions: Mollika Basu, Barb McNeil, Tracie Richardson, Robyn Young

Imaging and Multimedia: Lezlie Light

Composition and Electronic Capture: Amy Darga

Manufacturing: Cynde Bishop

For product information and technology assistance, contact us at
Gale Customer Support, 1-800-877-4253.
For permission to use material from this text or product,
submit all requests online at **www.cengage.com/permissions.**
Further permissions questions can be emailed to
permissionrequest@cengage.com

While every effort has been made to ensure the reliability of the information presented in this publication, Gale, a part of Cengage Learning, does not guarantee the accuracy of the data contained herein. Gale accepts no payment for listing; and inclusion in the publication of any organization, agency, institution, publication, service, or individual does not imply endorsement of the editors or publisher. Errors brought to the attention of the publisher and verified to the satisfaction of the publisher will be corrected in future editions.

EDITORIAL DATA PRIVACY POLICY. Does this product contain information about you as an individual? If so, for more information about our editorial data privacy policies, please see our Privacy Statement at www.gale.cengage.com.

Gale
27500 Drake Rd.
Farmington Hills, MI, 48331-3535

LIBRARY OF CONGRESS CATALOG CARD NUMBER 89-641100

ISBN-13: 978-0-7876-7795-4
ISBN-10: 0-7876-7795-7

ISSN 1040-5682

Printed in the United States of America
1 2 3 4 5 6 7 12 11 10 09 08

Contents

Introduction

Authors and Artists for Young Adults is a reference series designed to serve the needs of middle school, junior high, and high school students interested in creative artists. Originally inspired by the need to bridge the gap between Gale's *Something about the Author,* created for children, and *Contemporary Authors,* intended for older students and adults, *Authors and Artists for Young Adults* has been expanded to cover not only an international scope of authors, but also a wide variety of other artists.

Although the emphasis of the series remains on the writer for young adults, we recognize that these readers have diverse interests covering a wide range of reading levels. The series therefore contains not only those creative artists who are of high interest to young adults, including cartoonists, photographers, music composers, bestselling authors of adult novels, media directors, producers, and performers, but also literary and artistic figures studied in academic curricula, such as influential novelists, playwrights, poets, and painters. The goal of *Authors and Artists for Young Adults* is to present this great diversity of creative artists in a format that is entertaining, informative, and understandable to the young adult reader.

Entry Format

Each volume of *Authors and Artists for Young Adults* will furnish in-depth coverage of approximately twenty-five authors and artists. The typical entry consists of:

—A detailed biographical section that includes date of birth, marriage, children, education, and addresses.

—A comprehensive bibliography or filmography including publishers, producers, and years.

—Adaptations into other media forms.

—Works in progress.

—A distinctive essay featuring comments on an artist's life, career, artistic intentions, world views, and controversies.

—References for further reading.

—Extensive illustrations, photographs, movie stills, cartoons, book covers, and other relevant visual material.

A cumulative index to featured authors and artists appears in each volume.

Compilation Methods

The editors of *Authors and Artists for Young Adults* make every effort to secure information directly from the authors and artists through personal correspondence and interviews. Sketches on living authors and artists are sent to the biographee for review prior to publication. Any sketches not personally reviewed by biographees or their representatives are marked with an asterisk (*).

Highlights of Forthcoming Volumes

Among the authors and artists planned for future volumes are:

Algernon Blackwood	Paul Hornschemeier	Richard Serra
George Catlin	Elmer Kelton	Charles Simic
Thomas Cole	M. Alice Legrow	Jordan Sonnenblick
Joan Druett	Anita Loos	Wendy Corsi Staub
Ed Greenwood	Brian MacKay-Lyons	Laurie Faria Stolarz
D.W. Griffith	Paul Manship	Louis Comfort Tiffany
Zbigniew Herbert	Steven Pressfield	

Contact the Editor

We encourage our readers to examine the entire *AAYA* series. Please write and tell us if we can make *AAYA* even more helpful to you. Give your comments and suggestions to the editor:

BY MAIL: The Editor, *Authors and Artists for Young Adults*, 27500 Drake Rd., Farmington Hills, MI 48331-3535.

BY TELEPHONE: 1-800-877-4253

Authors and Artists for Young Adults
Product Advisory Boardc

The editors of *Authors and Artists for Young Adults* are dedicated to maintaining a high standard of excellence by publishing comprehensive, accurate, and highly readable entries on writers, artists, and filmmakers of interest to middle and high school students. In addition to the quality of the entries, the editors take pride in the graphic design of the series, which is intended to be orderly yet appealing, allowing readers to utilize the pages of *AAYA* easily, enjoyably, and with efficiency. Despite the success of the *AAYA* print series, we are mindful that the vitality of a literary reference product is dependent on its ability to serve its readers over time. As critical attitudes about literature, art, and media constantly evolve, so do the reference needs of students and teachers. To be certain that we continue to keep pace with the expectations of our readers, the editors of *AAYA* listen carefully to their comments regarding the value, utility, and quality of the series. Librarians, who have firsthand knowledge of the needs of library users, are a valuable resource for us. The *Authors and Artists for Young Adults* Product Advisory Board, made up of school, public, and academic librarians, is a forum to promote focused feedback about *AAYA* on a regular basis, as well as to help steer our coverage of new authors and artists. The advisory board includes the following individuals, whom the editors wish to thank for sharing their expertise:

- **Eva M. Davis,** Youth Department Manager, Ann Arbor District Library, Ann Arbor, Michigan

- **Joan B. Eisenberg,** Lower School Librarian, Milton Academy, Milton, Massachusetts

- **Susan Dove Lempke,** Children's Services Supervisor, Niles Public Library District, Niles, Illinois

- **Robyn Lupa,** Head of Children's Services, Jefferson County Public Library, Lakewood, Colorado

- **Caryn Sipos,** Community Librarian, Three Creeks Community Library, Vancouver, Washington

- **Stephen Weiner,** Director, Maynard Public Library, Maynard, Massachusetts

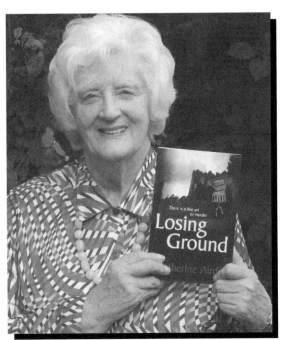

(Photograph by Anita Clarke. Reproduced by permission.)

Catherine Aird

■ Personal

Birth name K.H. McIntosh; born June 20, 1930, in Huddersfield, Yorkshire, England; daughter of Robert Aeneas Cameron (a physician) and V.J. McIntosh. *Education:* Attended Waverley School and Greenhead High School in Huddersfield, England.

■ Addresses

Home—Canterbury, Kent, England. *Agent*—Aitken and Stone Ltd., 29 Fernshaw Rd., London SW10 0TG, England.

■ Career

Writer. Former chair, Sturry Parish Council.

■ Member

Girl Guides Association (chair of finance committee), Crime Writers Association (chair, 1990-91).

■ Awards, Honors

A Most Contagious Game was selected by Anthony Boucher as one of the thirteen outstanding mystery novels of 1967; honorary M.A., University of Kent at Canterbury, 1985; made Member of British Empire, 1988.

■ Writings

"INSPECTOR SLOAN" MYSTERY NOVELS

The Religious Body, Doubleday (New York, NY), 1966.
Henrietta Who?, Doubleday (New York, NY), 1968.
A Late Phoenix, Doubleday (New York, NY), 1971.
His Burial Too, Doubleday (New York, NY), 1973.
Slight Mourning, Collins (London, England), 1975, Doubleday (New York, NY), 1976.
Parting Breath, Doubleday (New York, NY), 1977.
Some Die Eloquent, Doubleday (New York, NY), 1979.
Passing Strange, Doubleday (New York, NY), 1980.
Last Respects, Doubleday (New York, NY), 1982.
Harm's Way, Doubleday (New York, NY), 1984.
A Dead Liberty, Collins (London, England), 1986, Doubleday (New York, NY), 1987.
The Body Politic, Doubleday (New York, NY), 1990.
A Going Concern, Macmillan (London, England), 1993, St. Martin's (New York, NY), 1994.
After Effects, Macmillan (London, England), 1996.

Stiff News, St. Martin's (New York, NY), 1998.

Little Knell, St. Martin's (New York, NY), 2001.

Amendment of Life, St. Martin's (New York, NY), 2003.

A Hole in One, St. Martin's (New York, NY), 2005.

Losing Ground, Alison & Busby (London, England), 2007, St. Martin's (New York, NY), 2008.

OTHER

A Most Contagious Game, Doubleday (New York, NY), 1967, reprinted, Rue Morgue Press (Lyons, CO), 2007.

The Complete Steel, MacDonald & Co. (London, England), 1969, published as *The Stately Home Murder,* Doubleday (New York, NY), 1970.

The Story of Sturry (play), produced in Sturry, 1973.

The Catherine Aird Collection, Pan (London, England), 1993.

The Second Catherine Aird Collection, Pan (London, England), 1994.

Injury Time (story collection), St. Martin's (New York, NY), 1995.

The Third Catherine Aird Collection, Pan (London, England), 1997.

Chapter and Hearse and Other Mysteries, St. Martin's (New York, NY), 2004.

EDITOR; AS K.H. MCINTOSH

Sturry—The Changing Scene, 1972.

Fordwich—The Lost Port, 1975.

Chislet and Westbere, Villages of the Stour Lathe, 1979.

The Six Preachers of Canterbury Cathedral, 1982.

Hoath and Hern, The Last of the Forest, 1984.

In Good Faith, 1995.

■ Adaptations

Henrietta Who? was adapted for film in the Netherlands.

■ Sidelights

K.H. McIntosh, writing under the pseudonym Catherine Aird, has been grouped "among the more civilized practitioners of fictional homicide" by *Washington Post Book World* critic Jean M. White. A *Publishers Weekly* critic noted that, "like Agatha Christie, Aird . . . specializes in classic puzzles with ingenious, yet logical, surprise endings." Best known for her series of mystery novels featuring Inspector C.D. Sloan, nicknamed "Seedy" by his associates, Aird has chronicled the good inspector's investigations in the fictional English county of Calleshire for over forty years. Although Sloan's jurisdiction may seem rural and quiet, there are plenty of murders, usually involving an incident from the past that stirs present-day violence. Pearl G. Aldrich in the *St. James Guide to Crime and Mystery Writers* called Aird a master at writing "the leisurely, kinder, gentler crime novel." "Aird's contemporary British cozies," wrote GraceAnne A. DeCandido in *Booklist,* "display excellent, engaging dialogue as well as plots handled with deft, nononsense trajectory." Writing in the *Armchair Detective,* Martin H. Friedenthal stated: "All of Aird's books are delightful. She writes in an urbane, witty, civilized style, poking gentle, and often hilarious, fun at her characters, situations, and the particular mystery genre with which she is working."

A Medical Background

Aird was born in 1930 in Huddersfield, Yorkshire, England. Her father was a medical doctor and Aird once served as the manager of her father's medical practice. She attended Waverley School and Greenhead High School in Huddersfield, England. Her first mystery novel, *The Religious Body,* was published in 1966. It tells of a nun who is murdered at a convent in a small English town. Inspector Sloan, unfamiliar with the lives of nuns, must quickly learn about the ways of a nunnery. Soon, he must also learn the ways of agricultural institute students when one of them is found murdered as well, apparently by the same killer. The *Times Literary Supplement* critic believed Sloan displayed "the right stuff" in this debut novel. Anthony Boucher in the *New York Times Book Review* found that "Aird writes about a nunnery and its infinitely diverse nuns with far more insight and skill than the various mystery novelists . . . who have previously attempted it."

Sloan and his companions on the police force have formed the core characters in the continuing series. Aldrich explained: "The series' four continuing characters are Inspector C.D. Sloan; Superintendent Leeyes, his stupid, lazy, irascible boss; Detective Constable William Crosby, known throughout the force as the 'Defective Constable'; and Dr. Dabbe, the pathologist with a grim sense of humor." Superintendent Leeyes is devoted to taking Adult Education classes in order to improve himself. During the course of the series he takes classes in Norman History, French Literature, Eastern Philosophies

This 1967 mystery tells of the discovery of a centuries-old skeleton and its unexpected connection to a present-day murder. (Rue Morgue Press, 2007. Photograph by Tom Schantz. Reproduced by permission.)

for Inquiring Minds, Mathematics for the Average Adult, and a host of others. Whatever Leeyes half-learns in these classes appears in his police work, no matter how inappropriate, and much to the annoyance of Sloan. In *The Religious Body*, Sloan noted: "Superintendent Leeyes had started going to an Adult Education Class on Logic this autumn and it was playing havoc with his powers of reasoning." Sloan himself is a patient man who suffers fools with a bemused, polite manner. His wry comments about his colleagues are rarely meant to offend. Aird told Dale Salwak in *Clues: A Journal of Detection* that she conceived Inspector Sloan as "somebody a little bit sarcastic but not destructively so, just enough to keep the edge of authority over his subordinates. . . . I sort of try to see him as the ordinary man who has had his neck breathed on a bit from above, is a bit disappointed by the chap underneath him. But I see him as filling sort of a

symbolic role, a working policeman against all sorts of odds." Marv Lachman, writing in *Mystery News*, commented: "Throughout the series, Sloan proves to be a most likable character. . . . He is a conservative family man and wears a tie at all times, except when he is pursuing his hobby of gardening." A critic for *Publishers Weekly* described him: "Sloan is the kind of down-to-earth detective who makes you glad you aren't a criminal: gently persistent and full of wry observations, no superman but all the more believable because of that."

Sloan Investigates

Sloan next appeared in *Henrietta Who?* In this novel, he must discover just who the young girl Henrietta Jenkins is. A post-mortem examination of Henrietta's widowed mother proves that she never bore a child, causing Henrietta to question her true identity. But Sloan is more concerned with who killed Henrietta's supposed mother and why. A critic for the *Times Literary Supplement* called the novel "a nice puzzle and a nicely built tale." In *A Late Phoenix*, Sloan must identify a skeleton uncovered in a bombed-out building left over from World War II. M.K. Grant in the *Library Journal* called *A Late Phoenix* "another effective combination of past and present danger and strange traces of violence in a quiet English country town." In 1969's *His Burial Too*, a man is murdered in a church tower, and Inspector Sloan cannot understand how the killer escaped from the barricaded murder scene. In *Slight Mourning*, the death of a local man in what seems to be a routine car crash leads to a tangled mystery involving heirs who may or may not be murderers. Writing in the *Times Literary Supplement*, T.J. Binyon concluded that it was "a story for the connoisseur of the good old-fashioned detective novel."

Last Respects begins with a body found floating in a river near the village of Edsway. At first thought to be a drowning victim, the man was actually killed by falling from a great height. Sloan and Crosby's investigation soon leads them to the discovery of a sunken ship offshore and a possible murder by poisoning. Binyon found that this latest Sloan installment "maintains the usual high standard: carefully and originally plotted, it is also elegantly and amusingly written." In *The Body Politic*, Sloan investigates a murder during an historical reenactment. Alan Ottershaw is an English mining engineer working in the Sheikdom of Lassera. After he is involved in a fatal traffic accident, he flees the country. Unless he is returned from England to face trial, the country of Lassera will nationalize all British holdings, cutting off the supply of the rare mineral, queremite. But while taking part in a reenactment of the Battle of Lewes, Ottershaw falls dead. When Ottershaw is cremated, a hollow pellet made of queremite is discovered. Sloan must determine whether Ottershaw was murdered and, if so, prove it. Patricia Craig of the *Times Literary Supplement* concluded that "Aird is as mannered and clever a detective writer as Margery Allingham, and keeps us reading."

In the 1994 novel *A Going Concern,* elderly Octavia Garamond has died. Her will calls for police to be present at her funeral and that a doctor examine her body very carefully. Sole heir to Octavia's fortune is her Shakespeare-quoting grand-niece Amelia Kennerly, who knows nothing about her aunt's strange requests. But when a rare poison is found to be the cause of Octavia's death, Amelia remembers that her aunt conducted Army research work into chemical warfare during World War II. Sloan's investigation uncovers a link to two chemical companies, as well as a child born out of wedlock in 1940. Stuart Miller in *Booklist* found *A Going Concern* to be "a thoroughly entertaining mystery for those who like their procedurals on the lighthearted side." A critic for *Publishers Weekly* called it "intricate, witty and thoroughly delightful."

Sloan returns in *After Effects* as he investigates what seems to be a routine death at a local hospital. Mrs. Galloway died after a long illness. The doctors find nothing unusual about it. But her son, who is not satisfied with the quality of the care his mother received, asks the police to investigate it as a possible homicide. Soon the surprising suicide of Galloway's doctor and a tip from an anonymous informer convince Sloan that perhaps the death was not due to natural causes at all. Miller found *After Effects* to be "another humorous variation on the British police procedural delivered with the author's usual panache."

Stiff News finds Sloan investigating a local retirement home where a murderer may be on the loose. Almstone Manor is a fine old Tudor mansion that years ago was converted into a regimental rest home. One resident, Gertrude Powell, passes away, leaving behind a letter addressed to her son. In the letter, she claims that someone was trying to kill her. When Inspector Sloan is called to look into the matter, he uncovers a tangle of relationships among the nursing home's residents stretching back to their service together during World War II. Emily Melton in *Booklist* called *Stiff News* "a slow-paced, literate, witty, entertaining tale best suited for dedicated fans of the genre's intellectual, soft-boiled side." A reviewer for *Crime Buff* found that "the story is wry, sometimes humorous, witty, entertaining, full of

character and characters." Writing in the *Boston Herald,* Rosemary Herbert claimed that Aird "knows by heart the prescription for the classic English mystery: Mix untimely death with quirky characterization, quick wit and a goodly measure of wry wisdom."

A Surprise Mummy

Little Knell begins when a local museum is bequeathed a collection of valuable ancient Egyptian artifacts. But museum officials are stunned to learn that a 3,000-year-old sarcophagus contains, instead of the expected mummy, the relatively fresh corpse of a young woman accountant named Jill Carter. As Sloan and Crosby investigate, Jill's murder seems connected to a heroin-smuggling ring that uses fishing boats and a nearby nature reserve to bring in their drugs. "With methodical plotting and a few off the cuff, odd observances from Crosby," wrote Jennifer Monahan Winberry in the *Mystery Reader,* "Sloan is able to track down all the players and their motives, neatly connecting all the dots and tying up loose ends." Jenny McLarin in *Booklist* concluded: "For those who like quiet British procedurals, with the emphasis more on wit and sly turns of phrase than on mean streets, Aird's series is sure to please." A reviewer for *Crime Buff* dubbed the novel "a wry, entertaining British cosy."

In *Amendment of Life,* a dead body is found in a hedge maze on the grounds of Aumerle Court, a Tudor mansion presided over by its elderly chatelaine, Daphne Pedlinge. Sloan finds that the dead woman has a sickly child at the local hospital and was expected to have been at his bedside. Harriet Klausner, writing in *Best Reviews,* called *Amendment of Life* a "pleasurable tale that the audience will enjoy even as identifying the killer is as difficult to achieve as completing the maze that contained the deceased."

Aird tries her hand at a golf mystery in the 2005 novel *A Hole in One.* A novice golfer at the Berebury Golf Club in Calleshire follows her wayward ball into a sand trap. Repeated strokes to dislodge her golf ball only serves to dig a hole in the sand, in which she finds a partially buried corpse. Inspector Sloan is called in and soon finds that rival golf club members have been arguing over development of the club's property. With the questionable help of Constable Crosby, Sloan eventually sorts it out. Writing in *Booklist,* Bill Ott noted that "Sloan's asides to himself provide a running satirical commentary on the foibles of the private-club set." Sharon Katz, reviewing the novel for *Reviewing the*

Evidence, called it "a fun read filled with humor, slapstick, and great likeable characters." Writing for *Best Reviews,* Klausner concluded: "Aird's latest Sloan story is a fine entry in a strong series."

In addition to the many Sloan novels, Aird has also published *A Most Contagious Game,* the story of retired businessman Thomas Harding, who buys a country estate. When he finds a skeleton in a hidden room, the local police are not interested. The death must have happened centuries before and they have the murder of a local young woman to investigate. Harding decides to uncover the murderer himself by researching the history of the family that owned the estate before him. His efforts lead him to suspect a connection with the present-day murder. *A Most Contagious Game,* wrote Bridget Bolton in *Reviewing the Evidence,* "is a wonderful read." Sally Powers, reviewing the book for the *I Love a Mystery Newsletter,* found that "although strictly speaking this isn't a 'Golden Age' mystery (a term generally applied to books written between 1913 and 1953), the fact that there are no cell phones and no computers; the fact that Thomas Harding goes to the public library and the newspaper morgue to do his research in person; combined with the English village ambience, including the local constable arriving to investigate on his bicycle, and the gentile manner of the piece, all create a very Golden Age feel. HIGHLY RECOMMENDED."

If you enjoy the works of Catherine Aird, you may also want to check out the following books:

Josephine Tey, *Miss Pym Disposes,* 1998.
Ngaio Marsh, *Night at the Vulcan,* 1998.
Dorothy Simpson, *Dead and Gone,* 2001.

A Humorous Mystery

Aird broke from her usual serious approach to crime with the humorous *The Stately Home Murder.* In this novel, the murder of a wealthy lord's archivist, who has apparently discovered embarrassing information about the lord's ancestry, sets into motion this parody of the traditional British country manor mystery. The *Best Sellers* critic, while acknowledging the book' value as a spoof, found that "it can stand on its own merits as an entertainingly worked out mystery." Aldrich called *The Stately Home Murder* "an opera bouffe, complete with dotty aunts and cousins, three generations of a titled family, including a son born on the wrong side of the blanket— all, in effect, singing fortissimo. It's very funny, particularly the identity of the villain, and a tour de force." According to Tom and Enid Schantz in an article posted at the *Rue Morgue Press* Web site, *The Stately Home Murder* is "easily the funniest book in Aird's output."

Aird told Salwak that in her novels, she is "trying to postulate the age-old theory between right and wrong. Describing wrong and hoping that right is going to triumph. I think this is one of the reasons that I enjoy . . . detective fiction. It's very clear-cut. . . . With fiction anyway, you can always have good winning. I don't think it happens in real life by any means, but it's rather nice to be able to have it happen in fiction."

■ Biographical and Critical Sources

BOOKS

Mystery Voices: Interviews with British Crime Writers Catherine Aird, P.D.James, H.R.F.Keating, Ruth Rendell and Julian Symons, Borgo Press, 1991.
St. James Guide to Crime and Mystery Writers, 4th edition, St. James Press (Detroit, MI), 1996.

PERIODICALS

Armchair Detective, spring, 1986, review of *Harm's Way,* p. 196; spring, 1987, Martin H. Friedenthal, "The Calleshire Chronicles," pp. 138-145; winter, 1988, p. 61; winter, 1988, review of *A Dead Liberty,* p. 61; spring, 1992, p. 236; winter, 1997, review of *After Effects,* p. 105.
Best Sellers, December 1, 1966, review of *The Religious Body,* p. 26; November 1, 1967, review of *A Most Contagious Game,* p. 310; August 1, 1968, review of *Henrietta Who?,* p. 185; January 15, 1970, p. 29.
Booklist, January 1, 1987, review of *A Dead Liberty,* p. 685; August, 1994, Stuart Miller, review of *A Going Concern,* p. 2025; August, 1996, Stuart Miller, review of *After Effects,* p. 1884; December 1, 1998, Emily Melton, review of *Stiff News,* p. 652; February 15, 2001, Jenny McLarin, review of *Little Knell,* p. 1118; January 1, 2003, GraceAnne A. DeCandido, review of *Amendment of Life,* p. 854; January 1, 2004, Emily Melton, review of *Chapter and Hearse and Other Mysteries,* p. 829; July, 2005, Bill Ott, review of *A Hole in One,* p. 1903.

Books & Bookman, April, 1968, review of *Henrietta Who?*, p. 38.

Boston Herald, January 17, 1999, Rosemary Herbert, review of *Stiff News*, p. 51; February 28, 2003, Rosemary Herbert, review of *Amendment of Life*, p. 43.

British Medical Journal, October 19, 1996, Sarah Creighton, review of *After Effects*, p. 1020.

Clues: A Journal of Detection, spring/summer, 1984, Dale Salwak, "An Interview with Catherine Aird," pp. 73-90.

Kirkus Reviews, October 1, 1966, review of *The Religious Body*, p. 1071; August 15, 1967, review of *A Most Contagious Game*, p. 993; April 15, 1968, review of *Henrietta Who?*, p. 485; July 15, 1996, review of *After Effects*, p. 1009; January 1, 2003, review of *Amendment of Life*, p. 27.

Library Journal, February 1, 1967, review of *The Religious Body*, p. 599; October 1, 1967, review of *A Most Contagious Game*, p. 3450; June 1, 1968, review of *Henrietta Who?*, p. 2263; January 1, 1971, p. 96; February 1, 1981, Robin W. Winks, review of *Passing Strange*, p. 372; July, 1995, Rex E. Klett, review of *Injury Time*, p. 127; August, 1996, Rex E. Klett, review of *After Effects*, p. 118; April 1, 2001, Rex E. Klett, review of *Little Knell*, p. 137; February 1, 2003, review of *Amendment of Life*, p. 122; January, 2004, Rex E. Klett, review of *Chapter and Hearse and Other Mysteries*, p. 164; August 1, 2005, Rex E. Klett, review of *A Hole in One*, p. 59.

Los Angeles Times, February 27, 1981.

Mystery News, April-May, 2006, Marv Lachman, "Out of the Past: Catherine Aird," p. 3.

New Yorker, November 25, 1967, review of *A Most Contagious Game*, p. 247; April 4, 1970, p. 46.

New York Times Book Review, January 1, 1967, review of *The Religious Body*, p. 19; November 19, 1967, p. 78; December 1, 1968, review of *Henrietta Who?*, p. 46; February 1, 1970, p. 49; February 28, 1971, p. 33; December 17, 1978, review of *Parting Breath*, p. 29; March 28, 1982, review of *Passing Strange*, p. 35.

Observer (London, England), May 15, 1966, review of *The Religious Body*, p. 26; November 4, 1984, review of *Harm's Way*, p. 26.

Publishers Weekly, August 28, 1967, review of *A Most Contagious Game*, p. 276; April 22, 1968, review of *Henrietta Who?*, p. 51; May 8, 1978, review of *Part-ing Breath*, p. 71; February 8, 1980, review of *Some Die Eloquent*, p. 68; October 19, 1984, review of *Harm's Way*, p. 31; December 19, 1986, review of *A Dead Liberty*, p. 48; July 11, 1994, review of *A Going Concern*, p. 66; July 31, 1995, review of *Injury Time*, p. 72; December 7, 1998, review of *Stiff News*, p. 55; February 19, 2001, review of *Little Knell*, p. 72.

Saturday Review, July 27, 1968, review of *Henrietta Who?*, p. 34.

Times Literary Supplement, June 2, 1966, review of *The Religious Body*, p. 497; June 29, 1967, p. 583; April 11, 1968, review of *Henrietta Who?*, p. 380; November 6, 1970, review of *A Late Phoenix*, p. 1306; December 26, 1975, T.J. Binyon, review of *Slight Mourning*, p. 1544; October 29, 1982, T.J. Binyon, review of *Last Respects*, p. 1196; November 16, 1984, T.J. Binyon, review of *Harm's Way*, p. 1301; September 19, 1986, p. 1029; June 1, 1990, Patricia Craig, review of *The Body Politic*, p. 593.

Washington Post Book World, March 15, 1981.

ONLINE

Best Reviews, http://thebestreviews.com/ (December 14, 2002), Harriet Klausner, review of *Amendment of Life*; (July 15, 2005) Harriet Klausner, review of *A Hole in One*.

Catherine Aird Home Page, http://www.catherineaird.com (November 19, 2007).

Crime Buff, http://www.crimebuff.com/ (June 8, 2007), reviews of *Little Knell* and *Stiff News*.

I Love a Mystery Newsletter, http://www.iloveamysterynewsletter.com/ (May 1, 2007), Sally Powers, review of *A Most Contagious Game*.

Mystery Reader, http://www.themysteryreader.com/ (May 3, 2007), Jennifer Monahan Winberry, review of *Little Knell*.

Reviewing the Evidence, http://www.reviewingtheevidence.com/ (March, 2004), Mary A. Axford, review of *Chapter and Hearse and Other Mysteries*; (August, 2005), Sharon Katz, review of *A Hole in One*; (March, 2007), Bridget Bolton, review of *A Most Contagious Game*.

Rue Morgue Press, http://www.ruemorguepress.com/ (January, 2007), Tom and Enid Schantz, "Catherine Aird."*

(Photograph by Arthur B. Alphin. Reproduced by permission of the author.)

■ Personal

Born October 30, 1955, in San Francisco, CA; daughter of Richard E. (a United Nations procurement officer) and Janice (a collections agency executive) Bonilla; married Arthur B. Alphin (a retired army officer and president and CEO of two companies), May 9, 1982. *Education:* Rice University, B.A., 1977. *Hobbies and other interests:* Puzzles, dinosaurs, theater, needlework, collecting teddy bears and other stuffed animals, raising hamsters, gardening.

■ Addresses

Home—Madison, IN. *Agent*—Gloria R. Mosesson, 290 West End Ave., New York, NY 10023. *E-mail*—ElaineMAlphin@aol.com.

■ Career

Rice Thresher, Houston, TX, writer and department editor, 1974-76; *Houston* (magazine), Houston, TX, feature editor and writer, 1978-79; freelance writer,

Elaine Marie Alphin

1978—; A-Square Company, Cornwall-on-Hudson, NY, Madison, IN, and Bedford, KY, advertising manager and technical service, 1982-93; Hieroglyphics Unlimited, Madison, IN, and Bedford, KY, owner and cross-stitch designer, 1986—; Institute of Children's Literature, West Redding, CT, instructor, 1992—. Speaker at conferences, workshop, and schools.

■ Member

Authors Guild, Society of Children's Book Writers and Illustrators (Indiana chapter conference codirector, 1991-93), Association of American University Women, Central Indiana Writer's Association, Children's Reading Round Table of Chicago, Bloomington Children's Authors Group, Psi Iota Xi Philanthropic Sorority (corresponding secretary, 1992-93).

■ Awards, Honors

Thomas J. Watson research fellowship to study medieval history in Great Britain and Italy for *Tournament of Time,* 1977-78; works-in-progress grant, Society of Children's Book Writers and Illustrators, 1989, for *The Ghost Cadet;* Magazine Merit Award (fiction), Society of Children's Book Writers and Illustrators, 1989, for "A Song in the Dark"; honorable mention, Byline Children's Nonfiction, 1992, for "Balto Runs a Relay Race for Life"; *The Proving Ground* was a "Recommended Book for Reluctant Readers," American Library Association, 1993; Society of Children's Book Writers and Illustrators Magazine Merit Award (nonfiction category), for "Cornflower's Test," 1994; Virginia State Reading Association Young Readers Award for Best Book (elementary), 1995, for *A Bear for Miguel*, which was also included in the Consortium of Latin American Studies Programs Commended List, 1996; New Jersey Garden State Award nominee, 1999-2000, for *A Bear for Miguel*; Indianapolis Christian University International Washington Irving Literary Award for Outstanding Lifetime Achievement in Writing, 2000; *St. Louis Post Dispatch* Best Children's Books of 2000, Edgar Allan Poe Award for Best Young Adult Mystery, Mystery Writers of America, 2001, YALSA Quick Pick for Reluctant Young Adult Readers, 2001, and a nomination to the American Library Association Best Books for Young Adults List, 2002, all for *Counterfeit Son*.

■ **Writings**

The Ghost Cadet, Henry Holt (New York, NY), 1991.

The Proving Ground, Henry Holt (New York, NY), 1992.

101 Bible Puzzles, Standard, 1993.

Tournament of Time, Bluegrass Books, 1994.

Rainy Day/Sunny Day/Any Day Activities, Concordia (St. Louis, MO), 1994.

A Bear for Miguel, pictures by Joan Sandin, Harper-Collins (New York, NY), 1996.

Counterfeit Son, Harcourt (San Diego, CA), 2000.

Creating Characters Kids Will Love, Writer's Digest Books (Cincinnati, OH), 2000.

Ghost Soldier, Henry Holt (New York, NY), 2001.

Around the World in 1500, Benchmark Books (New York, NY), 2001.

Simon Says, Harcourt (San Diego, CA), 2002.

Germ Hunter: A Story about Louis Pasteur, Carolrhoda Books (Minneapolis, MN), 2002.

Picture Perfect, Carolrhoda Books (Minneapolis, MN), 2003.

Davy Crockett, Lerner (Minneapolis, MN), 2003.

(With husband, Arthur B. Alphin) *Dwight D. Eisenhower*, Lerner (Minneapolis, MN), 2004.

Dinosaur Hunter, HarperCollins (New York, NY), 2004.

The Perfect Shot, Carolrhoda Books (Minneapolis, MN), 2005.

Contributor of stories to anthologies, including, "Mystery of the Gobi Desert," in *The Favorites*, Institute of Children's Literature, 1991, and "A Song in the Dark" and "Beetle Bones," in *Success Stories*, Institute of Children's Literature, 1994; contributor of articles to anthologies, including "Ten Steps to That First Book Sale" in *Writer's Digest Children's Writers & Illustrator's Market*, Writer's Digest, 1992, and "Profiles: New Faces Make the Sale" in *Children's Magazine Market*, Institute of Children's Literature, 1993; contributor of stories and articles to periodicals, including *Cricket*, *Highlights for Children*, *Children's Digest*, *Child Life*, *Hopscotch*, *On the Line*, *Teen Quest*, and *Primary Treasure*; columnist for the newsletter *Children's Writer*, 1993—.

"HOUSEHOLD HISTORY" SERIES

Vacuum Cleaners, Carolrhoda Books (Minneapolis, MN), 1997.

Irons, Carolrhoda Books (Minneapolis, MN), 1998.

Toasters, Carolrhoda Books (Minneapolis, MN), 1998.

Telephones, Carolrhoda Books (Minneapolis, MN), 2000.

"POWER READING" SERIES

Power Reading Power Pak 3-A, National Reading Styles Insititue (Syosset, NY), 2001.

Power Reading Power Pak 6-A, National Reading Styles Insititue (Syosset, NY), 2001.

Power Reading Power Pak 6-A, National Reading Styles Insititue (Syosset, NY), 2002.

Power Reading Power Pak 2-C, National Reading Styles Insititue (Syosset, NY), 2002.

Power Reading Power Pak 6-B, National Reading Styles Insititue (Syosset, NY), 2002.

■ **Sidelights**

An award-winning author of several young adult novels, Elaine Marie Alphin focuses on young characters who overcome difficulties to take control of their own lives. Along the way, they learn the value of friendship and the need for honesty. Alphin once explained: "My novels deal with serious realities that young people face and overcome by the power of their imagination. There is often danger, and my heroes must find the courage and conviction to put themselves on the line for what they believe."

Alphin was born in San Francisco, California, in 1955. When she was in junior high school, her family moved to New York City, where her father served as a procurement officer for the United Nations. The family later moved to Houston, Texas, where Alphin attended Westchester High School. Alphin wanted to write since childhood. She explained on her Web site: "I started making up stories when I was very small, even before I could write them down. I always dreamed of writing my stories and seeing my books on library shelves one day, where everyone could read them."

Alphin was inspired to write by her father. She told *Authors and Artists for Young Adults* (*AAYA*): "I was an only child whose mother liked to sleep late whenever she could, so on the weekend my dad and I would get up early and go out for walks where I could make noise without waking Mom up. While we walked, Dad would tell me stories—I loved his stories, and I wanted to make up stories that were as good as his. So while he went to work during the week, I worked on making up stories, which I would proudly tell him during our weekend morning walks. I decided right then that I wanted to spend my life making up stories. I couldn't write yet, but I already knew I wanted to be a writer. I was three at the time, and I never wavered."

"I started my teen years in New York City at William H. Carr Junior High School," Alphin told *AAYA*, "and then moved to Houston, Texas and went to Westchester Senior High School. In both cities I was very active in the Drama Clubs, and in Houston I joined the International Thespian Society. I enjoyed acting, but I wasn't that great at it. What I was good at was being a director—guiding other actors in bringing stories to life on the stage. I think I saw it as an extension of writing, which was guiding characters to bring stories to life on the page. I was writing all this time—I worked on my schools' literary magazines and newspapers, and I wrote for my own pleasure. My projects were short stories and poetry while I lived in New York, but after I moved to Houston the short story ideas got larger until one of them grew to a novella and my next one was a full length novel. One of my high school teachers, Mr. Reveley, was a wonderful mentor. He taught physics and calculus, but still took the time to read my stories and encourage me. I wasn't writing all the time, of course. In addition to my thespian hobby I played basketball—an interest that paid off when I wrote *The Perfect Shot*, about a high school basketball player who becomes embroiled in a murder mystery." After graduating from Rice University in 1977, Alphin worked as a journalist and advertising manager for several years. She is currently the owner of Hieroglyphics Unlimited, for which she also designs cross-stitches.

Elaine Marie Alphin working at her computer. (Photograph by Arthur B. Alphin. From a jacket of her *Counterfeit Son*. Harcourt, 2000. Reproduced by permission of the author.)

A Ghostly Friendship

Alphin's first novel, *The Ghost Cadet*, exemplifies the author's concern with justice as well as another abiding interest—history. In this story of a young boy named Benjy, who helps the ghost of a Virginia Institute cadet restore his honor by finding a watch, Alphin combines the virtues of friendship and justice with the background of Virginia during the U.S. Civil War to create a "fine novel," noted David Haward Bain in the *New York Times*. Molly Kinney, writing in the *School Library Journal*, said that in this story of "friendship, trust, caring and self-discovery," Alphin has skillfully combined "fact, fiction, and emotion."

Alphin's next novel, *The Proving Ground*, features Kevin Spencer, the fourteen-year-old son of a military officer, who moves into the small town of Hadley where his father will be heading up an army testing facility. Due to the nature of Lieutenant-Commander Spencer's job, Kevin has changed schools frequently and often feels like an outsider. The same is true in Hadley. To make matters worse, local townspeople are resentful of the army's insensitivity in taking over farms in order to make room for the test facility, and this hostility spills over to Kevin as well, who is singled out as an "army brat." As he struggles to deal with the particularly rough treatment meted out to him by a girl named Charley and uncovers a plot that will sabotage the base, Kevin discovers that Hadley has provided him with an opportunity to test his own convictions. A reviewer for *Publishers Weekly* found *The Proving Ground* "a suspenseful, true-to-life coming-of-age story." Jack Forman of the *School Library Journal* praised Alphin for providing a "deft mixture of adventure, a romantic undercurrent, local politics, and development of character," all of which combine to create a "briskly paced, involving story."

Geared towards a younger set of readers, *A Bear for Miguel* nonetheless tells a "sensitive and compelling" tale, enthused Gale W. Sherman in the *School Library Journal.* Unfolding a straightforward narrative that tells the story of Maria's sacrifice to help her family, the tale is set against the backdrop of war-torn El Salvador. The story is told from Maria's perspective, as she helps her father trade the family's possessions, including her own stuffed bear, in order to buy some bare necessities. Maeve Visser Knoth, writing in *Horn Book,* remarked that although the details of war-torn El Salvador are "grim," they do not overpower the compassion with which Alphin tells the story.

Alphin's next novel, *Counterfeit Son,* was characterized as a "psychological thriller" by Miranda Doyle in the *School Library Journal.* Earning Alphin the Edgar Allan Poe Award of the Mystery Writers Association, this novel focuses on fourteen-year-old Cameron Miller as he struggles to find a place for himself in the world. Cameron is the son of a serial killer who preyed on young boys. After years of abuse and neglect suffered at the hands of his father, Cameron assumes the identity of one of his father's victims, Neil Lacey, and begins living with the Lacey family. He lives in fear of being discovered, though, and eventually someone from Cameron's past does threaten his existence with his adopted family, forcing Cameron to decide whether he wants to tell the Lacey family the truth. In addition to the moving interactions between Cameron and the Lacey family, Doyle also praised *Counterfeit Son* as a "solidly written, fast-paced read." *Booklist* contributor Todd Morning declared that "Alphin has done a creditable job" of depicting the psychology of a boy who had suffered horrible abuse and of his desire to find a safe, secure family. Similarly, a reviewer for *Publishers Weekly* lauded it as a "gripping novel," one that will leave readers "enthralled by [the] suspenseful plot."

Civil War Ghost Story

In 2001, Alphin issued *Ghost Soldier,* a story that combines the supernatural with elements of history and the military to tell the story of Alex Raskin and a young ghost from the Civil War. Alex has always been able to sense and hear spirits. His mother, who left him and his computer programmer father a few years ago, told him that he was special and therefore could communicate with people from the past. These sentiments are little consolation to Alex, however, as he travels with his father from Indiana to North Carolina to visit Paige Humbrick, his father's girlfriend. During a visit to an old Civil War battleground, Alex encounters the ghost of Richeson Francis Chamblee who wants help in tracing his family's history following the war. Alphin "provides an interesting lesson on how historical research occurs," *Booklist* critic Denise Wilms stated. According to Starr E. Smith in the *School Library Journal, Ghost Soldier* is "an entertaining blend of paranormal, historical, and family themes, with a well-crafted plot."

In this 2000 Edgar Award-winning thriller, the abused Cameron must take on a new identity to escape his tormented life. (Harcourt, Inc., 2000. Copyright © 2002 by Elaine Marie Alphin. Reproduced by permission of Harcourt, Inc. This material may not be reproduced in any form or by any means without the written permission of the publisher)

Alphin's young adult novel *Simon Says* grew out of one of the four books she wrote as a teenager at Rice University. The story concerns sixteen-year-old artist Charles Weston, who faces the challenge of living up to the expectations of others, or defying them and paying the cost of nonconformity. Charles sees life as a dangerous game of "Simon Says" in which he always loses. He wants nothing more than to stop playing and show his paintings to his family, to the friends he wishes he had, and to a wider audience. He transfers to a boarding school for the fine arts, desperately hoping that Graeme Brandt, another student, can show him how to escape the game. But Graeme and the other students prove to be master players themselves, and the final game of "Simon Says" that Charles is drawn into has high stakes and terrible consequences. "It is easy to relate to the loneliness and isolation Charles feels, and his desire to be accepted on his own terms," wrote Lyn Seippel in *Book Loons*. Similarly, Vicki Reutter in the *School Library Journal* found that readers "will relate to the disconnected characters who feel painfully alone and will be encouraged by the acceptance of their uniqueness." Jessica Swaim, reviewing the title for *Kliatt*, called *Simon Says* an "unusual and compelling novel."

In *Picture Perfect*, Ian Slater lives with his controlling father, who works as the school principal. To escape from home life, Ian takes to the woods where he and his friend Teddy Camden pursue their hobby of photography. Ian also drifts into a foggy mental state in which the outside world becomes a blur and the pain he feels subsides. When Teddy disappears, the police suspect that Ian may be responsible. He was in his withdrawn state and cannot remember what he was doing that day. His father's role in Teddy's disappearance brings Ian to an emotional and psychological awakening. "This psychological thriller," Debbie Carton admitted in *Booklist*, "has many twists and turns." The critic for *Publishers Weekly* called the novel "a compelling journey of self-discovery and self-protection." A *Kirkus Reviews* critic called the story "disturbing, engrossing, and thought-provoking."

Taking Responsibility for Justice

Alphin explores a violent tragedy in the novel *The Perfect Shot*. Brian Hammett's girlfriend, Amanda, her little brother, and her mother have been shot dead. Her father has been arrested for the murders, but Brian cannot believe he could do such a thing. Brian also feels guilty that he was out playing basketball when the tragedy occurred, trying to develop the perfect shot. A class lesson about the Leo Frank murder case in 1913, in which Frank was

This 2001 novel tells of Alexander, a teenaged boy who makes friends with the ghost of a Civil War soldier. (Henry Holt, 2001. Jacket illustration copyright © 2001 by Bob Crofut. Reprinted by permission of Henry Holt and Company, LLC.)

wrongfully accused, leads Brian to wonder about who committed the murders and whether he should speak up about a stranger he saw near Amanda's house that terrible day. The critic for *Publishers Weekly* noted that "the author explores themes of justice and an individual's civic and personal responsibility to see that justice is carried out." The *Kirkus Reviews* critic found: "With basketball action, a murder mystery, a compelling story from history, adolescent angst, racial and parental tension, Alphin offers something to please most young readers." Miranda Doyle in *Booklist* called *The Perfect Shot* an "engrossing thriller."

Alphin once explained that writing is not hard work. "For me, writing is a joy," she explained to *AAYA*. "The hardest part is the business of marketing the finished book! But before that becomes an issue, I love the planning and researching and the writing and the revision. Some writers worry about facing that blank page, but I love seeing a blank, inviting computer screen or sheet of paper, waiting for me to fill it up with ideas and characters." How does she create her characters? "I start by getting ideas from things I observe, things I've experienced, things that stick in my head and bother me. Then I try to work out how someone could find himself in that situation and what he might try to do to resolve the problem. I spend a great deal of time getting to know that main character, and the other characters around him, to develop what his strengths and weaknesses are and what he hopes for and what he fears, so I can see what he wants to try to do and why. Then I complicate the situation by introducing obstacles that will make him work harder to achieve his goal. These obstacles should test the main character, forcing him to prove himself, and discover who he is, inside. As he discovers this, I discover it, and that revelation becomes the heart of the book. While I'm getting to know my characters and develop the book, I make notes in plotting notebooks that I carry around with me, because ideas often strike when I'm somewhere outside my office. I also rely on a corkboard to organize the plot elements as they come into focus, using 'The Hero's Journey' to help pace the story, and using different color notecards to keep track of the different threads running through the book. Once I'm ready to start writing, I write the book in sequence, starting at page one and going on until I reach the end. Writing that first draft is definitely the most exciting part of the process as a whole, but I do love every step from the excitement of being struck by the idea through exploring what the characters will do to writing the first draft and even working through the revision process. It's all work, but when you love your work, it's a delight."

Speaking of her typical work day, Alphin noted: "I grew out of being a morning person over the years, so I don't start writing at five or six AM, as so many authors do. I usually try to wake up by watching some news, and then get to work on my Mac. I usually start the day with busy work like correspondence, or Web site updates, or going over what I wrote the day before. I like to read through what I wrote most recently to ease myself back into the world of the book, then I continue writing from where I left off. When I'm deeply engaged in the first draft of a novel, I often write late into the night, frequently until two or three AM. When I'm revising (which I normally do three or four times before sending to my editor, and then several more times as we ready the book for publication), I usually skip the busy work and plunge right into the job. But I don't work quite as late on revision as I do on the first draft, because writing the first draft is like being swept along on a roller coaster ride, and revising is tinkering with the track and the roller coaster carts to make sure it all runs as smoothly as possible. You can more easily get up from the tinkering and return to it later than you can get off the roller coaster as it rockets along.

"If I'm in the planning stages of a new book, as opposed to the writing stage, I usually spend the day doing a combination of research and working on plot and character development. All of my books, even my fiction, require a great deal of research because they're either influenced by real events (*Ghost Cadet* and *Ghost Soldier* involve real Civil War battles, for example, and *The Perfect Shot* uses a real murder case in 1913 Atlanta as its catalyst to unravel a contemporary mystery) or require specialized knowledge (*Counterfeit Son* required a lot of research into serial killers, and *Picture Perfect* required research into personality disorders and emotional abuse). I try to research the topics that will provide the background for the book in as much detail as I plan the fictional action of the book, so that once I'm ready to plunge into the writing I can enjoy the roller coaster ride without finding myself caught up short by a research question."

If you enjoy the works of Elaine Marie Alphin, you may also want to check out the following books:

Ann Rinaldi, *Amelia's War*, 2002.
Nancy Werlin, *The Rules of Survival*, 2006.
John Coy, *Crackback*, 2007.

In her free time, Alphin enjoys a number of activities: "When I have evenings or weekends free (when I'm not in the midst of a first draft), I like to read or watch DVDs or football in the fall, or go out to the theatre or a movie with my husband, of just have an adventure. Last weekend a restored B-17 was in town and we explored it and went on a flight. I like doing jigsaw puzzles. I live near a small lake, and I like watching the water, and looking at the ducks and geese and herons. I also like feeding the squirrels and chipmunks. I like traveling. I've lived in California, New York, Texas, Indiana, Montana, and even in England for a year. I like playing computer games on my Mac almost as much as writing stories on it, and I like playing on my Wii. I also like to read. I read kids' books and adult books, both fiction and nonfiction. I enjoy reading biographies, and I like history. I also like to read mysteries and scary books and realistic adventure stories."

Alphin also gets out and meets her readers: "I speak at schools, and at libraries and Young Author Conferences. I try to share with readers my love of writing, and let them see how they can come up with their own ideas and characters the same way I do. I advise them to read lots of different kinds of books, and think about what they like about each one, and also what they don't like. I advise them to write every day, whether it's writing a story or a poem, or writing in a journal or writing a blog. Most of all, I advise them to never give up. While I was growing up, teachers and even my parents advised me to write as a hobby, but to get a real job to support myself. But I loved writing so much that I didn't want to do it on the side, with only the energy left over after I worked at that 'real job.' In fact, that conflict inspired me to write the first draft of *Simon Says* while I was in college (even though it didn't get published until 2002). I think that adults too often discourage teenagers from holding onto their dreams, usually because the adults want to protect their students or sons and daughters from the realities of the world. But I feel that young people see the realities of the world and still, in spite of those realities, have dreams they want to follow. I encourage readers to follow their dreams and to work as hard as it takes to achieve them, no matter what any well-meaning adult tells them. That is what I did, and I've never regretted it."

■ Biographical and Critical Sources

PERIODICALS

Booklist, November 15, 1992, Janice Del Negro, review of *The Proving Ground*, p. 589; March 15, 1995, Carolyn Phelan, review of *Tournament of Time*, p. 1327; August, 1996, Carolyn Phelan, review of *A Bear for Miguel*, p. 1910; January 1, 1998, Denia Hester, review of *Vacuum Cleaners*, p. 796; September 15, 2000, Todd Morning, review of *Counterfeit Son*, p. 231; August, 2001, Denise Wilms, review of *Ghost Soldier*, p. 2118; August, 2003, Debbie Carton, review of *Picture Perfect*, p. 1970; September 1, 2003, Carolyn Phelan, review of *Dinosaur Hunter*, p. 127.

Horn Book Guide, spring, 1993, p. 79; spring, 1998, Barbara Barstow, review of *Vacuum Cleaners*, p. 138; fall, 1998, Barbara Bader, review of *Irons*, p. 391.

Horn Book Magazine, May-June, 1996, Maeve Visser Knoth, review of *A Bear for Miguel*, p. 331; January-February, 2004, Martha V. Parravano, review of *Dinosaur Hunter*, p. 78.

Kirkus Reviews, November 15, 1992, p. 1437; November, 1, 1997, review of *Vacuum Cleaners*, p. 1640; April 15, 1998, review of *Toasters*, p. 576; July 1, 2003, review of *Picture Perfect*, p. 905; September 1, 2003, review of *Dinosaur Hunter*, p. 1119; August 15, 2005, review of *The Perfect Shot*, p. 907.

Kliatt, September, 2005, Jessica Swaim, review of *Simon Says*, p. 17; November, 2005, Janis Flint-Ferguson, review of *The Perfect Shot*, p. 4; January, 2007, Stephanie Squicciarini, review of *Picture Perfect*, p. 20.

New York Times, May 19, 1991, David Haward Bain, review of *The Ghost Cadet*, p. 31.

Publishers Weekly, May 17, 1991, review of *The Ghost Cadet*, p. 64; November 16, 1992, review of *The Proving Ground*, p. 65; August 28, 2000, review of *Counterfeit Son*, p. 84; May 20, 2002, review of *Simon Says*, p. 68; August 4, 2003, review of *Picture Perfect*, p. 81; November 7, 2005, review of *The Perfect Shot*, p. 75.

School Library Journal, May, 1991, Molly Kinney, review of *The Ghost Cadet*, p. 91; January, 1993, Jack Forman, review of *The Proving Ground*, p. 96; June, 1996, Gale W. Sherman, review of *A Bear for Miguel*, p. 92; July, 1998, Stephanie Hutchinson, review of *Toasters and Irons*, p. 101; December, 2000, Miranda Doyle, review of *Counterfeit Son*, p. 138; August, 2001, Starr E. Smith, review of *Ghost Soldier*, p. 175; June, 2002, Vicki Reutter, review of *Simon Says*, p. 130; December, 2002, Anne Chapman Callaghan, review of *Davy Crockett*, p. 114; July, 2003, Donna Cardon, review of *Germ Hunter: A Story about Louis Pasteur*, p. 136; October, 2003, Lynn Evarts, review of *Picture Perfect*, p. 158; December, 2003, Anne Knickerbocker, review of *Dinosaur Hunter*, p. 102; January, 2005, Christine E. Carr, review of *Dwight D. Eisenhower*, p. 101; October, 2005, Miranda Doyle, review of *The Perfect Shot*, p. 150.

Voice Literary Supplement, February, 1993.

ONLINE

Book Loons, http://www.bookloons.com/ (March 27, 2007), Lyn Seippel, review of *Simon Says*.

Elaine Marie Alphin Web site, http://www.elainemariealphin.com (November 17, 2007).

John James Audubon

(Courtesy of Archive Photos/Getty Images.)

■ Personal

Born April 26, 1785, in Les Cayes, Haiti; died January 27, 1851, in New York, NY; buried in Trinity Cemetery in New York, NY; son of Jean Audubon (a French naval officer) and Jeanne Rabin; married Lucy Bakewell, April, 1807; children: Lucy, Rose, Victor Gifford, John Woodhouse.

■ Career

Artist, naturalist.

■ Writings

ORNITHOLOGICAL WORKS

The Birds of America, from Original Drawings, 4 volumes, privately printed, 1827–38, published as *The Birds of America, from Drawings Made in the United States and Their Territories,* 7 volumes, J.J. Audubon (New York, NY), 1840–44.

Ornithological Biography; or, An Account of the Habits of the Birds of the United States of America: Accompanied by Descriptions of the Objects Represented in the Work Entitled The Birds of America, and Interspersed with Delineations of American Scenery and Manners, 5 volumes, Dobson (Philadelphia, PA), 1831–39.

(With John Bachman) *The Viviparous Quadrupeds of North America,* 3 volumes, J.J. Audubon (New York, NY), 1845–54, published as *The Quadrupeds of North America,* 3 volumes, V.G. Audubon (New York, NY), 1849–54.

The Bird Biographies of John James Audubon, edited by Alice Ford, Macmillan (New York, NY), 1957.

John James Audubon: The Watercolors for "The Birds of America," edited by Annette Blaugrund and Theodore E. Stebbins, Jr., Villard (New York, NY), 1993.

JOURNALS AND CORRESPONDENCE

Audubon and His Journals, edited by Maria Audubon, 2 volumes, Scribner (New York, NY), 1897.

Audubon's Western Journal: 1849-1850, Arthur H. Clark (Cleveland, OH), 1906.

Journal of John James Audubon Made During His Trip to New Orleans in 1820-1821, edited by Howard Corning, Club of Odd Volumes (Boston, MA), 1929.

Journal of John James Audubon Made While Obtaining Subscriptions to His Birds of America, 1840-1843, edited by Howard Corning, Club of Odd Volumes (Boston, MA), 1929.

Letters of John James Audubon, 1826-1840, 2 volumes, edited by Howard Corning, Club of Odd Volumes (Boston, MA), 1930.

The 1826 Journal of John James Audubon, edited by Alice Ford, University of Oklahoma Press (Norman, OK), 1967.

Selected Journals and Other Writings, edited by Ben Forkner, Penguin (New York, NY), 1996.

OTHER

Delineations of American Scenery and Character, edited and with an introduction by Francis Hobart Herrick, Baker (New York, NY), 1926.

Audubon, by Himself, edited by Alice Ford, Harry N. Abrams (New York, NY), 1969.

My Style of Drawing Birds, Overland Press (Austin, TX), 1979.

Writings and Drawings, The Library of America (New York, NY), 1999.

The Audubon Reader, edited by Richard Rhodes, Everyman's Library, 2006.

Audubon's drawings have been issued in many editions. Many of his letters and manuscripts are housed at the American Museum of Natural History, New York City; the American Philosophical Society, Philadelphia; Audubon Memorial Museum, Henderson, Kentucky; Houghton Library, Harvard University, Cambridge, Massachusetts; National Audubon Society, New York City; Princeton University Library, Princeton; and Yale University Library, New Haven.

■ **Sidelights**

A gifted artist with a love of nature and a passion for discovery, John James Audubon was the greatest painter of birds of his time, an explorer, an important naturalist, and one of the forerunners of the contemporary environmental movement. "Audubon's reputation," according to Arthur Wrobel in the *Dictionary of Literary Biography,* "rests almost exclusively on his achievement as the artist of the monumental *The Birds of America, from Original Drawings* (1827-1838); his sharply detailed, anatomically accurate, and dramatically conceived representations of North American birds won him unqualified admiration and revolutionized all subsequent ornithological art." The artistic quality of *The Birds of America* surpassed that of its predecessors, and the work has not been equaled since in its scale, scope, and aesthetic appeal. Although he occasionally painted with oils, Audubon achieved his best effects using watercolors with an overlay of pastels

Audubon during a hunting trip on the American frontier. (Copyright © Bettmann/CORBIS.)

to enhance color and sharpen detail. Richard Rhodes, in his book *John James Audubon: The Making of an American,* argued: "Besides his art, which is as electrifying on first turning the pages of *The Birds of America* today as it was two centuries ago—no one has ever drawn birds better—Audubon left behind a large collection of letters, five written volumes, two complete surviving journals, fragments of two more, and a name that has become synonymous with wilderness and wildlife preservation."

Audubon was born in Les Cayes, Haiti, on April 26, 1785, the illegitimate son of Jean Audubon, a French naval officer, and Jeanne Rabin, a French servant girl from Brittany. His father had made a fortune as a planter, merchant, and slave dealer. After his mother's death, and a rebellion in Haiti, Audubon's father took him and a younger half sister to France, where he legally adopted his children in 1794. In school, Audubon early revealed his talents for drawing and music. He learned to play the violin and flute and by age fifteen had begun drawing birds and collecting birds' eggs. But Audubon chose to neglect most of his school studies. His stepmother, Anne Moynet, indulged him. "My father being mostly absent on duty," he once explained, "my mother suffered me to do much as I pleased; it was therefore not to be wondered at that, instead of applying closely to my studies, I preferred associating with boys of my own age and disposition, who were more fond of going in search of birds' nests, fishing, or shooting, than of better studies. Thus almost every day, instead of going to school when I ought to have gone, I usually made for the fields, where I spent the day; my little basket went with me, filled with good eatables, and when I returned home, during either winter or summer, it was replenished with what I called curiosities, such as birds' nests, birds' eggs, curious lichens, flowers of all sorts, and even pebbles gathered along the shore of some rivulet." It was during this time that Audubon first began to keep meticulous field notes of his observations.

Sent to America

In 1803, fearing that his son would be conscripted into Napoleon's army, the elder Audubon sent John James to Mill Grove, his farm near Valley Forge, Pennsylvania. At Mill Grove, Audubon lived the life of a country gentleman—fishing, shooting, and developing his skill at drawing birds. Eager to learn more of the movements and habits of the local birds, he tied bits of colored string onto the legs of several Eastern Phoebes and so proved that these birds returned to the same nesting sites the following year. He was the first to use banding, as it is now called, to track the migration patterns of birds. He also developed the technique of inserting wires into the bodies of freshly killed birds in order to manipulate them into natural positions for his sketching. In April of 1807, following a four-year engagement, Audubon married Lucy Bakewell, a girl of English descent who lived on a neighboring estate. The two spent much of their courtship in nearby caves, where Audubon enjoyed watching the birds who nested there. Of their four children, two sons—Victor Gifford and John Woodhouse—survived to adulthood and provided significant help to their father in his painting and publishing projects.

Soon after his marriage, Audubon and his wife headed for the American frontier. "Almost overnight, Audubon changed his silks for leather hunting clothes and let his hair grow down to his shoulders," according to Lewis Mumford in the *New York Review of Books*. He formed a partnership with Ferdinand Rozier, an older Frenchman whom his father had sent to look after him. They became frontier merchants, with stores in Kentucky, first in Louisville, then in Henderson, and finally in Ste. Genevieve, Missouri. Audubon was not cut out for the life of a businessman. Wrobel commented: "Differences in temperament, however, led to the dis-

solution of the partnership with Rozier in April 1811; Rozier's discipline and focus on business conflicted with Audubon's passion for natural history. In later years Audubon confessed in an autobiographical sketch entitled 'Myself' that studying, hunting, and drawing birds provided welcome relief from the irksome responsibilities of business." In a later journal entry, Audubon related: "Were I to tell you that once when travelling and driving several horses before me, laden with goods and dollars, I lost sight of the packsaddles and the cash they bore, to watch the motions of a warbler, I should only repeat occurrences which happened a hundred times and more in those days." Audubon entered into an ill-fated trade arrangement with his brother-in-law, Thomas Bakewell. In 1813, Audubon and a group of associates built a combination sawmill and gristmill in Henderson, Kentucky. In 1819 this enterprise failed and Audubon was plunged into bankruptcy, left with only the clothes he wore, his gun, and his drawings. This disaster ended his business career. After being imprisoned for debt, Audubon worked as a taxidermist for the Western Museum in Cincinnati. He earned additional income by doing crayon portraits for five dollars each. In 1820, he set out for New Orleans to continue work as an artist, but, more important, to add to his portfolio of bird paintings. His wife worked as a tutor to support the family, and the two endured many months apart before she joined him in Louisiana. When she joined him, Lucy obtained a position as a governess and later opened a school for girls. Thereafter she was the family's main support while Audubon tried to have his drawings published.

For Audubon, an avocation developed into a vocation, though it is not known precisely when the change occurred. In 1810, while he and Rozier were in their Louisville store, Alexander Wilson, the pioneer American ornithologist, showed them his

The 1836 painting "Roseate Spoonbill" by Audubon.
(Copyright © Bettmann/CORBIS.)

bird paintings and sought a subscription to support publication of his nine-volume *American Ornithology.* After seeing Wilson's work, Rozier remarked that his partner's paintings were better. By allowing Audubon to realize that his amateur work surpassed the work of a professional, this incident probably served as a catalyst to his fertile imagination.

An Ambitious Plan

Audubon gradually developed the idea for *The Birds of America,* an ambitious portfolio of all American species, life-size, in their natural habitats. In its scope, scale, and fidelity to nature, Audubon's work would eclipse that of his predecessors. In order to include all the known species, he would rely upon the discoveries and observations of others for some of his paintings, not limiting the work to his own observations as Wilson had done. By the time he

Audubon's painting "Golden Eagle." (Courtesy of The Library of Congress.)

left for New Orleans in late 1820, the outlines of the work, which would require almost two decades to complete, were formed.

In Audubon's time, a naturalist needed to collect specimens (usually by shooting), to record his observations in a journal, and to sketch or paint all that he found interesting. To collect specimens, he shot thousands of birds on his expeditions. "Audubon killed thousands of birds; before photography and high-resolution binoculars, that was the only possible way to render accurate images of them," explained Paul Gray in *Time.* "But before Audubon shot them, he watched his subjects intensively, noting how they moved and behaved, the plants or habitats they preferred. When he had his bird in hand, he used wires to arrange the specimen in a characteristic pose." Audubon, according to a writer for the *Wilson Quarterly,* "changed forever the way in which birds are illustrated. Before him, noted illustrators such as Alexander Wilson (1766-1813) used stuffed birds as models and produced accurate but stiff and static images." The collecting did not stop with birds: Audubon also gathered insects, reptiles, and mammals for many other scientists throughout the world. In his lengthy journals, often romantic and even grandiloquent in tone, he made detailed notes about bird sightings and behavior.

After his efforts to interest New York and Philadelphia publishers in his work failed, Audubon embarked in 1826 for England, where he was assured he would find a greater interest in his subject. He arrived at Liverpool in 1826, then moved on to Edinburgh and to London, being favorably received and obtaining wealthy subscribers for his volumes in each city. He was widely regarded as a natural untaught genius and became something of a celebrity, being named a fellow of the Royal Society. For *The Birds of America,* he sought two hundred subscribers willing to pay one thousand dollars each; he eventually obtained 161, about half of them from the United States. Subscribers paid for a set of five prints at a time, with eighty sets, or four hundred prints, projected.

The publication, requiring eleven years, began in 1827, in Edinburgh, under the engraver William Lizars. Audubon quickly changed to Robert Havell and Company in London, after Havell impressed the painter with his ability to reproduce color tones. The images were etched on copper plates using aquatint, producing shades of gray and black on a light background. They were engraved on sheets measuring thirty-nine and a half by twenty-six and a half inches, forming the Double Elephant Folio, one of the largest books ever printed. After the engraving, artists colored the prints professionally by hand to match Audubon's original paintings.

The painting "American Flamingo" by Audubon. (Copyright © Academy of Natural Sciences of Philadelphia/CORBIS.)

Completes His Masterwork

When completed, the work included life-size color prints of 489 species on 435 pages. The total number of bird paintings was 1,065, for Audubon attempted to illustrate different color phases of each species, and for birds of varied coloration he often produced several poses to reveal the colors more effectively. One of his own favorite paintings, that of the wood duck, includes four birds so positioned as to reveal the rich coloration of the species. His painting of the little blue heron shows a full-size adult in the foreground and, at a distance, standing in a marsh, the white immature representative of the species. One measure of the work's enduring importance occurred in 2000, when a complete set of the original Double Elephant Folio was sold at auction for $8.8 million.

After completing *The Birds of America*, Audubon issued the work in a smaller and less expensive edition. This version of the book sold very well, earning the Audubons a considerable sum of money. In 1841, they bought fourteen acres of land in New York along the Hudson River. They named the estate Minnie's Land, Minnie being an affectionate

Scottish term for "mother." The Audubon sons built houses next door to Minnie's Land.

In 1830, Audubon began writing *Ornithological Biography; or, An Account of the Habits of the Birds of the United States of America: Accompanied by Descriptions of the Objects Represented in the Work Entitled The Birds of America, and Interspersed with Delineations of American Scenery and Manners*. This five-volume work was to contain not only detailed information about bird species in America, but also personal stories of Audubon's adventures. Wrobel explained that Audubon "decided to imprint these writings as distinctively his by interspersing technical, ornithological material with more-personal material, namely anecdotes, reminiscences, and tales he had accumulated during a lifetime of pursuing new bird species from Florida to the lagoons of the Texas coast. These 'Episodes' or 'Delineations of American Scenery and Manners,' sixty in number, were to entertain and, more pragmatically, to enhance sales by tapping into the European fascination with the New World. The self-image he portrays in the 'Delineations,' that of the natural man responsive to instinct as he pursues a vision, appealed to the romantic imaginations of mid-nineteenth-century readers." Among the stories recounted by Audubon are his encounter with a runaway slave, his experience of an earthquake, his meeting with Daniel Boone, and his participation in a coon hunt. Other stories revolve around the customs and traditions of American frontier life, little known in the rest of America or in Europe. Whether all of these stories are literally true is still a matter of debate. At least some of them seem to be tall tales, common among frontiersmen of the time.

Audubon then turned to a new project, this time concerning North American mammals, *The Viviparous Quadrupeds of North America*, in collaboration with his friend, North Carolina minister and mammalogist John Bachman. Seeking specimens to paint, he organized his last great expedition in 1843, traveling up the Missouri River to the mouth of the Yellowstone in North Dakota. While the purpose of the journey was to gather information to use in the proposed book, it "also fulfilled Audubon's lifelong dream of seeing the western territories," Wrobel stated. "He carried with him letters of introduction from the political establishment in Washington, DC, which had also authorized his party to requisition any needed supplies. They set out in March 1843 from St. Louis aboard a steamer belonging to the American Fur Company in the company of buffalo hunters, whom Audubon described as 'the dirtiest of the dirty.' The journal of this expedition, subsequently known as the Missouri Journal, follows Audubon's party of five into Indian Territory to Fort Union, what is now North Dakota, near the confluence of the Missouri and Yellowstone Rivers, and back to St. Louis." The three-volume text by Bachman appeared between 1846 and 1854. Text and pictures were combined in later editions. Audubon's eyesight began to fail in 1846, and by the next year he had become senile. His sons completed the paintings, and with Bachman's help brought the project to a conclusion.

After age sixty, Audubon suffered a rapid decline in health, marked by a loss of mental powers. He died quietly at his New York home, Minnie's Land, on January 27, 1851, leaving completion of his work on the mammals to his sons and to Bachman. He is buried under a monument erected in his memory by the New York Academy of Sciences. In 1863 Lucy Audubon sold the original drawings for *The Birds of America* to the New York Historical Society for $2,000.

In ornithology, art, and conservation, Audubon's fame and influence have endured. During his time, taxonomy was in its early stages, and science developed largely through observation and compilation. Vast areas of the world lay unexplored and unstudied. To discover new species of flora or fauna was an obvious route to achievement, possibly even to fame. Never a theorist and little inclined toward experimentation, Audubon possessed intense curiosity about nature, keen eyes, and a questing, somewhat romantic nature. He discovered a dozen subspecies, more than twenty species, and one genus of American birds. According to Francis Hobart Herrick, in his introduction to *Delineations of American Scenery and Character:* "Beyond a doubt, John James Audubon was one of the most versatile and striking characters that has ever appeared in our history. In ardor and enthusiasm for the study of nature perhaps no one has ever surpassed him, and no one can measure the influence which his talents and devotion have exerted."

If you enjoy the artwork of John James Audubon, you may also want to check out the following:

The natural sculptural works of Andy Goldsworthy; the photography of Ansel Adams; and the nature paintings of Thomas Aquinas Daly.

The 1828 painting "California Vulture" by Audubon.
(Copyright © Geoffrey Clements/CORBIS.)

The name Audubon has become synonymous with the conservation of wildlife and, as Paul Gray noted in *Time*, "Audubon's bird illustrations have become part of the experience of living in America." Today, Audubon ranks among the leading figures in the history of environmentalism. Mumford maintained: "Audubon is one of the central actors in the conservation movement. He not merely demonstrated the richness of primeval America, but preserved as much of it as possible in lasting images of its flowers, shrubs, insects, butterflies, as well as birds and mammals. . . . If we manage to protect any part of the primeval habitat from the bulldozers, the highway engineers, the real estate speculators, and the National Parks bureaucrats, . . . it will be because Audubon stands in the way, reminding us that this birthright must not be exchanged for money or motor cars."

In 1886, his admirer, George Bird Grinnell, organized the first Audubon Society to help preserve the natural beauty and living creatures of the land Audubon loved. The National Audubon Society was founded in 1905. Audubon's home in Mill Grove, Pennsylvania, is now the John James Audubon Center at Mill Grove, a museum and bird sanctuary.

■ Biographical and Critical Sources

BOOKS

Adams, Alexander B., *John James Audubon, A Biography*, Putnam (New York, NY), 1966.

American Writers, Supplement XVI, Scribner (New York, NY), 2007.

Arthur, Stanley Clisby, *Audubon: An Intimate Life of the American Woodsman*, Fireside Press (Gretna, LA), 2000.

Audubon, Lucy Bakewell, *The Life of John James Audubon*, Scribner (New York, NY), 1897.

Audubon, Maria R., editor, *Audubon and His Journals*, Scribner's, 1897.

Bland, D.S., *John James Audubon in Liverpool, 1826-1827*, University of Liverpool (Liverpool, England), 1977.

Blaugrund, Annette, *John James Audubon*, Henry N. Abrams (New York, NY), 1999.

Boehme, Sarah E., *John James Audubon in the West: The Last Expedition: Mammals of North America*, Harry N. Abrams/Buffalo Bill Historical Center, 2000.

Burroughs, John, *John James Audubon*, Small, Maynard (Boston, MA), 1902.

Chalmers, John, *Audubon in Edinburgh*, NMS Publishing (Edinburgh, Scotland), 2003.

Chancellor, John, *Audubon: A Biography*, Viking Press (New York, NY), 1978.

DeLatte, Carolyn E., *Lucy Audubon: A Biography*, Louisiana State University Press (Baton Rouge, LA), 1982.

Dictionary of Literary Biography, Volume 248: *Antebellum Writers in the South*, Second Series, Gale (Detroit, MI), 2001.

DiSilvestro, Roger, *Audubon: Natural Priorities*, Turner Publishing (Atlanta, GA), 1994.

Dorman, James H., editor, *Audubon: A Retrospective*, Center for Louisiana Studies, University of Southwestern Louisiana (Lafayette, LA), 1990.

Durant, Mary, and Harwood, Michael, *On the Road with John James Audubon*, Dodd, Mead & Co. (New York, NY), 1980.

Ford, Alice, *John James Audubon*, University of Oklahoma Press (Norman, OK), 1964, revised edition, Abbeville Press (New York, NY), 1988.

Foshay, Ella M., *John James Audubon*, Harry N. Abrams/National Museum of American Art, Smithsonian Institution, 1997.

Fries, Waldemar H., *The Double Elephant Folio: The Story of Audubon's Birds of America*, American Library Association, 1973.

Herrick, Francis Hobert, *Audubon the Naturalist: A History of His Life and Time*, Appleton-Century (New York, NY), 1938.

Kastner, Joseph, *John James Audubon*, Harry N. Abrams (New York, NY), 1992.

Keating, L. Clark, *Audubon: The Kentucky Years*, University Press of Kentucky (Lexington, KY), 1976.

Kendall, Martha E., *John James Audubon: Artist of the Wild*, Millbrook Press, 1993.

Lindsey, Alton A., editor, *The Bicentennial of John James Audubon*, Indiana University Press (Bloomington, IN), 1985.

Low, Suzanne M., *A Guide to Audubon's Birds of America*, William Reese Company (New Haven, CT), 2002.

McDermott, John Francis, editor, *Up the Missouri with Audubon: The Journal of Edward Harris*, University of Oklahoma Press (Norman, OK), 1951.

McDermott, John Francis, editor, *Audubon in the West*, University of Oklahoma Press (Norman, OK), 1965.

Murphy, Robert Cushman, *John James Audubon (1785-1851): An Evaluation of the Man and His Work*, New York Historical Society Quarterly, 1956.

Nineteenth-Century Literature Criticism, Volume 47, Gale (Detroit, MI), 1995.

Peattie, Donald Culross, *Audubon's America: The Narratives and Experiences of John James Audubon*, Houghton Mifflin (Boston, MA), 1940.

Proby, Kathryn Hall, *Audubon in Florida, with Selections from the Writings*, University of Miami Press (Coral Gables, FL), 1974.

Rhodes, Richard, *John James Audubon: The Making of an American*, Knopf (New York, NY), 2004.

Rourke, Constance, *Audubon*, Harcourt (New York, NY), 1936.

Shuler, Jay, *Had I the Wings: The Friendship of Bachman and Audubon*, University of Georgia Press (Athens, GA), 1995.

Souder, William, *Under a Wild Sky: John James Audubon and the Making of The Birds of America*, North Point Press (New York, NY), 2004.

Steiner, Bill, *Audubon Art Prints: A Collector's Guide to Every Edition*, University of South Carolina Press (Columbia, SC), 2003.

Streshinsky, Shirley, *Audubon: Life and Art in the American Wilderness*, Villard Books (New York, NY), 1993.

Tyler, Ron, *Audubon's Great National Work: The Royal Octavio Edition of The Birds of America*, University of Texas Press (Austin, TX), 1993.

Vedder, Lee A., *John James Audubon's The Birds of America: A Visionary Achievement in Ornithological Illustration*, Huntington Library (San Marino, CA), 2006.

Weissmann, Gerald, *Darwin's Audubon: Science and the Liberal Imagination*, Plenum (New York, NY), 1998.

PERIODICALS

Antiques Magazine, November, 2002, Joseph Goddu, "The Making of Audubon's The Birds of America."

Blackwood's Edinburgh Magazine, July, 1898, A. Innes Shand, "A Great Naturalist," pp. 58-69.

Huntington Library Quarterly: Studies in English and American History and Literature, Volume 59, numbers 2-3, 1998, Linda Dugan Partridge, "By the Book: Audubon and the Tradition of Ornithological Illustration," pp. 269-301.

National Wildlife, October-November, 1994, Roger Di Silvestro, "Stories behind the Paintings," p. 52.

New Yorker, February 25, 1991, Adam Gopnik, "Audubon's Passion," pp. 96-104.

New York Review of Books, December 1, 1966, Lewis Mumford, "Larger Than Life," pp. 16, 18, 20, 22-24.

Princeton University Library Chronicle, June, 1944, Henry Lyttleton Savage, "John James Audubon: A Backwoodsman in the Salon," pp. 129-136; autumn, 1959-winter, 1960, Waldemar H. Fries, "John James Audubon: Some Remarks on His Writings," pp. 1-7; Numbers 1 and 2, 1960, Francis James Dallett, "Citizen Audubon: A Documentary Discovery," pp. 89-93.

Raritan: A Quarterly Review, fall, 1995, Christoph Irmscher, "Violence and Artistic Representation in John James Audubon," pp. 1-34.

Smithsonian, January, 1999, Bil Gilbert, "An Odd Fish Who Swam against the Tide," p. 112.

Southern Quarterly, Volume 29, number 4, 1990-91, Douglas Lewis, "John James Audubon (1785-1851): Annotated Chronology of Activity in the Deep South, 1819-1837," pp. 63-82.

Southwest Review, autumn, 1930, Samuel Wood Geiser, "Naturalists of the Frontier: Audubon in Texas," pp. 109-135.

Time, June 9, 1997, Paul Gray, "Inspired Naturalist: A Smithsonian Show Celebrates the Science and Art of America's Birdman, John James Audubon," p. 85.

Wilson Quarterly, summer, 1994, "The Birdman of America," p. 146.

ONLINE

John James Audubon Center at Mill Grove Online, http://pa.audubon.org/centers_mill_grove.html/ (August 20, 2007).

National Audubon Society, http://www.audubon.org/ (May 6, 2007).*

Catherine Clark

■ Personal

Born in Massachusetts; married; children: Cady. *Education:* Wesleyan University, B.A.; Colorado State University, M.F.A.

■ Addresses

Home—Minneapolis, MN. *E-mail*—frozen_rodeo @catherineclark.com.

■ Career

Works as a bookseller in Saint Paul, MN.

■ Awards, Honors

Frozen Rodeo and *The Alison Rules* were named to the New York Public Library Books for the Teen Age list, 2004; Minnesota Book Award nomination, 2005, for *The Alison Rules.*

■ Writings

Truth or Dairy, HarperCollins (New York, NY), 2000.

Wurst Case Scenario, HarperCollins (New York, NY), 2001.
Frozen Rodeo, HarperCollins (New York, NY), 2002.
The Alison Rules, HarperCollins (New York, NY), 2004.
Maine Squeeze, HarperCollins (New York, NY), 2004.
Icing on the Lake, HarperCollins (New York, NY), 2006.
So Inn Love, HarperCollins (New York, NY), 2007.

■ Sidelights

Catherine Clark is the author of a string of novels aimed at a teenaged female audience looking for light fun and a bit of romance. These books are, Paula Rohrlick wrote in *Kliatt*, "funny and appealing YA novels." Clark's books are "popular for their realistic characters and humorous situations," Amy Alessio noted in *TeenReads.com*.

A Childhood of Reading

Born in Massachusetts, Clark has lived all over the country, including Colorado, Maine, New York, and Minnesota. In a statement posted at her Web site, she remembered her reasons for wanting to write: "I did a lot of reading as a kid. We had a summer cabin with no TV or phone and only very sketchy radio reception. (Let's just say that I'm really good

Colleen must choose between old boyfriend Evan and current boyfriend Ben in this 2004 novel. (Avon Books, 2004. Cover copyright © 2004 by HarperCollins Publishers, Inc. Used by permission of HarperCollins Children's Books, a division of HarperCollins Publishers.)

at cribbage and Yahtzee.) (Okay, so Yahtzee is all luck, but still.) We used to drive to the library and take out about ten books at a time. Also, my father is an avid reader who taught high-school English, so we always spent time talking about writers and books. And then I got that D in Geometry, so the math/science thing was pretty much out of the question. . . ." She graduated from Wesleyan University, then earned a Master of Fine Arts degree at Colorado State University. "Those are my qualifications," Clark maintained on her Web site, "such as they are."

Clark's first novel, *Truth or Dairy*, is the story of seventeen-year-old Courtney Von Dragen Smith, a

Colorado high schooler who swears off boys after getting dumped by her college-bound boyfriend. She tries to get her mind off boys by getting involved in student government. But the student council has money problems, family members are bringing home their own troubles, and the ice cream store where Courtney works is increasingly boring. Told in diary format, the novel's many storylines are resolved in the end. Courtney's "misadventures will appeal to slightly brainy girls who sometimes need to be reminded that life is a journey," according to Karen Hoth in the *School Library Journal*. Speaking of Courtney's voice as she chronicles her activities in her diary, the critic for *Publishers Weekly* believed that "it is in her flaws that her voice rings true." Similarly, Gillian Engberg in *Booklist* concluded: "Irresistibly realistic, Courtney's voice will draw even reluctant readers into this enjoyable novel."

In *Wurst Case Scenario*, Clark picks up Courtney's story as she graduates high school and moves on to college in Wisconsin. Courtney has many of the usual problems new college students have. She gets a job at a bagel shop, where she finds it hard to make friends. Her vegetarian lifestyle is out of place in the local community. Her roommate seems completely at odds with her. Still, she eventually does develop some new friendships and begins to feel self confident again. "Teens eager to read about college," Engberg wrote, "will fly through this entertaining, often realistic offering."

High schooler Peggy Fleming Farrell lives in the small Western cattle town of Lindville in Clark's novel *Frozen Rodeo*. Peggy's summer between junior and senior years is filled with activity, including a job at a coffee house, a French class, and babysitting her younger siblings. While her mother prepares for the birth of another child, and her father hopes for a return to professional skating, Peggy plans for her life after high school. Engberg noted that some teen readers "may find the lack of drama refreshingly realistic." According to the critic for *Publishers Weekly*, "the various elements come together in a fun-filled, fever-pitch conclusion." Vicki Reutter in the *School Library Journal* called *Frozen Rodeo* "an amusing gem."

A Novel about Grieving

Clark tells a darker story in *The Alison Rules*, in which high schooler Alison is having a difficult time getting beyond her mother's death the previous summer. She has devised a set of rules to help her avoid the painful subject entirely. Working on the school newspaper as a reporter, Alison befriends the new boy, Patrick. But Patrick soon takes up with Alison's friend Laurie, driving a wedge between the two friends. When Laurie is involved in an accident, Alison finally confronts the grief she has been keeping inside of her. "It is a moving story," Miranda Doyle wrote in the *School Library Journal,* "especially when Alison's repressed emotions do explode." "Clark nicely captures the myopic, paralyzing ache of grief and the enormous strength required to survive great loss," Engberg wrote. "Alison learns that the pain of emotions rather than the numb existence she was striving for is actually better," Amy Alessio explained in *TeenReads.com,* "as it helps her heal."

Maine Squeeze tells of an awkward romantic situation. Colleen finds old flame Evan coming back into her life. But she is now involved with her new boyfriend Ben. Meanwhile, Colleen's parents are in Europe on a second honeymoon and expect her to maintain the house while they are away, and to not get into any trouble with boys. Nicole M. Marcuccilli, reviewing the title for the *School Library Journal,* called the novel "good beach reading for teens who are looking for a light, sitcomlike romance."

Teenaged Kirsten goes to Minnesota to help her older sister in *Icing on the Lake.* Her friends challenge her to find a date for a weekend trip, but Kirsten is busy helping her sister, who has a broken leg, and taking care of her nephew. In addition, she knows few people in town, and it is the middle of a snowy, cold, Minnesota January. Marsha Qualey, in a review posted at her Web site, called *Icing on the Lake* "a good mix of the St. Paul winter carnival, ice hockey, best friends, cool guys, and a nice dose of sibling relationship dysfunction." Writing in *Kliatt,* Joanna Solomon noted that "Clark skillfully portrays a smart and realistic character, chronicling accurately what dating at age seventeen feels like."

If you enjoy the works of Catherine Clark, you may also want to check out the following books:

Helen Fielding, *Bridget Jones's Diary,* 1996.
Karin Cook, *What Girls Learn,* 1997.
Joan Abelove, *Saying It Out Loud,* 2001.

This 2007 novel tells of Liza's complicated summer while working at a beach hotel. (HarperTeen, 2007. Cover art copyright © 2007 by Sasha Illingworth. Used by permission of HarperCollins Children's Books, a division of HarperCollins Publishers.)

So Inn Love finds Liza McKenzie's ideal summer falling apart. Promised an exciting job as desk clerk at the Tides Inn beach hotel, Liza soon loses that position and finds herself assigned to vacuuming duty. Worse, her friend Caroline begins to ignore her. And Liza has a crush on Hayden, a boy who only wants to see her when no one else is around. A reviewer for *Infodad.com* concluded: "It's all fluff, all forgettable and all summertime fun."

In a statement posted at her Web site, Clark explained how she comes up with ideas for her novels: "Basically I just listen to people and look around and try to remember funny, odd or intriguing things that I see and hear. (My friends always tease me

Kirsten, who has traveled to Minnesota to help her older sister, finds she has little time for herself in this 2005 novel. (Avon Books, 2006. Cover art copyright © 2006 by Sasha Illingworth. Used by permission of HarperCollins Children's Books, a division of HarperCollins Publishers.)

about writing stuff down on napkins at restaurants.) When I can't get a particular thing out of my mind for days on end, I decide to use it as a jumping-off point for a book, and build from there."

■ Biographical and Critical Sources

PERIODICALS

Booklist, April 15, 2000, Gillian Engberg, review of *Truth or Dairy*, p. 1537; September 15, 2000, Stephanie Zvirin, review of *Truth or Dairy*, p. 234; September 1, 2001, Gillian Engberg, review of *Wurst Case Scenario*, p. 96; February 15, 2003, Gillian Engberg, review of *Frozen Rodeo*, p. 1064; October 15, 2004, Gillian Engberg, review of *The Alison Rules*, p. 398.

Kirkus Reviews, February 15, 2003, review of *Frozen Rodeo*, p. 302; July 1, 2004, review of *The Alison Rules*, p. 626.

Kliatt, March, 2004, Paula Rohrlick, review of *Frozen Rodeo*, p. 17; July, 2004, Paula Rohrlick, review of *The Alison Rules*, p. 7; September, 2004, Rita Fontinha, review of *Maine Squeeze*, p. 19; September, 2005, Paula Rohrlick, review of *The Alison Rules*, p. 17; July, 2006, Joanna Solomon, review of *Icing on the Lake*, p. 18.

Publishers Weekly, May 1, 2000, review of *Truth or Dairy*, p. 72; January 6, 2003, review of *Frozen Rodeo*, p. 61; September 6, 2004, review of *The Alison Rules*, p. 64.

School Library Journal, July, 2000, Karen Hoth, review of *Truth or Dairy*, p. 100; October, 2001, Kim Harris, review of *Wurst Case Scenario*, p. 152; March, 2003, Vicki Reutter, review of *Frozen Rodeo*, p. 228; August, 2004, Miranda Doyle, review of *The Alison Rules*, and Nicole M. Marcuccilli, review of *Maine Squeeze*, p. 120.

ONLINE

Catherine Clark Home Page, http://www.catherineclark.com (November 19, 2007).

Infodad.com, http://transcentury.blogspot.com/ (July 26, 2007), review of *So Inn Love*.

Marsha Qualey Home Page, http://www.marshaqualey.com/journal/otherplaces.html/ (January 21, 2006), Marsha Qualey, review of *Icing on the Lake*.

TeenReads.com, http://www.teenreads.com/ (June 21, 2007), Amy Alessio, review of *The Alison Rules*.*

Chynna Clugston

■ Personal

Born August 19, 1975, in CA; married Guy Major (an artist; divorced); married Jonathan Flores, October 20, 2005. *Hobbies and other interests:* Reading, films, music, dancing.

■ Addresses

Home—San Diego, CA.

■ Career

Comic-book artist and author.

■ Awards, Honors

Eisner Award nominations for Best Limited Series, 2001, for "Blue Monday," 2002, for work on "Hopeless Savages," and 2002, for Best Writer/Artist-Humor; Russ Manning Award nomination, 2000; Harvey Award nomination.

■ Writings

GRAPHIC NOVELS

(Published under name Chynna Clugston-Major) *Blue Monday* (originally published in comic-book form), Oni Press (Portland, OR), 2000, second edition, 2005.

Scooter Girl, Oni Press (Portland, OR), 2003.
Queen Bee, Graphix (New York, NY), 2005.
Strangetown, Oni Press (Portland, OR), 2006.

Also author of minicomic "Bloodletting," Fantaco. Contributor of illustrations to "Action Girl" and "Buffy the Vampire Slayer" comic-book series, Dark Horse Comics, 2002; *Hopeless Savages,* by Jen Van Meter, Oni Press, 2001; *Atomics: Spaced out and Grounded,* Oni Press, 2003; *Ultimate Marvel Team-Up,* Marvel; *Four Letter Worlds,* Image Comics, 2005; and *Legion of Super-Heroes in the 31st Century,* DC Comics, 2007.

■ Sidelights

One of the new breed of trendy, indy comic-book artists that had caught the attention of mainstream New York City publishers by the early 2000s, Chynna Clugston is an American comic-book creator whose talent and hard work has propelled her into the stable of several well-respected presses. Clugston is best known for her "Blue Monday" and "Scooter Girl" series, humorous comics that reflect middle-school angst as it is lived in sunny southern California. Clugston's manga-influenced art also reflects her love of British pop music and culture, with its mod sensibility and unique slang. Describing Clugston's rise to acclaim in the *Comics Journal* online, Kristy Valenti noted that, "from her resumé, one might suspect that Clugston's artwork is slickly commercial, but her expressive style, though influenced both by Japanese-style manga and indy comics, is unmistakably her own. Although she collaborates frequently as an artist, she has a writer's ear for dialogue and a fine sense of characterization. Plus, her comics are damn funny."

Clugston was born in 1975, in southern California, and grew up in a home that was full of books and comic books. Although growing up in a single-parent household was difficult, she found solace in art and writing, telling Valenti: "I was very isolated much of the time, probably one of the reasons I did draw so much. It was the only way I could communicate my feelings to people without being yelled at. It was an environment full of contradictions."

Formative High-School Years

Although Clugston is basically a self-taught artist, she did attend Fresno's Roosevelt School of the Arts for a year in the early 1990s before leaving her mother's home to live with her father. At Roosevelt and, later, Yosemite High School in nearby Oakhurst, she discovered the comics of Evan Dorkin, "Ghost World" author Dan Clowes, and Japanese manga phenomenon Rumiko Takahashi. With a friend, Clugston created an original minicomic and self-published it for school-only circulation with the help of her grandmother, who worked at the *Fresno Bee.* Although Clugston originally intended to go into animation, after she was rejected from a summer animation program she decided to change course. Mixing the influences of her favorite indy and mainstream art comics creators with her own perspective on life gained as a California teen, Clugston developed the story and characters that would become the comic-book series "Blue Monday." "I had already been drawing a bit of 'Blue Monday' when I was 16," she told Valenti. "I came up with it when I was young. I went back to it and started drawing it in more of [a] . . . new style I was working on, and I was happy with it, so I just started pursuing bigger comic companies with that in tow."

Clugston's first published work was a minicomic about vampires titled "Bloodletting," which was published by the small press Fantaco. That experience, while not exactly resumé-building, opened the proverbial door, and soon she was doing art for Dark Horse Comics and working in collaboration with other comic-book creators. Her work soon appeared in indy comics such as "Action Girl," and was also tucked into the pages of issues of "Dark Horse Presents." Other early work included a stint with Marvel as well as work on Dark Horse Com-

ics' "Buffy the Vampire Slayer" series. Finally, when her Dark Horse editor moved to Portland, Oregon's Oni Press, Clugston followed.

Clugston started her comic-book career as Chynna Clugston-Major, but has been known as Chynna Clugston since her divorce from Guy Major, a comics colorist who continues to work on Clugston's books. In 2005, she remarried, to long-time friend Jonathan Flores, but has continued to work under her maiden name. Her first solo series, "Blue Monday," debuted at Oni Press in 1999, in "Oni Double Feature" number 11. Oni Press, the brainchild of Joe Nozemack and Bob Schreck, was founded in 1997 with the goal of publishing a creatively diverse selection of high-quality comics and graphic novels. Assembling a stable of indy talent, Oni has become one of independent comics' most respected and innovative publishers. Their

This 2005 title finds the new girl at middle school, who has paranormal powers, working hard to be popular. (Graphix, 2005. Cover art copyright © 2005 by Chynna Clugston. Reprinted by permission of Scholastic Inc.)

books' unique graphic style—achieved by publishing black-and-white contents wrapped in a stylish full-color cover—have made Oni's comics unique and highly sought by comic-book aficionados. Although the trend has begun turning toward book-bound graphic novels, Oni has continued to release series such as "Blue Monday" as serialized comics, as well as soft-cover compilations. As the company stated on its Web site, "many fans and retailers still prefer the nature of serialized comics, and we feel that audience deserves to have their say."

Publishes "Blue Monday"

Blue Monday originally appeared in four volumes: *The Kids Are Alright, Absolute Beginners, In Between Days,* and *Painted Moon.* In 2000 Oni reprinted Clugston's popular series into the two-volume miniseries *Blue Monday: The Kids Are Alright.* Volume One finds Bleu L. Finnegan frustrated over her attempts to get tickets for a totally crucial Adam Ant concert at a local club. Not only are tickets a problem, but she has to navigate annoying, sex-crazy adolescents while trying to get Mr. Bishop, her dishy substitute teacher to notice her. With best friend Clover as an ally, things eventually start looking up. By Volume Two, however, life for Bleu is back on the downslide when annoying boy friends Allan and Victor videotape her taking a bath and Bleu and Clover must find the original. A St. Patrick's Day bash involving embarrassing underwear is the focus of Volume Three, while in Volume Four Bleu becomes totally turned off by the annoyingly pathetic romantic attentions of Alan and Victor. A tour of the town's night life only makes her realize that Mr. Bishop is truly the answer to her dreams. But does she have the courage to tell him so?

Noting that the characters in the "Blue Monday" series are based on people she remembered from her own high-school experience, Clugston told Valenti: "There was so much time to waste; and you're just kind of loafing around and wishing you could be somewhere else, and getting destructive when you get bored. I really feel for teenagers that are stuck in places like that. I think a lot of books don't actually speak to those kids, and that's most of America, you know? It's just so sparse and so many people are kind of isolated from big cities. I think there's something there that you need to address, so people don't feel so alone. Hopefully those are the kids who will pick it up somehow and enjoy the book."

In addition to her original comics, Clugston has also continued her collaborations with other comic-book talents. Published in 2003 in full-color format as part of Mike Allred's "Madman" series, *Atomics: Spaced out and Grounded* finds four classic-style superheroes—It Girl, Mr. Gum, Crash Metro, and Spaceman—thrust into a villainous future. Another collaborative project involved co-illustrating writer Jen van Meter's comic-book series "Hopeless Savages." Geared for young teens, "Hopeless Savages" was praised by a *Publishers Weekly* contributor as a "fun, breezy series about a family sired by once-hip rock 'n' rollers Dirk Hopeless and Nikki Savage." In the series, the heroine is sixteen-year-old Zero Savage, a girl who tries to spark up her love life while her family goes under the camera à la *The Real World.* Clugston is also co-creator of "Strangetown," a miniseries about ten-year-old Vanora Finnar, a girl who mysteriously washed up onto Oregon's coastal shore in 1973.

Clugston's comic-book miniseries "Scooter Girl," published by Oni Press in graphic-novel format in 2004, is geared for older teen readers. As it plays out in Clugston's manga-inspired black-and-white art, the story follows California college student Ashton Archer, who, with his brains and his good looks, finds that everything comes easy. That is, until he meets Margaret Sheldon, a fellow student who does not fall under Aston's spell. "The world [Clugston's] . . . characters inhabit is an American neo Mod scene of sharp clothes, Vespa scooters, and dance clubs," noted *Library Journal* contributor Steve Raiteri, the critic noting that the intriguing "soundtrack" that runs through the book in the form of song titles from a variety of popular genres creates a "cinematic" quality to the work.

Moves toward Mainstream

While continuing with her "Blue Monday" series, as well as with her collaborative work, Clugston was wooed by Scholastic to write and illustrate one of the flagship volumes releases of Graphix, Scholastic's graphic-novel imprint for preteen readers. Dubbed a "bubbly, fun and smart new series" by a *Publishers Weekly* contributor, the graphic novel *Queen Bee* tells the story of Haley Madison, the new girl in town. Hoping to establish herself in the top tier of popularity in John F. Kennedy Intermediate School, the ambitious Haley devotes her summer vacation before school reinventing herself into a popular teen. She also works on a more unusual problem: she has psychokinetic (PK) powers that allow her to move things from a distance. After school starts up in the fall, Haley moves up the social ladder from shy Trini to a budding relationship with a school cutie. She soon comes face to face with competition in the form of Alexa Harmon, a beautiful girl who, with PK powers of her own, is not afraid of breaking a few rules on her way to the top of the social ladder.

If you enjoy the works of Chynna Clugston, you may also want to check out the following books:

Ariel Schrag, *Potential,* 2000.
Bryan Lee O'sMalley, *Lost at Sea,* 2006.
Mal Peet, *Tamar,* 2007.

In a *Booklist* review of *Queen Bee,* Francisca Goldsmith praised the balance between text and pictures and noted that Clugston's story "speaks to self-discovery, values, and the bitter truth about the social dynamics of middle-school." Calling the novel "highly entertaining," *Kliatt* contributor George Galuschak also noted the story's appropriateness for preteens, and Clugston's portrayal of Haley as "an intelligent, likable heroine who matures as the story progresses." Noting the manga influences in Clugston's art, *School Library Journal* contributor Sadie Mattox noted that, with his "spiky haircut and . . . 'London Calling' T-shirt, Haley's potential flame is "a nice change from the typical 'prince' love interest."

Clugston's career, which has gained a steady momentum due to her networking skills and her love of what she does, has also been fueled by three Eisner Award nominations, as well as nominations for both the Russ Manning and Harvey awards. Making her home in San Diego, California, she lives with her husband, an English bulldog named Buster, a cat, and a pet rabbit running around underfoot. Although her career requires her to keep up with modern culture, where she must be responsive to every new trend, in her free time Clugston enjoys reading the classics and historical biographies.

■ Biographical and Critical Sources

PERIODICALS

Booklist, September 15, 2005, Francisca Goldsmith, review of *Queen Bee,* p. 66.
Kliatt, January, 2006, George Galuschak, review of *Queen Bee,* p. 24.
Library Journal, November 1, 2004, Steve Raiteri, review of *Scooter Girl,* p. 66.
Publishers Weekly, September 22, 2003, review of *Hopeless Savages,* p. 86; August 8, 2005, review of *Queen Bee,* p. 219; August 22, 2005, Douglas Wolk, "The Road to Fruition," p. 30.
School Library Journal, January, 2006, Sadie Mattox, review of *Queen Bee,* p. 165.

ONLINE

Chynna Clugston Blog, http://girlmod.livejournal.com (November 19, 2007).
Comics Journal Online, http://www.tcj.com/ (July 11, 2006), Kristy Valenti, interview with Clugston.
Silver Bullet Comics Web site, http://www.silverbulletcomicbooks.com/ (June 25, 2007), interview with Clugston.*

Frank Deford

(Photograph courtesty of Rob Loud/Getty Images.)

■ Personal

Born December 16, 1938, in Baltimore, MD; son of Benjamin F., Jr. (a businessman) and Louise Deford; married Carol Penner, August 30, 1965; children: Christian McAdams, Alexandra Miller (deceased), Scarlet Faith. *Education:* Princeton University, B.A., 1962. *Politics:* Democrat. *Religion:* Episcopalian.

■ Addresses

Agent—Sterling Lord, Sterling Lord Literistic, 65 Bleecker St., New York, NY 10012; Brooks International Speakers Bureau, 763 Santa Fe Dr., Denver, CO 80204.

■ Career

Sports Illustrated (magazine), New York, NY, senior writer, 1962-89, senior contributing writer, 1998—; National Public Radio (NPR), Washington, DC, commentator, 1980—; Cable News Network (CNN), New York, NY, commentator, 1980-86; National Broadcasting Company (NBC), New York, NY, sports commentator, 1986-89; *National Sports Daily,* New York, NY, editor, 1989-91; ESPN, New York, NY, commentator, 1991-94; *Newsweek,* New York, NY, columnist, 1992, 1996-98; Home Box Office (HBO), New York, NY, correspondent and writer, 1995—.

■ Member

Cystic Fibrosis Foundation (trustee, 1973—; chairman, 1984-99).

■ Awards, Honors

Eclipse Award, National Racing Association, 1975, 1984; First Winner award, Center for Study of Sport in Society at Northeastern University, 1985, for excellence in sport journalism; award for distinguished service to journalism, University of Missouri, 1987; Emmy Award, 1988, for television writing and commentary; Sportswriter of the Year award, National Association of Sportswriters and Sportscasters, 1982, 1984, 1985, 1986, 1987, and 1988; National Magazine Writer of the Year award, *Washington Journalism Review,* 1987, 1988; America's Best Sportswriter award, *American Journalism Review,* 1992; National Magazine Award for Profiles, 1999; Peabody Award in writing, 1999, for HBO documentary *Dare to Compete;* elected to Hall of Fame, National Association of Sportscasters and Sportswriters, 1999; received Christopher Award.

■ Writings

There She Is: The Life and Times of Miss America, Viking (New York, NY), 1971.

Five Strides on the Banked Track, Little, Brown (Boston, MA), 1971.

Cut 'n' Run, Viking (New York, NY), 1973.

(With Arthur Ashe) *Arthur Ashe: Portrait in Motion,* Carroll and Graf (New York, NY), 1975.

Big Bill Tilden: The Triumphs and the Tragedy, Simon & Schuster (New York, NY), 1976.

The Owner, Viking (New York, NY), 1976.

(With Jack Kramer) *The Game: My Forty Years in Tennis,* Putnam (New York, NY), 1979.

Everybody's All-American, Viking (New York, NY), 1981.

(With Billie Jean King) *Billie Jean,* Viking (New York, NY), 1982, published as *The Autobiography of Billie Jean King,* Granada (London, England), 1982.

Alex: The Life of a Child, Viking (New York, NY), 1983.

The Spy in the Deuce Court, Putnam (New York, NY), 1986.

The World's Tallest Midget: The Best of Frank Deford, Little, Brown (Boston, MA), 1987.

(With Walter Iooss) *Sports People,* Harry N. Abrams (New York, NY), 1988.

Casey on the Loose, Viking (New York, NY), 1989.

Love and Infamy, Viking (New York, NY), 1993.

The Best of Frank Deford: I'm Just Getting Started, Triumph Books (Chicago, IL), 2000.

The Other Adonis: A Novel of Reincarnation, Sourcebooks Landmark (Naperville, IL), 2001.

An American Summer, Sourcebooks Landmark (Naperville, IL), 2002.

The Old Ball Game: How John McGraw, Christy Mathewson, and the New York Giants Created Modern Baseball, Atlantic Monthly Press (Berkeley, CA), 2005.

The Entitled, Sourcebooks Landmark (Naperville, IL), 2007.

Author of screenplay for *Trading Hearts,* 1988. Contributor to *Champions: Their Glory and Beyond,* Little, Brown (Boston, MA), 1993. Contributor to periodicals, including *Vanity Fair,* 1993-95.

■ Adaptations

Alex: The Life of a Child was adapted for a television movie by ABC-TV in 1986; *Everybody's All-American* was adapted for film in 1988; *Casey on the Loose* is being adapted as a Broadway musical.

■ Sidelights

Frank Deford approaches his sports writing seriously. A *Publishers Weekly* reviewer wrote: "If, as accepted wisdom has it, the sports department is the toy shop of journalism and sportswriters are the midgets of the literary world, Deford wants to be known as the world's tallest midget." Deford has demonstrated this ambition by writing in styles outside journalism, ranging from co-writing the autobiographies of tennis legends to authoring a mystery spoof set on the professional tennis circuit. Deford has also displayed larger concerns throughout much of his work. Michael M. Thomas explained in a *Washington Post Book World* review of *The World's Tallest Midget: The Best of Frank Deford,* "Sure, sports provides a framework, and these pieces were originally written for a sports-oriented magazine, but Frank Deford's real subject, like all the best American writing, is about being human."

During twenty-seven years with *Sports Illustrated,* Deford wrote profiles of coaches and athletes that explore their lives beyond the playing field, probing their emotions and goals. Deford also wrote book-length biographies of several athletes, including Billie Jean King, Arthur Ashe, and Bill Tilden, and has worked as a sports commentator for National Public Radio, CNN, and ESPN Radio. Since the 1990s, his articles have appeared in *Newsweek* and *Vanity Fair.*

A Happy Childhood

"For a writer, I had a terrible thing—a happy childhood," Deford remembered. "A writer should have a deprived and contentious childhood, but mine was especially peaceful and I had a mother and father who I adored." Born December 16, 1938, Deford grew up on the edge of Baltimore, Maryland, in an era when city could give way to country in the space of a block. "I grew up within the city limits," said Deford, "but down the street was what we called 'the mule pasture,' where a mule had been not long ago." His father, Benjamin, worked for a small company but was, according to his son, "a

Deford holds up the final issue of the *National*, the daily sports newspaper for which he wrote. (Photograph by Susan Ragan. AP Images.)

frustrated farmer—if he had the money he would have just raised chickens." Louise, his mother, raised Frank and his two younger brothers, Mac and Gill, and kidded her husband by making up stationary for the Mossway Poultry Farm that listed her as president. "That house on Mossway was the only one I ever knew," recalled Deford, "and when I got married and had kids I still came back and slept in the same bedroom I had when I was a kid."

Deford was a writer before he was a jock, as he learned when he was ten-years-old. "We would be assigned little compositions in class and I found out I loved to do it," he told Pendergast. Just as some kids learn that they can throw a ball better than others, Deford learned that he could write better and that it made others happy. "Teachers liked me because of it, and my friends liked me because of it," said Deford, who penned articles for the school newspaper, which he also edited. "I just loved to write and I did it well. Where I came from it was not considered sissy that I was a writer. It was something that made me more popular, more special."

Deford was also a jock from an early age, but insists that he wasn't very good at anything except basketball. "My problem was that I grew very late. I was so skinny. God, I was miserably skinny. Finally, I blossomed in my senior year and made all-city and everything else." Deford was good enough to make the Junior Varsity team at Princeton University, where he attended college beginning in 1957, but says that his career as a college athlete was summed up by his basketball coach, who told him, "Deford, you write basketball better than you play it." So Deford stuck to writing, running his college paper, the *Daily Princetonian,* writing two plays that

were produced on campus, and submitting his short fiction for publication. For two summers, Deford worked as a copy boy for the Baltimore *Evening Sun,* gaining practical experience as a journalist while he gained a degree in history and sociology.

Writes about Sports Figures

By the end of the 1960s, Deford had embarked on a new kind of sportswriting, the feature. Deford's features were personal profiles that explored the lives of interesting people who happened to be involved in sports, and he became known for his ability to offer insights into the inner workings of people's minds. Paul Loop, writing in the *Orange County Register,* described Deford's essays as "a mix of unlikely intellectualism, graceful, beautifully paced storytelling and a constant stretching for the essential detail that reveals character." For Deford, writing features was ideal: "I was extraordinarily happy doing features," he told Pendergast. "That's what I wanted to do and that's what I did best, and it didn't really make a hell of a lot of difference to me whether I was writing about sports guys or somebody else."

Among Deford's most notable features are those on University of Alabama football coach Bear Bryant, Indiana University basketball coach Bobby Knight, and East Mississippi Junior College football coach Bob "Bull" "Cyclone" Sullivan. The first two coaches were known for being tough, but Bull Cyclone, who no one outside of Scooba, Mississippi, had ever heard of, "was the toughest coach of them all," wrote Deford, "so tough he had to have two nicknames." People didn't have to be famous to be captured by Deford's pen, they just had to be interesting.

Deford described the process of interviewing for a feature as being "like a high school date. You are both trying to get something out of each other. You both want a good story, but your ideas of what makes a good story are two different things." One of the keys for Deford lies in being a sympathetic and nonconfrontational listener. "Part of it is a gift of getting people to talk, getting them to relax. I try to like people and find out what it is that they like, and to do that I have to be a bit of an actor. If I'm with someone who likes to stay up all night and party, for example, then I'll stay up all night and party. Then they think, 'Hey, this guy stays up all night and parties, he's my buddy.' But if someone wants to get up early and go to church, I'll go to church."

Sometimes just getting the story is the most difficult part, Deford told Pendergast. At one point Deford was asked to write a piece on Bobby Knight, who

"Frank Deford writes beautifully. It is not a book about football, but about relationships...between men and women, men and men, and gods and mortals."
—Dick Schaap

ONE OF SPORTS ILLUSTRATED'S TOP 25 SPORTS BOOKS OF ALL TIME

EVERYBODY'S ALL★AMERICAN

A NOVEL

WITH A NEW PREFACE BY THE AUTHOR FRANK DEFORD

This 1981 novel tells of a former football hero who cannot adjust to regular life after his playing days are over.
(Da Capo Press, 2004. Cover photograph © Getty Images.)

was hostile to *Sports Illustrated* because that magazine had often criticized him. "I wrote him a letter and we started a negotiation," remembered Deford, who joked that the North Korean nuclear arms negotiations could not have been any more elaborate than what he went through. "I remember early on I told him, 'Look, I've got no bone to pick with you, Bobby.' And the son-of-a-bitch had found a throwaway line about him I had put in a movie review two years before and read it back to me and said 'Oh, yeah?' I was just dead in the water." But the negotiations went on, and finally Knight agreed. "Once he agreed to go out with me—to have the high school date with me—then he wanted me to take him to the prom," laughed Deford. "He was going to do everything he could to show me what was good and bright about him." The article, titled "The Rabbit Hunter," was so successful that *Sports Illustrated* ran it in a commemorative edition in 1994.

Deford knew that he was doing a good job when his colleagues said: "Man, you really got him," but says that the meaning of "getting someone" has changed over the years. "When I started out, 'getting someone' was the supreme compliment, because it meant that I had captured them. Now when you say you got someone, it means you exposed them. In that way I am sort of a dinosaur, because what I want to do is capture somebody and describe them and paint them. I love to place people in their context of time and place, where they came from, what they're connected to, what makes them tick. All those things I just adore doing, those are my favorite kinds of stories, not only writing about someone, but explaining them, where they came from, who they are."

Looks at Miss America

In the 1970s, Deford began to attract attention with his features and a number of popular books. In *There She Is: The Life and Times of Miss America*, Deford described the "incredibly arbitrary, imperfect, and inconsistent" system that crowns the most beautiful girl in America. *There She Is*, a look at the inner workings of an American cultural institution, received more publicity and more reviews than any of Deford's other works, and Audrey Cahill of *Library Journal* praised Deford for his "insight" and "keen understanding of human nature." Also during the 1970s, Deford published biographies of tennis greats Bill Tilden and Arthur Ashe, and two novels. His first novel, *Cut 'n' Run*, combined pro football, top-secret army operations, and financial speculation in what *Library Journal* contributor Charles R. Andrews called "a neat little comic come-on for the pro football fan." *The Owner*, Deford's second novel, again combined sports and humor in its portrait of a sleazy owner of a hockey team.

In 1981 Deford published the novel *Everybody's All-American*, the story of Gavin Grey, a football player who must come to terms with his life once his college days are over. Known as "The Grey Ghost" in college, where he was a star player on a winning team, Grey finds that life in professional football is not as glamorous. He plays on losing teams and finds that fans are not as enthusiastic about him as they were in college. Slowly, his life begins to fall apart, ruining his marriage and the lives of those he loves. "This is not a book about football per se," explained the reviewer for *Curled Up with a Good Book*. "There are a scant three pages of description of actual football action. Deford's fascination is with Gavin Grey's life off the field and the interplay, sometimes subtle, between the action on the field and events off it."

In 1982, Deford was voted Sportswriter of the Year by the National Association of Sportswriters and Sportscasters, an award he owned for the next seven years. Critics have called him "the world's greatest sportswriter." The accolades confirmed what many had already been saying: Deford had arrived. But Deford refused to take this recognition too seriously: "I never set out to be the best sportswriter in the country," he recalled, "so being acclaimed as the best didn't mean that much to me. I don't mean I blew it off—I was delighted and proud of myself. But the award is kind of a fraud, because it's hard to know who is best when most sportswriters are writing for a local market. Plus, I always wanted to do something more or something else, and so I think that probably kept me in perspective."

Deford began to be known for more than his writing in the 1980s, as he began to offer radio and television commentary. "I was on CNN the first week it was on the air," he told Pendergast. "It was chaotic, but it was fun and it was like vaudeville: you could try stuff and fail and do wild things and have fun." Deford also began to do radio essays for NPR and ESPN radio. "I'm sort of a columnist of the air, which is great, because it's a lot of fun to come on and express an opinion." Though his radio and television commentaries are extremely popular—NPR audiences, who were thought to look down their noses at sports, have learned to treasure Deford's insights—Deford insists that these jobs are mere sidelines. *Publishers Weekly* interviewer Chris Goodrich asked Deford if he would quit doing commentary if he could support himself as a novelist. Deford's reply: "Would I? Watch my smoke!"

"It's tough being an old sportswriter," Deford told *AAYA*. In 1989, after twenty-seven years with *Sports Illustrated*, Deford was beginning to feel like an old sportswriter. "Back in my twenties I enjoyed it, but the players were my contemporaries and they weren't making two million dollars a year and didn't mind hanging out with sportswriters." "You can stay in politics your whole life because you're always dealing with adults," he told Goodrich, "but now it's very hard for me to go into a locker room and talk to naked young men." After all those years, it was beginning to feel like he was writing the same story over and over again. And so it was time to try something new. He planned to travel to Europe and work on a novel he had begun, but Peter O. Price, an old friend who was then publisher of the *New York Post*, called and made him an offer. Price wanted him to be the editor of a new sports daily for the United States.

Tries a Daily Sports Newspaper

With the backing of Mexican millionaire Emilio Azcarraga, Deford and Price set out to create the *National*, the nation's first all-sports daily. All-sports daily papers were popular in countries all over the world so, they reasoned, why not the United States? "We started with the premise that we were going to provide the best: the best newspaper writing, the best pictures, and the best numbers," Deford told *AAYA*. And, he told Melinda Beck of *Newsweek*: "This is the last challenge in daily journalism for the 20th century. . . . We'll give our readers the good parts of *USA Today*—but we'll go far beyond that. We're a paper for people who want to *read*."-First on the agenda was luring the best sportswriters in the country, which Deford and Price did by offering big salaries and room to stretch.

For Deford, the *National* was both a pleasant change of pace and a chance to prove wrong those who sneered at sportswriting. "As a feature writer you are always a lone wolf," Deford explained to *AAYA*, "but doing the *National* was a collaborative effort. It was fun to work with other people for once." Among those Deford worked with were tennis writer John Feinstein and columnist Mike Lupica, formerly with the *New York Daily News*. Moreover, the *National* would reveal "the dirty little secret of American publishers," Deford intimated in *U.S. News & World Report*: "It is the sports page that sells papers."

The *National* was aimed at young, fairly well-off males, but Deford hoped that it could lure others into reading. "We knew that it was difficult to get young people to read, especially young men," Deford explained to Pendergast, "and one way to do it is to entice them with sports. We thought that if we could get young people reading us on a daily basis they might get trapped in the habit and start reading real newspapers." Others in the publishing industry were not so optimistic. Sports was too local, they said. People won't buy a national sports page, especially one that comes out every day.

Critics who predicted that the paper would not succeed were right in the end, but for the wrong reasons. Readers liked the writing, and the staff was able to provide enough local coverage to build a following. But the staff was never able to solve the problem of distributing the paper widely enough to reach its admittedly discriminating audience. "People want papers at six o'clock in the morning on their doorstep, and with us only selling 150,000 papers a day nationwide, it was just too difficult to make it work," recalled Deford. The paper launched its first issue on January 31, 1990; eighteen months later, on June 13, 1991, the *National* closed its doors, and Deford looked for somewhere else to write.

It did not take Deford long to find a new home. *Sports Illustrated* offered to hire him again, despite the hard feelings that existed when Deford left the magazine in 1989. (Management thought he left the magazine to create a competitor; Deford felt that the *National* had a different audience.) But Deford told the editor he could not come home again and signed a contract with *Newsweek* to provide occasional pieces. Still, he wanted to write longer pieces than that magazine published, and late in 1992 he signed a contract with *Vanity Fair* to write three profiles a year.

Ironically, Deford's ability and ultimate need to write about "being human" is most evident in a work that does not focus on sports. *Alex: The Life of a Child* is a moving and emotional work detailing the life of Deford's daughter Alex and her long battle with and inevitable surrender to cystic fibrosis. Several critics praised Deford for the power of his deep respect and love for Alex. Martin Lieberman wrote in the *Los Angeles Book Review*: "His intense love for this remarkable child comes through on every page. . . . Through his eyes you come away feeling richer for the reading." Deford joined the Cystic Fibrosis Foundation and later became chair of the organization. The book was made into a movie and sold more copies than any of Deford's other works; Deford told *AAYA* that because of this publicity, "Alex has a legacy, even though she died when she was eight years old."

A Story of World War II

In his novel *Love and Infamy,* Deford tells the story of two best friends during the Japanese attack on Pearl Harbor in 1941. One is an American missionary raised in Japan, and the other is a Japanese man who was educated in the United States. "Writing [*Love and Infamy*] was fun, but it's also scary as hell since I don't know where this thing is going . . . and it's so different from anything else I've done," Deford told Meyers. Writing about Pearl Harbor was exciting for Deford, as he revealed to Goodrich: "I've always been fascinated by Pearl Harbor, because there's no way in the world it should have happened—politically, because we should have straightened things out before it ever came to that, and militarily because ninety-nine times out of one hundred an attack like that wouldn't work." The book also gave him a chance again to develop characters on his own, instead of writing about real

people. "I was intrigued by what became the confrontation between the two characters, the Japanese who didn't want to go to war and the American who did." "Your characters really do take on some kind of life on their own," he told Meyers. "It's fun to sit down at the typewriter and see where they're going to lead you today."

Deford was nervous as he awaited reviews of *Love and Infamy,* which was, after all, the first novel he had ventured to write outside the world of sports. But reviewers found in Deford's fiction the same lively pacing and vivid characters that had long characterized his sportswriting. "Deford's blend of history, irony, suspense, and romance is a skillful concoction," announced *Richmond Times-Dispatch* contributor Sharon Lloyd Stratton. "His novel is a remarkable piece of modern historical fiction." *Philadelphia Inquirer* reviewer Bill Kent praised Deford's even-handed treatment of the Japanese: "He has

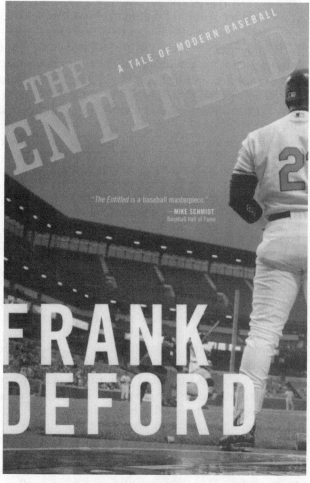

A major league baseball coach faces a tough decision about his star player in this 2007 novel. (Sourcebooks, Inc., 2007. Cover image copyright © CORBIS.)

shown us a way to see Japan as a nation that is not so exotic as it is complicated, contradictory and compellingly fascinating, and well worth learning to love." And a critic for *Publishers Weekly* called *Love and Infamy* "a consistently captivating story of romance, politics and the clash of two cultures."

Deford's 2001 novel *The Other Adonis: A Novel of Reincarnation* shuttles between modern day New York and 17th century Europe. The story revolves around Peter Paul Rubens's painting "Venus and Adonis." Magazine publisher Floyd Buckingham and financial analyst Constance Rawlings both believe they are the reincarnations of the painting's subjects. Under hypnosis, they learn they were indeed the models for Rubens' work, but they were not whom they think. The critic for *Publishers Weekly* found that "Deford keeps the tone light and humorous, mixing history and crime." Devon Thomas in the *Library Journal* called the novel "a light, enjoyable read."

Deford returned to fiction in 2002 with the novel *An American Summer*. Set among Baltimore's financial elite during the 1950s, the novel focuses on fourteen-year-old Christy Bannister, who has just moved with his father into the city's first subdivision. Christy soon makes friends with Kathryn, a woman in her twenties struck with polio and confined to an iron lung. Kathryn teaches Christy the butterfly stroke, hoping he will use it to win the community's swimming contest. Troubles with Kathryn's sister lead Christy into confrontations with older boys. The *Kirkus Reviews* critic found the novel to be "a story with an astute sense of the mores and tensions of a place." Deford, according to a reviewer for *Publishers Weekly*, "manages to twang the heart strings without being maudlin or sentimental, while delivering two memorable characters." In his review for *Booklist*, Wes Lukowsky concluded: "This is that rare literary effort that both entertains and inspires."

If you enjoy the works of Frank Deford, you may also want to check out the following books:

Gary Soto, *Baseball in April and Other Stories*, 1990.
Steve Craig, *Sports Writing: A Beginner's Guide*, 2002.
Tim Green, *Football Genius*, 2007.

A Baseball Novel

Howie Traveler, new manager for the Cleveland Indians baseball team, is the focus of Deford's 2007 novel *The Entitled.* Howie has been doing the hard work necessary to lay the groundwork for a championship team. But his efforts are derailed when his star player, Jay Alcazar, is accused of rape. Jay insists he is innocent, but Howie saw a disturbing incident outside Jay's hotel room and wonders if the star is hiding something. "The resolution won't please everyone," wrote the critic for *Publishers Weekly*, "but Deford tackles timely and provocative issues without flinching." Gilles Renaud of the *Library Journal* believed that "readers are exposed to a richly textured understanding of baseball and, no less, of estrangement, ambition, mendacity, and the search for one's destiny." A *Kirkus Reviews* writer concluded that *The Entitled* is "a decent book enhanced by Deford's great, conversational writing style."

Deford's vision of his own success seems not to rest upon what he has accomplished in the past but upon what he might accomplish in the future. Despite all the accolades, despite the fact that he is considered one of the better writers in America, despite his being "fringe famous," Deford can say: "I don't think I've ever taken myself all that seriously, because I have always had other goals that I have not achieved and that's probably very good that you never arrive where you set out to be. I always wanted to be a very successful novelist or playwright, and those things I have never achieved. That's been very good for me, it keeps me on my toes, let's me know you are not really that much of a hotshot, you're really not. So even though I am at the top of my profession, it isn't what I really want most of all, so I'm still struggling."

■ **Biographical and Critical Sources**

PERIODICALS

Aethlon: The Journal of Sport Literature, fall, 2003, Julian Meldon D'Arcy, "Gavin Grey and J.E.B. Stuart in Frank Deford's *Everybody's All-American*: A Confederate Last Stand on the Gridiron," pp. 1-9.

Booklist, September 1, 1981, review of *Everybody's All-American*, p. 26; September 15, 1983, p. 120; May 1, 1986, p. 1286; May 1, 1987, p. 1328; May 1, 1989, p. 1508; September 15, 2002, Wes Lukowsky, review of *An American Summer*, p. 206; February 15, 2005, Wes Lukowsky, review of *The Old Ball Game: How John McGraw, Christy Mathewson, and the New York Giants Created Modern Baseball*, p. 1050.

Connecticut Post, December 12, 1993, Joe Meyers, "Deford Shifts from Sports Writing to Historical Novel."

Editor & Publisher, June 22, 1991, George Garneau, "The 'National' Throws in the Towel," p. 10.

Hartford Courant, November 28, 1993, Jocelyn McClurg, "A Good Sport," November 28, 1993.

Inc., April, 1990, Edward O. Welles, "A Whole New Game," p. 58.

Journal of Library History, Philosophy & Comparative Librarianship, May 17, 1971, review of *Five Strides on the Banked Track*, p. 58.

Kirkus Reviews, April 15, 1971, review of *Five Strides on the Banked Track*, p. 474; August 1, 1981, review of *Everybody's All-American*, p. 952; August 1, 2001, review of *The Other Adonis: A Novel of Reincarnation*, p. 1047; June 15, 2002, review of *An American Summer*, p. 824; January 15, 2005, review of *The Old Ball Game*, p. 97; March 1, 2007, review of *The Entitled*, p. 186.

Library Journal, May 1, 1971, review of *Five Strides on the Banked Track*, p. 1632; October 15, 1971, p. 3337; December 1, 1972, p. 3929; October 15, 1981, review of *Everybody's All-American*, p. 2048; June 15, 1986, p. 76; June 1, 1987, p. 125; March 15, 2000, Morey Berger, review of *The Best of Frank Deford: I'm Just Getting Started*, p. 90; September 15, 2001, Devon Thomas, review of *The Other Adonis*,p. 110; July, 2002, A.J. Anderson, review of *An American Summer*, p. 115; March 1, 2007, Gilles Renaud, review of *The Entitled*, p. 69.

Los Angeles Times Book Review, November 6, 1983, p. 18.

Mediaweek, October 7, 1991, "Frank Deford to 'Newsweek,'" p. 33.

Newsweek, June 12, 1989, p. 53.

New York Times Book Review, August 17, 1986, p. 20; June 18, 1989, p. 20; February 1, 1998, p. 28; May 1, 2005, Alan Schwarz, review of *The Old Ball Game*, p. 13.

Nine, fall, 2006, Harry Jebsen, Jr., review of *The Old Ball Game*, p. 137.

Orange County Register, August 23, 1987, Paul Loop, "Deford Covers It All for *Sports Illustrated*.

People, August 18, 1986, Ned Geeslin, review of *The Spy in the Deuce Court*, p. 14; June 29, 1987, Campbell Geeslin, review of *The World's Tallest Midget: The Best of Frank Deford*, p. 16.

Philadelphia Inquirer, December 7, 1993.

Publishers Weekly, August 21, 1981, review of *Everybody's All-American*, p. 43; October 4, 1993, review of *Love and Infamy*, p. 63; December 6, 1993, p. 52; September 10, 2001, review of *The Other Adonis*, p. 59; July 1, 2002, review of *An American Summer*, p. 51; February 7, 2005, review of *The Old Ball Game*, p. 51; December 4, 2006, review of *The Entitled*, p. 30.

Richmond Times-Dispatch, January 2, 1994, Sharon Lloyd Stratton, "Friends Clash in Deford Novel."

Sports Illustrated, October 26, 1981, review of *Everybody's All-American*, p. 10.

Time, January 16, 1984, J.D. Reed, review of *Alex*, p. 72; November 29, 1993, R.Z. Sheppard, review of *Love and Infamy*, p. 82.

U.S. News & World Report, January 29, 1990, p. 11.

Washington Post Book World, October 4, 1981, p. 10; May 4, 1986, p. 12; August 17, 1986, p. 20; May 17, 1987, p. 11.

ONLINE

Curled Up with a Good Book, http://www.curledup.com/everyall.htm/ (June 27, 2007), review of *Everybody's All-American*.*

Jack Emmert

■ Personal

Born c. 1969. *Education:* University of Chicago, M.A. (ancient history); Ohio State University, M.A. (Latin and Greek). *Hobbies and other interests:* Comic books.

■ Addresses

Office—Cryptic Studios, Inc., 983-D University Ave., Los Gatos, CA 95032-7637. *E-mail*—PR@cryptic studios.com.

■ Career

Computer game developer. Cryptic Studios, Los Gatos, CA, cofounder, 2000, and chief creative officer. Speaker at conferences. Volunteer for animal rescue agencies.

■ Awards, Honors

Electronic Entertainment Expo Game Critics Award, 2003, for *City of Heroes.*

■ Writings

VIDEO GAMES

(Lead designer) *City of Heroes,* Cryptic Studios (Los Gatos, CA), 2004.

(Lead designer) *City of Villains,* Cryptic Studios (Los Gatos, CA), 2005.

Contributor to video games, including *Deadlands, Hell on Earth, DC Universe,* and *Marvel Superheroes.*

Emmert's games have been translated into other languages, including Korean.

OTHER

Author of strategy guides for computer games published by Prima Games. Contributor to periodicals, including *Game Designer.*

■ Sidelights

"City of Heroes. City of Tomorrow. Since 1931, when a prodigal son returned with the powers of an ancient god and called himself Statesman, Paragon City has been the center of the super-powered hero universe. Through the efforts of Statesman and those who joined him in the war against tyranny and crime, Paragon City truly became a beacon and inspiration for heroes world-wide. A true city of heroes." So reads the official backstory of *City of Heroes,* one of the most popular online role-playing games devised. The brainchild of game designer Jack Emmert, the "massively multiplayer online" (MMO) game allows players to create unique superhero alter-egos, and guide their adventures in an awe-inspiring, 3D graphical world. Based on the

comic-book worlds Emmert has loved since child-hood, *City of Heroes* won the 2003 Electronic Entertainment Expo Game Critics award, along with many other game-industry honors.

Born c. 1969, Emmert grew up with an abiding love of comic books. At age eight his favorite comics were *Hulk* and *Fantastic Four,* but by his teens he had graduated to *The X-Men* and *New Teen Titans.* Admitting to being little interested in video-gaming himself—Emmert reads widely in his free time—he enjoyed adopting the alter-ego Statesman and playing Dungeons and Dragons with friends. His professional career in the hobby game industry started at Showcase Comics, a small comic-book shop located on the outskirts of Philadelphia where he worked during the summer months.

Begins in Academia

Bookish by nature, Emmert assumed that his interests would lead him into academia. After earning a master's degree in ancient history from the University of Chicago, he pursued a second M.A. in classical languages at Ohio State University. Emmert's experience in the gaming industry started with a part-time job writing supplements for various gaming lines, such as *DC Universe, Deadlands, Hell on Earth,* and *Marvel Superheroes.*

Emmert had embarked on a Ph.D. program in preparation for his academic career, but he abandoned that career path in July of 2002 to join Michael Lewis and three other gaming visionaries as a cofounder of Cryptic Studios. Based in Los Gatos, California, Cryptic Studios was formed to develop subscription-based "massively multiplayer online" (MMO) "role playing games" (RPG's), for PC and next-generation machines. Brought into the limelight by the popularity of their masterwork, *City of Heroes,* the founders of Cryptic have also worked with Marvel Comics on the developing of Marvel Universe Online, an MMO game based on Marvel's superhero comics characters.

Creates *City of Heroes*

Released in 2004 and the winner of dozens of the gaming world's top honors, *City of Heroes* is an MMORPG published by NCSoft Corp. The game centers on Paragon City, a sprawling, urbanized area loosely based on New York City. In Paragon City, players design a unique superhero character, then direct that character through over sixteen zones, each housing an assortment of nasty threats.

As attackers approach, players can wonder: will they be forced to battle the alien Rikti, with their goal of vanquishing all superheroes, or outgun a mindless robot, vanquish a twisted god, destroy killer zombies, bring to justice some drug-addled gang bangers, thwart an evil corporate menace, or ferret out a secret society that menaces the city in the caverns beneath? The challenge to each player in *City of Heroes* was described by a *Game Developer* contributor in cinematic terms: "Once a bastion of decent people with a cadre of elite superheroes to defend them, Paragon City's old guard is gone. . . . Now, evil is loose on the streets, and it's your job to clean up."

For a monthly subscription fee comparable to the cost of a pair of movie tickets, players could login and experience their virtual life as a costumed crimefighter. Working up through the game's levels mimics the rise of a comic-book character: by vanquishing evildoers, performing good deeds, making newspaper headlines, and gaining the appropriate friends, players gain useful allies in city government and law enforcement, as well as a confidante that to serve as their own personal Kato. They also gain speed, endurance, new weapons, and various superpowers.

Emmert based *City of Heroes* on one key assumption: that most people raised in modern American culture, and exposed to comic books and other media, at some point dream of being a superhero. As he told *Jive* online interviewer Thomas L. Strickland, "Everybody remembers, at some point in their life, thinking about what superpowers would be the coolest or what costume would be awesome. . . . but more importantly I think that, given events in . . . North America, that every one of us has a deep desire to be a hero. Every one of us wants to save lives. Every one of us wants to be there to protect our family, our homes, our neighbor, our country. In *City of Heroes* they get to visualize that very deep, very sincere desire."

Based on the response of reporters and gamers alike, Emmert's assumption has been proved correct. While registering 100,000 subscribers is considered successful in an MMO, within months *City of Heroes* hit twice that number in the United States and Canada alone. The game has also been released around the world. As Emmert explained to *OGaming* online interviewer Scott Steinberg: "We were a no-name developer working on an idea which had never translated well in the PC medium. I believe that the success of [*City of Heroes*] is due mainly to its accessibility; players of all skill levels can get into the game and have fun within fifteen minutes."

Continual Creation

Much of the challenge for Emmert and the Cryptic Studios team has been to sustain the game's appeal, especially for hard-core gamers. To this end, Emmert works with three writers who design the expansions that are issued every four to six months. In addition to patches designed to repair technical issues, subscribers can look forward to new missions, new content and expanded features at no additional cost. In the first expansion, titled "Through the Looking Glass" and issued three months after the game's April, 2004, debut, players were treated to three new villain groups, two new high-level zones, and the services of a superhero fashion service that allowed them to refine their character's work attire. With a nod to players in other parts of the world, costume options in *City of Heroes* now include a panda mascot perched on one's shoulder and the always awe-inspiring open brain pan.

With expansion three, writers created a cataclysmic event that affected the whole of Paragon City. Other enhancements to *City of Heroes* include mini-events scattered into the action. For example, superheroes grappling with ne'er-do-wells along the city's murky shoreline might do well to keep on the lookout for a ghost ship, or even a giant octopus. Badges were added during another upgrade, allowing the game's appeal to extend to players more interested in exploring Paragon City's geographical realms than wrestling with evil. A chance at some much-needed R & R was provided with the addition of customized home bases, which gave players the chance to choose the decor in their own personal superhero retreat.

Enter *City of Villains*

In a move reflecting the ying and yang of crime-fighting, Emmert and the Cryptic Studios team released *City of Villains* in October of 2005. A stand-alone game that links to *City of Heroes, City of Villains* is designed for those who realize that power corrupts. Instead of fighting a mind-numbed zombie or evil megalomaniac, players in this game can now be one. Not surprisingly, the action is more aggressive, as theft, kidnapping, arson, murder, and world domination are all worthy goals. Technologically, as a second-generation product, *City of Villains* contains more sophisticated graphics and visual effects. The product was so impressive, in fact, that Marvel Comics partnered with Emmert and Cryptic Studios to develop *Marvel Universe Online*, an MMORPG featuring the comic' publishers stable of classic superheroes.

If you enjoy the works of Jack Emmert, you may also want to check out the following games:

The Sims: Complete Collection, 2005.
Sid Meier's Civilization IV, 2005.
Age of Empires III, 2005.
Crimson Skies, 2006.

Emmert drew on his training as a classical scholar in devising the basic villain archetypes available in *City of Villains*. The Brute's goal is to create havoc and destruction, and he is motivated by a blind fury. The appeal of this character to young adolescent players is easy to explain. More complex is The Stalker, who specializes in orchestrating surprise attacks on groups of civilians, while The Corrupter looks for weakness and capitalizes on it. The Dominator wants total control. Once he—or she—has it, watch out, while The Mastermind plays Mafioso and lets underlings do the work. While *City of Heroes* focused on preserving the status quo, *City of Villains* is about tearing things apart, and in the place were the two games intersect game developers created Player vs. Player or PvP zones. The victor in these classic battles between good and evil reaps a reward that moves him or her further up the hierarchy. Team-building among players has been another outgrowth of the game, as Emmert's virtual world has taken on a life of its own.

Player-initiated activities like team building do not go unnoticed by Emmert, who considers the social ramifications of the interactive gaming experience in his design process. In his view, playing MMORPG's such as *City of Heroes* offer more than just entertainment; they have the potential to foster collaboration, leadership, and player-to-player education, and provide players with a chance to work out virtual interpersonal relationships that parallel those in the real world.

While Emmert's shift from academia to video game design might seem unusual to some, the career choice has been a wise one in his own view. While devoting his time to the study of Greek literature and the classics, "I was writing stuff that maybe one hundred people would read, that maybe only one hundred people in the world could understand," he explained to Jonathan Sidener in the *San Diego Union-Tribune Online*. "Now I've helped create a game that hundreds of thousands of people play." Emmert, in his Statesman guise, is one of those hundreds of thousands of people. When the rapid-fire action and stress of saving the world gets too much, he returns to his roots, however, and joins friends for a session of Dungeons and Dragons every other Tuesday.

■ Biographical and Critical Sources

PERIODICALS

Game Developer, January, 2007, "Test of Design: A Game Designer Exam for Finding the Right Candidates," p. 41.

ONLINE

Boomtown Web site, http://www.boomtown.net/en_uk/ (January 20, 2006), Jakob Paulsen, interview with Emmert.

City of Heroes Web site, http://www.cityofheroes.com/ (June 27, 2004).

CMP Game Group Web site, http://www.cmpgame.com/ (June 27, 2007), "City of Heroes Creator to Explore How Social and Behavioral Aspects of Player-to-Player Interaction Can Address Challenges Beyond Entertainment.

Cryptic Studios Web site, http://www.crypticstudios.com/ (June 27, 2007).

Game Spy, http://archive.gamespy.com/ (October, 2001), James Fudge, interview with Emmert.

Game Zone, http://pc.gamezone.com/ (September 7, 2007), Michael Lafferty, interview with Emmert.

ign.com, http://pc.ign.com/ Steve Butts, "City of Villains Interview: Lead Designer Jack Emmert Proves It's Good to Be Bad."

Jive Online, http://www.jivemagazine.com/ (September 16, 2004), Thomas L. Strickland, interview with Emmert.

OGaming, http://www.ogaming.com/ (June 27, 2007), Scott Steinberg, interview with Emmert.

San Diego Union-Tribune Online, http://www.signonsandiebo.com/uniontrib/ (July 26, 2004), Jonathan Sidener, interview with Emmert.*

Sharon G. Flake

■ Personal

Born in Pittsburgh, PA; children: Brittney. *Education:* Attended college.

■ Addresses

Home—Pittsburgh, PA. *E-mail*—ShrFla9@aol.com.

■ Career

Center for the Assessment and Treatment of Youth in Philadelphia, Philadelphia, PA, youth counselor; Katz Business School, University of Pittsburgh, Pittsburgh, director of publications.

■ Awards, Honors

Winner of August Wilson Short Story Contest; scholarship recipient, *Highlights for Children*'s writers' conference; Best Book for Young Adult Readers selection, Quick Pick for Reluctant Readers selection, American Library Association, Top Ten Books for Youth selection, *Booklist*, Best Children's Book of 1999 selection, Bank Street College of Education, Coretta Scott King/John Steptoe Award for new authors, and New York Public Library Book for the Teen Age selection, 1999, all for *The Skin I'm In*; Coretta Scott King Award, 2002, for *Money Hungry*.

■ Writings

The Skin I'm In, Jump at the Sun (New York, NY), 1998.

Money Hungry, Jump at the Sun (New York, NY), 2001.

Begging for Change (sequel to *Money Hungry,*), Jump at the Sun (New York, NY), 2003.

Who Am I without Him?: Short Stories about Girls and the Boys in Their Lives, Jump at the Sun (New York, NY), 2004.

Bang!, Jump at the Sun (New York, NY), 2005.

The Broken Bike Boy and the Queen of 33rd Street, Jump at the Sun (New York, NY), 2007.

■ Adaptations

The Skin I'm In was adapted for audio, Recorded Books, 2004.

■ Sidelights

Coretta Scott King Award-winner Sharon G. Flake writes novels about black teens in the inner city. "Her novels, which explore the lives of African-

American teenagers, are known for their honest depiction of gritty urban life and racism, as well as the universal themes of teen insecurity and angst," according to Andrea Sachs in an article for *Time. com*. Flake told Abby Mendelson in *Pop City:* "The inner city is not all about broken glass. There's crystal goblets, too. That's what my books do—put the broken glass and the crystal goblets in the same context." While her books have become part of the required reading at middle and high schools across the country, they have also proved popular with readers of all ages and backgrounds. Some half a million copies of Flake's books have been sold.

A Philadelphia Childhood

"I grew up in North Philadelphia with three brothers, two sisters, my mom and my dad," Flake told *Authors and Artists for Young Adults (AAYA)*. "I was

Teenager Raspberry Hill works hard to get the money she and her mother need in this 2003 novel. (Jump at the Sun/ Hyperion Books For Children, 2003. Reproduced by permission of Hyperion Books For Children.)

shy, but never lonely. In middle school I stayed to myself a lot; reading books, watching television, and spending time with my family. I don't ever remember anyone saying that I had writing talent when I was young, and frankly I don't think I did." She did enjoy reading. "Primarily I read lots of young adult romance and a nice helping of Langston Hughes," Flake told *AAYA*. "That's probably why most of my books have a romantic thread that runs through them and my inner city characters have a lot of dignity and inner strength." Flake remembered: "Middle school was hard for me. Nobody chased me home or beat me up but like most children that age I was shy, insecure, and didn't see my own strength and talent. In eighth grade one of my best friends was left back and it scared me to death because even though I was a good student most of my life, at the time I was kind of lackadaisical. So that experience made me work even harder in high school. One of my favorite classes was social studies because the teacher was really cute and he ran the hostelling club." "I tell people that I am a writer in spite of myself," she explained to Holly Atkins in the *St. Petersburg Times*. "I didn't write in middle or high school. And I went to college to be a doctor, only I stank at science. I changed my major a lot, from premed to psychology to accounting. Only I wasn't good at so many things—math, stuff like that. But I seemed to do well at writing, so I took more and more of those classes."

Publishes First Novel

In Flake's first novel, *The Skin I'm In*, thirteen-year-old Malika Madison is a bright student who is taunted because her grades are too high, her skin is too dark, and because she wears handmade clothing. Maleeka tries to fit in by hanging out with Charlese, the toughest girl in the school. Her life changes when Miss Saunders becomes her new English teacher. The woman's face is disfigured by a large birthmark, making her a target of hostility, to which Malika contributes. However, her perception changes when the teacher singles Malika out as a talented writer and inspires the girl to enter a writing contest which she wins. She is also inspired by the teacher's strength and spirit, and ultimately, Malika's own integrity breaks through. *Booklist* reviewer Hazel Rochman felt that Flake's "characters are complex," while a *Publishers Weekly* contributor wrote that "those identifying with the heroine's struggle to feel comfortable inside the skin she's in will find inspiration here."

"I would say Malika in *The Skin I'm In*, is probably still my favorite character because she goes through so much and learns so much," Flake recounted to

AAYA. "And if she was a real person I think she would be so excited about how many young people see themselves in her and learn from her experiences."

The protagonist in *Money Hungry* is thirteen-year-old Raspberry Hill, who lives with her mother in a housing project. Prior to this, they slept on the street and on friends's couches after they left Raspberry's drug-addicted father. Now her mother works two jobs and is back in school. Raspberry's best friends include Mia, whose parents are Korean and black but who will only identify herself as black; Ja'nae, who lives with loving grandparents but longs for her flaky mother; and Zora Mitchell, whose divorced doctor father's efforts to pursue a relationship with Raspberry's mother are upsetting both girls. Determined to move into a better neighborhood, Raspberry will do just about anything to earn money; anything except illegal things, like selling dope or shoplifting. She sells pencils and candy, cleans houses, and washes cars. Rather than eat, she adds her lunch money to her hoard, and her stinginess eventually causes problems. When Raspberry's mother finds her bankroll, she thinks the money is stolen and throws it from the window. When everything they own is stolen, Raspberry and her mom once again find themselves on the street to begin again with the support of caring neighbors. A *Publishers Weekly* contributor said that Flake "candidly expresses the difficulty in breaking the cycle of poverty and leaves it up to the reader to judge Raspberry's acts." *School Library Journal* reviewer Gail Richmond wrote that Flake "does a stunning job of intertwining Raspberry's story with daily urban scenes, and she writes smoothly and knowingly of teen problems." Gillian Engberg commented in *Booklist* that Flake's "razor-sharp dialogue and unerring details evoke characters, rooms, and neighborhoods with economy and precision, creating a story that's immediate, vivid, and unsensationalized."

In *Begging for Change,* Raspberry is rebuilding her nest egg. Her character is flawed in this outing, as she steals cash from friends, raising issues of trust. But her motives are pressing: her mother has been hospitalized after being hit with a pipe. The teen also continues to earn extra money honorably, most of which is taken by her homeless father. When Raspberry and her mother finally move to a better neighborhood, the girl confesses her crimes and begins to repair her ways. A *Publishers Weekly* writer felt that, "touching upon issues of prejudice, street violence, homelessness, and identity crises, this poignant novel sustains a delicate balance between gritty reality and dream fulfillment." Engberg said

Stories about teenaged girls and the boys in their lives are found in this 2004 collection. (Jump at the Sun/Hyperion Books For Children, 2004. Reproduced by permission of Hyperion Books For Children.)

that "although vivid images of urban poverty, violence, and drug addiction clearly illustrate why Raspberry is so afraid, Flake never sensationalizes."

A Look at Bad Boyfriends

Who Am I without Him?: Short Stories about Girls and the Boys in Their Lives is a collection addressing the problem of "girls who confuse having a boy's attention with having personal worth," as Jenny Morris explained in the *Decatur Daily.* Most, but not all, of the ten stories are written from a girl's point of view. The girls are lonely and insecure unless they have a boyfriend in their lives, and so they will tolerate almost any behavior just to have a boyfriend. Flake's stories contain no obscenity or sex, and as Rochman noted, while "there are messages, . . . the narrative is never preachy or uplifting; it's honest about the pain." Morris wrote: "The girls in it are not positive role models. The boys are at times little more than thugs. But the stories are an excellent springboard for a thorough discussion of a young woman's legitimate needs and how she should seek to meet them. A *Kirkus Reviews* critic felt that Flake's handling of her subject "shines with an awareness of the real-life social, emotional, and physical pressures that teens feel about dating." In one story not narrated by a girl, a father writes a letter to his daughter, telling her not to settle for someone like him. Mary N. Oluonye wrote in the *School Library Journal* that this story "is sad, poignant, and loving. Flake has a way of teaching a lesson without seeming to do so." Laurence Adams, writing in the *Horn Book Magazine,* found that "Flake's stories go right to the deepest longings, fears, and needs of teens. In ten first-person narratives, Flake holds back nothing but judgment, allowing these young black women and men plenty of room for missteps in their search for love and self-esteem." *Who Am I without Him?* won Flake the prestigious Coretta Scott King Award.

Speaking about *Who Am I without Him?* with Holly Atkins in the *St. Petersburg Times,* Flake explained: "I come from a generation that didn't talk about relationships with young people. So when I started dating in college, I didn't know all that much about things, especially how to ask for what you want in relationships, how boys should treat girls and the like. When you don't know, you make a lot of mistakes and establish patterns for yourself that might not be so healthy. I didn't want that for my daughter, who is a teenager, or for other young girls and boys."

Confronts Street Violence

In the novel *Bang!,* Flake confronts violence in the urban black community. She tells the story of Mann Martin as he tries to cope with the loss of his younger brother, Jason, in a street shooting. His father, wanting to toughen the boy up for life in the streets, takes Mann and his friend Kee-lee into the woods and leaves them there, hoping that the ordeal will make men of them. Flake explained to Heidi Henneman in *BookPage* what inspired her to write the story: "Like a lot of U.S. cities, Pittsburgh goes through seasons where there seem to be a lot of killings in the inner city. Two years ago, this was the case. It made me sad, and I wanted to do something about it, so I started writing a short story about a boy who would solve the problem. It didn't work well, so I dropped the idea. Then a year later the shootings started again, and *Bang!* was born." She recounted that a school principal told her that

when asked if they knew someone who had been shot, an entire classroom raised their hands. "That's when I started asking students the same question after I read a chapter of *Bang!* to them. It stunned me—no matter the city, many hands would go up, sometimes all of them. Some black, some white, some Hispanic. It let me know that there are many, many students in our schools who are grieving, or angry, at the very least hurting over loss, and I wondered, who is talking them through their pain? I'm hoping that *Bang!* will do that, as well as provide a platform for them to discuss the issue of violence and what it does to individuals and families."

In *The Broken Bike Boy and the Queen of 33rd Street,* Queen is a teenaged girl who treats everyone in her life as if they are beneath her. She has no friends, and even the teacher at school dislikes her. When a new boy, Leroy, comes to school, riding a broken bike and wearing old clothes, Queen targets him for special ridicule. Even though her parents tell her to treat the newcomer nicely, Queen refuses. She thinks he is telling lies to everyone, especially about really being an African prince. But then he shows her old gold coins from Africa and an elephant tusk. Is Leroy telling the truth about his royal background? When she begins snooping into Leroy's private life to discover the truth about him, Queen meets his older friend Cornelius Junction the Fourth, a former actor now suffering from a phobia that stops him from going outside of his house. "Her efforts to undermine Leroy and regain the sole position of royalty seem to do nothing but alienate everyone," according to Sonja Bolle in *Newsday.* Terrie Dorio in the *School Library Journal* especially singled out Queen as a memorable character: "Flake has created a character who is difficult and unlikable but at the same time sympathetic." Robin Smith in *Horn Book Magazine* praised the book, finding that the "complex intergenerational characters and a rich urban setting defy stereotyping." The critic for *Publishers Weekly* concluded: "Multi-dimensional characters and frequently affecting dialogue make this a memorable work of fiction."

Speaking of how she writes her stories, Flake revealed to *AAYA:* "For the most part none of my characters are based on real people. I begin a book with very little information. For example, in *The Skin I'm In,* I knew I wanted to write about a dark skinned girl. In *Money Hungry,* I knew I wanted to write about a girl who wanted money. I don't predetermine the beginning, middle, or end. I don't know what people's names will be. I just know that my characters will probably be African American, and the setting is usually inner city. It's like trying to get to Mississippi without knowing it's in the U.S. or the South. That means lots of interesting twists and turns; some dead ends, but a wonderful journey."

If you enjoy the works of Sharon G. Flake, you may also want to check out the following books:

Sharon Mathis, *A Teacup Full of Roses*, 1987.
Langston Hughes, *The Best of Simple*, 2000.
Nikki Grimes, *The Road to Paris*, 2006.

Flake enjoys visiting schools across the country, reading from her works, and personally meeting her readers. "The biggest surprise," she told *AAYA*, "is that so many different audiences have embraced my work—middle and high school students, boys, adults, even college professors. I love visiting schools, and talking to young people, and hearing what they think about the book. Not only that, I love to hug them, and laugh and joke with them. That's the fun part to me."

In an interview with Kenya Jordana James in *Blackgirl Magazine*, Flake spoke of how she became a writer: "I think a lot has to do with God pushing me and knowing what was better for me than what I knew for myself, and now I am so glad and I love what I am doing."

■ Biographical and Critical Sources

PERIODICALS

Blackgirl Magazine, July, 2004, Kenya Jordana James, interview with Sharon G. Flake; September-October, 2004, review of *Who Am I without Him?*, p. 6.

Booklist, September 1, 1998, Hazel Rochman, review of *The Skin I'm In*, p. 110; June 1, 2001, Gillian Engberg, review of *Money Hungry*, p. 1880; August, 2003, Gillian Engberg, review of *Begging for*

Change, p. 1980; April 15, 2004, Hazel Rochman, review of *Who Am I without Him?: Short Stories about Girls and the Boys in Their Lives*, p. 1440; May 1, 2006, Anna Rich, review of *Bang!*, p. 97; June 1, 2007, Hazel Rochman, review of *The Broken Bike Boy and the Queen of 33rd Street*, p. 68.

Decatur Daily (Decatur, AL), October 8, 2006, Jenny Morris, "'Who Am I' Examines Girls' Self-worth."

Horn Book Magazine, July-August, 2004, Laurence Adams, review of *Who Am I without Him?*, p. 451; July-August, 2007, Robin Smith, review of *The Broken Bike Boy and the Queen of 33rd Street*, p. 395.

Kirkus Reviews, June 1, 2003, review of *Begging for Change*, p. 803; April 15, 2004, review of *Who Am I without Him?*, p. 393; April 15, 2007, review of *The Broken Bike Boy and the Queen of 33rd Street*.

Kliatt, November, 2004, Samantha Musher, review of *Begging for Change*, p. 16.

Newsday, June 3, 2007, Sonja Bolle, review of *The Broken Bike Boy and the Queen of 33rd Street*.

Publishers Weekly, November 9, 1998, review of *The Skin I'm In*, p. 78; December 21, 1998, "Flying Starts," p. 28; June 18, 2001, review of *Money Hungry*, p. 82; June 9, 2003, review of *Begging for Change*, p. 52; May 10, 2007, review of *The Broken Bike Boy and the Queen of 33rd Street*, p. 60.

St. Petersburg Times (St. Petersburg, FL), March 28, 2005, Holly Atkins, "Meeting Yourself on a Book's Page," p. 6E.

School Library Journal, July, 2001, Gail Richmond, review of *Money Hungry*, p. 107; July, 2003, Sunny Shore, review of *Begging for Change*, p. 129; May, 2004, Mary N. Oluonye, review of *Who Am I without Him?*, p. 147; June, 2006, Claudia Moore, review of *Bang!*, p 86; June, 2007, Terrie Dorio, review of *The Broken Bike Boy and the Queen of 33rd Street*, p. 144.

ONLINE

BookPage, http://www.bookpage.com/ (September, 2005), Heidi Henneman, "Guiding Kids Through a Violent World."

New York Public Library Web site, http://www.nypl.org/ (July 18, 2002), transcript of live chat with Flake.

Pop City, http://www.popcitymedia.com/ (July 11, 2007), Abby Mendelson, "Pop Star: Sharon Flake."

Sharon G. Flake Home Page, http://www.sharongflake.com (November 19, 2007).

Time Online, http://www.time.com/time/ (September 25, 2005), Andrea Sachs, "Tales from the Hood."

Steve Hamilton

(Author Steve Hamilton. Copyright © Jerry Bauer. Reproduced by permission.)

■ Personal

Born January 10, 1961, in Detroit, MI; son of Robert G. (a small-business owner) and Nonna L. (a graduate studies coordinator) Hamilton; married Julia L. Antonietta, June 8, 1991; children: Nicholas G., Antonia. *Ethnicity:* "Caucasian." *Education:* University of Michigan, B.A., 1983. *Politics:* Independent. *Religion:* Reformed Church of America. *Hobbies and other interests:* Golf.

■ Addresses

Home—Cotlekill, NY. *Agent*—Jane Chelius, 548 Second St., Brooklyn, NY 11215. *E-mail*—Steve@authorstevehamilton.com.

■ Career

Novelist. International Business Machines (IBM), Poughkeepsie, NY, information developer, 1983—.

■ Member

Mystery Writers of America, Private Eye Writers of America, Sisters in Crime.

■ Awards, Honors

Hopwood Award, University of Michigan, 1983; Best First Private-Eye Novel, St. Martin's Press/Private-Eye Writers of America, 1997, Edgar Allan Poe Award, Mystery Writers of America, for best first novel, 1999, and Shamus Award for best first private-eye novel, 1999, all for *A Cold Day in Paradise;* Shamus Award nomination, 2003, for *North of Nowhere;* Michigan Author Award, Michigan Center for the Book, 2006; Nero Award nomination, 2007, for *A Stolen Season.*

■ Writings

"ALEX MCKNIGHT" MYSTERY SERIES

A Cold Day in Paradise, St. Martin's Press (New York, NY), 1998.

Winter of the Wolf Moon, St. Martin's Press (New York, NY), 2000.

The Hunting Wind, St. Martin's Press (New York, NY), 2001.

North of Nowhere, St. Martin's Press (New York, NY), 2002.

Blood Is the Sky, St. Martin's Press (New York, NY), 2003.

Ice Run, St. Martin's Press (New York, NY), 2004.

A Stolen Season, St. Martin's Press (New York, NY), 2006.

OTHER

Night Work, St. Martin's Press (New York, NY), 2007.

Contributor to magazines, including *Ellery Queen's Mystery Magazine* and *Pirate Writings.*

■ Adaptations

Several of Hamilton's books have been adapted for audiocassette.

■ Sidelights

Steve Hamilton's mystery novels are set in Michigan's Upper Peninsula and feature the character of Alex McKnight, a divorced, one-time minor league baseball player and former Detroit cop. McKnight was wounded during a shootout with a criminal suspect; his partner died in the event. Since the shooting, McKnight carries with him a bullet lodged so close to his heart that it cannot be removed. On cold days, he can sometimes feel the bullet inside his chest. McKnight makes a quiet living by renting out a few cabins his father built to hunters, fishermen, and tourists. When not working, he enjoys drinking at a little tavern in the nearby town of Paradise. Although he has tried to isolate himself from the problems of the larger world, McKnight is dragged into problems nonetheless, most of them criminal. As Hamilton explained it in an interview with *Shots* magazine: "Alex is a very reluctant PI [private investigator], somebody who got roped into it against his better judgement and now regrets every minute of it—and who has absolutely NO interest in ever doing anything remotely resembling PI work again. Every book, he has to be dragged into it by somebody. Good thing he's a total sap at heart." David Pitt in *Booklist* described McKnight as "the kind of fellow you'd like to meet—he'd shake your hand, buy you a beer, and, as long as you didn't get on his wrong side, be your friend for life." Speaking of the "McKnight" books, Anthony Rainone of *January Magazine* concluded: "Hamilton has so far eschewed the high-caliber pyrotechnics of many contemporary novels—action that emphasizes the heroic elements of this genre, but too often stretches believability. Yet he delivers all of the modern detective fiction essentials, including plot twists that the reader flat-out never sees coming." Andi Schechter, writing in the *Library Journal,*

claimed that "Hamilton's Alex McKnight private investigator series has long attracted fans and critical raves for its vigorous prose, gripping suspense, and fully rounded characters."

Hamilton was born in Detroit, Michigan, in 1961. His father was the owner of a small business, and his mother worked as a graduate studies coordinator. Hamilton told *Authors and Artists for Young Adults (AAYA)*: "I was born and raised in the suburbs of Detroit. One brother, three years younger than me. As far as I can remember, I've wanted to write stories ever since Elementary School, when I first fell in love with reading. If you go back in a time machine to the late sixties and ask me what I want to be when I grow up, that's my answer. (So maybe if I ever do grow up, I can make that come true.)" His love of reading began early: "I read all the time. I was partial to mysteries, ghost stories, anything dark and suspenseful. I used to LOVE those old Alfred Hitchcock paperbacks, then later everything by Agatha Christie." Hamilton explained in an interview posted at the *Fiction Addiction* Web site: "I always hoped I'd be a writer of some sort, going back to when I was a little kid. Of course, I REALLY wanted to write mysteries back then—I even sent a short story to *Ellery Queen's Mystery Magazine* when I was like twelve years old. They didn't buy it, of course. It wasn't that good."

Early Writing Ambition

Hamilton told *AAYA* that he was shy in high school: "Lots of good friends, but all male. I was terrified of the opposite sex until very recently. Like when I turned 40." Hamilton earned a degree at the University of Michigan, where he also won the school's prestigious Hopwood Award in 1983 for his writing. Even though he had dreamed of writing, Hamilton found himself working as an information developer for International Business Machines (IBM). "I help people who use the biggest IBM mainframes to get their work done," he explained to *AAYA.* "Answering questions, writing instructions, putting stuff on the Web. The best part is that the people I work with at IBM have been amazingly supportive of my 'other' life in fiction." After ten years of working at IBM and trying to write and sell his fiction, he was unsuccessful. "Then a friend at work told me about a writing group he was in," Hamilton told Claire E. White for *Writers Write.* "Every Thursday night, they'd meet down in the basement of this little library. I started going, and besides all the other good reasons to be there, the best of all was the simple fact that now I had this external deadline. Every Thursday night, they'd be waiting, so I'd better get a short story done. That's really what got me back in the game."

Introduces Alex McKnight

Hamilton's first novel, *A Cold Day in Paradise,* won three major awards in the mystery field: the Best First Private Eye Novel from St. Martin's Press and the Private-Eye Writers of America (PWA), the Edgar Allan Poe Award from the Mystery Writers of America, and the Shamus Award from the PWA. As Barbara Franchi noted in *Reviewing the Evidence:* "This book won both the Edgar and Shamus awards. No other first mystery novel has ever done that." The novel was written for a writing contest. Hamilton explained: "When I decided to try entering the contest, I figured I should try to write a novel that was true to the private eye 'formula'—you know, with the wise-cracking private eye sitting in his office, waiting for the next client to walk in. I couldn't do it." Frustrated, Hamilton sat down at his keyboard and let the story develop naturally. In an online interview with Rainone, Hamilton explained: "I don't want to make it sound mystical—like this voice came to me from the heavens—but I got this idea for a character in the same mood I was in. Someone who was feeling like a failure, and he was by himself, like I felt by myself that night. So I started asking myself who this guy was and why he was feeling that way. And I got this idea for a character and started following it." That first novel, Hamilton recounted, "was really more of a suspense story than a classic private eye story, so I figured I had no chance of winning the contest. But then Robert Randisi, the president of PWA, called me one night to tell me I had won."

A Cold Day in Paradise tells of former-cop McKnight's move from Detroit to the small town of Paradise, Michigan, on the shore of Lake Superior. There he runs the camp his father left to him, renting out cabins to hunters, and only gets drawn back into his former life when two friends, a lawyer and a millionaire with a gambling problem, ask for his help. McKnight is reluctant to investigate, but when two bookmakers associated with the millionaire are murdered and the millionaire himself disappears under suspicious circumstances, McKnight is forced to become involved. The mystery deepens when it seems as if the man who shot McKnight years before, and who is now sitting in prison, actually masterminded the murders. "Hamilton's writing is brisk and Alex McKnight is a welcome addition to the ranks of PI heroes," stated Rick McMahan in a review for *Over My Dead Body Magazine.* A *Publishers Weekly* reviewer praised the novel's "clear, crisp writing, wily, colorful characters and an offbeat locale," calling *A Cold Day in Paradise* "an impressive debut."

Hamilton set this first story in Michigan's remote and rugged Upper Peninsula (popularly called the "U.P." by locals). The area is better known for its fishing and hunting than for its detectives. "Michigan's Upper Peninsula, not used as a setting for a mystery since perhaps Robert Traver's *Anatomy of a Murder* in the mid-1950s, is lovingly and well described and is a perfect metaphor for the isolation that McKnight both feels and seeks," according to Michael Grollman in *Reviewing the Evidence.* McKnight, Hamilton explained to Gary Warren Niebuhr in *Mystery News,* "lives in a cabin on an old logging road, and some days the only person he even talks to is his friend Jackie at the Glasgow Inn. Jackie will be the first one to tell you that, yes, Alex is hiding from the world. But of course the world keeps finding him. . . . He has to deal with what's happened in the past, but he does get over it. He has to—to save his own life in the first book and to help somebody else in the second. It's kind of a cliche to say it this way, but isn't overcoming fear more heroic than not feeling fear in the first place?" Hamilton told *AAYA* that McKnight is "really not based on anyone real, no. When I tried to write a traditional Private Eye and utterly failed, he was sort of just there, waiting. He's a very lonely person, actually. That was the first thing I knew about him."

The rugged setting for the series is based on Hamilton's own visits to the Upper Peninsula. The town of Paradise, which is the closest community to McKnight's isolated cabin, actually exists. "A few years ago," Hamilton told *AAYA,* "Paradise got six feet of snow in one day. Six feet of snow. And they still call it Paradise. That's maybe everything you need to know about the place right there. But seriously, it's such a remote place, and so beautiful in its own stark way. It just felt like the right place for Alex. I try to get back up to the U.P. at least once or twice a year. There's nowhere else like it!" "Growing up in the Detroit area," Hamilton told an interviewer for *Mystery Ink,* "we'd go 'Up North' (as they say in Michigan) every summer. It's such a great place and, in a country that's all starting to look alike, the U.P. is still totally unique. I still get back up there every year, and ironically I'm getting to know the U.P. even better now, even though I live in New York now."

McKnight returns in the novel *Winter of the Wolf Moon.* In this story the former cop subs as a hockey referee for a local team, but ends up defending an abused woman from her drug-dealing boyfriend. When the woman disappears, apparently kidnaped, McKnight and his Ojibway Indian friend Leon set out to find her. McKnight also has to convince the disbelieving police that there is a woman missing at all. Martha Moore in the *Mystery Reader* argued that "the one thing that can be said about Alex McKnight is that he is tenacious. Stupid and tenacious like a pit bull sometimes, but this man doesn't let up. . . . *Winter of the Wolf Moon* is carried largely by the first-person narrative. Alternating between comical, angry and determined, Alex McKnight is a formidable presence. Hamilton also succeeds with his supporting cast of characters, from the hard-nosed chief of police to the Scots bartender. And of course, the frozen and fierce winter setting plays a pivotal role as the mystery unfolds." *Booklist*'s Pitt claimed the story is, "start to finish, an excellent mystery," while a critic for *Publishers Weekly* judged *Winter of the Wolf Moon* to be "a most entertaining tale, peppered with wry humor and real, amusing characters."

The Hunting Wind finds McKnight reunited with an old buddy from his minor-league baseball days. The friend wants McKnight's help in tracking down a girlfriend he has not seen in some thirty years. Although reluctant, McKnight agrees to help, and soon the pair are combing through old public records in an inept effort to find the woman. Their search unwittingly stirs up violent trouble, though, and McKnight must find out just why. A *Publishers Weekly* contributor found that "Hamilton's prose moves us smoothly along and his characters are marvelously real," concluding that *The Hunting Wind* is an "exceptionally entertaining novel." Connie Fletcher, writing in *Booklist*, claimed that "the surprise ending delivers a satisfying jolt."

McKnight Turns Fifty

McKnight turns fifty years old in *North of Nowhere*, an event that leads him into depression and an almost hermit-like isolation. His friend Jackie Connery, owner of the local pub, decides to take drastic action to cheer up McKnight, and drags his buddy off to a poker game at a local millionaire's summer house. But the friendly game is interrupted by robbers, who force the millionaire to open his safe and clean it out. The local police chief is convinced that McKnight's poker-playing friends were in on the robbery, and the only way to clear them is for the reluctant ex-cop to discover the true culprits. According to a *Kirkus Reviews* critic, Hamilton "spins a brisk, well-plotted tale brightened by his usual deft way with local color." "Hamilton keeps the action fast and furious," according to a critic for *Publishers Weekly*, "and manages to keep the reader off balance almost as much as his hero." "The plot is wonderfully complex and takes several twists and turns, many of which are unexpected but none of which are implausible," wrote Maddy Van Hertbruggen in *Reviewing the Evidence*. "The setting, as always, is almost like another character. Add to that Hamilton's wit, smoothly written prose and impeccable sense of pacing, and you have a winner."

Blood Is the Sky finds McKnight trying to rebuild a cabin his father had first built, assisted by his friend Vinnie LeBlanc. But Vinnie soon faces a family crisis.

His parolee brother Tom, a professional guide, has been reported missing in the Canadian woods with a party of hunters. Because Tom has violated parole by leaving the country, Vinnie dares not report the disappearance to the authorities. Instead, he and McKnight set out to locate the missing men. Along the way, they uncover secrets stretching back many years, and find that Tom made friends with the wrong people. On his Web site, Hamilton explained that he got the novel's plot from going with friends into remote northern Ontario on fishing trips: "The last time I went up there, I spent a lot of time imagining all of the bad things that can happen to you if you're stranded a hundred miles away from the nearest phone, or the nearest building, or the nearest anything. What happens if you get sick? Or if you have an accident? What do you do if you have to wait six or seven days for help to arrive? Worse yet, what do you do if you suddenly realize that the men who are finally flying out to you aren't coming to help you at all?" A contributor to *Kirkus Reviews* called *Blood Is the Sky* a "smart, brisk, twisty tale." Andy Plonka, reviewing the title for *Mystery Reader*, concluded: "The plot is distinctive and flawless, a tale you literally cannot stop reading until it is done."

A Prohibition Mystery

Ice Run finds McKnight in the beginnings of a relationship with Canadian Constable Natalie Reynaud. While the two lovers try to spend time together, McKnight receives a mysterious message that pulls him into a mystery that goes back to Prohibition days, when smugglers brought liquor across the frozen St. Mary's River from Canada. His investigation results in a severe beating administered by three strangers and, even more painful, the loss of Natalie's affection. Connie Fletcher in *Booklist* allowed that Hamilton "delivers powerful suspense and a socko climax." "Hamilton expertly delivers sharply etched characters, a vivid setting and a thoroughly enjoyable hero, leaving us breathless, perched at the edge of our seats for this chilly ride," according to a *Publishers Weekly* reviewer. A *Kirkus Reviews* critic praised the novel, calling it "character-driven, briskly paced, occasionally witty, even wise: Hamilton's best, better than Edgar-winning *A Cold Day in Paradise*."

In *A Stolen Season*, the legendary cold weather of the Upper Peninsula has gone on much longer than usual. On a chilly Fourth of July night, McKnight helps rescue the passengers of a speedboat accident. The good deed leads him into investigating a criminal prescription drug ring. Meanwhile, Natalie is sent to Toronto to work undercover against a gun runner. A *Kirkus Reviews* writer noted that "the cast is strong and the local color vivid as ever," while Connie Fletcher in *Booklist* praised the novel's "hair-raising suspense with poignant characterization." "Plot turnarounds and double-crosses," wrote a critic for *Publishers Weekly*, "ensure a startling conclusion." According to Derek Hill in *Mystery Scene:* "This seventh novel in the McKnight series continues Hamilton's deft handling of straightforward plotting and complex yet familiar characters, dished up with the proper hardboiled backwoods style that his fans demand."

In 2007 Hamilton took a break from Alex McKnight to try his hand at a stand-alone crime novel. *Night Work* features Joe Trumbull, a New York probation officer who comes to realize that he is being stalked. In fact, the deaths of two women, including his own fiancée, are connected to the stalker, who is trying to frame him for the crimes. According to Dianne Day of *Mystery Scene,* "there's a twist at the end that's as tense as it is unexpected." A critic for *Kirkus Reviews* admitted: "It's hard not to like a good guy like Joe." Oline H. Cogdill, writing in the *South Florida Sun-Sentinel,* found that "Hamilton's shaping of Joe as a man whose life has been destroyed excels as does the setting of historic Kingston and the Hudson River landscape." David Pitt of *Booklist* found the novel to be "smartly paced with well-drawn characters and a constant claustrophobic sense of evil, as though something is about to lunge out of the darkness at us." According to Robert Wade, in a review for *Sign on San Diego,* Hamilton "displays here the same unrelenting suspense and emotional intensity that have made the McKnight stories so popular."

Hamilton told *AAYA:* "This new book is about a probation officer—and even though I intended it to be a stand-alone, I'm sure I'll probably write about Joe Trumbull again. I'd be an idiot not to, because he has the perfect license to be involved in other people's business every day. As for Alex, yes, I'll definitely go back to him! I can't imagine ever not wanting to know what's up with him next."

If you enjoy the works of Steve Hamilton, you may also want to check out the following books:

Robert Traver, *Anatomy of a Murder*, 1957.
Chuck Logan, *Hunter's Moon*, 1996.
William Kent Krueger, *Iron Lake*, 1999.
Julia Spencer-Fleming, *In the Bleak Midwinter*, 2002.

In an interview with Kevin Tipple at the *Hardluck Stories* Web site, Hamilton explained his writing process: "When I have an interesting situation that would make a good beginning, I just go. I don't have a map. I don't have any research. (I might do some of that after the fact). I've got nothing but that beginning and maybe just a vague feeling of how it MIGHT turn out—and I'm usually wrong about that." In his interview with Schechter, Hamilton remarked: "Winning the St. Martin's contest was a great way to break into the business, obviously. But years from now, it'll be the answer to a trivia question. The books are what you hope will last. If I can keep getting better and if people keep enjoying the books, I'll be holding up my end of the bargain." Asked by Martina Bexte of *Bookloons* about his writing schedule, Hamilton revealed: "My wife Julia is great and amazing, first of all. My two kids are great and amazing. When they all go to bed, that's when I do my thing. I'm upstairs in my office, telling these stories to myself and leading this secret fantasy life as a writer. I still can't quite believe that I get to keep doing it."

■ **Biographical and Critical Sources**

PERIODICALS

Booklist, February 15, 2000, David Pitt, review of *Winter of the Wolf Moon*, p. 1088; August, 2000, Karen Harris, review of *A Cold Day in Paradise* (audio edition), p. 2163; May 1, 2001, Connie Fletcher, review of *The Hunting Wind*, p. 1630; March 1, 2002, Connie Fletcher, review of *North of Nowhere*, p. 1095; January 1, 2003, Ted Hipple, review of *North of Nowhere* (audio edition), p. 920; May 1, 2003, Connie Fletcher, review of *Blood Is the Sky*, p. 1545; May 1, 2004, Connie Fletcher, review of *Ice Run*, p. 1508; July 1, 2006, Connie Fletcher, review of *A Stolen Season*, p. 37; July 1, 2007, David Pitt, review of *Night Work*, p. 35.

Capital Times (Madison, WI), June 28, 2002, Rob Thomas, review of *North of Nowhere*, p. 13A.

Evening Standard (London, England), October 24, 2006, Paul Connolly, review of *A Stolen Season*, p. 28.

Globe & Mail (Toronto, Canada), July 6, 2002, Margaret Cannon, review of *North of Nowhere*, p. 1; June 12, 2004, Margaret Cannon, review of *Ice Run*, p. D14; September 2, 2006, review of *A Stolen Season*, p. D12.

Kirkus Reviews, March 1, 2002, review of *North of Nowhere*, p. 292; April 1, 2003, review of *Blood Is the Sky*, p. 508; May 1, 2004, review of *Ice Run*, p. 424; August 1, 2006, review of *A Stolen Season*, p. 755; August 15, 2007, review of *Night Work*.

Library Journal, January, 2000, Rex E. Klett, review of *Winter of the Wolf Moon*, p. 166; May 1, 2003, Jo Ann Vicarel, review of *Blood Is the Sky*, p. 155; June 1, 2004, Rex E. Klett, review of *Ice Run*, p. 107; September 1, 2006, Andi Schechter, "Q & A: Steve Hamilton," p. 122; July 1, 2007, Roland Person, review of *Night Work*, p. 59.

Mystery News, February/March, 2000, Gary Warren Niebuhr, "No Interest in Being a Private Eye: The Reluctant Career of Alex McKnight," pp. 6-7.

Mystery Scene, fall, 2006, Derek Hill, review of *A Stolen Season*; fall, 2007, Dianne Day, review of *Night Work*, p. 67.

New York Times Book Review, February 6, 2000, Marilyn Stasio, review of *Winter of the Wolf Moon*, p. 24; June 24, 2001, Marilyn Stasio, review of *The Hunting Wind*, p. 22; May 19, 2002, Marilyn Stasio, review of *North of Nowhere*, p. 44; September 17, 2006, Marilyn Stasio, review of *A Stolen Season*, p. 35.

Plain Dealer (Cleveland, OH), December 7, 2000, Michele Ross, review of *Winter of the Wolf Moon*, p. 6E.

Publishers Weekly, July 6, 1998, review of *A Cold Day in Paradise*, p.53; January 17, 2000, review of *Winter of the Wolf Moon*, p. 46; May 21, 2001, review of *The Hunting Wind*, p. 85; March 18, 2002, review of *North of Nowhere*, p. 80; May 12, 2003, review of *Blood Is the Sky*; May 24, 2004, review of *Ice Run*, p. 48; July 10, 2006, review of *A Stolen Season*, p. 57; July 9, 2007, review of *Night Work*, p. 32.

South Florida Sun-Sentinel (Fort Lauderdale, FL), June 28, 2002, Oline H. Cogdill, review of *North of Nowhere*; September 9, 2007, Oline H. Cogdill, review of *Night Work*.

Tampa Tribune (Tampa, FL), September 17, 2006, Larry Gandle, "Boat Wreck on Michigan Lake Draws Retired Cop into Mystery," p. 9.

ONLINE

Bookloons, http://www.bookloons.com/ (September, 2006), Martina Bexte, "Steve Hamilton Creates a Different Kind of Private Eye."

Fiction Addiction, http://interviews.fictionaddiction.net/ (May 6, 2007), interview with Steve Hamilton; Veronica Tammaro, review of *The Hunting Wind*; Robert Ryan Langer, review of *Blood Is the Sky* (audio edition).

Hardluck Stories, http://www.hardluckstories.com/ (June 23, 2007), Kevin Tipple, "Steve Hamilton Interview."

January Magazine, http://www.januarymagazine.com/ (May, 2002), Anthony Rainone, "The Education of Steve Hamilton" (interview).

Mystery Ink, http://www.mysteryinkonline.com/ (July 2, 2003), "Interview with Steve Hamilton"; David J. Montgomery, review of *Blood Is the Sky*.

Mystery Reader, http://www.themysteryreader.com/ (August 22, 2007), Martha Moore, reviews of *A Cold Day in Paradise* and *Winter of the Wolf Moon*, and Andy Plonka, reviews of *The Hunting Wind*, *North of Nowhere*, and *Blood Is the Sky*.

Over My Dead Body Magazine, http://www.overmydeadbody.com/ (May 6, 2007), Rick McMahan, review of *A Cold Day in Paradise*; Karen Meek, reviews of *Ice Run*, *Blood Is the Sky*, and *North of Nowhere*.

Reviewing the Evidence, http://www.reviewingtheevidence.com/ (June, 2002), Barbara Franchi, review of *A Cold Day in Paradise*, Michael Grollman, review of *North of Nowhere*, and Maddy Van Hertbruggen, review of *North of Nowhere*, (July, 2002), Barbara Franchi, review of *Winter of the Wolf Moon*; (April, 2003), Sharon Katz, review of *Blood Is the Sky*; (August, 2003), Sarah Dudley, review of *Blood Is the Sky*; (September, 2006), P.J. Coldren, review of *A Stolen Season*; (August, 2007), Sharon Katz, review of *Night Work*.

Shots, http://www.shotsmag.co.uk/ (May 6, 2007), interview with Steve Hamilton.

Sign on San Diego, http://books.signonsandiego.com/ (October 21, 2007), Robert Wade, review of *Night Work*.

Steve Hamilton Web site, http://www.authorstevehamilton.com (November 19, 2007).

Writers Write, http://www.writerswrite.com/ (May 6, 2007), Claire E. White, "A Conversation with Steve Hamilton."

James Hilton

(Photograph copyright © Bettmann/CORBIS.)

■ Personal

Born September 9, 1900, in Leigh, Lancashire, England; immigrated to the United States, 1937, naturalized U.S. citizen, 1948; died December 20, 1954, of cancer of the liver; son of John (a headmaster of an elementary school) and Elizabeth (a teacher) Hilton; married Alice Brown (divorced, April 13, 1937); married Galina Kopineck (an actress), April 20, 1937 (divorced, 1945). *Education:* Attended Leys School, Cambridge; Christ's College, Cambridge, B.A., 1921.

■ Career

Novelist, screenwriter, and journalist, 1921-54. Instructor at Cambridge University, 1921-32. Host and editor of *Hallmark Playhouse,* a radio broadcast, beginning 1948.

■ Awards, Honors

Hawthornden Prize, 1934, for *Lost Horizon;* Academy Award for Best Screenplay, 1942, for *Mrs. Miniver.*

■ Writings

Catherine Herself, Unwin (London, England), 1920, Avon (New York, NY), 1946.

Storm Passage, Unwin (London, England), 1922.

The Passionate Year, Butterworth (London, England), 1923, Little, Brown (Boston, MA), 1924.

The Dawn of Reckoning, Butterworth (London, England), 1925.

The Meadows of the Moon, Butterworth (London, England), 1926, Small, Maynard (Boston, MA), 1927.

Terry, Butterworth (London, England), 1927.

The Silver Flame, Butterworth (London, England), 1928.

And Now Good-bye: A Novel, Benn (London, England), 1931, Morrow (New York, NY), 1932.

(Under pseudonym Glen Trevor) *Murder at School: A Detective Fantasia,* Benn (London, England), 1931, published as *Was It Murder?,* Harper (New York, NY), 1933, published under name James Hilton, Harper (New York, NY), 1935.

Rage in Heaven, King (New York, NY), 1932.

Contango: A Novel, Benn (London, England), published as *Ill Wind,* Morrow (New York, NY), 1932.

Knight without Armour, Benn (London, England), 1933, published as *Without Armor,* Morrow (New York, NY), 1934.

Lost Horizon, Morrow (New York, NY), 1933.

Good-bye, Mr. Chips, Little, Brown (Boston, MA), 1934.

We Are Not Alone, Little, Brown (Boston, MA), 1937.

To You, Mr. Chips, Hodder & Stoughton (London, England), 1938.

Random Harvest, Little, Brown (Boston, MA), 1941.

So Well Remembered, Little, Brown (Boston, MA), 1945.

Three Loves Had Margaret, Avon (New York, NY), 1946.

Nothing So Strange, Little, Brown (Boston, MA), 1947.

Twilight of the Wise, St. Hugh's (London, England), 1949.

Morning Journey, Little, Brown (Boston, MA), 1951.

Time and Time Again, Little, Brown (Boston, MA), 1953.

SCREENPLAYS

(With Zoe Akins and Frances Marion) *Camille*, Metro-Goldwyn-Mayer (MGM), 1936.

(With Milton Krims) *We Are Not Alone*, Warner Brothers, 1939.

The Tuttles of Tahiti, RKO, 1942.

(With Arthur Wimperis, George Froeschel, and Claudine West) *Mrs. Miniver*, MGM, 1942.

(With Charles Bennett, C.S. Forester, and others) *Forever and a Day*, RKO, 1943.

Collaborator, with Robert Benchley, on dialogue for film *Foreign Correspondent*, 1940; narrator, *Madame Curie*, 1943.

OTHER

(With Barbara Burnham) *Good-bye Mr. Chips: A Play in Three Acts*, Hodder & Stoughton (London, England), 1938.

Address by James Hilton on the Present War and Our Hopes for the Future, [New York], 1943.

The Story of Dr. Wassell, Little, Brown (Boston, MA), 1943.

H.R.H.: The Story of Philip, Duke of Edinburgh, Little, Brown (Boston, MA), 1956.

Contributor to periodicals, including *Atlantic Monthly, Manchester Guardian*, and *Ellery Queen's Mystery Magazine*. Columnist, *Irish Independent*; fiction reviewer, *Daily Telegraph*

■ **Adaptations**

Lost Horizon was filmed by Frank Capra for Columbia in 1937; and filmed as a musical by Columbia in 1973. *Goodbye, Mr. Chips* was filmed by MGM, with Robert Donat in the title role, in 1939; filmed by MGM, with Peter O'Toole in the title role, in 1969; filmed by the British Broadcasting Corp. (BBC) as a six-episode television miniseries in 1984; and filmed by SMG Television Productions Limited for the Public Broadcasting System (PBS) in 2002. *Goodbye, Mr. Chips* was also adapted as the Portuguese television series *Adeus, Mr. Chips* by TV Tupi in 1959. *Knight without Armour* was filmed by London Film Productions in 1937. *Rage in Heaven* was filmed by MGM in 1941. *Random Harvest* was filmed by MGM in 1942. *So Well Remembered* was filmed by Alliance Productions in 1947. *And Now Goodbye* was adapted for the New York stage and produced in 1937.

■ **Sidelights**

Although he was a novelist and screenwriter for many years, James Hilton is best known for two novels with continuing audience appeal: *Lost Horizon*, the story of a hidden utopia called Shangri-La, and *Good-bye, Mr. Chips*, the nostalgic story of a beloved British school teacher. Both best-selling novels were also made into successful films. Hilton, always more popular with the public than with literary critics, once modestly called himself a "novelist who sells the reader a good time." Rose Feld, writing in the *New York Times Book Review*, maintained: "Hilton has an enormous preoccupation with the past and the hidden, both in terms of civilization and of human beings. Wedded to that preoccupation is a masterly ability to create a mood in his writing which carries the reader along with him."

Hilton was born in Leigh, Lancashire, England, in 1900. His father, John Hilton, was a teacher, as was his mother, Elizabeth Hilton. In 1902, his father became headmaster at an elementary school in London. James Hilton attended Leys School in Cambridge and, after graduation, moved on to Christ's College in Cambridge. While still attending college, he published his first novel, *Catherine Herself*, which made little impression on the reading public. After graduating from college in 1921, Hilton found it difficult to find steady work. The post-World War I economy was in a slump. For several years he worked as an instructor at Cambridge and as a journalist. He wrote a weekly newspaper column under a pseudonym and reviewed books for the *Daily Telegraph*.

Decade of Teaching

During the 1920s, Hilton continued to write and publish a string of novels with little success while continuing his teaching career. His 1923 novel *The*

Passionate Year tells the story of a schoolmaster who marries the daughter of the head of the school. His wife is unable to provide him support as she leads a tumultuous life of her own and eventually commits suicide. A *Boston Transcript* reviewer found the story good for its portrayal of the "depressing and constrained life" at an English boarding school, but called the author a "poor diagnostician of the heart." A *Times Literary Supplement* reviewer noted that though the story is at times melodramatic, the author makes the reader identify with the characters in his realistic depiction of them.

In 1931, Hilton found unexpected success with two books. Under the pseudonym Glen Trevor, he published a mystery novel, *Murder at School: A Detective Fantasia.* The book sold so well that it was reprinted in the United States as well. The story features amateur detective Colin Revell, who returns to Oakington, the boarding school he attended, to investigate the strange death of one of the students. Robert Marshall died when a gas fixture fell on him while he was sleeping. Two more deaths occur before Revell solves the mystery. "The unusual setting and Hilton's use of a witty amateur detective nicely balance the morbid events," wrote Marvin S. Lachman in the *Dictionary of Literary Biography.* Lachman concluded: "The book's denouement, in which the true killer is revealed, is a small masterpiece."

And Now Good-bye: A Novel is a more serious novel. It was praised by several critics for its provincial sense of Englishness and its ability to tell a sentimental story without becoming maudlin. The story concerns a priest suffering from a mental breakdown, whose life is later changed when he meets the daughter of a parishioner. After being injured in a train accident, the priest has a long recuperation before he returns to the pulpit. A *Boston Transcript* critic called the story "absolutely satisfying" and *Yale Review* critic Helen McAfee remarked that Hilton is good at capturing "the slow erosion of daily life." With the financial success of these two books, Hilton was able to quit teaching and devote himself to writing.

In 1932 Hilton published *Ill Wind*, which consists of several short stories linked through the chance meetings of the characters. The premise met with mixed reviews from critics. A *Books* reviewer commented that even though the technique seems heavy-handed at times, the result is a "moving and extraordinary book." But V.S. Pritchett of *New Statesman and Nation* called the link between the stories "not strong enough" and claimed that too much is left to chance. A *Saturday Review* critic overlooked the literary device and wrote that the sincerity and originality of the effort stands on its own.

Hilton gives the reader a taste of Russian history in *Knight without Armour,* the story of a British spy's encounters during the Russian revolution. Many critics remarked on Hilton's knowledge of Russian history, which gives "the air of having been obtained first hand" and seems "the illusion of an actual biography," according to a writer for the *Saturday Review of Literature.* Graham Greene of the *Spectator* attributed the book's plainness to its factual prose. McAfee admitted that the book was hard to put down because of its exciting portrayal of historical events, though she deemed the novel not as "fine" as Hilton's previous work.

Creates a Utopia

With his 1933 novel *Lost Horizon*, Hilton had his first bestseller. The novel tells of the crash of a British plane high in the remote Himalayan Mountains

The 2004 edition of the classic tale about a utopian community in the remote mountains of Tibet. (Perennial, 2004. Reprinted by permission of HarperCollins Publishers Inc.)

The poster for the 1937 film version of Hilton's popular novel, *Lost Horizon,* **directed by Frank Capra.** (Courtesy of Columbia/ The Kobal Collection/The Picture Desk, Inc.)

of Tibet. The plane's passengers have been escaping a revolution in a nearby country when they were kidnapped by the plane's pilot. He flew them to an unknown location where he crash-landed, killing himself. The crash survivors find themselves lost in a snow-covered rugged terrain until they stumble upon an isolated valley that is free of snow. Here they find Shangri-La, a lamasery (a residence for monks) in the Valley of the Blue Moon.

Shangri-La is an ageless society, whose inhabitants keep their youth and live far beyond the usual life span of humans from the outside world. "The very highest attainments in all fields are possible," John W. Crawford explained in *Extrapolation.* "Besides meeting the basic needs, the most exquisite things are to be found here—from collections of art, to music, to knowledge, to religion. The whole illustrates a balance and rarity so fragile that it could be easily destroyed at any time by those who do

not understand or appreciate its worth." The community is led by the High Lama, who has lived for some two hundred years. Visitors to Shangri-La are welcome, but they are not allowed to leave. Shangri-La does not want the outside world, which they see as corrupt, to know about them. Each Western character represents a mode of thinking that is in contrast to the Eastern idea expressed in Shangri-La: moderation in all things to avoid stress or conflict. The leader of the Westerners, the diplomat, adventurer, and patriot "Glory" Conway, falls in love with Shangri-La and its goals. However, his deputy counsel Mallinson is unhappy with life there and persuades Conway to lead him and some others back to the outside world. Conway barely survives the trip, and as the novel closes he is struggling to find his way back to the elusive Shangri-La.

A critic for the *Times Literary Supplement* at the time concluded: "Hilton always writes well and with imagination; his characters are clearly drawn and revealed in constant dramatic movement; his dialogue is excellent." "It quite definitely establishes Mr. Hilton as a writer to read now and to watch for in the future," wrote George Dangerfield in the *Saturday Review of Literature.*

Lost Horizon was an enormously popular novel, selling millions of copies worldwide. It also became the first book to be reprinted as a paperback. President Franklin Roosevelt named his country retreat Shangri-La (later changed to the present-day name of Camp David). Even an aircraft carrier was named after the utopian community in 1944. The reading public of the time, with memories of the horrors of World War I still fresh in their minds and now coping with the Great Depression, welcomed this vision of a utopian hideaway of peace and plenty. "In *Lost Horizon* James Hilton, playing Alice, takes us through the Looking Glass into a land of make-believe," according to James W. Poling in the *New York Herald Tribune Books.* "This novel, so fantastic and incredible in conception, is a strange and interesting example of that romantic 'escape' literature which, today, many of our better writers are turning to. . . . There are several truly dramatic moments, some moments of quiet beauty and others of pleasant satire and humor. The idea behind the book and its implied philosophy are mentally provocative, and it is all told in the same terse and imaginative prose which distinguish the author's earlier work." Writing in *Geographical,* Jules Stewart noted that, "above all, *Lost Horizon* is a thumping great adventure yarn, but the reader is confronted with deeper metaphysical issues" as well. "Hilton's *Lost Horizon,*" wrote an essayist for the *St. James Guide to Fantasy Writers,* "is one of those rare books which have added a new concept to the English language. The name of Shangri-La, the Tibetan lamasery situated above a preternaturally fertile mountain-rimmed valley, whose inhabitants enjoy a long-extended youth, has come to be used with reference to any remote and idyllic retreat from the hostile and confusing world."

"Many of [Hilton's] books," declared Lauren H. Pringle in the *Dictionary of Literary Biography,* "wistfully evoke a rosy image of Victorian and Edwardian life, . . . that humane, genteel, balanced atmosphere which Hilton—and his readers—felt was destroyed in the ferocity and barbarism of the world war." Shangri-La in *Lost Horizon* is in many ways a tribute to the English society that Hilton felt had fallen prey to such outside influences as the Great Depression and political unrest in India. "To a man of Hilton's tastes and turn of mind," wrote Harold C. Martin in his introductory essay to an American edition of *Lost Horizon,* "these events must have seemed not only dreadful in themselves but a threat to the way of life he most cherished." "The next

Peter O'Toole as Mr. Chipping in a still from the 1969 film version of *Goodbye, Mr. Chips.* (Copyright © Bettmann/ CORBIS.)

war," Hilton told Grant Uden in a 1934 interview for the *Bookman,* "will be more than a waste—it will mean practically total annihilation of everything decent and beautiful." "Just as eighteenth-century England became enamored of Orientalism," Crawford stated, "so does the twentieth-century Englishman begin seeing man's hope resting in the isolated, primitive setting of marble palaces, running streams, flowing fountains, and afternoon teas in shady bowers—a virtual Edenic Shangri-La." In 1937 Columbia released a film version of *Lost Horizon* directed by Frank Capra. Many editions of the novel have appeared over the years since its initial release.

A Fond Look at Teaching

While *Lost Horizon* has enjoyed a lasting popularity, it was not an immediate success. The book only caught widespread attention following the release of the 1934 novel *Good-bye, Mr. Chips.* In December of 1933, Hilton agreed to write a long Christmas story for the magazine *British Weekly.* But he could not come up with an idea. Finally, during an early morning bicycle ride, he began thinking about his childhood school days. Four days later, *Good-bye, Mr. Chips* was finished. While the story's reception in England was favorable, its April, 1934, appearance in the American *Atlantic Monthly* magazine drew an enthusiastic response. Later that same year, the story was published as a novel in the United States.

Good-bye, Mr. Chips tells the story of the life of Mr. Chipping, a classics master at the small, fictional English school of Brookfield. "Mr. Chips," as his students cheekily call him, originally harbored ambitions to become a teacher at a first-rate school when he started at Brookfield in 1870. Instead, he finds that his life becomes inextricably intertwined with Brookfield, teaching Greek and Latin to his boys, then to the sons of his boys, and finally, to the grandsons of his original students. He marries a much younger woman in the 1890s, but loses her

and their child during childbirth. Although he retires from active teaching in 1913 at the age of sixty-five, he returns to Brookfield three years later to serve as headmaster. "Throughout the 1920s he lived on his memories," explained Patrick Scott in the *South Atlantic Quarterly*, "but in 1933 he died quite suddenly, having fallen into an unexplained faint, following exposure to the chilling air of autumn." Three generations of students, who had come to know and love his gentle humor, mourned him.

While a tribute to the English school system, *Good-bye, Mr. Chips* is also a paean to a way of life that is ending. Chips's turn as headmaster shows the effects of World War I on Brookfield. He is only asked to fill the role because there are no younger men available. Chips himself struggles against change in the form of a new headmaster who stresses teaching science rather than the classics. In the process,

Actor Peter O'Toole with school boys in a still from the 1969 film version of *Goodbye, Mr. Chips*. (MGM/The Kobal Collection/The Picture Desk, Inc.)

Mr. Chips comes to represent the best of Brookfield and Victorian England itself—"an embodiment of beloved tradition," stated a *New York Times Book Review* critic. "To Brookfield boys," wrote Florence Haxton Britten in the *New York Herald Tribune Books,* "he gave a little and very salutary taste of the best of the old and the pre-war which must so inevitably yield its place to the new." "As Chips grows older, in spite of all the jolly protestations that he will live forever," declared Scott, "we know that Chips must die. He knows more about Brookfield than anyone else and is acclaimed as the upholder of the Brookfield tradition, but we know that his memories will come to mean less and less to his visitors, for whom the world, even of school, has changed." Britten called the novel "a little masterpiece" and praised "the grace and style and sympathetic delicacy of this gently told story." The *New York Times Book Review* critic concluded that *Good-bye, Mr. Chips* is "a minor miracle—one of those rare and living pieces of writing which transcend classification. . . . Above all, it creates in Mr. Chips himself a memorable and living character."

A Life in America

Hilton and his wife, Alice, came to the United States in November of 1935 to advise on the filming of *Lost Horizon.* Hilton soon became involved in writing screenplays for Hollywood studios. In 1937, he became a permanent resident of the United States and, in 1948, an American citizen. Also in 1937, Hilton filed for a Mexican divorce from his first wife and, seven days after it was granted, married Galina Kopineck. She was to divorce him in 1945.

As a screenwriter, Hilton wrote several noteworthy Hollywood films. *Mrs. Miniver,* for which he and his co-writers won an Academy Award for the screenplay, highlights the struggle of British civilians during World War II. It tells the story of the happy Miniver family, whose idyllic life in a town outside London, England, is shattered when the war brings tragedy to their doorstep. Friends and family members are killed by low-flying Nazi bombers during air raids. To keep their spirits up, the local vicar prepares a patriotic speech that transcended the film and became a rallying cry for the Allies. "This film packed a tremendous emotional wallop back in 1942," Jamie Gillies wrote in the *Apollo Guide,* "as one of the first major films that depicted the effects of the Second World War on the British population. Winston Churchill said that *Mrs. Miniver* was more vital to the nation than a flotilla of destroyers." The film, which won numerous Academy Awards, was a box-office success and became Hilton's most successful screenplay. Hilton also contributed dialogue to the 1940 Alfred Hitchcock

thriller *Foreign Correspondent,* and cowrote 1943's *Forever and a Day,* a wartime patriotic feature starring a host of prominent actors, including Claude Rains, Ida Lupino, Merle Oberon, Ray Milland, Charles Laughton, Elsa Lanchester, Sir Cedric Hardwicke, Sir C. Aubrey Smith, and Buster Keaton.

Hilton continued to write novels, even as he enjoyed success as a Hollywood screenwriter. *Random Harvest* is the story of a man who must piece together three years of his life, lost to him through amnesia. English soldier Charles Rainier loses his memory during a World War I bombing attack. When he is sent back home to England, he is hospitalized. But he escapes from the hospital and, still under amnesia and unaware of his true identity, marries a young girl. But when his memory returns, he forgets her and returns to his pre-war life. Only through true love does the couple ultimately meet again and find happiness. *Boston Transcript* reviewer Marian Wiggen praised the story for its realistic portrayal of events that "could so easily have happened," and compared the book favorably to *Lost Horizon* and *Good-bye Mr. Chips. Churchman* reviewer G.F. Taylor praised the novel's presentations of "shell shock, a changing social order, and a good love story." Muriel Burns of the *New Republic* praised the characters in the story, even though she found the story tinged with a "faintly mauve sentimentalism." "Hilton," according to Clifton Fadiman in the *New Yorker.* "has cranked out another deft piece of storytelling. . . . There are certainly very few writers as sheerly ingenious as he is, or as able to cut out and put together the complex jigsaw-puzzle kind of story of which *Random Harvest* is so good an example." "*Random Harvest* is, as a whole, so good a book that one forgets its minor flaws," Rose Feld noted in the *New York Times Book Review.* "It is Rainier who makes the tale and he is completely real and convincing." Hilton sold the film rights to the story for $50,000 and it was filmed by MGM in 1942. In addition to his film work, Hilton served as host and editor of the popular radio program *Hallmark Playhouse* beginning in 1948.

If you enjoy the works of James Hilton, you may also want to check out the following books:

W.H. Hudson, *Green Mansions,* 1989.
Lois Lowry, *The Giver,* 1994.
Heinrich Harrar, *Seven Years in Tibet,* 1997.
Tobias Wolff, *Old School,* 2005.

In 1954, Hilton died of cancer of the liver. A writer for *Time* magazine stated at the time: "Millionaire novelist Hilton served up a mellow blend of worldly wisdom and well-bred British morality that delighted the book clubs, Hollywood producers, and the general public, but alienated first-line critics." Hilton's unfailing ability to fashion a story that readers enjoyed was remarked upon by Isabelle Mallet in the *New York Times:* "Hilton's gift as a raconteur has reached a pitch where he could if necessary tell an absorbing and expert story about almost nothing. . . . He has evolved a smooth blend of worldly wisdom, charming simplicity and delightful ease with words which could conceivably carry the multiplication table to dramatic heights. But the moralist in Mr. Hilton demands that, however cunning the design of his embroidery, the material used must project its author's straightforward belief in human nature, his positive reverence for decency."

■ **Biographical and Critical Sources**

BOOKS

Dictionary of Literary Biography, Gale (Detroit, MI), Volume 34: *British Novelists, 1890-1929: Traditionalists,* 1985, Volume 77: *British Mystery Writers, 1920-1939,* 1988.

Hammond, John R., *Lost Horizon Companion: A Guide to the James Hilton Novel and Its Characters, Critical Reception, Film Adaptations and Place in Popular Culture,* McFarland & Co. (Jefferson, NC), 2008.

Martin, Harold C., introduction to *Lost Horizon* by James Hilton, Houghton (Boston, MA), 1962.

Modern British Literature, 2nd edition, St. James Press (Detroit, MI), 2000.

Mott, Frank Luther, *Golden Multitudes: The Story of Best Sellers in the United States,* Macmillan (New York, NY), 1947.

Reference Guide to Short Fiction, St. James Press (Detroit, MI), 1994.

St. James Guide to Fantasy Writers, St. James Press (Detroit, MI), 1996.

Sibley, Carrol, *Barrie and His Contemporaries: Cameo Portraits of Ten Living Authors,* International Mark Twain Society (Missouri), 1936.

Stevens, George, *Lincoln's Doctor's Dog and Other Famous Best Sellers,* Lippincott (Philadelphia, PA), 1938.

Twentieth Century Literary Criticism, Volume 21, Gale (Detroit, MI), 1986.

Weeks, Edward, foreword to *Good-bye Mr. Chips* by James Hilton, Little, Brown (Boston, MA), 1962.

PERIODICALS

Atlantic Monthly, April, 1937; June, 1938, pp. 28-40; April, 1951; September, 1953; November, 1980.

Bookman, July, 1934, p. 192.

Books, February 21, 1931, p. 2; April 10, 1932, p. 15; November 20, 1032, p. 10.

Bookweek, May 2, 1943, p. 6; August 5, 1945, p. 5.

Boston Transcript, March 29, 1924, p. 15; March 9, 1932, p. 2; December 28, 1932, p. 2; December 22, 1934, p. 10; March 13, 1937, p. 11; January 25, 1941, Marian Wiggen, review of *Random Harvest,* p. 1.

Canadian Forum, December, 1933; July, 1037; April, 1941; November, 1953.

Catholic World, May, 1937; March, 1941; October, 1945; May, 1951; November, 1953.

Chicago Tribune, December 22, 1934, p. 10; March 13, 1937, p. 21; February 18, 1951, p. 3; August 23, 1953, p. 3; April 22, 1956, p. 6.

Choice, December, 1986, p. 597.

Christian Century, March 5, 1941; August 15, 1945; August 26, 1953.

Christian Science Monitor, July 1, 1933, p. 10; June 23, 1937, p. 10; March 15, 1941, p. 10; April 27, 1943, p. 14; August 1, 1945, p. 12; October 20, 1947, p. 16; February 24, 1951, p. 9; August 20, 1953, p. 11; April 19, 1956, p. 7.

Churchman, March, 1941, G.F. Taylor, review of *Random Harvest.*

Commonwealth, August 31, 1934; April 9, 1937; May, 1940, p. 75; February 28, 1941; August 31, 1945; December 12, 1947.

Cuyahoga Review, spring-summer, 1984, John W. Crawford, "The Utopian Dream, Alive and Well," pp. 27-33.

Extrapolation, summer, 1981, John W. Crawford, "Utopian Eden of 'Lost Horizon,'" pp. 186-190.

Far Eastern Review, August 22, 1996, pp. 45-46.

Forum, August, 1934.

Geographical, July, 2005, Jules Stewart, review of *Lost Horizon,* p. 88.

Hiltonian, 2005—.

James Hilton Newsletter, 2005—.

Library Journal, January 1, 1941.

Literary Review, May 17, 1924, p. 764.

Literature/Film Quarterly, Volume 17, number 4, 1989, Brian McFarlane, "Re-Shaped for the Screen: 'Random Harvest,'" pp. 268-273.

Malcolm Lowry Newsletter, fall, 1982, pp. 7-10.

Manchester Guardian, April 6, 1937, p. 7; October 3, 1941, p. 3; November 30, 1951, p. 4.

Margin: Life & Letters in Early Australia, November, 2006, Victor Crittenden, "'Watkin Tench,' 'La Perouse,' and 'Lost Horizon,'" p. 4.

Nassau Review, Volume 4, number 3, 1982, Francis S. Heck, "The Domain as a Symbol of a Paradise Lost: 'Lost Horizon' and 'Brideshead Revisited,'" pp. 24-29.

Nation, February 22, 1941; May 15, 1943.

Natural History Review, April, 1983, pp. 54-62.

New Republic, July 23, 1924; July 18, 1934, pp. 271-272; March 17, 1937, pp. 173-174; March 17, 1941, Muriel Burns, review of *Random Harvest.*

New Statesman and Nation, September 12, 1931; September 3, 1932; October 20, 1934; April 10, 1937; November 14, 1953.

New Statesman & Society, May 13, 1933; October 20, 1934, pp. 550, 552; July 21, 1989, p. 33.

New Yorker, January 25, 1941, Clifton Fadiman, review of *Random Harvest,* pp. 60, 62; April 24, 1943; October 18, 1947; February 24, 1951; August 29, 1953.

New York Herald Tribune Books, October 15, 1933, James W. Poling, review of *Lost Horizon,* p. 14; June 10, 1934, Florence Haxton Britten, review of *Goodbye, Mr. Chips,* p. 5; October 19, 1947, p. 4; February 18, 1951, p. 5; August 23, 1953, p. 1; May 6, 1956, p. 6.

New York Times, November 20, 1932, p. 7; March 14, 1937, p. 7; May 14, 1943, p. 6; October 19, 1947, p. 4; February 18, 1951, p. 5.

New York Times Book Review, April 20, 1924, p. 27; February 21, 1932, p. 7; October 15, 1933, pp. 8-9; March 11, 1934, p. 24; June 17, 1934, p. 9; January 26, 1941, Rose Feld, review of Random Harvest, p. 4; August 5, 1945, Isabelle Mallet, "Mr. Hilton's Cunning Embroidery," p. 5; June 23, 1985, p. 32; January 26, 1941, p. 4; August 5, 1945, p. 5; August 23, 1953, p. 4.

Observer (London, England), November 23, 1969, p. 27; April 13, 1997, p. 18.

p.o.v: A Danish Journal of Film Studies, December, 2006, Richard Raskin, "The Three Endings of Capra's 'Lost Horizon' (1937)," pp. 89-94.

Publishers Weekly, August 15, 1966, p. 67; May 1, 1967, p. 57; September 15, 1969, p. 62.

San Francisco Chronicle, October 26, 1947, p. 13; March 8, 1951, p. 20; September 6, 1953, p. 19; June 24, 1956, p. 23.

Saturday Review of Literature, May 21, 1932; September 3, 1932; November 12, 1932; May 13, 1933; October 14, 1933, George Dangerfield, review of *Lost Horizon,* p. 181; April 21, 1934; June 9, 1934, p. 739; October 13, 1934; March 13, 1937; January 25, 1941; May 15, 1943; December 13, 1947; March 17, 1951; August 29, 1953.

South Atlantic Quarterly, autumn, 1986, pp. 319-328.

Spectator, August 29, 1931; September 17, 1932; June 16, 1933; April 16, 1937; October 10, 1941.

Springfield Republican, July 22, 1934, p. E7; March 14, 1937, p. E7; November 16, 1947, p. B10; May 13, 1951, p. A20; August 30, 1953, p. C5; April 29, 1956, p. C8.

Time, March 15, 1937; October 27, 1947; March 12, 1951; August 24, 1953.

Times Literary Supplement, December 6, 1923, p. 853; August 27, 1931, p. 646; September 8, 1932, p. 622; May 18, 1933, p. 346; September 28, 1933, review of *Lost Horizon,* p. 648; November 22, 1934, p. 826; September 10, 1941, p. 469; December 14, 1951; November 13, 1953, p. 721.

Virginia Quarterly Review, spring, 1980, p. 79.

Wilson Library Bulletin, October, 1924; April, 1932; July, 1934; April, 1937; November, 1947; March, 1951; July, 1953; May, 1956; March, 1980, p. 453.

Yale Review, summer, 1932; spring, 1934; winter, 1934; spring, 1937; spring, 1941; summer, 1943.

ONLINE

Apollo Guide, http://www.apolloguide.com/ (June 15, 2007), Jamie Gillies, review of *Mrs. Miniver.*

James Hilton Society Web site, http://www.james hiltonsociety.co.uk/ (June 15, 2007).*

Sarah Orne Jewett

(Copyright © Bettmann/CORBIS.)

■ Personal

Born September 3, 1849, in South Berwick, Maine; died of a cerebral hemorrhage, June 24, 1909, in South Berwick, ME; daughter of Theodore Herman (a physician) and Caroline Frances Jewett. *Education:* Attended Miss Payne's School; graduated from Berwick Academy, 1866.

■ Career

Writer.

■ Awards, Honors

Honorary doctorate from Bowdoin College, 1901.

■ Writings

SHORT STORIES

Deephaven, J.R. Osgood (Boston, MA), 1877.

Old Friends and New (contains "A Lost Lover," "A Sorrowful Guest," "A Late Supper," "Mr. Bruce," "Miss Sydney's Flowers," "Lady Ferry," and "A Bit of Shore Life"), Houghton, Osgood (Boston, MA), 1879.

Country By-Ways (contains "River Driftwood,""Andrew's Fortune," "An October Ride," "From a Mournful Villager," "An Autumn Holiday," "A Winter Drive," "Good Luck: A Girl's Story," and "Miss Becky's Pilgrimage"), Houghton Mifflin, 1881.

The Mate of the Daylight, and Friends Ashore (contains "The Mate of the Daylight," "A Landless Farmer," "A New Parishioner," "An Only Son," "Miss Debby's Neighbors," "Tom's Husband," "The Confession of a House-Breaker," and "A Little Traveler"), Houghton Mifflin, 1884.

A White Heron, and Other Stories (contains "A White Heron," "The Gray Man," "Farmer Finch," "Marsh Rosemary," "The Dulham Ladies," "A Business Man," "Mary and Martha," "The News from Petersham," and "The Two Browns"), Houghton Mifflin, 1886, title story published separately as *A White Heron: A Story of Maine,* illustrations by Barbara Cooney, Crowell, 1963, with illustrations by Vera Rosenberry, Creative Education, 1983.

The King of Folly Island, and Other People (contains "The King of Folly Island," "The Courting of Sister Wisby," "The Landscape Chamber," "Law Lane," "Miss Peck's Promotion," "Miss Tempy's Watchers," "A Village Shop," and "Mere Pochette"), Houghton Mifflin, 1888.

Strangers and Wayfarers (contains "A Winter Courtship," "The Mistress of Sydenham Plantation," "The Town Poor," "The Quest of Mr. Teaby," "The Luck of the Bogans," "Fair Day," "Going to Shrewsbury," "The Taking of Captain Ball," "By the Morning Boat," "In Dark New England Days," and "The White Rose Road"), Houghton Mifflin, 1890.

Tales of New England (contains "Miss Tempy's Watchers," "The Dunham Ladies," "An Only Son," "March Rosemary," "A White Heron," "Law Lane," "A Lost Lover," and "The Courting of Sister Wisby"), Houghton Mifflin, 1890.

A Native of Winby, and Other Tales (contains "A Native of Winby," "Decoration Day," "Jim's Little Woman," "The Failure of David Berry," "The Passing of Sister Barsett," "Miss Esther's Guest," "The Flight of Betsey Lane," "Between Mass and Vespers," and "A Little Captive Maid"), Houghton Mifflin, 1893.

The Life of Nancy (contains "The Life of Nancy," "Fame's Little Day," "A War Debt," "The Hiltons' Holiday," "The Only Rose," "A Second Spring," "Little French Mary," "The Guests of Mrs. Timms," "A Neighbor's Landmark," and "All My Sad Captains"), Houghton Mifflin, 1895.

The Country of the Pointed Firs, Houghton Mifflin, 1896.

The Queen's Twin, and Other Stories (contains "The Queen's Twin," "A Dunnet Shepherdess," "Where's Nora?," "Bold Words at the Bridge," "Martha's Lady," "The Coon Dog," "Aunt Cynthy Dallett," and "The Night before Thanksgiving"), Houghton Mifflin, 1899.

The Only Rose and Other Tales, introduction by Rebecca West, Cape, 1937.

Lady Ferry, introduction by Annie E. Mower, Colby College Press, 1950.

The Uncollected Short Stories of Sarah Orne Jewett, edited by Richard Cary, Colby College Press (Waterville, ME), 1971.

The Irish Stories of Sarah Orne Jewett, edited by Jack Morgan and Louis Renza, Southern Illinois University Press (Carbondale, IL), 1996.

NOVELS

A Country Doctor, Houghton Mifflin (Boston, MA), 1884, reprinted with an introduction by Joy Gould Boyum and Ann R. Shapiro, New American Library (New York, NY), 1986.

A Marsh Island, Houghton Mifflin, 1885.

The Tory Lover, Houghton Mifflin, 1901.

FOR CHILDREN

Play Days: A Book of Stories for Children (contains "The Story of a Story Writer," "The Water Dolly,"

"Prissy's Visit," "Woodchucks," "Marigold House," "The Desert Islanders," and "Beyond the Tollgate"), Houghton, 1878.

(And compiler) *Katy's Birthday, with Other Stories by Famous Authors*, D. Lothrop (New York, NY), 1883.

The Story of the Normans, Told Chiefly in Relation to Their Conquest of England (history), Putnam (New York, NY), 1887.

Betty Leicester: A Story for Girls, Houghton Mifflin, 1890.

Betty Leicester's English Xmas: A New Chapter of an Old Story, privately printed (Baltimore, MD), 1894, published as *Betty Leicester's Christmas*, Houghton Mifflin, 1899.

(Editor) Celia Thaxter, *Stories and Poems for Children*, Houghton, 1895.

OMNIBUS VOLUMES

Stories and Tales, seven volumes, Houghton Mifflin, 1910, Volume 1: *Deephaven*, Volume 2: *Tales of New England*, Volume 3: *A Country Doctor*, Volume 4: *The Queen's Twin, and Other Stories*, Volume 5: *The Life of Nancy*, Volume 6: *A Native of Winby*, Volume 7: *The Country of the Pointed Firs*.

The Night before Thanksgiving [and] *A White Heron* [and] *Selected Stories by Sarah Orne Jewett*, with introductory materials by Katharine H. Shute, Houghton, 1911.

The Best Stories of Sarah Orne Jewett, two volumes, selected and arranged with a preface by Willa Cather, Houghton Mifflin, 1925, in one volume, Peter Smith, 1965.

The Country of the Pointed Firs, and Other Stories (contains "The Country of the Pointed Firs," "A White Heron," "The Dulham Ladies," "Miss Tempy's Watchers," "Going to Shrewsbury," "The Town Poor," "The Hiltons' Holiday," "The Only Rose," "The Guests of Mrs. Timms," "The Flight of Betsey Lane," "Martha's Lady," "The Queen's Twin," "Aunt Cynthy Dallett," "A Dunnet Shepherdess," and "William's Wedding"), preface by Willa Cather, Doubleday, 1954, Centennial edition, edited, and with introduction by Sarah Way Sherman, University Press Of New England (Hanover, NH), 1997.

The World of Dunnet Landing: A Sarah Orne Jewett Collection, edited by David Bonnell Green, University of Nebraska Press (Lincoln, NE), 1962, Peter Smith, 1972.

Deephaven, and Other Stories, edited by Richard Cary, College & University Press, 1966.

The Country of the Pointed Firs, and Other Stories (contains "The Country of the Pointed Firs," "A Dunnet Shepherdess," "The Foreigner," "The Queen's Twin," "William's Wedding," "A White Heron," "Miss Tempy's Watchers," "Martha's

Lady," and "Aunt Cynthy Dallett"), selected with an introduction by Mary Ellen Chase, illustrations by Shirley Burke, Norton, 1968.

Short Fiction of Sarah Orne Jewett and Mary Wilkins Freeman, edited with an introduction by Barbara H. Solomon, New American Library, 1979.

The Country of the Pointed Firs, and Four Stories (contains "The Country of the Pointed Firs," "A White Heron," "The Dulham Ladies," "Miss Tempy's Watchers," and "Going to Shrewsbury"), illustrations by Kevin King, limited edition, Franklin Library, 1984.

Sarah orne Jewett: Novels and Stories, Library of America (New York, NY), 1994.

The Irish Stories of Sarah Orne Jewett, edited and introduced by Jack Morgan and Louis A. Renza, Southern Illinois University Press (Carbondale, IL), 1996.

The Dunnet Landing Stories, Modern Library (New York, NY), 1996.

OTHER

(Editor) *The Poems of Celia Thaxter,* Houghton, 1896.

An Empty Purse: A Christmas Story, privately printed (Boston, MA), 1905.

(Editor) *Letters of Sarah Wyman Whitman,* Houghton, 1907.

Letters of Sarah Orne Jewett, edited by Annie Fields, Houghton, 1911.

Verses, edited by M.A. DeWolfe Howe, privately printed (Boston, MA), 1916.

Letters of Sarah Orne Jewett Now in the Colby College Library, with explanatory notes by Carl J. Weber, Colby College Press, 1947.

Sarah Orne Jewett Letters, edited with an introduction and notes by Richard Cary, Colby College Press, 1956, enlarged and revised edition, 1967.

The Complete Poems of Sarah Orne Jewett, Ironweed (Forest Hills, NY), 1999.

Contributor of sketches and short stories to periodicals, including *Atlantic Monthly, Riverside, Our Young Folks,* and the *Independent,* under pseudonyms A.D. Eliot, Alice Eliot, and Sarah C. Sweet. Collections of Jewett's manuscripts, letters, and journals are found at the Houghton Library at Harvard University, the Society for the Preservation of New England Antiquities in Boston, Colby College in Waterville, Maine, the Folger Shakespeare Library, and the Library of Congress.

■ Adaptations

The White Heron (film), Jane Morrison, 1978; *Master Smart Women* (film), Jane Morrison and Peter Namuth, 1984; *The Country of the Pointed Firs,* in Black-

stone Audiobooks (audiotape; recorded by Audio Bookshelf); "The Courting of Sister Wisby," in *Great American Short Stories: Vol. 3* (audiotape); "The White Heron," in *Women in Literature: The Short Story* (audiotape); "Editha" by William Dean Howells, "The Courting of Sister Wisby" by Sarah Orne Jewett (audiotape), Commuter's Library; "Miss Tempy's Watchers" (audiotape), Commuter's Library; "The Only Rose" (audiotape), Commuter's Library; "A White Heron and Other New England Tales" (audiotape; recorded by Audio Bookshelf); *Stories of New England: Then and Now,* Volumes 1 & 2 (audiotape; recorded by Audio Bookshelf); *The Country of the Pointed Firs* (play), Pontine Movement Theatre, Portland, Maine, Dartmouth College, Hanover, New Hampshire.

■ Sidelights

Sarah Orne Jewett is regarded as one of the premier writers of American regional fiction. As one of the prominent members of the "local color movement," she portrayed a specific geographical setting in prose with a fidelity to the history, speech, and mannerisms of the region. Jewett once observed that "a dull little village is just the place to find the real drama of life." Seeking to preserve the rural past of her native Maine through her works, Jewett faithfully depicted the characters, culture, and flavor of her predominantly New England settings. Although she wrote several novels, short stories, verses, and one volume of history, Jewett is best known for her sketches about provincial life in New England during the 1800s. Melanie Kisthardt in the *Dictionary of Literary Biography* explained: "'Don't try to write about people and things, tell them just as they are.' Sarah Orne Jewett quoted this advice from her father. . . . Jewett often repeated this suggestion to novice writers, and it lies at the core of her aesthetic, 'imaginative realism.' She attributed her capacity for keen observation, joy in simple things, and impatience with affectation and insincerity to her father's influence. Knowledge of human nature and attention to detail served Jewett well throughout her career, but her sketches of country life reveal more than chronicling a waning culture. Her themes transcend 'local color' and speak to generations of readers about the value of community and the nurturing wisdom of women." David D. Anderson in the *Dictionary of Literary Biography* wrote: "One of the most prolific contributors to American literature of her time and to the canon of the literature of her region, Jewett has a small but secure place in literary history. The bulk of her work consists of clear, careful expositions of some of the great themes of American and New England history: America's decline as a seafaring nation, the transition from a rural and village economy to urban industrialism, the cross-cultural impact of immigration, the decline of individualism and craftsmanship, and the great migrations to the towns and the cities. . . . The time, place, and people of late-nineteenth-century New England have had no more faithful chronicler, and they endure in her work."

A Comfortable Childhood

Jewett was born September 3, 1849, in South Berwick, Maine. She was the middle of three daughters born to Caroline F. Perry and Theodore H. Jewett, a wealthy Maine physician. She was raised in her grandparents' home. Her grandfather was a retired sea captain and the family was financially comfortable. Jewett remembered reading the books in her grandparents' library, including those by Jane Austen and Harriet Beecher Stowe. Her formal education was erratic; Jewett suffered from arthritis for most of her life and was often ill as a child. As a form of open-air therapy, she frequently accompanied her father when he made his rounds by carriage to his patients' homes. This early exposure to New England coastal life combined with Jewett's avid reading greatly influenced the author early in her literary career. She attended the Berwick Academy from 1861 to 1865. Financial independence allowed her to write at her leisure and, by 1867, she began submitting short stories to magazines under the pseudonyms A.D. Eliot, Alice Eliot, and Sarah C. Sweet.

Over the next several years a number of her sketches about village life off the coast of Maine were published in the *Atlantic Monthly*. William Dean Howells, an *Atlantic* editor and novelist, suggested that Jewett collect and revise the stories for publication in a single volume. She created two fictional personas—narrator Helen Denis and her friend Kate Lancaster, two Bostonians spending the summer in an old house in a Maine fishing village—to frame and unite the stories; the resulting episodic work was published in 1877 as *Deephaven*.

The decline of the fishing industry and the mass exodus of young men from the East for new employment opportunities in the West left an aging, predominantly female population in nineteenth-century New England. A wave of immigration beginning in the latter half of the century contributed to the urbanization of the dying coastal fishing villages. The heroines of *Deephaven* function as outside observers who meet up with rural characters of the old guard on the east coast, including aged spinsters, long-winded old sea captains, indigent farmers, and an eccentric herbalist. In her preface to

the 1893 edition of *Deephaven*, Jewett recalled the purpose that she hoped her book would serve: "[I] was possessed by a dark fear that townspeople and country people would never understand one another, or learn to profit by their new relationship. . . . There is a noble saying of Plato that the best thing that can be done for the people of a state is to make them acquainted with one another."

Reviews of *Deephaven* upon its initial publication focused mainly on Jewett's talent for depicting in rich detail the folklore, traditions, and people of a rural New England community facing urbanization. Howell praised *Deephaven* in a review for the *Atlantic Monthly* as "studies, so refined, so simple, so exquisitely imbued with a true feeling for the ideal within the real." In his essay from *Appreciation of Sarah Orne Jewett* Paul John Eakin remarked that "the presence of the visitor . . . provide[s] the occasion for the revelation of the knowledge available only to the native, and the sympathy and appreciation of the native could [in turn] be acquired by the visitor."

This episodic 1877 novel tells of the decline of a New England fishing village due to urbanization. (Cover of *"Deephaven,"* written by Sarah Orne Jewett, photograph.)

Late twentieth-century criticism of *Deephaven* echoes the book's first public reception. Anderson contended that Jewett's attempt to give the stories a coherent structure by inserting the characters of the two female visitors to the town fails. "The work suffers from attempting to become what it is not, a nearly chronological story of the girls' experiences and observations during the summer." "Neither the best nor the most enduring of her work," Anderson continued: "*Deephaven* is, however, not entirely the 'beginning raw work' that Willa Cather called it." As to the question of whether *Deephaven* is an "enduring" piece of literature, Patti Capel Swartz argues in *Gay and Lesbian Literature* that the book continues to hold something for lesbian readers: "The relationship of Kate and Helen in Jewett's *Deephaven*, particularly the scene where they dance in the moonlight, has touched deeply the hearts of lesbian readers attempting to find themselves in literature." Josephine Donovan, writing in her biography of the author, *Sarah Orne Jewett*, acknowledges the flaws of *Deephaven* but asserts its continued value for the reader interested in the development of Jewett's themes, the evolution of her skill as a writer, and for an early portrait of the locale that would figure largely throughout the rest of Jewett's fiction. "If only for its extraordinary veracity of detail *Deephaven* still deserves to be read. In this regard it has the value of charming and well-edited oral history," Donovan wrote.

Befriends Annie Fields

From the late 1870s through the early 1880s Jewett joined the literary circle that revolved around *Atlantic* publisher James T. Fields and his wife, socialite and biographer Annie Fields, who had been a close friend of Jewett's since childhood. After the death of her husband in 1881, Annie drew on that longstanding friendship and, despite her vast social contacts, turned primarily to Jewett for comfort and companionship. Jewett responded in turn; as Anderson suggested, "the relationship . . . replaced Jewett's earlier closeness to her father as the central relationship in her life." The two women toured Europe, visiting such notable writers as English poets Christina Rossetti and Alfred Tennyson. Returning to Fields' home in Boston—where Jewett would make her home with Annie for six months of every year after 1882—the two women entertained such literati as Oliver Wendell Holmes, Thomas Bailey Aldrich, and Harriet Beecher Stowe. Their close relationship, which was common among financially independent, intellectual, proto-feminists of the day who chose to live together as a couple, was characterized as a "Boston marriage." Much speculation has since been made on whether Fields and Jewett were in fact engaged in a lesbian

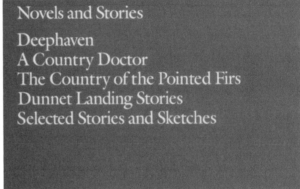

Novels and Stories

Deephaven
A Country Doctor
The Country of the Pointed Firs
Dunnet Landing Stories
Selected Stories and Sketches

Jewett's primary novels and stories are found in this 1994 collection. (The Library of America, 1994. Reproduced by permission.)

relationship. Most certainly, their close, loving relationship served as an example to lesbian writer Willa Cather, who would be a protegee of Jewett's in later years and who also sought the elder writer's counsel in matters of the heart. However, warned Jewett biographer Paula Blanchard, there is a danger in applying twentieth-century social standards to the nineteenth century: "Sarah Orne Jewett's love for other women was as passionate and absorbing as any heterosexual man's," Blanchard noted in *Sarah Orne Jewett: Her World and Her Work*, "but from all available evidence it never led to direct sexual expression."

It was during these first years of her relationship with Fields that Jewett published the well-received short story collections *Old Friends and New, Country By-Ways,* and *The Mate of Daylight, and Friends Ashore.* The first volume, *Old Friends and New,* consists of stories previously published in periodicals, and one additional tale titled "Lady Ferry," about an old woman who seems destined to live forever. It takes the kiss of a little girl to end this unusual fable and release Lady Ferry from her seemingly endless life. French novelist and critic Maria Therese Blanc, writing under the pseudonym Bentzon, commented on Jewett's collection in an essay reprinted in *Appreciation of Sarah Orne Jewett*. Referring to a streak of "insanity" running through "Lady Ferry," Bentzon considered the story's ending "a moral conclusion ingeniously contrived." She explained, "This world is a school that prepares us for larger horizons. . . . We learn . . . how redoubtable such a fate would be, that this arid and desolate lesson has belatedly had an end, that the immortal one is dead."

The stories in the 1881 collection *Country By-Ways* once again depict a world of the past and revolve around elderly women. The narrator of the sketches observes the New England scenery through the seasonal changes and describes a variety of eccentric characters who live along the shore—often old women facing their fate with grace and dignity. The author's next collection, the 1884 publication *The Mate of Daylight, and Friends Ashore*, was dedicated to Annie Fields. In addition to Jewett's usual stock of situations and characters, the volume contained an experimental tale of role reversal titled "Tom's Husband." In the story, Tom's wife, Mary, opts to run the family's mill while her husband attends to the domestic chores. Mary becomes a successful businesswoman while Tom, who had initially enjoyed his new role, grows tired of housework. In what Richard Cary termed an "anti-feminist" ending in his book *Sarah Orne Jewett*, the couple abandons the arrangement, and husband and wife reassume their respective stereotypical roles. But Josephine Donovan argued in the *Massachusetts Review* that the story's conclusion "should be read rather as an example of Jewett's awareness of the tedium of housework and of how no man would endure it—a decidedly feminist point." Donovan excerpted lines from the story that support her claim: "[Tom developed] an uneasy suspicion that [Mary] could get along pretty well without him. . . . He seemed to himself to have merged his life in his wife's . . . he felt himself fast growing rusty and behind the times, and to have somehow missed a good deal in life."

First Novel Appears

Jewett expanded on the theme of women in the work force in her 1884 novel *A Country Doctor*. Widely regarded as her most feminist work, the semiautobiographical narrative follows orphan Nan

Price from her childhood accompaniment of her guardian, Dr. Leslie, on his country rounds, through her adult decision to pursue a career in medicine. Though briefly diverted by a suitor, George Gerry, whom she seems in a way to genuinely love, Nan reasons by the book's end—as excerpted by Donovan—"It is not easy to turn away from him. . . . I know all tradition fights on his side, but I can look forward, and see something a thousand times better than being his wife, and . . . keeping his house, and trying to forget all that nature fitted me to do." Bentzon speculated that Jewett's goal in *A Country Doctor* was "to obtain the grace of the strong woman, the free woman, to show what her strength and liberty cost her" and to admit to a nineteenth-century reality: that a woman was not "adequate for a double mission" in the way that a man was. Donovan echoed Bentzon's sentiment, proclaiming that through the book, Jewett was "perhaps most of all . . . lamenting the lack of emotional possibility which cursed the world she knew. In this sense," Donovan continued, "she is a modern: her theme is alienation—especially as it affected women."

A Country Doctor received mixed reviews. Critics praised Jewett's authentic portrayal of rural character and setting but censured the author for her bland and unrealistic depiction of the romance between Nan and George. Jewett "was never able to portray lovers convincingly," judged Cross. Reviews of *A Marsh Island*, Jewett's next novel, pointed to the same problem: although the story deals with a woman's involvement in a love triangle, it lacks elements of passion and romance. Protagonist Doris Owen, a marsh island farm girl, is happy with her country blacksmith beau, Dan Lester, until an outsider arrives on the scene. Dick Dale, an artist from the city, spends the summer on the island painting landscapes and becomes interested in Doris. While Dick takes pleasure in the natural simplicity of the country, he ultimately decides that he prefers city life. An infatuated Doris visits the city with Dick but feels out of place. In the end both return to their natural element: Dick has a successful exhibition of his paintings back in the city, and Doris returns home to declare her love for Dan, who later marries her. Critics suggested that Jewett had used the courtship technique to reinforce her themes of serenity and simplicity in nature and to attempt a reconciliation of clashing urban and rural values. Reviewers once again commended the author for her vivid descriptions of setting but decried the absence of dramatic action.

Berthoff contended that Jewett's almost asexual depiction of love, a motif evident even in her earliest writings, functioned to establish women as "the guardians and preservers of a community," figures dedicated "to preservation of the past, to intercourse with nature, to disguising and delaying [society's] inevitable dissolution." For instance, "A Lost Lover," one of Jewett's first short stories, contains "no marriage at all," commented Bertoff, "simply the desertion." In the story, an elderly woman takes on a widow's status even though her lover, supposedly lost at sea, ran off before they could be married. "On the basis of this lie, [the woman becomes] a person of consequence in the village as well as in her own eyes," theorized Berthoff. Donovan agreed, pointing to the title story in *A White Heron, and Other Stories*, a collection published in 1888. One of Jewett's most frequently anthologized pieces, the story revolves around a young country girl who is asked by an ornithologist to betray the nesting place of the white heron. Although she is fascinated by the outsider, the girl vows not to jeopardize the bird's life and consequently does not help the hunter in his search. Donovan argued that an underlying conflict "between women's loyalty to community versus the male will to destroy and isolate" could be seen in the young girl's "reject[ion of] a potential suitor" in an act of fidelity "to the sanctity of the natural community to which she belongs." Marilee Lindemann in *Modern American Women Writers* found it to be "the most famous of [Jewett's] writings about nature."

Some of Jewett's oddest characters appear in her short fiction pieces collected in the late 1880s. The two sisters in "The Dulham Ladies," a tale from *A White Heron*, cover their thinning hair with shaggy, poodle-like wigs in an attempt to preserve their social status. Mrs. Goodsoe in "The Courting of Sister Wisby," a story published in 1888's *The King of Folly Island, and Other People*, is an eccentric herbalist who trusts intuition over the book knowledge of doctors. The spirit of Miss Tempy in "Miss Tempy's Watchers," also contained in *The King of Folly Island*, is resurrected from the dead on the night before her funeral to share her wisdom with the women who are guarding her body for the night.

Publishes Her Masterpiece

While the stories from these volumes are considered among her strongest short works, Jewett's 1896 collection *The Country of the Pointed Firs* remains her undisputed masterpiece. "A delicately connected series of sketches narrated by a summer visitor to a village on the Maine coast," as Lindemann described the book, "*Pointed Firs* is vintage Jewett in its deft interweaving of tales of excursions, visits, eccentrics, and elderly women, quiet comedy, and the simple pleasures and inevitable privations of rural life." The narrator is a writer from the city visiting the Maine coastal village of Dunnet Landing for the summer. Her landlady, the feisty widow Almira Todd, is an herbalist living in complete communion with her environment. "*Pointed Firs* offers a vision of a world in which community and empathetic imagination flourish beyond the larger, more hectic world," according to Melanie Kisthardt in the *Dictionary of Literary Biography*. "Into this 'centre of civilization' comes the narrator, a harried writer whose stay in Dunnet Landing proves an education in the importance of recognizing one's roots. Like Kate and Helen in *Deephaven*, this narrator is seduced by the spell of the place and its inhabitants, especially Almira Todd, herbalist, homeopathic healer, mentor, and eventually, dear friend." Donovan noted that in Jewett's fiction strong female characters "seem to have the power to help people to overcome isolation and poverty." The character of Mrs. Todd takes on epic proportions—Jewett repeatedly compares her to ancient Greek figures—and functions as a "beneficent witch," the "town healer," proposed Donovan. In *The Country of the*

A photograph of Jewett working. (Photograph courtesy of Bettmann/CORBIS.)

Pointed Firs, Jewett endows Mrs. Todd with transcendent powers: "it seemed sometimes as if love and hate and jealousy and adverse winds at sea might also find their proper remedies along with the curious wild-looking plants in Mrs. Todd's garden."

During her stay, the narrator of *Pointed Firs* encounters an array of interesting rustic people, including Captain Littlepage, an old sea captain who longs for a return of the olden days. He tells the narrator of a trip he made long ago to a supernatural village in the Arctic—a sort of limbo for souls caught between this world and the next. Following her meeting with the captain, the visitor accompanies Mrs. Todd to Green Island, the home of Mrs. Todd's mother, Mrs. Blackett, and brother, William. The circle of pointed firs on the Blackett property serves as a center of stability and perpetuity for the entire coastal community. But even if Jewett's pastoral narrative "seeks to present a vision of life held in stasis," asserted David Stouck in an essay from *Appreciation of Sarah Orne Jewett*, "it nevertheless ultimately recognizes the inevitable truth of mutability." The narrator in *The Country of the Pointed Firs* learns of lost and lonely souls inhabiting Dunnet Landing: the old fisherman Elijah Tilley, for instance, dedicates his life to preserving his dead wife's memory; and Joanna Todd, the victim of a love affair gone wrong, lives alone on a nearby island in self-imposed exile. Donovan echoed Stouck's sentiment, commenting that social rituals in Jewett's world "are the only thing[s] that give human life significance, that enable a measure of transcendence. The final parting between the narrator and Mrs. Todd fittingly summarizes the theme of the preciousness and transitoriness of relationships—the fragility of community. . . . 'So we die before our own eyes; so we see some chapters of our lives come to their natural end.'"

The Country of the Pointed Firs met with an enthusiastic reception upon its initial publication and, almost a century later, is considered among the finest pieces of local color fiction ever written. Lindemann called it "the work that nearly a century of popular and critical response has embraced as Jewett's masterpiece." In her preface to *The Best Stories of Sarah Orne Jewett*, American writer Willa Cather, who was also Jewett's protegee, named *The Country of the Pointed Firs*, along with Nathaniel Hawthorne's *The Scarlet Letter* and Mark Twain's *Huckleberry Finn*, one of the finest and most enduring works by an American writer. "I can think of no others that confront time and change so serenely," Cather wrote. "Several waves of criticism have washed over American literature since it was published almost a century ago," Blanchard noted, "but *The Country of the Pointed Firs* has held its own place and remains as much loved and as much read

This 1996 collection gathers Jewett's stories set in Ireland. (Southern Illinois University, 1996. Originally published, Scribner's Magazine, 1898.)

as another offbeat classic, Walden. Like that book too it has continued to provoke new interpretations, depending on the generation and experience of its readers." Francis O. Matthiessen, in his *Sarah Orne Jewett*, judged the book "impressive in its quietness" and possessive of a "radiant simplicity . . . which bathed [the author's] scenes and characters in its own delicate, but uncompromising light."

Recent critical studies of *The Country of the Pointed Firs* point to this novel as an example of Jewett's movement beyond the realist school which was popular at the time and with which she is often associated. That is, like *A White Heron* and other Jewett narratives, this novel contains a fairly explicit critique of the masculine world of science, which values evidence over experience, and the material world over the spiritual. In addition to the explicit stories of the town's inhabitants, Michael Holstein, writing in *Studies in American Fiction*, finds a secondary narrative thread in which the narrator as author attempts to find "a stance adequate to her subject and her needs as a writer," and arrives at the role of healer. "The narrator finds positive models for her healing art in three distinct types of her Dunnet neighbors: the herbalist, the spiritualist, and the solitary. They possess the traits necessary to the writer who also would heal the spirit."

Jewett's last volume of short fiction, *The Queen's Twin, and Other Stories,* was published in 1899. The collection includes two additional sketches set in Dunnet Landing. The first, titled "The Queen's Twin," reunites the unnamed narrator-observer with Mrs. Todd, and together they call on an old widow named Abby Martin. With subtle humor Jewett comments on the power of the human imagination: because she was born on the same day as England's Queen Victoria, Mrs. Martin has come to regard herself as a sort of psychic twin to the queen. In the other story, titled "A Dunnet Shepherdess," Mrs. Todd's brother, William, and the narrator enjoy trout fishing and then visit William's longtime love, Esther. A later unfinished story by Jewett joined the couple in marriage following the death of Esther's aged mother.

The author's final novel signaled a departure from the short rustic fiction that had made her famous. A historical novel titled *The Tory Lover,* the book was a financial, but not a literary success. Shortly after the publication of *The Tory Lover* in 1901, Henry James urged Jewett to return to her "country of the pointed firs" and pen loosely structured novels from sketches and short, regional prose pieces. A fall from a carriage on her fifty-third birthday, however, left Jewett with severe head and spinal injuries that put an end to her literary career. The author spent the last years of her life counseling Cather on the art of composing regional fiction. In June of 1909, three months after suffering a stroke, Jewett died of a cerebral hemorrhage at her home in South Berwick, Maine.

"Jewett's reputation," wrote Gwen L. Nagel in the *Dictionary of Literary Biography,* "rests on *The Country of the Pointed Firs* and a body of short works that portray provincial life in nineteenth-century New England. Her fictive world is a limited one, but she perfected her craft, deepening her characterizations and gaining control of subtleties of tone and atmosphere. She has been declared one of the foremost writers of regional fiction, but she avoided the excesses of dialect and caricature that mar much of the work of the local-color school. She is a realist whose work bears the mark of a sympathetic and feeling observer. Like many of her fictive characters who confront change by guarding the artifacts,

traditions, and values of the past, Jewett recorded for all time the essence of life in her country of the pointed firs. Her canon of finely wrought fiction will remain an enduring memorial to a way of life that has long since vanished."

If you enjoy the works of Sarah Orne Jewett, you may also want to check out the following books:

Harriet Beecher Stowe, *The Pearl of Orr's Island,* 1862.
Mary Wilkins Freeman, *A Humble Romance and Other Stories,* 1887.
Rose Terry Cooke, *Huckleberries Gathered from New England Hills,* 1891.
Hildegarde Hawthorne, *Faded Garden: The Collected Ghost Stories of Hildegarde Hawthorne,* 1985.

Summarizing the enduring appeal of Jewett's fiction, Martha Hale Shackford contended in the *Sewanee Review* that Jewett's simple, reserved, and undramatic stories derived great power from their restraint: "[Jewett's] tales are disconcerting, tiresome to those whose logical powers are developed at the expense of their imagination and their love of romantic waywardness. . . . She had something better than formal skill,—wisdom, matured understanding of life, individual insight. . . . She shows people living simple, normal, average lives, and the tissue of their existence is not external event but slow pondering of life, and still slower exchange of comment about it." Writing in her book *Sarah Orne Jewett,* Margaret Farrand Thorp claimed: "Anyone from another part of the United States, anyone from another part of the world, who wants to understand New England might do well to begin with the stories of Sarah Orne Jewett."

"With the recent resurgence of interest in Sarah Orne Jewett," wrote an essayist for *Feminist Writers,* "more and more of her previously out-of-print works have been reprinted. Modern readers now have the opportunity to discover her infectious optimism about the multi-dimensional potential of women's relationships and the richness of middle-aged and older women's experience. Portraits of vigorous, independent, rock-solid, mature women have been especially lacking in American literature, and Jewett's oeuvre can be celebrated for broadening narrow, conventional literary conceptions of the female experience." Swartz concluded her essay for *Gay and Lesbian Literature* with the following accolade: "Sarah Orne Jewett's vision was and is a wonderfully kind vision, one in which each individual can recognize her or his potential and one in which difference is cause for celebration."

■ Biographical and Critical Sources

BOOKS

Auchincloss, Louis, *Pioneers and Caretakers: A Study of Nine American Women Novelists,* University of Minnesota Press, 1965.

Blanchard, Paula, *Sarah Orne Jewett: Her World and Her Work,* Addison-Wesley (Reading, MA), 1994.

Cary, Richard, *Sarah Orne Jewett,* Twayne (New York, NY), 1962.

Cary, Richard, editor, *Appreciation of Sarah Orne Jewett: Twenty-nine Interpretive Essays,* Colby College Press (Waterville, ME), 1973.

Cather, Willa, *Not under Forty,* Alfred A. Knopf (New York, NY), 1936.

Church, Joseph, *Transcendent Daughters in Jewett's Country of the Pointed Firs,* Associated University Presses (Cranbury, NJ), 1994.

Commager, Henry Steele, *The American Mind: An Interpretation of American Thought and Character since the 1880s,* Yale University Press, 1950.

Dictionary of Literary Biography, Gale (Detroit, MI), Volume 12: *American Realists and Naturalists,* 1982; Volume 74: *American Short-Story Writers before 1880,* 1988; Volume 221: *American Women Prose Writers, 1870-1920,* 2000.

Donovan, Josephine, *Sarah Orne Jewett,* Ungar (New York, NY), 1981.

Donovan, Josephine, *Master Smart Woman: A Portrait of Sarah Orne Jewett,* North Country Press, 1988.

Faderman, Lillian, *Chloe plus Olivia: An Anthology of Lesbian Literature from the Seventeenth Century to the Present,* Penguin (New York, NY), 1994.

Feminist Writers, St. James Press (Detroit, MI), 1996.

Fetterley, Judith and Marjorie Pryse, *American Woman Regionalists: 1850-1910,* Norton (New York, NY), 1992.

Frost, John Eldridge, *Sarah Orne Jewett,* Gundalow Club (Kittery Point, ME), 1960.

Gay and Lesbian Biography, St. James Press (Detroit, MI), 1997.

Gay and Lesbian Literature, Volume 2, St. James Press (Detroit, MI), 1998.

Hicks, Granville, *The Great Tradition: An Interpretation of American Literature since the Civil War,* Macmillan (New York, NY), 1933, revised edition, 1935.

Howard, June, *New Essays on "The Country of the Pointed Firs,"* Cambridge University Press (New York, NY), 1994.

Koppelman, Susan, *Two Friends and Other Nineteenth-Century Lesbian Stories by American Women,* Penguin (New York, NY), 1994.

Martin, Jay, *Harvests of Change: American Literature, 1865-1914,* Prentice-Hall (New York, NY), 1967.

Matthiessen, Francis Otto, *Sarah Orne Jewett,* Houghton Mifflin (Boston, MA), 1929.

Modern American Women Writers, Scribner (New York, NY), 1991.

Nagel, Gwen L., editor, *Critical Essays on Sarah Orne Jewett,* G.K. Hall (Boston, MA), 1984.

Nagel, Gwen L. and James Nagel, *Sarah Orne Jewett: A Reference Guide,* G.K. Hall (Boston, MA), 1978.

Renza, Louis A., *"A White Heron" and the Question of Minor Literature,* University of Wisconsin Press (Madison, WI), 1984.

Roman, Margaret, *Sarah Orne Jewett: Reconstructing Gender,* University of Alabama Press (Tuscaloosa, AL), 1992.

Sexual Theory, Textual Practice: Lesbian Cultural Criticism, Blackwood, 1993.

Sherman, Sarah Way, *Sarah Orne Jewett: An American Persephone,* University Press of New England (Hanover, NH), 1989.

Short Story Criticism, Volume 6, Gale (Detroit, MI), 1991.

Silverthorne, Elizabeth, *Sarah Orne Jewett: A Writer's Life,* Overlook Press (Woodstock, NY), 1993.

Sougnac, Jean, *Sarah Orne Jewett,* Jouve et Cie (Paris, France), 1937.

Thorp, Margaret Farrand, *Sarah Orne Jewett,* University of Minnesota Press, 1966.

Twentieth-Century Literary Criticism, Gale (Detroit, MI), Volume 1, 1978, Volume 22, 1987.

Weber, Clara Carter and Carl J. Weber, *A Bibliography of the Published Writings of Sarah Orne Jewett,* Colby College Press (Waterville, ME), 1949.

Westbrook, Perry D., *Acres of Flint: Writers of Rural New England, 1870-1900,* Scarecrow Press, 1951.

Ziff, Larzer, *The American 1890s: Life and Times of a Lost Generation,* Viking (New York, NY), 1966.

PERIODICALS

American Literary Realism, fall, 1967, pp. 61-66; fall, 1969, Clayton L. Eichelberger, "Sarah Orne Jewett (1849-1909): A Critical Bibliography of Secondary

Comments," pp. 189-262; autumn, 1984, Gwen L. Nagel, "Sarah Orne Jewett: A Reference Guide—An Update," pp. 227-263.

American Literature, May, 1955, Ferman Bishop, "Henry James Criticizes *The Tory Lover,*" pp. 262-264; June, 1967, Paul John Eakin, "Sarah Orne Jewett and the Meaning of Country Life."

Atlantic Monthly, June, 1887, p. 759; October, 1904, Charles M. Thompson, "The Art of Miss Jewett," pp. 485-497; July, 1915, pp. 21-31.

Berwick Scholar, October, 1887, Sarah Orne Jewett, "My School Days."

Bloomsbury Review, October, 1991, p. 23.

Booklist, January 1, 1989, p. 42; April 15, 1994, Wilma Longstreet, review of *The Country of Pointed Firs* audiobook, p. 1546.

Colby Library Quarterly, June, 1964, John Eldridge Frost, "Sarah Orne Jewett Bibliography: 1949-1963," pp. 405-417, Robin Magowen, "The Outer Island Sequence in *Pointed Firs,*" pp. 418-424, and Richard Cary, "Jewett on Writing Short Stories," pp. 425-440; June, 1965, Richard Cary, "Jewett's Literary Canons," pp. 82-87; September, 1967, Richard Cary, "Miss Jewett and Madame Blanc," pp. 467-488; September, 1968, Richard Cary, "Some Bibliographical Ghosts of Sarah Orne Jewett," pp. 139-145; December, 1970, Richard Cary, "Violet Paget to Sarah Orne Jewett," pp. 235-243; December, 1974, Katherine T. Jobes, "From Stowe's Eagle Island to Jewett's 'A White Heron,'" pp. 515-521; March, 1975, Catherine B. Stevenson, "The Double Consciousness of the Narrator in Sarah Orne Jewett's Fiction," pp. 1-12, and Richard Cary, "Jewett to Dresel: 33 Letters," pp. 13-49; December, 1975, pp. 219-229; June, 1976, Randall R. Mawer, "Setting as Symbol in Jewett's *A Marsh Island,*" pp. 83-90; September, 1978, Theodore R. Hovet, "America's "Lonely Country Child': The Theme of Separation in Sarah Orne Jewett's 'A White Heron,'" pp. 166-171; September, 1979, Mary C. Kraus, "Sarah Orne Jewett and Temporal Continuity," pp. 157-174; September, 1980, Malinda Snow, "'That One Talent': The Vocation as Theme in Sarah Orne Jewett's *A Country Doctor,* pp. 138-147; March, 1981, Charles W. Mayer, "'The Only Rose': A Central Jewett Story," pp. 26-33; September, 1983, Laurie Crumpacker, "The Art of the Healer: Women in the Fiction of Sarah Orne Jewett," pp. 155-166; March, 1985, Kelley Griffith, Jr., "Sylvia as Hero in Sarah Orne Jewett's 'A White Heron,'" pp. 22-27; June, 1985, Edward J. Piacentino, "Local Color and Beyond: The Artistic Dimension of Sarah Orne Jewett's 'The Foreigner,'" pp. 92-98; September, 1985, Richard G. Carson, "Nature and the Circles of Initiation in *The Country of Pointed Firs,*" pp. 154-160; March, 1986, Elizabeth Ammons, "The Shape of Violence in Jewett's 'A White Heron,'" pp. 6-16, Marilyn E.

Mobley, "Rituals of Flight and Return: The Ironic Journeys of Sarah Orne Jewett's Female Characters," pp. 36-42, and Gwen L. Nagel, "'This prim corner of land where she was queen': Sarah Orne Jewett's New England Gardens," pp. 43-62.

College English, December, 1994, pp. 877-895.

Comparative Literature, fall, 1964, Robin Magowan, "Fromentin and Jewett: Pastoral Narrative in the Nineteenth Century," pp. 331-337.

Down East, August, 1977, Marie Donahue, "Sarah Orne Jewett's 'Dear Old House and Home,'" pp. 62-67.

Emerson Society Quarterly, Number 19, 1973, Michael W. Vella, "Sarah Orne Jewett: A Reading of *The Country of the Pointed Firs,*" pp. 275-282.

Florida State University Studies, no. 5, 1952, pp. 113-121.

Frontiers: A Journal of Women's Studies, fall, 1979, pp. 26-31; January, 1980, Josephine Donovan, "The Unpublished Love Poetry of Sarah Orne Jewett," pp. 26-31.

Horn Book, May 1987, p. 366.

Massachusetts Review, summer, 1980, Josephine Donovan, "A Woman's Vision of Transcendence: A New Interpretation of the Works of Sarah Orne Jewett," pp. 365-381.

MELUS, fall, 1999, Kristin Johansen, review of *The Irish Stories of Sarah Orne Jewett,* p. 202.

New England Quarterly, September, 1945, Carl J. Weber, "Whittier and Sarah Orne Jewett," pp. 401-407; September, 1946, pp. 338-358; December, 1956, Eleanor M. Smith, "The Literary Relationship of Sarah Orne Jewett and Willa Sibert Cather," pp. 472-492; June, 1957, Ferman, Bishop, "Sarah Orne Jewett's Idea of Race," pp. 243-249; March, 1959, Warner Berthoff, "The Art of Jewett's *Pointed Firs,*" pp. 31-53; December, 1961, David Bonnell Green, "The World of Dunnet Landing," pp. 514-517; June, 1963, Robin Magowan, "Pastoral and the Art of Landscape," pp. 229-240.

New Republic, May 17, 1954, Irving Howe, "Cameos from the North Country," pp. 24-25.

Observer, April 23, 1995, p. 21.

School Library Journal, March, 1989, p. 209.

Sewanee Review, winter, 1922, Martha Hale Shackford, "Sarah Orne Jewett," pp. 20-26.

Signs, Volume 13, 1988, Sandra Zagarell, "Narrative of Community: The Identification of Genre," pp. 498-527.

Studies in American Fiction, spring, 1988, pp. 39-49.

Studies in Short Fiction, summer, 1972, Susan A. Toth, "Sarah Orne Jewett and Friends: A Community of Interest," pp. 233-241; winter, 1973, pp. 85-91; volume 17, 1980, pp. 21-29; winter, 1986, pp. 43-48.

Studies in the Literary Imagination, Number 16, 1983, Elizabeth Ammons, "Going in Circles: The Female Geography of Jewett's 'Country of the Pointed Firs,'" pp. 83-92.

Tribune Books (Chicago, IL), December 4, 1994, p. 1.

Twentieth Century Literature, July, 1959, Hyatt H. Waggoner, "The Unity of *The Country of the Pointed Firs,*" pp. 67-73.

Western Humanities Review, autumn, 1957, Clarice Short, "Studies in Gentleness," pp. 387-393.

Women's Studies, Number 2, 1974, Carolyn Forrey, "The New Woman Revisited," pp. 37-56.

Yale Review, October, 1913, Edward M. Chapman, "The New England of Sarah Orne Jewett," pp. 157-172.*

Lael Littke

■ Personal

Born December 2, 1929, in Mink Creek, ID; daughter of Frank George and Ada Geneva (Petersen) Jensen; married George C. Littke (a college professor), June 29, 1954; children: Lori S. *Education:* Utah State University, B.S., 1952; graduate study at City College (now City University of New York), 1955-59, and University of California—Los Angeles, 1968. *Politics:* Democrat. *Religion:* Church of Jesus Christ of Latter-day Saints (Mormon). *Hobbies and other interests:* Travel.

■ Addresses

Home—Pasadena, CA. *Agent*—Jack Byrne, 3209 S. Fifty-fifth St., Milwaukee, WI 53219-4433.

■ Career

Gates Rubber Co., Denver, CO, secretary, 1952-54; Life Insurance Association of America, New York, NY, secretary, 1954-60; worked as a medical secretary for a physician in New York, NY, 1960-63; writer, 1963—. Taught writing classes in writers' programs at Pasadena City College and University of California—Los Angeles, 1978-88.

■ Member

Society of Children's Book Writers and Illustrators, Council on Children's Literature.

■ Awards, Honors

Southern California Council on Children's Literature Award for notable work of fiction, 1992, for *Blue Skye;* Best Books for the Teen Age, New York Public Library, 2003, and International Reading Association Award, both for *Lake of Secrets.*

■ Writings

Wilmer the Watchdog, Western (New York, NY), 1970.

Tell Me When I Can Go, Scholastic (New York, NY), 1978.

Cave-In!, illustrated by Tom Dunnington, Children's Press (New York, NY), 1981.

Trish for President, Harcourt (New York, NY), 1984.

Shanny on Her Own, Harcourt (New York, NY), 1985.

Loydene in Love, Harcourt (New York, NY), 1986.

Where the Creeks Meet, Deseret (Salt Lake City, UT), 1987.

Prom Dress, Scholastic (New York, NY), 1989.

Blue Skye, Scholastic (New York, NY), 1990.

Who Painted the Porcupine Purple?, illustrated by Ann Grifalconi, Silver Burdett (Morristown, NJ), 1992.

The Watcher, Scholastic (New York, NY), 1994.

Haunted Sister, H. Holt (New York, NY), 1998.

Lake of Secrets, H. Holt (New York, NY), 2002.

(With Richard E. Turley and James Michael Pratt) *Stories from the Life of Joseph Smith,* Deseret Book Company (Salt Lake City, UT), 2003.

King of the Knock Jokes, Dominic Press (Carlsbad, CA), 2003.

The Cookie Quest, Dominic Press (Carlsbad, CA), 2003.

Space Slug, Dominic Press (Carlsbad, CA), 2003.

Searching for Selene, Deseret Book Company (Salt Lake City, UT), 2003.

"TALL TALE" SERIES; WITH CASSETTE RECORDINGS

Olympia Odette Presents Paul Bunyan's Blue Ox Blues, illustrated by Tom and Carol Newsom, Thinking Well (East Moline, IL), 1990.

Olympia Odette Presents Davy Crockett's Bear-ly Believable Sneeze, illustrated by Tom and Carol Newsom, Thinking Well (East Moline, IL), 1990.

Olympia Odette Presents Nellie Bly's "In a Jam" Telegram, illustrated by Tom and Carol Newsom, Thinking Well (East Moline, IL), 1990.

"PEANUT BUTTER POND" SERIES; WITH CASSETTE RECORDINGS

The Day Woodchuck Would Chuck Wood at Peanut Butter Pond, illustrated by Stephanie McFetridge Britt, Thinking Well (East Moline, IL), 1990.

The Day Porcupine Put on the Dog at Peanut Butter Pond, illustrated by Stephanie McFetridge Britt, Thinking Well (East Moline, IL), 1990.

The Day Snake Saved Time at Peanut Butter Pond, illustrated by Stephanie McFetridge Britt, Thinking Well (East Moline, IL), 1990.

"BEE THERES" SERIES

Getting Rid of Rhoda, Deseret Book Company (Salt Lake City, UT), 1992.

The Mystery of Ruby's Ghost, Deseret Book Company (Salt Lake City, UT), 1992.

Star of the Show, Deseret Book Company (Salt Lake City, UT), 1993.

There's a Snake at Girls' Camp, Deseret Book Company (Salt Lake City, UT), 1994.

The Bridesmaid Dress Disaster, Deseret Book Company (Salt Lake City, UT), 1994.

Run, Ducky, Run, Deseret Book Company (Salt Lake City, UT), 1996.

The Phantom Fair, Deseret Book Company (Salt Lake City, UT), 1996.

OTHER

Contributor of stories to anthologies, including *Best Short Stories of 1973*, 1973, *Miniature Mysteries*, 1981, *Ellery Queen's Masters of Mystery*, 1987, and *Mystery Cats*, 1995. Contributor to magazines, including *Ellery Queen's Mystery Magazine, Seventeen, Ladies' Home Journal, McCall's, Boy's Life, Young Miss,* and *Co-ed.*

■ Sidelights

In Lael J. Littke novels, teenage girls become involved in romance, adventure, and mystery. In books such as *Shanny on Her Own, Loydene in Love,* and *Blue Skye,* Littke presents young female characters who mature quickly through the course of their adventures. In other works—including *Prom Dress, The Watcher, Haunted Sister,* and *Lake of Secrets*—Littke has written suspense tales that *School Library Journal* contributor Audrey Eaglen claimed "could have been written by either [popular authors Christopher] Pike or [R.L.] Stine."

An Idaho Childhood

"I was born and grew up in Mink Creek, a tiny farming community in the mountains of southeastern Idaho," Littke once explained. "People in other parts of the county used to say that the way to get to Mink Creek was to go as far back in the hills as you can—then go a little farther. We didn't even have a paved highway when I was growing up, and a trip to Preston, the county seat twenty miles away (population 4,000), was like a journey to another planet. What I liked most of all there was the Carnegie Public Library."

"I loved books from the time my mother bought a copy of *Three Little Pigs* for me when I was about four," the author continued. "I read all the books that my mother owned plus all of those in our little country school. My idea of heaven was when big crates of books would arrive from the State Circulating Library in Boise."

Speaking of her early reading interests with Ann Stalcup in an interview posted at the *California Readers* Web site, Littke recounted: "I remember loving Anne of Green Gables. At the time I read it, I had already determined that I was going to be a writer, and I hoped that I could someday write like L.M. Montgomery. I also loved Mark Twain's Tom Sawyer and the way it was written. Later, when I was 13, I read A Tree Grows in Brooklyn, by Betty Smith. I totally identified with the character of Francie, even though she lived in the tenements of Brooklyn and I lived on an Idaho ranch. I began to see the power of writing when I read that book."

This 2002 novel tells of Carlene's investigation into her younger brother's supposed drowning years before. (Henry Holt, 2002. Jacket copyright © Photonica. Reprinted by permission of Henry Holt and Company, LLC.)

Littke's love for books soon grew into a desire to write. Doing chores around the family ranch, she related, "was my favorite time to dream and I thought of the time when I would become a writer and write about the valley which spread before me and the people who lived there." Many of her first short stories were set in Mink Creek, as well as several of her novels, for which she renamed the town "Wolf Creek" and "Blue Creek." Littke's first stories were sold to *Ellery Queen's Mystery Magazine*, *Ladies' Home Journal*, and *Seventeen*.

First Young Adult Novels

In the mid-1980s, after publishing several titles for young readers, Littke began writing novels for young adults. *Shanny on Her Own* and *Loydene in Love* are companion books featuring Los Angeles native Shanny Adler, a fifteen-year-old girl who in *Shanny on Her Own* learns about growing up during a stay at her Aunt Adabelle's Idaho ranch. Littke reverses the circumstances in *Loydene in Love*, when Shanny's friend from Wolf Creek visits her in California. Once in Los Angeles, Loydene must decide whether the excitement of tinseltown and a new boyfriend are enough reason not to return home. While critics have occasionally faulted Littke's romances for having predictable characterization and plotlines, others have complimented Littke on her pacing and clever dialogue. For example, in a review of *Shanny on Her Own*, *School Library Journal* contributor Ruth Horowitz complained that Littke's heroine is "cardboard," but added that Shanny's "clever first-person narrative" makes the book "better than most." Similarly, *Voice of Youth Advocates* reviewer Kathy Fritts remarked on the novel's quick pace, humor, and "charm," yet found the growth of the protagonist to be handled in an unskilled fashion. Of the book's sequel, *School Library Journal* contributor Betty Ann Porter found that Littke's "message is well taken without being overbearing" and described the protagonist as "a believable and engaging young woman."

Littke's *Blue Skye* is a similar tale of a young girl who finds herself in an unfamiliar but positive environment. Eleven-year-old Skye, who has become used to a vagabond life of traveling with her mother, is left at her grandfather's home in Idaho when her mother decides to marry. At first, Skye feels abandoned and resentful, but she gradually grows to love her extended family, including all the aunts and cousins she meets. When her mother finally returns, the young protagonist decides to remain with her new family. Several reviewers commended Littke for her characterizations and handling of the subject matter, including a *Publishers Weekly* critic who praised the novel's "energetic and heartening" plot and "dynamic" characters, and also appreciated Littke's "easy, blues rhythm writing style that envelops the reader." "Thoughtful and solidly entertaining" are the words a *Kirkus Reviews* contributor used to sum up this award-winning novel.

A lighter problem faces the protagonist of *Trish for President*, who runs for class office to attract the attention of a boy, only to question her feelings about the race. "It's an enjoyable (and funny!) read with food for thought besides," Judith A. Sheriff observed in *Voice of Youth Advocates*, while a *Publishers Weekly* critic called this "first-rate" story a "fast, suspenseful, funny chronicle."

Turns to Thrillers

Prom Dress and *The Watcher* deal with suspense of a more sinister kind as the protagonists become involved in mysteries that could endanger their lives. In *Prom Dress*, for instance, the wearers of an irresistible but cursed dress feel great about themselves until tragedy strikes, while in *The Watcher*, soap opera fan Catherine Belmont is harassed by someone who replays events of a television show by using Catherine as a subject. When Catherine is almost killed in a stage "accident," she begins to suspect several of the people closest to her. Comparing Littke's suspense thrillers to those of genre favorites Stine, Richie Cusick, and Diane Hoh, *Voice of Youth Advocates* reviewer Marylee Tiernan commented that "kids will love the fast-paced, suspenseful plot" of *The Watcher*. *Kliatt* reviewer Gail E. Roberts also praised this novel, particularly the story line, with its "convincing red herrings" and surprising ending.

Haunted Sister is a thriller in which the teenaged Janine suffers a serious car accident, during which she has an out-of-body experience and meets the spirit of her deceased twin sister, Lenore, who died in a swimming accident as a child. Lenore enters Janine's body, sharing her thoughts and emotions as Janine recovers from her injuries. Because Lenore is more impulsive than Janine, her actions endanger not onlt Janine's relationships with family and friends, but her life as well. Their struggle for control makes for what Mary Ann Capan described as an "intriguing story line" in her *Voice of Youth Advocates* review. *Booklist*'s Anne O'Malley concluded: *Haunted Sister* "is a fast read and should prove a popular choice with younger teens." "Part ghost story, part psychological drama," wrote the critic for *Publishers Weekly*, "this eerie account of a near-death experience is sure to draw teenage thrill-seekers."

If you enjoy the works of Lael J. Littke, you may also want to check out the following books:

Gail Jarrow, *If Phyllis Were Here*, 1987.
Carol Plum-Ucci, *The Night My Sister Went Missing*, 2006.
Neal Shusterman, *Everlost*, 2006.

Lake of Secrets revolves around the disappearance of Carlene's brother Keith, who disappeared at the age of four and is believed to have drowned. But when Carlene visits the lake town where the tragedy took place, she is haunted by events and people she has never seen before. A woman who drowned the same day her brother disappeared, and a small boy who may be his reincarnation, move Carlene to investigate further, unraveling the mystery of her brother's disappearance. A critic for *Publishers Weekly* found that the small resort town "provides an appropriately haunting backdrop, and Carlene's resentment of her mother's absorption in her missing brother provides an interesting tension." "The handful of main characters are well developed, the small town has just enough eccentrics to keep things interesting, and Carlene is a well-rounded, typical teenager," according to a critic for *Kirkus Reviews*. "Carlene is a likable, believable character whose struggle with the shadow of her brother, her relationship with her mother, and reincarnation as a concept is interesting and engaging," wrote Saleena L. Davidson in the *School Library Journal*. *Horn Book*'s Kitty Flynn called the novel "a riveting tale of acceptance and forgiveness, with a touch of supernatural mystery." Frances Bradburn, writing in *Booklist*, concluded: "The realistic characters and plot make the idea compelling, and the story will intrigue teens."

Speaking to Ann Stalcup in an interview posted at the *California Readers* Web site, Littke explained how she got the idea for *Lake of Secrets*: "I got the idea back in 1991 when there was an article in the *Los Angeles Times* about Lake Isabella up near Kernville. This was a time of drought, and the man-made lake had receded so much that the foundations of the old town that was covered up when the area was flooded were visible after being covered by water for over forty years. I was so intrigued by the idea that I went to Kernville to see where the old town had been and to walk along the old streets. I knew there was a story there somewhere. And there was!"

Littke once commented: "After teaching writing classes for several years, I have decided that the difference between a successful author and one who gets only rejections is often a matter of discipline: the discipline to stick with a project to completion, to revise it endlessly if necessary, and to send it out again and again if it keeps coming back. It takes a hard disciplinarian to sit oneself down at a cold typewriter each morning and go at it again, but that's what it takes. I had a friend who kept her ironing board set up next to her typewriter, and each morning she told herself that if she didn't write, she would have to iron, a task she hated more than scrubbing bathrooms. Even so, she often spent the day ironing. That's how hard it is to become a successful writer. But most of us agree that it's worth every effort we've made."

■ Biographical and Critical Sources

PERIODICALS

Booklist, February 15, 1979, review of *Tell Me When I Can Go,* p. 927; September 15, 1981, Stephanie Zvirin, review of *Cave-In!,* p. 99; October 1, 1998, Anne O'Malley, review of *Haunted Sister,* p. 324; March 1, 2002, Frances Bradburn, review of *Lake of Secrets,* p. 1131.

Bulletin of the Center for Children's Books, February, 1986, review of *Shanny on Her Own,* p. 113; March, 1987, Zena Sutherland, review of *Loydene in Love,* p. 130; March, 1993, Roger Sutton, reviews of *Getting Rid of Rhoda* and *The Mystery of Ruby's Ghost,* p. 217.

Horn Book, May, 2002, Kitty Flynn, review of *Lake of Secrets,* p. 334.

Kirkus Reviews, November 1, 1991, review of *Blue Skye,* p. 1405; February 15, 2002, review of *Lake of Secrets,* p. 261.

Kliatt, July, 1994, Gail E. Roberts, review of *The Watcher,* pp. 9-10.

Publishers Weekly, January 18, 1985, review of *Trish for President,* p. 74; April 25, 1986, review of *Trish for President,* p. 87; October 18, 1991, review of *Blue Skye,* p. 63; August 31, 1998, review of *Haunted Sister,* p. 77; February 18, 2002, review of *Lake of Secrets,* p. 97.

School Library Journal, September, 1981, F. Crabbe, review of *Cave-In!,* p. 118; December, 1985, Ruth Horowitz, review of *Shanny on Her Own,* pp. 103-104; March, 1987, Betty Ann Porter, review of *Loydene in Love,* p. 172; December, 1989, Audrey Eaglen, "New Blood for Young Readers, "p. 49; September, 1991, p. 256; October, 1998, Janet Hilbun, review of *Haunted Sister,* p. 138; March, 2002, Saleena L. Davidson, review of *Lake of Secrets,* p. 234.

Voice of Youth Advocates, April, 1985, Judith A. Sheriff, review of *Trish for President,* p. 50; April, 1986, Kathy Fritts, review of *Shanny on Her Own,* p. 32; April, 1990, Rosie Peasley, review of *Prom Dress,* pp. 38-39; August, 1994, Marylee Tiernan, review of *The Watcher,* pp. 157-158; February, 1999, Mary Ann Capan, review of *Haunted Sister,* p. 437.

ONLINE

California Readers, http://californiareaders.org/ (November 19, 2007), Ann Stalcup, "Meet Lael Littke."

Deseret Book Web site, http://deseretbook.com/ (June 15, 2003), Doug Wright, "Everyday Lives, Everyday Values: Interview with Richard Turley and Lael Littke about Stories from the Life of Joseph Smith."*

Sujata Massey

■ Personal

Born 1964, in Sussex, England; immigrated to the United States; married Tony Massey (a U.S. Navy medical officer); children: Pia, Neel. *Education:* Johns Hopkins University, graduated 1986.

■ Addresses

Home—Minneapolis, MN. *E-mail*—sujatamassey @mac.com.

■ Career

Writer. *Baltimore Evening Sun,* Baltimore, MD, journalist; freelance writer, 1997—.

■ Awards, Honors

Malice Domestic Unpublished Writers grant, 1996, and Agatha Award for Best First Novel, 1998, both for *The Salaryman's Wife;* Agatha Award nomination for best novel, 2005, for *The Pearl Diver.*

■ Writings

"REI SHIMURA" MYSTERY SERIES

The Salaryman's Wife, HarperCollins (New York, NY), 1997.

Zen Attitude, HarperCollins (New York, NY), 1998.

The Flower Master, HarperCollins (New York, NY), 1999.

The Floating Girl, HarperCollins (New York, NY), 2000.

The Bride's Kimono, HarperCollins (New York, NY), 2001.

The Samurai's Daughter, HarperCollins (New York, NY), 2003.

The Pearl Diver, HarperCollins (New York, NY), 2004.

The Typhoon Lover, HarperCollins (New York, NY), 2005.

Girl in a Box, HarperCollins (New York, NY), 2006.

■ Sidelights

Sujata Massey is the creator of the "Rei Shimura" mystery series, featuring a twenty-something Japanese-American woman who lives in Tokyo. In the course of buying and selling antiques for her shop, Rei stumbles across murder mysteries which she is compelled to solve. Along the way, the reader learns about contemporary Japanese culture. "With her wry humor and her multicultural background," Jenny McLarin stated in *Booklist,* "Rei is one of the most complex female protagonists around." An essayist for *VG: Voices from the Gaps* found that "the Rei Shimura novels are not merely a great mystery series; they are a venue in which Sujata Massey discusses serious societal issues. . . . Her works serve as an excellent example of the genre of feminist mystery writing." Speaking with Betty Shimabukuro in the *Honolulu Star-Bulletin*, Massey maintained: "In the end, my sleuth and I both share a belief that everyone is human, no matter how badly he or she behaves."

A Multicultural Background

Sujata Massey was born in Sussex, England, in 1964, the daughter of a father from India and a mother from Germany. When she was five years old, her parents immigrated to the United States. Massey grew up in Pennsylvania, California, and Minnesota, but never became totally Americanized because her family often returned to England; she remains a citizen of the United Kingdom, but is a legal resident of the United States.

Massey graduated from Johns Hopkins University in Baltimore, Maryland, in 1986, and then worked as a journalist for the *Baltimore Evening Sun* newspaper. She met Tony Massey, a U.S. Navy medical officer, and they eventually married. When Tony Massey was posted to Japan, the couple moved there in 1991, returning to the United States in 1993.

While in Japan, Massey became fascinated with Japanese culture and history. She united this interest with her love of mystery novels to begin writing mysteries with Japanese characters. These mysteries feature the character Rei Shimura. Rei, like Massey, is a multicultural woman. Born in California to a Japanese father and an American mother, she speaks Japanese well. At her Web site, Massey noted: "The most important similarity I share with my sleuth is confusion over cultural identity." Rei is torn between her two cultures, enjoying Japanese art and aesthetics, but also enjoying the freedom she has as an American woman. Rei has moved to Japan to teach English, but discovers her real interest in antiques. She is soon developing a business as an antiques dealer in Tokyo, Japan, catering to wealthy clients. According to Robin Agnew in the *Mystery Readers Journal*, "Rei is a fascinating and sometimes frustrating character . . . she's smart, well educated and thinks things through in unusual ways which often help her get to the bottom of a situation." Writing for the *Mystery Ink Web site*, David J. Montgomery stated: "Rei is a fascinating character: bold, unique, spirited and intelligent." While working on her first novel, *The Salaryman's Wife*, Massey entered the Malice Domestic Unpublished Writers Grant Contest. She won and, with the help of the grant, was able to finish her novel, find an agent, and sell her book.

Rei Shimura becomes involved in the murder of a young comic book writer in this 2001 novel. (Avon Books, 2001. Reprinted by permission of HarperCollins Publishers Inc.)

Introduces Rei Shimura

In *The Salaryman's Wife*, Rei is teaching English to the employees of a kitchenware company in Tokyo. While on a New Year's holiday at a ski resort in the Japanese Alps, Rei stumbles across the body of a salaryman's wife outside the communal bathhouse. (A salaryman is a Japanese nickname for a businessman or a corporate middle manager.) The police ask her to serve as a translator while they interrogate the English-speaking guests at the resort. One of them, a Scotsman by the name of Hugh Glendinning, is initially a suspect but when he is released, he and Rei team up to find the actual killer. Diane Skoss, in a review for *Koryu.com Book Reviews*, concluded: "Mystery fans will enjoy the well-crafted plot, lively characters, and satisfying denouement."

In a review for *Over My Dead Body Magazine,* Cherie Jung wrote: "With a cup of green tea in hand, retire to a comfy chair, and curl up with this book. You'll soon find yourself immersed in the people and places of Japan." *The Salaryman's Wife* won Massey the Agatha Award for best first novel.

Zen Attitude finds Rei opening her own antiques shop in Tokyo. She is also living with Hugh Glendinning, the Scotsman from the previous novel. When a con man sells Rei a fake antique tansu, or chest of drawers, she vows to get her money back. But the seller, Mr. Sakai, is found dead in a parked car. Rei must suddenly look into her clients who wanted the chest, discovering some family secrets along the way. In a review for *City Paper Online,* Jack Purdy called *Zen Attitude* "a tightly plotted and culturally rich mystery." Cherie Jung wrote: "Each time I read one of Ms. Massey's books, I feel like I've gotten a free trip to Japan, complete with a charming guide!"

In *The Flower Master,* Rei is living in Tokyo, working as an antiques dealer. When her Aunt Norie, a master of traditional Japanese flower arranging, or *ikebana,* tells her she should enroll in a flower-arranging class, Rei does so. Norie hopes that ikebana may lead to Rei finding a suitable husband. But Rei turns out to be so exceptionally untalented at ikebana that she is publicly reproved by her teacher, which leads to a counter-attack by her aunt. Both women plan to make their apologies by presenting the teacher with a pair of scissors; but the teacher is stabbed to death with the scissors and Rei becomes the prime suspect in the murder. To clear her name, Rei must uncover the killer. Among the suspects are some of her classmates and a Japanese activist who claims that his country's demand for fresh flowers is endangering the thousands of Colombian workers who come into contact with the dangerous pesticides used to raise them. Cherie Jung stated: "Massey manages to combine just enough Japanese culture with sleuthing to make reading about Rei's adventures exciting and educational." The *Publishers Weekly* critic praised "the richly detailed Tokyo setting, from ancient tea houses to arcane rituals involving the cherry blossom festival." In the *Washington Post Book World,* Paul Skenazy commented that Massey "provides us with a wonderfully detailed tour of Japan, and of *ikebana.*"

A Baby from India

In 2000 Massey and her husband adopted a daughter, Pia, who was born in South India. Massey stayed in India with Pia from December 1998 through February 1999. Although she was under contract at the time to complete her novel *The Floating Girl,* she was unable to travel with a laptop computer because she had too much baby equipment. She took discs with her to India and worked on computers whenever she could find one available.

While in India, a computer virus erased half of the novel she was working on, but she had printed out much of her material. When she returned to Baltimore with Pia, Tony typed all of these pages into their home computer, and it took Massey five more months to complete the novel. She wrote on her Web page: "Now I'm happy to report having a baby has not slowed me down too much as a writer." She writes during her daughter's naps, and hires a babysitter occasionally when she needs more time.

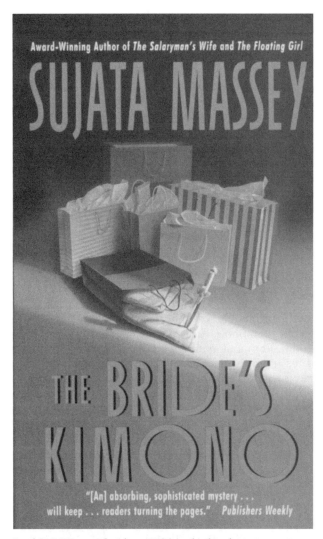

In this 2002 novel, when Rei is asked to lecture on some rare Japanese kimonos, it leads to murder. (Avon Books, 2002. Reprinted by permission of HarperCollins Publishers Inc.)

Rei discovers manga in *The Floating Girl*. Asked to write a magazine article about the Japanese comics form manga, Rei begins to explore the world of Japanese comics. She finds an entire subculture of manga fans, who often dress up as their favorite characters. She is drawn to one comic in particular, *Mars Girl*, but when she attempts to track down the elusive artist, she finds herself caught up in a world of Japanese gangsters. Soon after she interviews the young American man who writes the story for the *Mars Girl* comic, he turns up dead, and her editors ask her to continue her investigation in order to increase the magazine's sagging circulation. "Deftly sketching everyday life in parts of Tokyo rarely seen by tourists," a *Publishers Weekly* reviewer wrote, "Massey tells a series of overlapping stories about identity, the popular media and the hilarious frenzy of contemporary comic book culture." "In portraying a modern young Japanese-American in Japan today," wrote Andi Shechter in *Reviewing the Evidence*, "[Massey] offers a lot to think about, and a suspenseful story to accompany all the information."

Rei Goes Home

In *The Bride's Kimono*, Rei returns for a visit to the United States after several years away from home. Because she has been building up a business in Japanese antiques, with a specialty in textiles and clothing, Rei is asked to undertake a delicate mission: to accompany a collection of valuable 19th century kimonos from Tokyo to Washington for an exhibit at the Museum of Asian Arts, where she will also deliver a lecture on the garments. En route, she meets a Japanese office worker who is heading to a mall to shop for her wedding. This woman is murdered, and the body is initially identified as being Rei. When she clarifies the mistaken identity with the police, Rei then faces another problem: a bride's kimono is stolen from her Washington hotel room. Romantic entanglements, as well as family issues, complicate the story. In *Publishers Weekly*, a reviewer called *The Bride's Kimono* an "absorbing, sophisticated mystery." Jenny MaLarin praised the book's "astute character development and fascinating use of Japanese history." In the *Washington Post Book World*, Patrick Anderson wrote that Shimura, "sexy, breezy, and smart, holds our interest even as the novel veers off in unexpected directions."

Rei uncovers a disturbing family secret in *The Samurai's Daughter*. While researching her family history during a visit with her parents in San Francisco, Rei finds that her great-grandfather tutored the young Japanese Emperor Hirohito. He also wrote a textbook that may have encouraged the emperor's later attack on Pearl Harbor, triggering America's involvement in World War II. Rei's boyfriend, Hugh Glendinning, a lawyer involved in a class-action lawsuit filed against Japanese companies for enslaving Asians as slave labor during the war, shows up at Rei's home to visit. While there, one of his contacts, Rosa Munoz, is murdered. Then the young student boarder at her parents' house disappears. Rei and Hugh join forces to investigate the murder, which leads them back to Tokyo. "Massey poses some deeply resonating questions about guilt and responsibility," the critic for *Publishers Weekly* wrote, "while Rei faces some universal truths about families, loyalty and dealing with the past no matter how unpleasant it may be." Jenny McLarin concluded: "Massey deftly weaves fascinating historical and cultural detail into a suspenseful plot."

After having been deported from Japan for events recounted in the previous novel, Rei and Hugh are living in Washington, DC, and planning their wedding in *The Pearl Diver*. Rei is pleased and surprised when restaurateur Marshall Zanger hires her to furnish the upscale Japanese restaurant he is opening. In the middle of all this, Rei's cousin Kendall, who is working with her to prepare for the opening night festivities, is abducted. Rei and the owner investigate, and Rei discovers that the owner's mother, a pearl diver in her native Japan, disappeared thirty years before. The two disappearances may be connected. Rex E. Klett, writing in the *Library Journal*, praised the novel for its "genteel prose, a forthright but tactful protagonist, and a riveting story line." According to Beverly J. DeWeese, writing in *Mystery Scene*, "Rei's love affair with Hugh, the sympathetic picture of interracial relationships, and the unique background coalesce into a very good mystery." "Adept at crafting dead-on dialogue and juggling serious issues with humor, Massey has produced another triumph," according to a critic for *Publishers Weekly*.

In *The Typhoon Lover*, Rei is sent back to Tokyo by the Smithsonian to help uncover the whereabouts of an ancient pitcher stolen from Iraq's national museum. The valuable relic may be in the private collection of a wealthy Japanese. Rei soon discovers that an old boyfriend, Takeo Kayama, may be involved with a ring of antiques smugglers. Under cover of a typhoon that paralyzes Tokyo, Rei goes searching for the missing artifact by breaking into a country estate. "This is another excellent book in the series," wrote Shirley H. Wetzel in a review for *Over My Dead Body Magazine*. "Massey writes beautifully, and her descriptions of the settings, in Washington and Japan, are vivid." A critic for *Publishers Weekly* noted that "Massey gleefully contrasts the young, bizarrely garbed generation . . . with traditional Japanese society." Barbarra Franchi of *Reviewing the Evidence* concluded: "Even if you haven't read any of the other books, this one will entrance you."

Girl in a Box finds Rei working undercover at a Japanese department store. It seems that Tokyo retailer Mitsutan is making exorbitant profits and officials at the Organization for Cultural Intelligence want to know the real source of the money. Though she tries hard to work in a Japanese company, Rei has trouble with the long hours and the necessity for constant humility. She also begins to have romantic feelings about her boss. "Readers will find Rei's cross-cultural escapades as engrossing as the department store's shenanigans," wrote a *Publishers Weekly* reviewer. "A voyeur's tour of consumption-crazed Tokyo is the real point here," according to a critic for *Kirkus Reviews*, "with Rei-san, as always, a companionable guide."

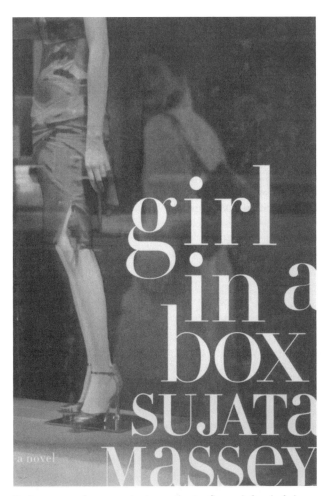

Rei goes undercover to investigate financial misdoings at a Tokyo department store in this 2006 mystery. (Harper-Collins, 2006. Reprinted by permission of HarperCollins Publishers Inc. Massey, Sujata, photograph. Copyright © Jerry Bauer. Reproduced by permission.)

If you enjoy the works of Sujata Massey, you may also want to check out the following books:

Jonathan Gash, *Jade Woman*, 1990.
Asa Nonami, *The Hunter*, 2006.
Miyuki Miyabe, *The Devil's Whisper*, 2007.

Speaking of the "Rei Shimura" series as a whole, Lynn Kaczmarek in *Mystery News* explained that Massey has "traveled a number of places . . . always with a sense of openness to the discovery of new things. And she brings all her experiences, curiosity, and respect for cultural differences to the pages of her books. Sujata Massey has given us a view of Japan that most of us will never experience first hand, but which through her words, we too have come to respect."

What is Massey's advice for aspiring writers? She noted on her Web site: "I rewrote my first book more than fifty times before submitting it to an agent. There is something to be said for not proceeding until you are as polished as you can be."

■ Biographical and Critical Sources

PERIODICALS

Booklist, April 15, 1999, review of *The Flower Master*, p. 1482; May 1, 2000, Jenny McLarin, review of *The Floating Girl*, p. 1622; May 1, 2001, Merle Jacob, review of *The Flower Master*, p. 1607; August, 2001, Jenny McLarin, review of *The Bride's Kimono*, p. 2098; February 15, 2003, Jenny McLarin, review of *The Samurai's Daughter*, p. 1055; July, 2004, Jenny McLarin, review of *The Pearl Diver*, p. 1825; September 1, 2005, Jenny McLarin, review of *The Typhoon Lover*, p. 70; August 1, 2006, Sue O'Brien, review of *Girl in a Box*, p. 51.

Honolulu Star-Bulletin, July 31, 2005, Betty Shimabukuro, "She Dunit: The Author of the Rei Shimura Series of Whodunits Is Writing a Hawaii-based Mystery."

Kirkus Reviews, August 1, 2001, review of *The Bride's Kimono*, p. 1071; January 15, 2003, review of *The Samurai's Daughter*, p. 114; June 1, 2004, review of *The Pearl Diver*, p. 521; July 15, 2005, review of *The Typhoon Lover*, p. 768; July 1, 2006, review of *Girl in a Box*, p. 657.

Library Journal, April 15, 1999, Francine Fialkoff, review of *The Flower Master,* p. 149; April 1, 2000, Dean Jones, review of *The Flower Master,* p. 160; February 15, 2003, Jackie Cassada, review of *The Samurai's Daughter,* p. 173; August, 2004, Rex E. Klett, review of *The Pearl Diver,* p. 59.

Mystery Readers Journal, spring, 2007, Robin Agnew, review of *Girl in a Box,* pp. 68-69.

Mystery News, June-July, 2000, Lynn Kaczmarek, "Sujata Massey: Speaking the Language of Mystery," pp. 1-3.

Mystery Scene, fall, 2004, Beverly J. DeWeese, review of *The Pearl Diver;* Issue 92, 2005, Derek Hill, review of *The Typhoon Lover.*

New York Times Book Review, May 2, 1999, Marilyn Stasio, review of *The Flower Master,* p. 28; August 22, 2004, Marilyn Stasio, review of *The Pearl Diver,* p. 15.

People, November 17, 1997, J.D. Reed, review of *The Salaryman's Wife,* p. 43.

Publishers Weekly, April 13, 1998, review of *Zen Attitude,* p. 72; April 5, 1999, review of *The Flower Master,* p. 225; April 17, 2000, review of *The Floating Girl,* p. 54; August 6, 2001, review of *The Bride's Kimono,* p. 66; February 24, 2003, review of *The Samurai's Daughter,* p. 56; July 19, 2004, review of *The Pearl Diver,* p. 148; August 15, 2005, review of *The Typhoon Lover,* p. 37; July 10, 2006, review of *Girl in a Box,* p. 52.

USA Today, September 21, 2006, Carol Memmott, review of *Girl in a Box,* p. 4D.

Washington Post Book World, October 10, 1999, Paul Skenazy, review of *The Flower Master,* p. 13; October 14, 2001, Patrick Anderson, review of *The Bride's Kimono,* p. 13.

ONLINE

City Paper Online, http://www.citypaper.com/ (September 9, 1998), Jack Purdy, review of *Zen Attitude.*

Koryu.com Book Reviews, http://www.koryu.com/ books/massey.html/ (June 20, 2007), Diane Skoss, review of *The Salaryman's Wife.*

Mystery Ink Web site, http://www.mysteryinkonline. com/ (August 18, 2007), David J. Montgomery, review of *The Typhoon Lover.*

Over My Dead Body Magazine, http://www. overmydeadbody.com/ (May 6, 2007), Cherie Jung, reviews of *The Bride's Kimono, The Floating Girl, The Flower Master, Girl in a Box, The Pearl Diver, The Salaryman's Wife, The Typhoon Lover,* and *Zen Attitude;* and Shirley H. Wetzel, review of *The Typhoon Lover.*

Reviewing the Evidence, http://www. reviewingtheevidence.com/ (June, 2000), Andi Shechter, review of *The Floating Girl;* (December, 2001), Barbara Franchi, review of *The Bride's Kimono;* (June, 2003), Lane Wright, review of *The Samurai's Daughter;* (October, 2005), Barbara Franchi, review of *The Typhoon Lover.*

Sujata Massey Web site, http://www.interbridge. com/sujata (November 19, 2007).

VG: Voices from the Gaps, http://voices.cla.umn.edu/ VG/index.html/ (May 7, 2002), "Biography/ Criticism."

Women's Fiction @ Suite 101, http://womensfiction. suite101.com/ (August 25, 2006), Andree Lachapelle, "Sujata Massey: Woman of Mystery."

Writers Write, http://www.writerswrite.com/ (October, 1998), Claire E. White, "A Conversation with Sujata Massey."*

(Courtesy of AP Images.)

■ Personal

Born August 3, 1943, in New York, NY; son of Milton (a professor of English) Millhauser; married Cathy Allis, 1984; children: one son, one daughter. *Education:* Columbia College, B.A., 1965; graduate study at Brown University, 1968-71, 1976-77.

■ Addresses

Home—Saratoga Springs, NY. *Office*—Department of English, Skidmore College, Palamountain Hall 307, 815 North Broadway, Saratoga Springs, NY 12866; fax: 518-580-5189. *Agent*—Amanda Urban, International Creative Management, 40 W. 57th St., New York, NY 10019. *E-mail*—smillhau@skidmore.edu.

■ Career

Writer and educator. Williams College, visiting associate professor of English, 1986-88; Skidmore College, Saratoga Springs, NY, associate professor, 1988-92, professor of English, 1992—.

Steven Millhauser

■ Member

American Academy of Arts and Sciences.

■ Awards, Honors

Prix Medicis Etranger (France), 1975, for *Edwin Mullhouse: The Life and Death of an American Writer, 1943-1954, by Jeffrey Cartwright;* American Academy/ Institute of Arts and Letters Award for literature, 1987; World Fantasy Award, 1990; Lannan Literary Award for fiction, 1994; Pulitzer Prize for fiction, 1997, for *Martin Dressler: The Tale of an American Dreamer.*

■ Writings

NOVELS

Edwin Mullhouse: The Life and Death of an American Writer, 1943-1954, by Jeffrey Cartwright, Alfred A. Knopf (New York, NY), 1972.
Portrait of a Romantic, Alfred A. Knopf (New York, NY), 1977.
From the Realm of Morpheus, William Morrow (New York, NY), 1986.
Martin Dressler: The Tale of an American Dreamer, Crown Publishers (New York, NY), 1996.

SHORT FICTION

In the Penny Arcade (stories and novella), Alfred A. Knopf (New York, NY), 1986.

The Barnum Museum (stories), Poseidon Press (New York, NY), 1990.

Little Kingdoms (three novellas), Poseidon Press (New York, NY), 1993.

The Knife Thrower and Other Stories, Crown Publishers (New York, NY), 1998.

Enchanted Night: A Novella, Crown Publishers (New York, NY), 1999.

The King in the Tree: Three Novellas, Alfred A. Knopf (New York, NY), 2003.

OTHER

Contributor of short stories to periodicals, including *New Yorker, Tin House, Grand Street, Harper's,* and *Antaeus.* Contributor to *The New Yorker out Loud* (CD), 1998.

■ Adaptations

Martin Dressler was released in an audio version by Guidall, 1997; *Enchanted Night* was released in audio versions by Dove Audio, 1999; "Eisenheim the Illusionist," a story in *The Barnum Museum,* was adapted as the film *The Illusionist,* starring Edward Norton and Paul Giamatti, released by Yari Film Group, 2006.

■ Sidelights

"I'd wish the reader, in the course of falling into one of my stories, to grow more and more estranged from the familiar, until by the end of the story he or she, if only for a moment, sees the world as a mysterious and surprising place." So explained Steven Millhauser during an interview with Marc Chénetier of *Transatlantica: American Studies Journal.* The winner of a host of literary prizes, including a Pulitzer Prize, Millhauser has been hailed by many critics as one of America's finest writers. "The two main concerns of Millhauser's fiction," Michael Adams wrote in the *Dictionary of Literary Biography,* "are literature and childhood. His novels contain parodies of specific writers and genres and are heavily allusive. But more important is Millhauser's unsentimental presentation of the pains and pleasures of childhood, a period he rescues from the

cliches of popular culture and the stereotypes of the sociologists and psychologists." An essayist for *Contemporary Novelists* found that Millhauser's characters "are disappointed dreamers who long to see their fantasies realized, though each meets with varying degrees of success." Speaking of Millhauser's style of writing, a contributor to the *St. James Guide to Fantasy Writers* described it as "a languid, lapidary prose that evokes the literature of Romantic decadence."

Steven Millhauser was born August 3, 1943, in New York CIty and raised in Connecticut. His father, Milton Millhauser, was a professor of English at the University of Bridgeport. Millhauser earned a B.A. from Columbia University in 1965, later doing graduate study at Brown University. Since 1988, Millhauser has been teaching English at Skidmore College in Saratoga Springs, NY. In 1984 he married Cathy Allis. They have two children.

A Fictitious Biography

Millhauser made his first entry onto the literary scene with *Edwin Mullhouse: The Life and Death of an American Writer, 1943-54, by Jeffrey Cartwright.* It is the fictitious biography of an eleven-year-old novelist as penned by the novelist's twelve-year-old companion. The young novelist, Edwin Mullhouse, completed only one work, the masterpiece *Cartoons,* prior to his untimely death at age eleven. His biographer records Mullhouse's interest in baseball cards and novelty-shop gifts while unwittingly revealing his own obsessions with Mullhouse and *Cartoons.* As the biographer's self-created rivalry with the late Mullhouse develops, *Edwin Mullhouse* evolves into both a parody of literary biographies and a sardonic portrait of the artist.

Published in 1972, *Edwin Mullhouse* was acclaimed by many reviewers. William Hjortsberg, writing in *New York Times Book Review,* called Millhauser's work "a rare and carefully evoked novel, . . . displays an enviable amount of craft, the harsh discipline that carves through the scar tissue of personality painfully developed during the process known as 'growing up.'" J.D. O'Hara, reviewing the work for *Washington Post Book World,* noted that Millhauser's "characters, like J.D. Salinger's in one way . . . are absurdly precocious children, but their story is for adults." A *New Republic* reviewer was equally impressed with Millhauser's work, calling it "a mature, skillful, intelligent and often very funny novel."

Millhauser continues his depiction of childhood in his second novel, *Portrait of a Romantic.* Arthur Grumm, the twenty-nine-year-old protagonist, gives an account of his life between the ages of twelve and fifteen. He sees himself as a sickly, bored only child who says that "by some accident the children in my neighborhood were older than I and so excluded me from their dusty games." Grumm reveals himself as a vaguely suicidal adolescent divided by the polarized beliefs of his two friends, William Mainwaring, an avowed realist whom Grumm refers to as "my double," and Philip School-craft, an equally vehement romantic referred to by Grumm as "my triple." Schoolcraft introduces Grumm to the romantic life, typified by decay, contemplation, and despair—they pass time pondering Poe and playing Russian roulette. Grumm later forms suicide pacts with the pathetic Eleanor Schumann and eventually with the disillusioned Mainwaring. The bizarre events caused by Grumm's suicide pacts provide an offbeat context for his own internal conflict between realism and romanticism and his weighing of the harsh repercussions inherent in submitting to either attitude.

According to John Calvin Batchelor of *Village Voice*, Millhauser, in his attempts to capture completely every detail, writes "with sometimes suffocating amount of sights and sound." *Times Literary Supplement* critic William Boyd noted that too much effort is lavished on "pages of relentlessly detailed description." Nevertheless, *Portrait of a Romantic* stands as a "remarkable book" by a very talented writer, according to George Stade in *New York Times Book Review*. Stade added: "Once you reread the book the particulars begin to look different. The foreshadowings become luminous with afterglow. What first seemed merely realistic . . . becomes symbolic. What seemed mere fantasy . . . becomes the workings of an iron psychological necessity." William Kennedy, who reviewed the novel for *Washington Post Book World*, also responded with respect and praise, declaring that Millhauser's "achievement is of a high order."

Carl Hausman, the young narrator of Millhauser's 1986 novel *From the Realm of Morpheus*, is watching a baseball game. He chases a foul ball and finds an opening to the underworld, which he immediately investigates, and readers are plunged, *Alice in Wonderland*-style, into the world of Morpheus, the God of Sleep. In what John Crowley in *New York Times Book Review* dubbed "a book, wholly odd yet purposefully unoriginal," Millhauser takes readers on a literary tour that parodies a variety of genres and where characters from history, literature, and legend converse and philosophize in a series of disconnected episodes. While Rob Latham, in the *St. James Guide to Fantasy Writers*, contended that this experiment in mock epic writing falls short of

its intended goal, *Washington Post Book World* contributor Michael Dirda praised *From the Realms of Morpheus* as "beautifully composed"and "utterly entrancing."

Prize-winning Novel

Millhauser's Pulitzer Prize-winning *Martin Dressler: The Tale of an American Dreamer* tells the story of a quintessential Gilded-Age American entrepreneur, his dreams, and his disappointments. The title character works his way up from his father's cigar shop through a dreamy series of promotions, schemes, and machinations to become the owner and proprietor of a Manhattan hotel, The Grand Cosmo, that is "a leap beyond the hotel" in its fantastical atmosphere and consumerist excess. Janet Burroway, writing for *New York Times Book Review*, described the novel as "a fable and phantasmagoria of the sources of our century," calling Martin "not a parody but a paradigm of the bootstrap capitalist." Critics cited the novel for its imaginative and piercing glimpse into the American psyche and the American dream; *Martin Dressler* explores not only Dressler's business success, but also his personal failures and ultimate unhappiness. A *Booklist* reviewer observed that Millhauser "brings descriptive delicacy to this chronicle of Martin's 'falling upwards' and the forces behind the fall." A *Kirkus Reviews* critic described the novel as "a chronicle of obsession, self-indulgence, and, in a curious way, moral growth, expertly poised between realistic narrative and allegorical fable."

In addition to longer works, Millhauser has also authored many short stories and novellas, most of which have been included in published collections. A writer for *Contemporary Literary Criticism Yearbook 1997* commented that the author "writes of the world of the imagination. The subject of his stories is frequently the artist and the dreamer, the illusionist who creates words to satisfy the needs of others for fantasy. Millhauser's artistic motivation is summarized in a line of his short story, 'Eisenheim the Illusionist' from the collection *The Barnum Museum*: 'Stories, like conjuring tricks, are invented because history is inadequate to our dreams.'"

Publishes Story Collections

In his first collection of short stories, *In the Penny Arcade*, Millhauser continues his pursuit of "fiction as a mysterious, magical, enlightening experience" according to Robert Dunn in *New York Times Book Review*. The book is divided into three sections, the

This 1986 title, Millhauser's first collection, contains seven stories, including "Snowmen" and "Cathay." (Dalkey Archive, 1998. Cover art copyright © by David Shannon. Reproduced by permission.)

first containing the novella *August Eschenburg*, a long story about a German boy who is possessed by the desire to create mechanical devices that approximate life. Creating lifelike models for store windows and for an automaton theater, he dreams about infusing these automatons with life. But when a rival exploits this craft for pornographic purposes, August returns to his home and dreams his dreams in solitude.

The second section of *In the Penny Arcade,* comprised of three stories about real-life characters, contrasts to the artificial-life stories of sections one and three. These stories are more delicate; they are subtle, revealing the "fragility of moods in which nothing much actually happens," according to Al J. Sperone in *Village Voice Literary Supplement.* Similarly Irving Malin, in *Review of Contemporary Fiction* contended, "These stories vary in length and setting and time, they must be read as variations on a theme—the

'perfection' of art. . . . They surprise us because they are less interested in plot, character, and philosophy than in magic, dream, and metaphor." Among the three stories in the final section is the title story, in which a young boy returns to an arcade he has idealized in his mind, seeing it in all its seediness. Robert Dunn noted in *New York Times Book Review* that Millhauser "creates for us this splendid arcade. And he asks us also to be vigilant as we venture with him into the common corners of our ragged world, where the marvelous glows and the true meanings breathe life."

The Barnum Museum collects stories that seek a reconciliation between the worlds of illusion and reality. In "The Sepia Postcard," the narrator buys an old post card and finds that as he examines it more closely the figures on it come alive. In "Rain," a man walks out of a theater and into a storm. As he walks on, he washes away as if he were a watercolor painting. Taken as a whole, this collection addresses the broader issue of imagination, according to Jay Cantor in a review for *New York Times Book Review.* The critic wrote that Millhauser "imagines the imagination as a junk shop with a warren of rooms, one chamber linked to another without any reason except the bewildering reason of the heart." This junk shop is the Barnum Museum, which is "named for the patron saint of charming bunco," P.T. Barnum. Many of the ten stories in the collection engage the reader in what Catherine Maclay in *World and I* dubbed "a playful examination of the imaginary and the real . . . [and the attempt to find] a reconciliation of these opposites." In blurring the lines between these two, Millhauser's postmodern stories help us "find a way to maintain a bridge" between them, according to Maclay.

His third short-story collection, *The Knife Thrower and Other Stories,* showcases Millhauser's "rich, sly sense of humor" and a characteristic "tone of whimsy" that "conceals disturbing subversive energies" noted Patrick McGrath in the *New York Times Book Review.* In the dozen stories included in this collection the author proves himself to be "American literature's mordantly funny and unfailingly elegant bard of the uncanny," according to a *Publishers Weekly* reviewer, who added that the collection addresses two themes: When does the "pursuit of transcendent pleasure degrade rather than exalt?" and can the pursuit of pleasure be sated "without our becoming jaded or corrupt?" In the tales "Flying Carpets" and "Clair de Lune" he addresses these questions in stories imbued with a fairy tale quality that recalls childhood. "The Sisterhood of Night" and "Balloon Flight, 1870," about a hot-air balloonist during the Franco-Prussian war, in contrast, "suggest new avenues of thought in Millhauser's fiction," according to McGrath. In the title story, according to *Washington Post Book World* reviewer A.S. Byatt, the author "steps beyond the bounds of the comfortable" in describing a virtuoso knife thrower in whose public performances are couched private fantasies. Praising "Paradise Park," Byatt added that the strength of this story lies in "Millhauser's ability to weave detail into detail, the lovingly real and possible into the extravagantly impossible." Commenting on the collection in *Boston Globe*, Margot Livesey concluded that Millhauser's characters are intent upon escape. "Sometimes they go too far . . .," the critic added, "but in their struggles between the real and surreal, the effable and the ineffable, art and life, these characters and their creator illuminate our struggles to live our daily lives and still keep something larger in mind."

Millhauser's first collection of novellas, *Little Kingdoms*, includes *The Little World of J. Franklin Payne, The Princess, the Dwarf, and the Dungeon,* and *Catalogue of the Exhibition: The Art of Edmund Moorash 1810-1846*. Each of these works continues their author's exploration of the theme of the relationship between the life of the world and the life of imagination, according to Michael Dirda in *Washington Post Book World*. Dirda added that these three stories as grouped "subtly question each other about imagination and its power." In the first, J. Franklin Payne, a newspaper cartoonist, becomes obsessed with the making of an animated cartoon film. In doing so, Nicholas Delbanco, writing for the *Chicago Tribune*, noted that he "invents his own reality—not so much in compensation for artistic disappointment as in an effort to improve upon the diurnal world. What seems vivid to him is his own imagination; reality looks dull." In his fixation on the cartoons he is creating, we are reminded of August Eschenburg's fixation on mechanical figures.

The Princess, the Dwarf, and the Dungeon plays with the conventions of the fairy tale genre: a late-medieval time setting, castles, dungeons, evil, dwarves, jealous princes, and virtuous maidens. Frederick Tuten noted in *New York Times Book Review* that "embedded in this story is the narrator's meditation on the art of his time, paintings so life-like as to cause a dog to lick the portrait of his master." Millhauser's blurring of the lines between reality and imagination is a continuation of the same techniques in his *Barnum Museum* stories. *Catalogue of the Exhibition: The Art of Edmund Moorash 1810-1846* is perhaps the most clever. In a writing style Daniel Green described in *Georgia Review* as "typically energetic," the story is presented as an extended commentary on an exhibition of paintings by the fictional painter Edmund Moorash. Through a close reading of the explanations of the paintings, however, readers see the world of the painter complete with intimations of incest, devil worship,

romance, and betrayal. There are four characters in the tale: Moorash, his sister Elizabeth, his friend William Pinney, and William's sister, Sophia. However, as Dirda pointed out, "passion's cross-currents disturb friendship's pallid surface." The result is that these four end up as figures as tragic as the subjects of the paintings at the exhibition. This novella is a work of art about art works and the theme of imagination and reality and the lines between them. Elizabeth keeps a diary in which she writes, "Edmund wants to dissolve forms and reconstruct them so as to release their energy. Art as alchemy." Delbanco noted in *Chicago Tribune* that this is "the credo of the whole" story. But it very well fits as the credo of all Millhauser's works.

Donna Seaman, in her review of Millhauser's 1999 work *Enchanted Night: A Novella* for *Booklist*, noted that the author "has been drifting into fantasy . . . and now he weaves pure magic in this dreamy tale of one fateful summer night." *Enchanted Night*, which is comprised of seventy-four short prose sections with chapters sometimes only one page long, conjures up toys and a mannequin coming to life, an unsuccessful author and his unsuccessful relationship with the mother of a childhood friend, teenage girls breaking into a house leaving cryptic notes, a lonely drunk stumbling home, and a girl waiting for a lover who may be real or may be fantasy.

The three-novella collection published as *The King in the Tree* focuses on the consequences of forbidden amours. In *An Adventure of Don Juan*, based on Gabriel Tellez's sixteenth-century writings about the legendary Spanish lover, the thirty-year-old Don Juan finds his plans to seduce two sisters frustrated when he inadvertently falls in love with one of them. According to *World and I* contributor Edward Hower, Millhauser's protagonist "experiences the sort of conflict shared by many of this author's characters: how to reconcile the sometimes seductive demands of the outer world with the longings that spring from the inner recesses of the soul." The title story also focuses on obsession, retelling the medieval legend of Tristan and Ysolt while also adding psychological depth. As Michael Dirda noted in his *Washington Post Book World* review, in Millhauser's version "all loyalties, strongly felt and believed in—loyalty to one's sovereign, to the marriage vows, to honor, friendship and ones' very self—are ripped apart by the remorseless claims of passionate love." The short novella *Revenge* takes the form of a monologue as a widow gives a tour of her home—and her own life—to a prospective home buyer who, the reader soon discovers, is actually a former rival for the narrator's late husband's affections.

If you enjoy the works of Steven Millhauser, you may also want to check out the following books:

Richard Bruatigan, *Trout Fishing in America*, 1997.
Edward Carey, *Observatory Mansions*, 2000.
Georges Rodenbach, *Bruges-la-Morte*, 2005.
Jorge Luis Borges, *Labyrinths: Selected Stories and Other Writings*, 2007.

Praising *The King in the Tree* as being "rich in verbal dexterity, ambitious romantic imagery, and fascinating insights into the darker regions of the human heart," Hower commented that Millhauser's construction of a "world of artifice" serves to distill from his characters' lives "the most intense emotional expression and meaning." In *Los Angeles Times* Jeff Turrentine cited Millhauser's "Gothicism" as well as his love for the nineteenth century that permeates the collection. *The King in the Tree* "is a moving, melancholy book about the unlovely toll exacted by love on those it has abandoned," added Turrentine. A *Kirkus Reviews* writer maintained that "some of the best writing of Millhauser's increasingly brilliant career appears in this collection."

Millhauser's fiction remains widely heralded for its perceptive exploration of the problems and pleasures of youth, and the author continues to be lauded for both his stylistic virtuosity and his capacity to evoke the undercurrents of ordinary life. As Dirda commented in the *Washington Post Book World*: "Reading Millhauser, there are times when you simply lay the book aside and say to yourself, 'I had not known that sentences could be so simple and so beautiful.'"

■ **Biographical and Critical Sources**

BOOKS

Chénetier, Marc, *Beyond Suspicion: New American Fiction since 1960*, University of Pennsylvania Press (Philadelphia, PA), 1996.
Chénetier, Marc, *Steven Millhauser: La précision de l'impossible*, Belin (Paris, France), 2003.
Contemporary Literary Criticism, Gale (Detroit, MI), Volume 21, 1982, Volume 54, 1989, Volume 109, 1999.

Contemporary Novelists, 7th edition, St. James Press (Detroit, MI), 2001.
Dictionary of Literary Biography, Volume 2: *American Novelists since World War II*, First Series, Gale (Detroit, MI), 1978.
Fehn, Ann and others, editors, *Neverending Stories: Toward a Critical Narratology*, Princeton University Press (Princeton, NJ), 1992.
Freese, Peter and Charles B. Harris, editors, *The Holodeck in the Garden: Science and Technology in Contemporary American Fiction*, Dalkey Archive (Normal, IL), 2004.
Iftekharrudin, Farhat, and others, editors, *Postmodern Approaches to the Short Story*, Praeger (New York, NY), 2003.
St. James Guide to Fantasy Writers, St. James Press (Detroit, MI), 1996.
Short Story Criticism, Volume 57, Gale (Detroit, MI), 2003.

PERIODICALS

Antioch Review, summer, 1986, review of *In the Penny Arcade*, p. 381.
Biography, Volume 5, number 3, 1982, Timothy Dow Adams, "The Mock-Biography of Edwin Mullhouse," pp. 205-214; Volume 11, number 1, 1988, John D. Boyd, "The Double Vision of *Edwin Mullhouse*," pp. 35-46.
BOMB, spring, 2003, Jim Shepard, interview with Steven Millhauser, pp. 76-80.
Booklist, September 1, 1977, review of *Portrait of a Romantic*, p. 24; June 15, 1990, review of *The Barnum Museum*, p. 1958; April 1, 1996, review of *Martin Dressler: The Tale of an American Dreamer*; September 15, 1999, Donna Seaman, review of *Enchanted Night: A Novella*, p. 233; December 15, 2002, Brad Hooper, review of *The King in the Tree: Three Novellas*, p. 708.
Boston Book Review, December, 1999, review of *Enchanted Night*, p. 40.
Boston Globe, May 17, 1998, Margot Livesey, review of *The Knife Thrower and Other Stories*, p. D1; March 9, 2003, David Rollow, review of *The King in the Tree*.
Chicago Tribune, October 3, 1993, Nicholas Delbanco, review of *Little Kingdoms*, p. 5.
Christian Science Monitor, October 15, 1997, Ron Charles, review of *Martin Dressler*, p. 8.
Contemporary Literature, Volume 42, number 3, 2001, Arthur Saltzman, "A Wilderness of Size: Steven Millhauser's *Martin Dressler*, pp. 589-616.
Critique, Volume 37, number 2, 1996, Douglas Fowler, "Steven Millhauser, Miniaturist," pp. 139-148.

Denver Post, February 9, 2003, John Freeman, review of *The King in the Tree,* p. EE3.

Denver Quarterly, Volume 36, numbers 3-4, 2002, Catherine Kasper, "Steven Millhauser's American Gothic," pp. 88-93.

Dreiser Studies, Volume 30, number 1, 1999, Nancy Warner Barrineau, "Theodore Dreiser and *Martin Dressler:* Tales of American Dreamers," pp. 35-45.

Entertainment Weekly, May 17, 1996, p. 55; April 10, 1998, review of *Little Kingdoms,* p. 61; March 14, 2003, Troy Patterson, review of *The King in the Tree,* p. 71.

Esquire, February, 1986, David Leavitt, review of *In the Penny Arcade,* pp. 117-118.

Fantasy Review, June, 1986, review of *In the Penny Arcade,* p. 20.

Georgia Review, winter, 1995, Daniel Green, review of *Little Kingdoms,* pp. 960-967.

Hudson Review, winter, 1991, Gary Krist, review of *The Barnum Museum,* p. 691.

Journal of the Fantastic in the Arts, Volume 1, number 4, 1988, Douglas Fowler, "Millhauser, Suskind, and the Postmodern Promise," pp. 77-86.

Kirkus Reviews, November 1, 1985, review of *In the Penny Arcade,* p. 1155; March 1, 1996, review of *Martin Dressler;* August 15, 1999, review of *Enchanted Night,* p. 1248; December 15, 2002, review of *The King in the Tree.*

Library Journal, January, 1986, Thomas Lavoie, review of *In the Penny Arcade,* pp. 103-104; September 1, 1986, Patricia Dooley, review of *From the Realm of Morpheus,* p. 216; June 1, 1990, Mary Soete, review of *The Barnum Museum,* p. 182; August, 1993, Brian Geary, review of *Enchanted Night,* pp. 156-157; April 15, 1996, Anne Irvine, review of *Martin Dressler,* p. 123; February 15, 1998, Jo Carr, review of *Martin Dressler,* p. 183; June 1, 1998, Christine DeZelar-Tiedman, review of *The Knife Thrower and Other Stories,* p. 165.

Los Angeles Times Book Review, January 8, 1986, Richard Eder, review of *In the Penny Arcade,* p.6; October 31, 1999, review of *Enchanted Night,* p. 29; March 16, 2003, Jeff Turrentine, review of *The King in the Tree.*

Mosaic: A Journal for the Interdisciplinary Study of Literature, September, 2002, Alejandro Herrero-Olaizola, "Writing Lives, Writing Lies: The Pursuit of Apocryphal Biographies," pp. 73-88.

Nation, September 17, 1977, J.D. O'Hara, "Two Mandarin Stylists," pp. 250-252; May 6, 1996, p. 68; May 25, 1998, Benjamin Kunkel, review of *The Knife Thrower and Other Stories,* p. 33.

New Republic, September 16, 1972, review of *Edwin Mullhouse: The Life and Death of an American Writer, 1943-1954, by Jeffrey Cartwright.*

Newsweek, March 17, 1986, David Gates, review of *In the Penny Arcade,* p. 74.

New Yorker, July 27, 1998, review of *The Knife Thrower and Other Stories,* p. 77; March 24, 2003, review of *The King in the Tree,* p. 85.

New York Review of Books, August 14, 2003, Gabriele Annan, review of *The King in the Tree,* p. 25.

New York Times, April 9, 1997, Dinitia Smith, "Shy Author Likes to Live and Work in Obscurity," p. 13.

New York Times Book Review, September 17, 1972, p. 2; October 2, 1977, pp. 13, 30; January 19, 1986, p. 9; January 19, 1986, Robert Dunn, review of *In the Penny Arcade,* p. 9; October 12, 1986, Robert Dunn, review of *In the Penny Arcade,* p. 9; June 24, 1990, Jay Cantor, review of *The Barnum Museum,* p. 16; October 3, 1993, p. 9, p. 11; May 12, 1996, p. 8; May 10, 1998, Patrick McGrath, review of *The Knife Thrower and Other Stories,* p. 11; November 14, 1999, Tobin Harshaw, review of *Enchanted Night,* p. 109; March 9, 2003, Laura Miller, review of *The King in the Tree,* p. 1; March 23, 2003, review of *The King in the Tree,* p. 22.

Publishers Weekly, August 8, 1986; May 6, 1996, Jennifer Schuessler, "Steven Millhauser: The Business of Dreaming," pp. 56-57; March 23, 1998, review of *The Knife Thrower and Other Stories,* p. 78; January 20, 2003, review of *The King in the Tree,* p. 55.

Review of Contemporary Fiction, summer, 1986, Irving Malin, review of *In the Penny Arcade,* pp. 146-147; fall, 1998, Christopher Paddock, review of *The Knife Thrower and Other Stories,* p. 235; spring, 1994, Irving Malin, review of *Little Kingdoms,* p. 212; summer, 2000, Brian Evenson, review of *Enchanted Night,* p. 180; spring, 2003, Christopher Paddock, review of *The King in the Tree,* p. 136; spring, 2006, Steven Millhauser issue, p. 7.

Salmagundi, fall, 1991, Mary Kinzie, "Succeeding Borges, Escaping Kafka: On the Fiction of Steven Millhauser," pp. 115-144.

Saturday Review, September 30, 1972; October 1, 1977, p. 28; June, 1986, Bruce Allen, review of *In the Penny Arcade,* p. 74.

Spectator, March 7, 1998, Caroline Moore, review of *Martin Dressler,* p. 32.

Time, July 2, 1990, Stefan Kanfer, review of *The Barnum Museum,* p. 67; June 10, 1996, p. 67.

Times Literary Supplement, July 28, 1978, William Boyd, review of *Portrait of a Romantic;* April 3, 1998, review of *Martin Dressler,* p. 23.

Village Voice, March 6, 1978, John Calvin Batchelor, review of *Portrait of a Romantic,* pp. 70-73; October 26, 1999, Ben Marcus, review of *Enchanted Night,* p. 90.

Village Voice Literary Supplement, February, 1986, Al. J. Sperone, review of *In the Penny Arcade,* pp. 3-4.

Virginia Quarterly Review, winter, 1994, review of *Little Kingdoms;* spring, 2000, review of *Enchanted Night,* p. 64

Wall Street Journal, April 24, 1996, Donna Rifkind, "Stories for a Stormy Night," p. A12.

Washington Post Book World, September 24, 1972, p. 8; October 9, 1977, p. E5; September 21, 1986, pp. 1, 14; June 18, 1990, Michael Dirda, review of *The Barnum Museum,* pp. B1, B10; September 5, 1993, p. 5, p. 14; April 28, 1996, p. 3; June 14, 1998, A.S. Byatt, review of *The Knife Thrower and Other Stories,* pp. 1, 10; February 9, 2003, Michael Dirda, review of *The King in the Tree,* p. 1.

World and I, December, 1990, review of *The Barnum Museum,* pp. 406-410; October, 1998, review of *The Knife Thrower and Other Stories,* p. 280; June, 2003, Edward Hower, review of *The King in the Tree,* p. 230.

World Literature Today, winter, 1999, review of *The Knife Thrower and Other Stories,* p. 148; September-December, 2004, Marvin J. LaHood, review of *The King in the Tree,* p. 95.

Yale Review, winter, 1988, Maureen Howard, review of *In the Penny Arcade,* p. 243; Volume 85, number 1, 1997, Sven Birkerts, review of *Martin Dressler,* pp. 144-155.

ONLINE

Transatlantica: American Studies Journal, http://www.transatlantica.org/document562.html/ (June 28, 2007), Marc Chénetier, "An Interview with Steven Millhauser."*

Stephan Pastis

■ Personal

Born 1968, in San Marino, CA; married; wife's name Staci; children: Tom, Julia. *Education:* University of California at Berkeley, B.S., 1989; University of California, Los Angeles, J.D., 1993.

■ Addresses

Home—Santa Rosa, CA. *E-mail*—theratandpig@aol.com.

■ Career

Attorney and comic-strip creator. Insurance litigator in San Francisco, CA, 1993-2004; Estate of Charles Schultz, Santa Rosa, CA, estate attorney and co-curator of Charles M. Schultz Museum. "Pearls before Swine" (comic strip), creator, 2001—, e-published, then syndicated by United Features Syndicate, 2002—.

■ Member

National Cartoonists Society.

■ Awards, Honors

Best Newspaper Comic Strip Award, National Cartoonists Society, nomination, 2002 and 2006, awarded, 2004.

■ Writings

COMIC-STRIP COMPILATIONS

Pearls before Swine: BLTs Taste So Darn Good (originally published in comic-strip format), Andrews McMeel (Kansas City, MO), 2003.

Sgt. Piggy's Lonely Hearts Club Comic: A Pearls before Swine Treasury, (originally published in comic-strip format), Andrews McMeel (Kansas City, MO), 2004.

This Little Piggy Stayed Home (originally published in comic-strip format), Andrews McMeel (Kansas City, MO), 2004.

Nighthogs: A Pearls before Swine Collection (originally published in comic-strip format), Andrews McMeel (Kansas City, MO), 2005.

Lions and Tigers and Crocs, Oh My!: A Pearls before Swine Treasury (originally published in comic-strip format), Andrews McMeel (Kansas City, MO), 2006.

The Ratvolution Will Not Be Televised: A Pearls before Swine Collection (originally published in comic-strip format), Andrews McMeel (Kansas City, MO), 2006.

Pearls Before Swine
by Stephan Pastis

BLTs Taste So Darn Good

This 2003 title is the first collection of the popular comic strip. (Andrews McMeel Publishing, 2003. Reproduced with permission of United Media.)

Da Brudderhood of Zeeba Zeeba Eata: A Pearls before Swine Collection (originally published in comic-strip format), Andrews McMeel (Kansas City, MO), 2007.

The Sopratos: A Pearls before Swine Collection (originally published in comic-strip format), Andrews McMeel (Kansas City, MO), 2007.

■ **Sidelights**

Inspired by the late Charles M. Schulz's famous "Peanuts" comic strip, Stephan Pastis turned his back on a promising law career to write for the funny papers. Actually, the law career promised more headaches than rewards, and the funny papers meant a coveted spot in the roster of the United Features Syndicate, which placed Pastis's comic strip, "Pearls before Swine," into the *Washington Post*, the *Philadelphia Inquirer*, and the *Seattle Post-Intelligencer* almost overnight. In 2004, the same year it began syndication, "Pearls before Swine" was awarded Best Newspaper Comic Strip honors by the National Cartoonists Society.

While Pastis's work seemed to appear overnight, his road to a career as a comic-strip creator actually stretched all the way back to childhood. Born in San Marino, a suburb of Los Angeles, California, in 1968, Pastis developed an interest in drawing as a result of an annual bout with bronchitis, which affected him every winter despite southern California's mild climate. Absent from school and stuck in bed for weeks, he doodled with pen and paper, copying his favorite figures from Schulz's "Peanuts" strip. By the time he reached high school, Pastis had become a competent artist, and his sharp wit and powers of observation found an effective outlet in his comic doodlings. Although he considered becoming a syndicated cartoonist, he was far too practical; for every 2,000 strips submitted, the top syndicates accepted only a handful of artists, then put them through their paces to see if they could generate sufficient high-quality material to sustain reader interest in a competitive market. Instead, Pastis opted for a career in law.

After attending the University of California at Berkeley, where he graduated in 1989 with a degree in political science, Pastis enrolled at UCLA's Law School and earned his law degree. During particularly boring classes, he doodled in his notebooks, and out of these doodlings was born an arrogant rodent. The frustrated law student felt an instant affinity with this rat character, and it soon appeared throughout his doodles. Reworking Rat countless times, the rodent's strong personality took shape.

Doodling with a Purpose

In 1993 Pastis passed the bar and joined a law practice in the San Francisco Bay area. Now married and raising two children, he enjoyed the salary from his practice, but did not enjoy the law any more than he had in college. Turning again to his cartooning, he developed several strips that featured his rat character. Submitting them to the syndicates in 1996, his submissions received the expected rejection. Undeterred, he continued to work to refine his comics, tempering Rat with a pig character. As Pastis recalled to *Columbus Dispatch* interviewer Tom Reed of his sticktoitiveness in the face of rejection, "Law had a huge effect on me. If you want to become a syndicated cartoonist and have some staying power, I think you should be a litigation lawyer for seven years. You will hate it so much; you will work like crazy to make sure you never, ever have to go back to being a lawyer."

While Pastis continued to refine his ideas, he stayed with the arrogant rat character, which Pastis has admitted is actually a kind of alter-ego. With Pig as a foil, Rat's abrasiveness became less biting. To work on building the dialogue and timing that generate

A page from the 2003 title featuring Pig and Rat. (Andrews McMeel Publishing, 2003. Reproduced with permission of Universal Press Syndicate.)

humor, his core curriculum was Scott Adams' entire "Dilbert" oeuvre. After creating "Pearls before Swine" and completing 200 individual comic strips, he put them aside for over a year, once again fearful of the syndicate's reaction. One spring day in 1999, Pastis arrived at work with all 200 strips, and had his colleagues select the top forty. Packaging these up, he submitted them to the three top syndicates, then sat back and waited for the inevitable rejection.

No rejection came. In fact, all three syndicates were interested in "Pearls before Swine," so Pastis chose United Features Syndicate (UFS), the home of his beloved "Peanuts." By the end of 1999, although he was officially on board, Pastis's hard work was not over yet. In the process of working out a development strategy, staffers at UFS became concerned that a feature strip about a pig and a rat had no clear target audience. Suddenly, the start date in 2000 began to look shaky. Fortunately, Pastis got the proverbial lucky break when the syndicate decided to include "Pearls before Swine" on its Comics.com Web site. Up and running by late 2000, the strip got a respectable 2,000 hits per day, but this was not

This 2004 collection also includes a behind-the-scenes look at the comic strip's creation. (Andrews McMeel Publishing, 2005. Reproduced with permission of United Media.)

enough to convince UFS to take the risk of running it in print. Then Scott Adams came to the rescue, by talking up Pastis's comic on his own Web site and newsletter. From 2,000 hits, "Pearls before Swine" was soon logging almost 100,000 hits, a jump that impressed UFS. When Bill Amend's popular long-running "Fox Trot" comic strip made the shift to Sundays only, the dailies had an open spot for a black-and-white comic, and UFS chose "Pearls before Swine" to fill it. While continuing its run on the Internet, Pastis's strip began its run in over forty newspapers in January of 2002.

Remarking on those who helped him achieve success, Pastis told J.D. Bliss on the *JDBliss Blog*: "Other cartoonists were very helpful to me. Charles Schulz and *Peanuts* had a huge influence on me throughout my life. I got to meet him when I was still developing my ideas in the mid 90s and he was tremendously encouraging. As the strip developed he continued to be very helpful. Scott Adams, the creator of *Dilbert*, encouraged me after my strip started running on the Internet. Darby Conley, who draws the *Get Fuzzy* strip, is a friend who taught me a lot and walked me through much of what I needed to know." Speaking to Mindie Paget of *LJWorld.com* about his lack of artistic talent, Pastis claimed: "I think if it hadn't have been for *Dilbert* and his art 'quality,' so to speak, I wouldn't have made it. I think *Dilbert* showed that if you could write a decent joke, even if you couldn't draw that well, that your lack of drawing would one day be called style. If something is successful and it's funny enough, people will sort of accept the art."

Rat, Pig, and Company

With a title drawn from the Bible's New Testament, "Pearls before Swine" features megalomaniacal Rat and formidably foolish Pig. Reflecting Pastis's verbal focus, the relationship between the two characters is a complex one that often finds Rat twisting Pig's innocent statements into logical absurdities. Other characters in the strip include aggressive Duck, smart-aleck Goat, and contentious Zebra. Through this scruffy menagerie, Pastis skewers the nonsensical side of pop culture, politics, and modern society. Of Greek descent, Pastis also takes aim at Greek culture and, to the dismay of his young son, disparages Jim Davis's *Garfield* characters along with several other comic-strip regulars, including Jeffy from *Family Circle*. Pastis has a distinctly strange and wicked sense of humor. In various strips, he has sent the Care Bears to Iraq and a lonely pancake to the local IHOP restaurant in search of friends.

"I first drew Rat while bored during a class on the European Economic Community in law school," Pastis explained in a statement on the *Comics.com*

Pearls Before Swine
by Stephan Pastis

Nighthogs

The outrageously funny adventures of Pig, Rat, Zebra, and Goat continue in this 2005 title. (Andrews McMeel Publishing, 2005. Reproduced with permission of United Media.)

rather poor drawing. There's an old adage in cartooning, which is that good writing can carry bad art, but good art cannot carry bad writing." His advice to other beginning comics creators? "Learn the economy of words. Learn the rhythm of humor. . . . Once you think you've got a handle on it, write a whole mess of strips and show them to people who don't particularly like you and who are willing to tell you the truth. See if they laugh. If you can't make the guy sitting next to you laugh, you probably can't make the eight million readers laugh either."

If you enjoy the works of Stephan Pastis, you may also want to check out the following books:

Darby Conley, *I'm Ready for My Movie Contract: A Get Fuzzy Collection,* 2007.
Bill Amend, *And When She Opened the Closet, All the Clothes Were Polyester,* 2007.
Scott Adams, *Positive Attitude: A Dilbert Collection,* 2007.

Web site. "I still have the first strip. Rat gets killed. Kind of an inauspicious start. The pig was taken from a strip I used to draw about an attorney, called 'The Infirm.' In one strip, I had an attorney defending an evil pig farmer, and I liked the way I drew the pigs. One day, I just stuck one of the pigs with the rat. The zebra came from one of the strips . . . the one where he appears at Rat's front door selling cookies to raise money for automatic weapons (to use against the lions, of course). People liked him, so I kept him. The goat came from Amy Lago, my former editor at United. I needed a smart character and I suggested a few possible animals to Amy. (I think there was a bear, a cow, a sheep and a goat.) Amy chose the goat. The crocodiles were introduced in January, 2005. In the past, Zebra's predators were generally unseen and in some remote place. I thought that introducing them into the neighborhood could really ramp up Zebra's stress level and provide more fodder for jokes."

A self-taught artist, Pastis uses a Japanese pen to create his initial cartoon image, then refines his work using the computer. In his view, however, the most crucial part of his comic is the writing. "The concept [behind "Pearls before Swine"] is very Dilbert-based," he explained to a *Phi Kappa Forum* interviewer; "If you can write decently and produce a good joke, then people will let you get away with

Reflecting on his dramatic career shift with *U.S. News & World Report* contributor Andrew Curry, Pastis noted that each of his two vocations required distinctly different qualities. "To be a good litigator you have to be strategic, distrustful, aggressive," he explained. "Cartooning is as diametrically opposed to that as could be. You need to be childlike, walk lightly, and absorb everything to bring joy to people." "The worst day of cartooning is better than the best day of being a lawyer," Pastis summed up for Brad Stone in *Newsweek.* Happy in the latter role, he divides his six-day work week between cartooning, spending time with his family, and serving as co-curator of the Charles M. Schulz Museum, which is housed in the Santa Rosa estate of Pastis's lifelong idol.

■ Biographical and Critical Sources

PERIODICALS

Columbus Dispatch, January 1, 2007, Tom Reed, interview with Pastis.

Editor & Publisher, January 7, 2002, David Astor, "There's Life after the Web for 'Pearls before Swine,'" p. 20; January 9, 2003, David Astor, "Tales of Starting, and Doing," p. 25.

Napa Valley Register, September 2, 2006, Kathleen Dreessen, "A Pig, a Rat and a Goat."

Newsweek, July 1, 2005, Brad Stone, "A Pearl of a Strip."

Phi Kappa Phi Forum, summer, 2004, interview with Pastis, p. 34.

U.S. News & World Report, March 25, 2002, Andrew Curry, interview with Pastis, p. 6.

ONLINE

Charles M. Schulz Museum Web site, http://www.schulzmuseum.org/ (November 6, 2007).

Comics.com, http://www.comics.com/ (September 14, 2007), "Frequently Asked Questions (FAQs) of Stephan Pastis."

Crescent Blues, http://www.crescentblues.com/ (November 6, 2007), Richard L. Smith, "Stephan Pastis: Animal Attitude."

Daily Cartoonist, http://dailycartoonist.com/ (October 16, 2007), Alan Gardner, "Brian Walker, Stephan Pastis to Co-curate Exhibits for Schulz Museum."

JDBliss Blog, http://www.jdblissblog.com/ (November 6, 2006), J.D. Bliss, "Interview: Stephan Pastis: Attorney Turned Cartoonist."

LJWorld.com, http://www2.ljworld.com/ (December 24, 2006), Mindie Paget, "Strip Deals Wry Pearls of Wisdom."

Pearls before Swine Web site, http://www.comics.com/comics/pearls/ (November 19, 2007).

Washington Post.com, http://www.washingtonpost.com/ (September 24, 2004), Suzanne Tobin, "Comics: Charles Schulz Museum/Stephan Pastis."*

(Courtesy of The Bancroft Library, University of California, Berkeley.)

Clark Ashton Smith

annual Fantasy Faire, a convention of genre fans in Southern California; January 10-16, 1993, was proclaimed Clark Ashton Smith Week in the city of Auburn to mark the centenary of the writer's birth.

■ Personal

Born January 13, 1893, in Long Valley, CA; died August 14, 1961, in Pacific Grove, CA; son of Timeus (a hotel night clerk) and Mary Frances Smith; married Carolyn Emily Jones Dorman, 1954. *Education:* Self-educated.

■ Career

Writer. Writer of fiction and essays; poet; journalist; painter and sculptor; also performed odd jobs and manual labor. Columnist, *Auburn Journal,* 1923-26. Exhibitions of his artwork held in San Francisco, Los Angeles, and New York City.

■ Awards, Honors

The road in Auburn, California, nearest to the former Smith property is now named Poet Smith Drive, while another nearby street is named Smith Court; from 1978 to 1985, the International Clark Ashton Smith Poetry Award was presented at the

■ Writings

FICTION

The Immortals of Mercury, Stellar (New York, NY), 1932.

The Double Shadow and Other Fantasies, privately printed (Auburn, CA), 1933.

Out of Space and Time, Arkham House (Sauk City, WI), 1942.

Lost Worlds, Arkham House (Sauk City, WI), 1944.

Genius Loci, and Other Tales, Arkham House (Sauk City, WI), 1948.

The Abominations of Yondo, Arkham House (Sauk City, WI), 1960.

Tales of Science and Sorcery, Arkham House (Sauk City, WI), 1964.

Other Dimensions, Arkham House (Sauk City, WI), 1970.

Zothique, edited with an introduction by Lin Carter, Ballantine (New York, NY), 1970.

The Mortuary, Roy Squires (Glendale, CA), 1971.

Xiccarph, edited with an introduction by Carter, Ballantine (New York, NY), 1972.

Hyperborea, edited with an introduction by Carter, Ballantine (New York, NY), 1973.

Poseidonis, edited with an introduction by Carter, Ballantine (New York, NY), 1973.

Prince Alcouz and the Magician, Roy Squires (Glendale, CA), 1977.

The City of the Singing Flame, edited by Donald Sidney-Fryer, Pocket Books (New York, NY), 1981.

The Last Incantation, edited with an introduction by Donald Sidney-Fryer, Pocket Books (New York, NY), 1982.

The Monster of the Prophecy, edited by Sidney-Fryer, Pocket Books (New York, NY), 1983.

Untold Tales, Cryptic (Bloomfield, NY), 1984.

The Unexpurgated Clark Ashton Smith, six volumes, edited by Steve Behrends, Necronomicon (West Warwick, RI), 1987–88.

A Rendezvous in Averoigne: Best Fantastic Tales of Clark Ashton Smith, introduction by Ray Bradbury, illustrated by Jeffrey K. Potter, Arkham House (Sauk City, WI), 1988.

Strange Shadows: The Uncollected Fiction and Essays of Clark Ashton Smith, edited by Behrends, Sidney-Fryer, and Rah Hoffman, Greenwood Press (Westport, CT), 1989.

Tales of Zothique, edited by Will Murray and Steve Behrends, Necronomicon (Warwick, RI), 1995.

The Book of Hyperborea, edited by Will Murray, Necronomicon (Warwick, RI), 1996.

The Witchcraft of Ulua, Necronomicon (Warwick, RI), 1998.

The Black Diamonds, edited by S.T. Joshi, Hippocampus Press (New York, NY), 2002.

The Emperor of Dreams, Orion/Gollancz, 2002.

Red World of Polaris: The Adventures of Captain Volmar, Night Shade (San Francisco, CA), 2003.

The Double Shadow, Wildside Press, 2003.

The Sword of Zagan and Other Writings, Hippocampus Press (New York, NY), 2004.

The White Sybil and Other Stories, Wildside Press, 2005.

The Maker of Gargoyles and Other Stories, Wildside Press, 2005.

Star Changes: The Science Fiction of Clark Ashton Smith, Darkside Press (Seattle, WA), 2005.

Lost Worlds, University of Nebraska Press (Lincoln, NE), 2006.

Out of Space and Time, University of Nebraska Press (Lincoln, NE), 2006.

The End of the Story: The Collected Fantasies of Clark Ashton Smith, Volume 1, Night Shade (San Francisco, CA), 2007.

The Door to Saturn: The Collected Fantasies of Clark Ashton Smith, Volume 2, Night Shade (San Francisco, CA), 2007.

The Black Abbot of Puthuum, RAS Press (Glendale, CA), 2007.

The Return of The Sorcerer: The Best of Clark Ashton Smith, Wildside Press, 2007.

POETRY

The Star Treader and Other Poems, A.M. Robertson (San Francisco, CA), 1912.

Odes and Sonnets, Book Club of California (San Francisco, CA), 1918.

Ebony and Crystal: Poems in Verse and Prose, privately printed, 1922.

Sandalwood, privately printed, 1925.

Nero and Other Poems, Futile Press (Lakeport, CA), 1937.

The Ghoul and the Seraph, Gargoyle Press (Brooklyn, NY), 1950.

The Dark Chateau, and Other Poems, Arkham House (Sauk City, WI), 1951.

Spells and Philtres, Arkham House (Sauk City, WI), 1958.

The Hill of Dionysus, a Selection, privately printed, 1962.

Cycles, Roy Squires (Glendale, CA), 1963.

Poems in Prose, illustrated by Frank Utpatel, Arkham House (Sauk City, WI), 1964.

The Tartarus of the Suns, Roy Squires (Glendale, CA), 1970.

The Palace of Jewels, Roy Squires (Glendale, CA), 1970.

In the Ultimate Valleys, Roy Squires (Glendale, CA), 1970.

To George Sterling: Five Poems, Roy Squires (Glendale, CA), 1970.

Selected Poems, introduction by Benjamin DeCasseres, Arkham House (Sauk City, WI), 1971.

Sadastor, Roy Squires (Glendale, CA), 1972.

From the Crypts of Memory, Roy Squires (Glendale, CA), 1973.

Grotesques et Fantastiques, Gerry de le Ree (Saddle River, NJ), 1973.

Fugitive Poems, four volumes, privately printed, 1974–75.

Klarkash-Ton and Monstro Ligriv, Gerry de le Ree (Saddle River, NJ), 1974.

The Titans in Tartarus, Roy Squires (Glendale, CA), 1974.

A Song from Hell, Roy Squires (Glendale, CA), 1975.

The Potion of Dreams, Roy Squires (Glendale, CA), 1975.

The Fanes of Dawn, Roy Squires (Glendale, CA), 1976.

Seer of the Cycles, Roy Squires (Glendale, CA), 1976.

The Burden of the Suns, Roy Squires (Glendale, CA), 1977.

Nostalgia of the Unknown: The Complete Prose Poetry of Clark Ashton Smith, edited by Marc and Susan Michaud, Necronomicon (Warwick, RI), 1988.

The Hashish-Eater; or, The Apocalypse of Evil, Necronomicon (Warwick, RI), 1989.

The Last Oblivion: Best Fantastic Poetry of Clark Ashton Smith, Hippocampus Press (New York, NY), 2002.

The Complete Poetry and Translations of Clark Ashton Smith, edited by David E. Schultz and S.T. Joshi, Hippocampus Press (New York, NY), 2007.

OTHER

The Fantastic Art of Clark Ashton Smith, Mirage Press (Baltimore, MD), 1973.

Planets and Dimensions: Collected Essays of Clark Ashton Smith, Mirage Press (Baltimore, MD), 1973.

The Black Book of Clark Ashton Smith, Arkham House (Sauk City, WI), 1979.

Clark Ashton Smith: Letters to H.P. Lovecraft, edited by Steve Behrends, Necronomicon (Warwick, RI), 1987.

The Devil's Notebook: Collected Epigrams and Pensées of Clark Ashton Smith, Starmont House (Mercer Island, WA), 1990.

Live from Auburn: The Elder Tapes, Necronomicon (Warwick, RI), 1995.

Selected Letters of Clark Ashton Smith, Arkham House (Sauk City, WI), 2003.

The Shadow of the Unattained: The Letters of George Sterling and Clark Ashton Smith, Hippocampus Press (New York, NY), 2005.

Smith's manuscripts are housed in the Smith Collection at the John Hay Library of Brown University and at the Berg Collection at the New York Public Library.

■ **Sidelights**

"The short stories and poems of Clark Ashton Smith," John Kipling Hitz stated in *Studies in Weird Fiction,* "display a freshness of conception and a coincidence of thematic treatment that establish him as the one author who reflects, most nearly, the versatile genius of Edgar Allan Poe." Smith is recognized by many critics of fantasy and science fiction as one of the foremost authors in the genre known as "weird fiction." H.P. Lovecraft, an acclaimed horror writer himself, defined a "true weird tale" in his *Supernatural Horror in Literature* as "something more than secret murder, bloody bones, or a sheeted form clanking chains according to rule.

A certain atmosphere of breathless and unexplainable dread of outer, unknown forces must be present." Locating his stories in such mythical lands as Zothique (a futuristic realm where magic has replaced science), Smith distinguished his prose from the formulaic pulp stories of the day by fashioning fantastic plots and bizarre imagery out of poetic, and sometimes archaic, language. "Smith was one of the most important writers of fantasy fiction appearing in the pulp magazines," wrote Douglas Robillard in *Supernatural Fiction Writers.* Smith's fiction, Robillard argued, "seeks to disorient the readers' senses by removing familiar landmarks. Some of the best supernatural stories of other authors make their point by the frightful events that occur in familiar surroundings, but Smith usually plunges his readers outside their normal world and lets them flounder toward some uneasy familiarity with strange circumstances." In the introduction to *Strange Shadows: The Uncollected Fiction and Essays of Clark Ashton Smith,* Robert Bloch styled the author "an inhabitant of realms beyond the reaches of reality. His imaginative genius gives us glimpses of grotesquery and grandeur." In a letter written to Lovecraft, Smith explained his own view of what his fiction was meant to accomplish: "My own standpoint is that there is absolutely no justification for literature unless it serves to release the imagination from the bounds of everyday life."

Writing in a tradition which traces its roots back to the works of Edgar Allan Poe and other nineteenth-century writers of the macabre, Smith and fellow contributors Lovecraft and Robert E. Howard defined the "golden age" of the pulp magazine *Weird Tales* during the 1930s. Although the works of Lovecraft and Howard are still widely appreciated by readers of horror and fantasy literature—tales by both authors have been adapted into films—Smith's stories, despite their critical acclaim, are known only to a smaller and more specialized audience. "Of these three gifted men (who were all good friends and correspondents although I do not believe they ever actually met), it is Clark Ashton Smith alone who has yet to achieve the wide recognition his artistry so richly deserves," observed Lin Carter in his introduction to Smith's paperback anthology *Zothique.*

A Life in California

Born in Long Valley, California, in 1893, Smith never ranged far from the place of his birth. A bout with scarlet fever at the age of four, left the only child physically weak for many years. In 1902 his father had saved enough money from working as night clerk at the Hotel Truckee to purchase a 44-acre sec-

This 2002 supernatural adventure novel, written when Smith was fourteen years old, is set in a mythical Arabia. (Hippocampus Press, 2002. Reproduced by permission.)

tion of land near Auburn, California, where, over the next several years, Smith and his father constructed a four-room house for the family. Although his formal education ended at grammar school, Smith read and wrote stories and poems from the age of eleven with the intention of devoting his life to literature, specifically poetry. "While his withdrawal from the normal schoolboy milieu may or may not have made him a better poet, it also, probably, contributed to his later frustrating difficulties in making a living," de Camp pointed out in *Literary Swordsmen and Sorcerers*. During his writing career, Smith was sometimes forced to cut wood and pick fruit to make ends meet. In a quote published in *Literary Swordsmen and Sorcerers*, Smith described his struggle with poverty: "If I work for a living, I will have to give up my art. I've not the energy for both. And I hardly know what I could do—I'm 'unskilled labor' at anything except draw-

ing and poetry. . . . Nine hours of work on week days leaves me too tired for any mental effort." Smith also suffered from ill health during this period, but he would improve physically by the late 1920s, finding the energy from 1929 to 1936 to complete more than one hundred short stories.

Although Smith is remembered for his "weird" stories, he perceived himself as primarily a poet. L. Sprague de Camp remarked in *Literary Swordsmen and Sorcerers* that Smith's poems, "once compared to those of [nineteenth-century English poets Lord] Byron, [John] Keats and [Algernon Charles] Swinburne, are known today to few outside of some science-fiction and fantasy fans. Few of those who nowadays make a stir in the poetic world have even heard of Clark Ashton Smith." Smith's 1912 collection, *The Star-Treader and Other Poems* immediately marked him as a poet to watch. Porter Garnett in the *San Francisco Call* labeled Smith "a true poet." Garnett praised Smith's poetry for possessing "a rare and symmetrical beauty." John Jury of the *San Jose Mercury and Herald* called the book "most certainly an extraordinary work for so young a man." Writing in the *New York Times Book Review*, Shamus O'Sheel found that "the best poems in the book are astonishingly splendid and majestic treatments of cosmic themes, in a style of high and radiant rhetoric." Some one thousand copies of *The Star-Treader and Other Poems* were sold.

As Smith's poetry met with success, he was encouraged to contact George Sterling, one of his favorite poets and the leader of an artists' colony in Carmel, California. Sterling, a protege of author and journalist Ambrose Bierce, wrote poems reminiscent of French "Decadent" literature, a pessimistic movement that acknowledged the inevitability of moral decline and exulted unrepentingly in it. According to Brian Stableford in *The Second Dedalus Book of Decadence: The Black Feast,* Sterling's verse (the poem "A Wine of Wizardry," for example) "placed morbid meditations on destiny within a peculiar cosmic perspective." A friendship developed between Smith and Sterling—with the older poet serving as a mentor—that continued until Sterling's suicide in 1926. After Sterling introduced Smith to the writings of prominent Decadent author Charles Baudelaire, the champion and translator of Poe into French during the mid-nineteenth century, Smith, in turn, learned French and translated Baudelaire's poems into English. Sterling also served as the subject for one of Smith's numerous essays, many of which dealt with authors Smith deemed influential. According to William Thompson on the *SF Site,* "it was as a poet, influenced by the 19th century French Decadence movement and the later California Romantics, that [Clark] was to gain his first, if regional, attention." Fred Chappel, in an article for *Lost Worlds,* argued that Smith's poetry is closely attuned to the spirit of the French Symbolist poet Charles Baudelaire. "If I knew a young poet who wanted to understand something of Baudelaire but had not had opportunity to study French," Chappell wrote, "I would confidently recommend a list of Smith's poems to communicate a vivid impression of what the Symbolist master had accomplished."

Despite the critical acclaim, Smith learned that there was no money to be made as a poet. His 1918 collection *Odes and Sonnets*, published by the Book Club of California, earned critical praise but sold few copies. *Ebony and Crystal: Poems in Verse and Prose* (1922) and *Sandalwood* (1925) were printed by Smith himself at the offices of the *Auburn Journal* newspaper, where he worked for a time. Reviewing *Ebony and Crystal*, William Foster Elliott in the *Fresno Bee* claimed that "the poetry of Clark Ashton Smith is authentic poetry, of which there is not enough in the world. . . . He has a vivid imagination, a copious and personal vocabulary, an unfaltering sense for literary form." But such enthusiastic praise were not matched by book sales. Smith ended up giving away most of the copies of these two volumes. But this early poetry attracted the attention of fledgling writer H.P. Lovecraft, who introduced him by mail to a number of other writers and poets. Lovecraft also suggested that Smith turn from writing poetry to writing fiction. Although the pulp magazines of the time paid only a penny or two a word, that was still more than Smith could earn selling poems. By 1928, Smith had begun writing short stories. The same "cosmic themes" that critics found in his poetry were also present in his fiction. Charles K. Wolfe, writing in *Nyctalops,* argued that from the beginning, although he wrote primarily for the money, Smith also was concerned with writing quality literature: "Smith was one of our foremost practitioners of fantasy, but he was also a writer very much aware of exactly what he was doing and why he was doing it. Unlike some of his contemporaries, who all too often saw themselves as entertainers rather than artists, Smith from the very beginning of his writing career saw himself as a serious artist, and saw his work as the realization of a cogent and well-formed aesthetic theory."

A Burst of Creativity

During Smith's most fertile period of creativity, from about 1930 to 1936, he had switched over to writing fiction and was completing at least one story a month. De Camp suggests in *Literary Swordsmen and Sorcerers* that this burst of productivity is related to the fact that Smith (who was also looking after his aging parents) was making more money by writing—"even at the low rates and late payments of

Weird Tales"—than through jobs requiring manual labor. "He regarded himself mainly as a poet who wrote prose only to pay his decrepit parent's bills," de Camp stated. "The stories which Smith produced during this brief professional phase constitute one of the most remarkable oeuvres in imaginative literature," according to Brian Stableford, writing in *American Supernatural Fiction: From Edith Wharton to the "Weird Tales" Writers.*

Smith's stories are clearly identifiable by his unique writing style; in the introduction to *Zothique*, Carter noted: "The short stories of Clark Ashton Smith are very much his own, and nothing quite like them has been written in America, at least since Poe." "The most compelling feature of Smith's weird fiction," Hitz wrote, "which represents the lion's share of his output, is an initially overwhelming stylistic virtuosity. . . . His painstaking attention to phonetic pattern, often fashioned to the point of ostentation, is combined with an abundance of visual detail and figurative language. It is a very rhythmical and ornate style, comparable to Poe." Various critics have observed the influence on Smith's fiction of Sterling, Bierce, and French author Gustave Flaubert (notably the novels *Salammbo* and *Tentation de Saint Antoine*). English author William Beckford's gothic novel *Vathek*, as well as the fantasies of Irish writer Lord Dunsany and supernatural stories by Lovecraft,have also been cited as important references in the formation of Smith's prose. Gahan Wilson commented in the *Magazine of Fantasy and Science Fiction* that Smith's stories "were beautifully constructed, full of lovely images and absolutely sumptuous English." Smith's penchant for choosing obscure and archaic words, de Camp suggested in *Literary Swordsmen and Sorcerers*, stemmed from the author's self-educational technique; he would "read an unabridged dictionary through, word for word, studying not only the definitions of the words but also their derivations from ancient languages. Having an extraordinary eidetic memory, he seems to have retained most or all of it."

The author's enchantment with language—as well as his instinct for horror—is apparent in "The Garden of Adompha," a tale of Zothique. As the story begins, Adompha (the decadent ruler of an island kingdom), has instructed the wizard Dwerulas to create a secret garden in which the king might "search for novel pleasures and violent or rare sensations." Smith's prose describes the garden in the following passage: "There were many . . . weird plants, diverse as the seven hells, and having no common characteristics other than the scions which Dwerulas has grafted upon them here and there through his unnatural and necromantic art. . . . These scions were the various parts and members of human beings. Consummately, and with never failing success, the magician had joined them to the half-vegetable, half-animate stocks, on which they lived and grew thereafter, drawing an ichor-like sap. . . . On palmy boles, beneath feathery-tufted foliage, the heads of eunuchs hung in bunches."

Zothique was to be the setting for many of Smith's stories. The last continent at the end of the world, when the dying sun gives out only a weak light, Zothique was described by Smith in a letter to L. Sprague de Camp: "Zothique, vaguely suggested by Theosophic theories about past and future continents, is the last inhabited continent of Earth. The continents of our present cycle have sunk, perhaps several times. Some have remained submerged; others have re-arisn, partially, and re-arranged themselves. Zothique, as I conceive it, comprises Asia Minor, Arabia, Persia, India, parts of Northern and eastern Africa, and much of the Indonesian archipelago. A new Australia exists somewhere to the south. To the west, there are only a few known islands, such as Naat, in which the black cannibals survive. To the north are immense unexplored deserts; to the east, an immense unvoyaged sea. . . The science and machinery of our present civilization have long been forgotten, together with our present religions. But many gods are worshipped; and sorcery and demonism prevail again as in ancient days." Smith was to write a total of sixteen stories, one poem, and one verse drama set in Zothique. The land is, according to Jim Rockhill in an essay for *The Freedom of Fantastic Things: Selected Criticism on Clark Ashton Smith*, Smith's "most sustained contribution to created-world fantasy literature." Douglas Robillard in *Supernatural Fiction Writers* believed that "among Smith's created lands, the most vivid is probably Zothique. . . . The sun has become dim, whatever is left of the world is old and decadent, the world we live in is as ancient to that future as Hyperborea is to us. The concept has within it an almost hypnotic power, and it yields often to Smith's most incantatory style: 'I tell the tale as men shall tell it in Zothique, the last continent, beneath a dim sun and sad heavens where the stars come out in terrible brightness before eventide.'"

This 2006 collection includes tales set in Averoigne and others set in the world of the Cthulhu mythos. (University of Nebraska Press, 2006. Cover illustration copyright © Stasys Eidiejus/iStockphoto. Reproduced by permission of the University of Nebraska Press.)

Imaginative Settings

The settings of most of Smith's stories can be divided into several different worlds. In addition to the continent of Zothique, he created the locales of Hyperborea (an arctic land of ancient Earth), Poseidonis (Atlantis), Averoigne (medieval France), and Xiccarph (a region on the planet Mars). Many of Smith's fictional heroes find themselves transported into alternative realities via space travel, enchantment, or a portal to another dimension. In the story "City of the Singing Flame," the narrator discovers an invisible gateway in the rugged California countryside that leads to an alien realm. Joining other creatures of all description who are drawn to a strange monolithic city by a flame that radiates mesmerizing music, the narrator witnesses—several times—the voluntary sacrifice of certain pilgrims. "The narrator . . . ends the tale by saying that he will return to the City and immolate himself in the Flame, that he might merge with the unearthly beauty and music that he had sampled and lost," according to Steve Behrends in *Studies in Weird Fiction*. Two prominent, award-winning science fiction authors have both credited "City of the Singing Flame" as a major source of inspiration. In the introduction to Smith's *A Rendezvous in Averoigne: Best Fantastic Tales of Clark Ashton Smith*, Ray Bradbury recalled that "City" and "Master of the Asteroid" were the two tales that "more than any others I can remember had everything to do with my decision, while in the seventh grade, to become a writer." In a letter published in *Emperor of Dreams: A Clark Ashton Smith Bibliography*, Harlan Ellison related that "City of the Singing Flame" specifically influenced his career when he discovered an anthology containing the story in his high school library. (Ellison was so impressed, he admitted in the letter that he stole the volume, writing, "I own it to this day.") Ellison further commented, "I owe the greatest of debts to Clark Ashton Smith, for he truly opened up the universe for me."

Gahan Wilson wrote that, upon their first publication, Smith's stories "stood out rather starkly" in the formulaic realm of pulp writing. Indeed, some of Smith's more violent and nihilistic tales were severely edited, with changes to the endings and reductions in the stylistic flourishes. Nevertheless, Wilson declared, the author's work reveals "sly and subtle jibes at mankind's aspirations, chilling little fables of a startling bleakness. [The stories] were beautifully constructed, full of lovely images and absolutely sumptuous English, but they were deadly. Reading them was a tiny bit like being skillfully murdered with a Cellini stiletto, or dining well at the Borgias."

The theme of loss has appeared frequently in Smith's fiction. Behrends explained: "Smith created scores of situations in which individuals lose the things closest to their hearts, and live on only to regret their loss and to contrast their fallen state with the glory they once knew. He gave his characters the capacity to realize the extent of their loss, and to express the pain they felt." The story "The Last Incantation," according to Behrends, "contains some of Smith's finest descriptions of the emotions of loss." The plot concerns the elderly wizard Malgyris who uses magic to bring a lover, long dead, back to life. "But, once she is back, he learns with disappointment how different from his memories of her she now seems. He is disillusioned to learn that what he cannot call back is his own youth with all its idealism," stated Douglas Robillard in *Supernatural Fiction Writers*.

Among Smith's Martian stories is "The Vaults of Yoh-Vombis," about an archaeological expedition that discovers an ancient tomb in the planet's unexplored wastelands. As the archaeologists venture into the ruins of Yoh-Vombis, unaccompanied by their reluctant Martian guides, they encounter a mummified being in an inner vault whose head is covered with a mysterious black cowl; the cowl, in fact, is a brain-feeding leech-like creature. By suddenly attaching itself to the head of an expedition member, the creature controls its host and frees others of its kind. Although the story is ostensibly

science fiction, Carter, writing in the introduction to Smith's paperback anthology *Xiccarph*, perceives it as a superior hybrid of genres: "Read the tale and savor the prose style: this rich, bejeweled, exotic kind of writing is the sort we most often think of as being natural to the heroic fantasy tale of magic kingdoms and fabulous eras of the mysterious past. Finally, read the story straight through and notice the actual plot. As you will find, it is precisely the sort of thing we call weird or horror fiction." Donald Sidney-Fryer stated in the introduction to Smith's paperback collection *The Last Incantation* that "The Vaults of Yoh-Vombis" is "one of the most purely horrific stories that Smith ever created" and has "obvious parallels with such Lovecraftian masterpieces as 'The Color Out of Space' and 'The Shadow Out of Time,' as well as with such a recent 'Lovecraftian' film as *Alien*."

If you enjoy the works of Clark Ashton Smith, you may also want to check out the following books:

Charles Baudelaire, *Flowers of Evil and Other Works*, 1992.
H.P. Lovecraft, *Tales of the Cthulhu Mythos*, 1998.
Thomas Ligotti, *The Shadow at the Bottom of the World*, 2005.
Gene Wolfe, "The Book of the New Sun" series.

Turns Away from Fiction

Smith abruptly ceased to write fiction after the deaths of his parents (his mother died in September of 1935, his father in December of 1937). Although he would write the occasional story, "the tales actually completed after 1937 could be counted on the fingers of two hands," de Camp remarked in *Literary Swordsmen and Sorcerers*. Having also shown a flair for the visual arts throughout his life, Smith turned more to rendering his fantastic visions in paintings and sculptures. Eleanor Fait reported in a December, 1941, article in the *Sacramento Union* that Smith started sculpting out of native rock in 1935. "Visiting his uncle who owned a copper mine . . . he picked up a piece of talc, took it home, and casually carved it into a figure one day. Pleased by the result, since then, he has done more than two hundred pieces." Smith exhibited his sculptures, most of them the size of a fist, in the California cities of Auburn, San Francisco, Sacramento, and Los Angeles. He also had an exhibition in New York City's Salon des Independents. In May of 1956, Smith's paintings and sculptures were on display at the Cherry Foundation in Monterey, California. This exhibit was one of the few times when Smith gave a public reading of his poetry. The 1973 title *The Fantastic Art of Clark Ashton Smith* contains photographs of many of Smith's sculptures, paintings, and drawings.

After a number of relationships over the years, including one long-term relationship that ended badly, Smith married Carolyn Emily Jones Dorman in 1954. He moved into her home in Pacific Grove, California, with her three children from an earlier marriage. Smith was working as a gardener when he suffered a number of strokes in 1961 and died in his sleep on August 14, 1961. His ashes are buried near a boulder on his family's old property near Auburn. His unique contributions to the field of imaginative fiction were summed up by H.P. Lovecraft, who wrote to Smith in 1923 (in a letter quoted in *Howard Phillips Lovecraft: Dreamer on the Nightside*), "No author but yourself seems to have glimpsed fully those tenebrous wastes, immeasurable gulfs, grey topless pinnacles, crumbling corpses of forgotten cities, slimy, stagnant, cypress-bordered rivers, and alien, indefinable, antiquity-ridden gardens of strange decay with which my own dreams have been crowded since earliest childhood." In the *St. James Guide to Horror, Ghost and Gothic Writers*, Stefan Dziemianowicz maintained that Smith's works "feature some of the most original and imaginative horrors in 20th-century weird fiction," and in the introduction to *Strange Shadows*, Robert Bloch praised Smith thus: "Let us rejoice in our legacy—the art and artistry, the prose and poetry of one whose imagination did indeed soar beyond space and time."

■ Biographical and Critical Sources

BOOKS

Barrass, Glynn, *A Clark Ashton Smith Bibliography & Checklist*, Blackgoat Books, 2007.

Behrends, Steve, *Clark Ashton Smith*, Starmont House (Mercer Island, WA), 1990.

Bleiler, E.F., editor, *Supernatural Fiction Writers*, Scribner (New York, NY), 1985.

Chalker, Jack L., editor, *In Memoriam Clark Ashton Smith*, Anthem (Baltimore, MD), 1963.

Connors, Scott, editor, *The Freedom of Fantastic Things: Selected Criticism on Clark Ashton Smith*, Hippocampus Press (New York, NY), 2006.

Contemporary Literary Criticism, Volume 43, Gale (Detroit, MI), 1987.

de Camp, L. Sprague, *Literary Swordsmen and Sorcerers*, Arkham House (Sauk City, WI), 1976.

Long, Frank Belknap, *Howard Phillips Lovecraft: Dreamer on the Nightside*, Arkham House (Sauk City, WI), 1975.

Lovecraft, H.P., *Dagon and Other Macabre Tales*, Arkham House (Sauk City, WI), 1965.

Lovecraft, H.P., *Supernatural Horror in Literature*, Ben Abramson, 1945.

Rickard, Dennis, *The Fantastic Art of Clark Ashton Smith*, Mirage (Baltimore, MD), 1973.

St. James Guide to Fantasy Writers, St. James Press (Detroit, MI), 1996.

St. James Guide to Horror, Ghost and Gothic Writers, St. James Press (Detroit, MI), 1998.

St. James Guide to Science Fiction Writers, 4th edition, St. James Press (Detroit, MI), 1996.

Science Fiction Writers, 2nd edition, Scribner (New York, NY), 1999.

Sidney-Fryer, Donald, *The Sorcerer Departs: Clark Ashton Smith (1893-1961)*, 1963, revised edition, Silver Key Press, 2007.

Sidney-Fryer, Donald, *The Last of the Great Romantic Poets*, Silver Scarab (Albuquerque, NM), 1973.

Sidney-Fryer, Donald, *Emperor of Dreams: A Clark Ashton Smith Bibliography*, Donald M. Grant (West Kingston, RI), 1978.

Smith, Clark Ashton, *Zothique*, Ballantine (New York, NY), 1970.

Smith, Clark Ashton, *Selected Poems*, Arkham House (Sauk City, WI), 1971.

Smith, Clark Ashton, *Xiccarph*, Ballantine (New York, NY), 1972.

Smith, Clark Ashton, *The Last Incantation*, Pocket Books (New York, NY), 1982.

Smith, Clark Ashton, *A Rendezvous in Averoigne: Best Fantastic Tales of Clark Ashton Smith*, Arkham House (Sauk City, WI), 1988.

Stableford, Brian, editor, *The Second Dedalus Book of Decadence: The Black Feast*, Dedalus, 1992.

Supernatural Fiction Writers, Volume 2, Scribner (New York, NY), 1985.

PERIODICALS

Acolyte, spring, 1946, Richard Stockton, "Appreciation of the Prose Works of Clark Ashton Smith."

Argonaut, December 16, 1922, Morton Todd, "Clark Ashton Smith's New Volume, *Ebony and Crystal*, Marks Another Stage in the Development of a California Genius," pp. 387-388; November 14, 1925, "The Bard of Auburn," p. 9.

Boston Evening Transcript, April 2, 1913, William Stanley Braithwaite, review of *The Star Treader and Other Poems*, p. 24.

Current Opinion, February, 1913, review of *The Star Treader and Other Poems*, p. 150.

Dark Eidolon, winter, 1993, S.T. Joshi, "What Happens in 'The Hashish Eater?'"

Fantasy Review, February-March, 1949, Arthur F. Hillman, "The Lure of Clark Ashton Smith," pp. 25-26.

Firsts: The Book Collector's Magazine, October, 2000, Don Herron, "Collecting Clark Ashton Smith," pp. 26-39.

Fresno Bee (Fresno, CA), December 30, 1922, William Foster Elliot, review of *Ebony and Crystal: Poems in Verse and Prose*.

Lost Worlds: The Journal of Clark Ashton Smith Studies, Number 2, 2005, Fred Chappell, "Communicable Mysteries: The Last True Symbolist."

New York Review of Science Fiction, July, 2001, Arinn Dembo, "Offerings at the Tomb," pp. 1, 4-9; September, 2001, Scott Connors and Arinn Dembo, "The Last Continent: An Exchange," pp. 18-19.

New York Times Book Review, January 26, 1913, Shamus O'Sheel, "A Young Poet. He Has Quality, but Also the Faults of Youth," p. 38; November 19, 1944, Marjorie Farber, "Atlantis, Xiccarph."

Niekas, July, 1998, Mary Ann Brandenberger, "The Poetic Devices Found in 'The Empire of the Necromancers,'" pp. 87-89.

Nyctalops, Number 7, 1972, Charles K. Wolfe, "A Note on the Aesthetics of Fantasy."

Paradoxa: Studies in World Literary Genres, Volume 5, numbers 13-14, 1999-2000, Lauric Guillaud, "Fantasy and Decadence in the Work of Clark Ashton Smith," pp. 189-212, and Peter H. Goodrich, "Sorcerous Style: Clark Ashton Smith's *The Double Shadow and Other Fantasies*," pp. 213-225.

Poetry: A Magazine of Verse, April, 1913, Harriet Monroe, review of *The Star Treader and Other Poems*, pp. 31-32.

Sacramento Bee, December 30, 1922, "A California Poet. Clark Ashton Smith of Auburn Reveals Unusual Talents in New Volume," p. 26.

San Francisco Call, December 1, 1912, Porter Garnett, review of *The Star Treader and Other Poems*, p. 6.

San Francisco Chronicle, November 15, 1942, Anthony Boucher, review of *Out of Space and Time*, p. 31.

San Francisco Evening Post, November 23, 1912, Sophie Treadwell, review of *The Star Treader and Other Poems*, p. 2.

San Francisco Examiner, December 17, 1922, "Boy Publishes More Poems," p. 20.

San Jose Mercury and Herald, December 8, 1912, John Jury, review of *The Star Treader and Other Poems*, p. 2.

Studies in Fantasy Literature: A Scholarly Journal for the Study of the Fantasy Genre, Number 1, 2004, Steve Tompkins, "Coming in from the Cold: 'Incursions of Outsideness' in Clark Ashton Smith's Hyperborea," pp. 12-28.

Studies in Weird Fiction, spring, 1996, Dan Clore, "The Babel of Visions: The Structuration of Clark Ashton Smith's 'The Hashish-Eater,'" pp. 2-12; summer, 1996, John Kipling Hitz, "Clark Ashton Smith: Master of the Macabre," pp. 8-15; summer, 2001, Scott Connors, "Gesturing toward the Infinite: Clark Ashton Smith and Modernism," pp. 18-28.

Tumbrils, June, 1945, Don Herron, "Eblis in Bakelite."

Wasp, November 23, 1912, "Clark Ashton Smith: California Boy-Poet, Whose Muse Gives Promise of Masterpieces of Melody," p. 16

ONLINE

Eldritch Dark, http://www.eldritchdark.com/ (November 19, 2007).

SF Site, http://www.sfsite.com/ (November 19, 2007), William Thompson, review of *Emperor of Dreams.**

Robert Smithson

(Courtesty of Jack Robinson/Hulton Archive/Getty Images.)

■ Personal

Born January 2, 1938, in Passaic, NJ; died in a plane crash, July 20, 1973; married Nancy Holt (an artist), 1963. *Education:* Attended Art Students League; attended Brooklyn Museum School, 1956.

■ Career

Painter, sculptor, and collage artist. *Exhibitions:* Work included in numerous group exhibits, internationally; solo exhibits staged at Dwan Gallery, New York, NY; Corcoran Gallery, Washington, DC; Detroit Art Institute, Detroit, MI; Museum of Modern Art, Oxford, England; San Francisco Museum of Art, San Francisco, CA; Portland Center for the Visual Arts, Portland, OR; Walker Art Institute, Minneapolis, MN; Museum of Contemporary Art, Chicago; John Weber Gallery, New York, NY; Centre d'Art Contemporain, Geneva, Switzerland; Art Gallery of Ontario, Toronto, Ontario, Canada; Galleria Emi Fontana, Milan, Italy; National Museum of Contemporary Art, Oslo, Sweden; Vancouver Art Gallery, Vancouver, British Columbia, Canada; and Whitney Museum of American Art, New York, NY, among many others.

■ Writings

(With wife, Nancy Holt) *Swamp* (film), 1969.
Spiral Jetty (film), 1970.
Writings of Robert Smithson, edited by wife, Nancy Holt, New York University Press (New York, NY), 1979, revised and expanded as *Robert Smithson: The Collected Writings,* edited by Jack Flam, University of California Press, 1996.
The Writings of Robert Smithson, edited by Robert Hobbs, Cornell University Press (Ithaca, NY), 1981.
Robert Smithson Unearthed: Drawings, Collages, Writings, text by Eugenie Tsai, Columbia University Press (New York, NY), 1991.

Contributor to periodicals, including *Harper's Bazaar, Artforum, Arts, Art Voices, Aspen, Art International, Studio International, Documentario,* and *Sculptors.* Images of Smithson's work appear in numerous exhibition catalogues, including *Robert Smithson Sculpture 1968-69, Robert Smithson's Partially Built Woodshed, Robert Smithson: PhotoWorks, Robert Smithson: Mapping Dislocations, Robert Smithson in Vancouver: A Fragment of a Greater Fragmentation,* and *Robert Smithson: Operations on Nature.*

■ Sidelights

An American artist who, through the monumental quality of his work, made a significant impact on the art world during his lifetime, Robert Smithson was a painter, essayist, photographer, and filmmaker. In his more radical guise, he was also a sculptor whose "clay" was the earth itself; Smithson's artistic works, created out of tons of dirt and rocks, include the "Spiral Jetty" located in Utah's Great Salt Lake, Holland's "Broken Circle/Spiral Hill," and the "Floating Island" that toured the waters around Manhattan in 2005 as a posthumous reminder of Smithson's vision. Gary Shapiro, in his study *Earthwards: Robert Smithson and Art after Babel*, stated that Smithson "is acknowledged as a major figure of the American and global avant-garde of the 1960s and 1970s."

Born in Passaic, New Jersey, in 1938, Smithson grew up with an interest in both drawing and natural history, and his collection of fossils and other artifacts, as well as reptiles, soon developed into an informal museum housed in his parents' home. Growing up across the river from Manhattan, he took every opportunity to visit the New York Museum of Natural History as a teen, where the collection of dinosaur bones captured his imagination. As a high-school student, he was honored with a scholarship to attend night classes at New York City's Art Students League. Following graduation, he studied for a year at the Brooklyn Museum School. Unsure of his future, he spent several months in the Army Reserves, but by 1957 the nineteen-year-old Smithson was living in New York City, determined to make a career as a painter.

Under the influence of the abstract artists of the period, Smithson's early paintings were characterized by their loose, gestured brushstrokes and symmetrical motifs. Even in these early works, the artist's interest on the interplay of opposites—good versus evil, heaven versus hell, black versus white—could be discerned. Tapping into the city's arts and intellectual life, Smithson also established friendships with writers, such as poets Richard Baker and Allan Brilliant, and became reacquainted with artist Nancy Holt. A former childhood friend, Holt shared Smithson's interest in nature. In addition to becoming his wife, she also encouraged the young artist to explore three-dimensional work that would draw on his fascination with organic objects.

Art as Context

Understanding that a work of "art" is defined by its context, Smithson began assembling natural objects into displays that show the interplay between shape and form. Sponges, bones, chemicals, minerals, and other substances were incorporated into works of "art" that were organized to call attention to

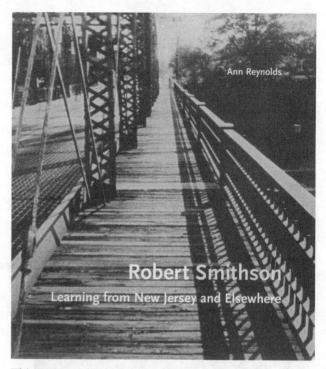

This 2001 study draws heavily on the Smithson materials at the Archives of American Art. (MIT Press, 2003. Reproduced by permission of The MIT Press, Cambridge, MA.)

meaningful relationships. These works led to the "Oppositions" sculptures he created from 1964 to 1965. Large in scale, works such as 1965's "Enantiomorphic Chambers" and "Mirror Strata," are nonetheless minimalist in the artist's approach; they focus on geometric precision and a logical interplay of line and balance. As his early paintings reflected the trend toward abstraction, Smithson's new sculptures mirrored the minimalist approach of painters such as Sol LeWitt, Donald Judd, and Robert Morris. In "Enantiomorphic Chambers," for example, his focus is the molecular structure of crystalline compounds composed of mirrored elements. In his sculpture, Smithson captures the essence of a crystalline compound: creating a steel framework, he incorporates mirrors positioned in such a way that a person looking into one of these mirrors can see, not him-or herself, but only reflections of reflections, as in a fun-house illusion. Interestingly, by reflecting no part of its surrounding, and mirroring only itself, the simulated crystalline structure acts to shatter the viewer's efforts to understand its function from a logical framework.

In "Mirror Strata," which Smithson included in the first of many solo exhibits he would stage at New York City's Dwan Gallery, the artist again used reflection to embody a concept, but this time he layers transparent sheets of glass over a central mirrored object to create a whole that, in order to be viewed as sculpture, requires the viewer to see through and ignore its transparent casing. The visual dimension it projects forces a shift of perception, much as would watching a television screen for what it project rather than for the sheet of glass or other material that it, in fact, is. Even more conceptual, Smithson's "Mirror Displacements" series, temporary installations erected in the Yucatan peninsula, featured nine square mirrors which, positioned amid varied surroundings, distorted the world around them by serving as both an intrusive alien object and a void or hole containing a reflection of a different space.

Although his first solo show would be held in December of 1966, Smithson was already expanding his vision beyond something that could be contained by gallery walls. Much as did nineteenth-century landscape architect Frederick Law Olmsted, Smithson began to view man's attempts to terraform the earth as a form of conceptual art. Frequently joined by Holt, he made several excursions to quarries and other "exposed-earth" sites in and around his boyhood home in New Jersey, mapping the terrain in drawings that reflected his own perception and vision. He recounted these experiences in a series of articles he published in magazines such as *Artforum, Arts,* and *Art International.* In his article "A Tour of the Monument of Passaic, New Jersey," published in *Artforum* in December of 1967, he presented a photo essay of his New Jersey home town that expressed his fascination with entropy as a physical force: the erosion and decay that, as in nature, culminates the efforts of man to build upon the earth. As he wrote in his article, "One's mind and the earth are in a constant state of erosion, mental rivers wear away abstract banks, brain waves undermine cliffs of thought, ideas decompose into stones of unknowing, and conceptual crystallizations break apart into deposits of gritty reason." Many of these influential articles, together with other writings by the artist, were collected by Holt and later published as *The Writings of Robert Smithson.*

In his sculpture series "Site/NonSite" Smithson expresses his vision as it expanded as a result of his mapping expeditions. In the "Non-Site" portion of the work, he arranged, geometrically, various uniquely shaped metal containers filled with samples of material from the specific location under focus. The "Site" itself is captured in photographs and maps that, uniquely shaped to correspond to the relevant bin of site materials, are also displayed in the installation. The arrangement creates a fluid relationship among the viewer, the artist, the work of sculpture created by the artist, and the root source—in nature—of the materials used in that sculpture.

From his Nonsite works was a short step to his Earthworks phase, the first of which, 1969's "Asphalt Rundown," found Smithson in Rome, Italy, supervising a dump truck's worth of asphalt pouring over a cliff. According to Shapiro, "the hillside was already eroded, exhibiting a first level of entropy; the asphalt, following in its flow the gullies and fissures wrought by earlier erosion, both highlights the earlier process and overlays it with a second." "Asphalt Rundown," was followed later in 1969 by two similar works: "Concrete Pour," in which a truckload of wet concrete was poured down a ravine near Chicago, Illinois, and "Glue Pour," in which bright orange glue was poured down an eroded hillside near Vancouver, British Columbia, Canada. Robert Fiori's film *Rundown* documents the creation and aftermath of the three works. That same year, Smithson spent months working on a proposed "Island of Broken Glass" on Miami Islet near Vancouver. The small rocky outcropping would be covered with broken glass. Over centuries, Smith believed, the actions of nature would eventually reduce the broken glass to sand. At first, it seemed as if the project was coming along fine. Smith was even given the small island as a gift from Queen Elizabeth II. But local environmental groups protested Smithson's project, stopping dump trucks filled with broken glass at the Canadian border. They believed that covering the small island with glass would harm the local bird population. Their protests eventually killed the project.

Creates "Spiral Jetty"

In 1970 Smithson was back in the United States, on the campus of Ohio's Kent State University, enacting "Partially Buried Woodshed," in which bulldozers piled rocks and dirt on the roof of a wood-frame shed until the roof beam gave way. That same year Smithson began construction of what would be his masterwork, "Spiral Jetty," which is located on Rozelle Point, on (or under) Utah's Great Salt Lake. Formed by reconfiguring over 6,500 tons of indigenous black basalt rocks, mud, salt crystals, and lake water, he created a fifteen-foot-wide outcropping that coils, counterclockwise, like a pathway from the surrounding desert into the lake's reddish expanse. Measuring a total length of 1,500 feet, and with a construction cost of sixteen hundred dollars, Smithson's coiled pathway was constructed atop an abandoned oil rig site. From the air, it has the symbolic effect of an ancient earth mound while also being a work of art. While constructing "Spiral Jetty," Smithson filmed the process, and also wrote about the project. These actions proved providential, for the site was eventually submerged under the lake's constantly fluctuating surface. Given to New York City's Dia Center for the Arts by Smithson's Estate in 1999, "Spiral Jetty" reemerged following a widespread drought in 2002. Because its remote location makes it difficult to find, a trip to "Spiral Jetty" was described by *Architecture* contributor Abby Bussel as "a pilgrimage for land-art enthusiasts," Bussel noting that "the jetty's disappearing act has only added to its mystique." A visit to "Spiral Jetty" involves travelling back roads in the Utah desert. The site is some fifteen miles from the visitor center of the Golden Spike National Historic Site. The official directions on the "Spiral Jetty" Web site warn that, at one point, "Travel slowly—the road is narrow, brush might scratch your vehicle, and the rocks, if not properly negotiated, could high center your vehicle." Because of the difficulties involved in visiting the site, Michael Kimmelman, writing in the *New York Times Magazine,* described "Spiral Jetty" as "the most famous work of American art that almost nobody has ever seen in the flesh."

Smithson told Moira Roth in a 1973 interview included in *Robert Smithson* that "I was never too interested in works without substantial permanence." Yet, he realized that changes to his earthwork structures were inevitable: "'The Spiral Jetty' right now is under water. Because it's eighty percent rock it won's erode completely. It holds its shape but it's affected by the climate changes. In the late summer it will evaporate and the whole thing will develop salt. . . . So I'sm interested in something substantial enough that's permeate—perhaps permeate is a better word than permanent—in other words, something that can be permeated with change and different conditions."

If you enjoy the artwork of Robert Smithson, you may also want to check out the following artists:

The sculptor and conceptual artist Robert Morris, the environmental installation artists Christo and Jeanne-Claude, and James Turrell, creator of Roden Crater.

As his vision evolved, Smithson found his canvas in land reclamation projects, a way to mediate the opposing interests of naturalists and industry. Seeking out appropriate sites throughout the world, he styled himself a land-reclamation artist/consultant, his mission to reconceptualize abandoned or otherwise unusable sites as sculptural works on a grand scale. One such side was a quarry in Emmen, Netherlands, which, in 1971, became "Broken Circle/Spiral Hill." The work—build, in oppositional fashion, half on land and half on water—consists of two semi-circles that mirror each other. Broken Circle features the smooth surface of the canal, while Spiral Hill traces out a path along a jetty. Two years later, on July 20, 1973, Smithson died in an airplane crash, while undertaking the preliminary research for a land reclamation project in Amarillo, Texas.

Smithson's final project, the "Amarillo Ramp," was completed following his death by his widow, Holt, and friends Richard Serra and Tony Shafrazi. Another of his visions, the creation of a floating island pulled by a tugboat through the waters surrounding Staten Island, New York, was also left unfunded at his death, but was realized in September of 2005. Noting the millions of years and many physical forces that create most islands, *New York Times* contributor Randy Kennedy noted that Smithson's "Floating Island" "was formed over about a week, in a ragged-looking barge yard on Staten Island, shaped by a public art group, a landscape architect, a contractor, an engineer, a project manager and various other dedicated conceptual art workers using a 30-by-90-foot flat-decked barge, ten [full-grown] trees, three huge rocks, a bunch of shrubs, rolls of sod, a whole lot of dirt and even more ingenuity." The "Floating Island" project was funded by the Whitney Museum of American Art, which sponsored the moveable sculpture to coincide with a retrospective of Smithson's art. As Catherine Slessor noted in *Architectural Review* with a nod to Smithson's love of Manhattan, his respect for Olmsted, and his overarching view of opposition and circularity, "as Central Park is, in effect, an artificial model of nature, so the floating island is an artificial model of Central Park."

Noting the renewed interest in Smithson's work as environmental awareness increased in the early twenty-first century, Peter Schjeldahl offered a reason in his commentary for the *New Yorker.* "As a figure of freedom, temerity, and lyrical prophecy," Schjeldahl maintained, "Smithson stirs nostalgia among artists and others in the art world, which, for all its wealth and popularity, feels increasingly constricted, faltering, and prosaic. . . . Smithson's example suggests not only that anything can be art but that anyone, with proper fire in the belly, can become a great artist, even without being much good at it." Carter Ratliff presented a more nuanced assessment in *Art in America.* Along with fellow

Earth Art adherents Holt, Michael Heizer, James Turrell, Walter De Maria, and Dennis Oppenhelm, Ratliff noted: "Smithson gave American art the literal scale of the American landscape and in the process subjected the venerable idea of the sublime to shocks we still feel."

■ Biographical and Critical Sources

BOOKS

Adamson, Glenn, *Thinking Through Craft*, Berg (New York, NY), 2007.

Baker, George, *Robert Smithson: Spiral Jetty: True Fictions, False Realities*, University of California Press (Berkeley, CA), 2005.

Battcock, Gregory, editor, *Minimal Art: A Critical Anthology*, [New York, NY], 1968.

Boettger, Suzann, *Earthworks: Art and the Landscape of the Sixties*, University of California Press (Berkeley, CA), 2002.

Casey, Edward S., *Earth-mapping: Artists Reshaping Landscape*, University of Minnesota Press (Minneapolis, MN), 2005.

Cummings, Paul, *Artists in Their Own Words: Interviews*, St. Martin's Press (New York, NY), 1979.

Graziani, Ron, *Robert Smithson and the American Landscape*, Cambridge University Press (Cambridge, MA), 2004.

Hobbs, Robert Carleton, *Robert Smithson—Sculpture*, Cornell University Press (Ithaca, NY), 1981.

Kastner, Jeffrey, and Brian Wallis, editors, *Land and Environmental Art*, Phaidon (London, England), 1998.

Kwon, Miwon, *One Place after Another: Site-Specific Art of the 1960s*, MIT Press (Cambridge, MA), 2002.

Reynolds, Ann, *Robert Smithson: Learning from New Jersey and Elsewhere*, MIT Press (Cambridge, MA), 2001.

Roberts, Jennifer L., *Mirror-Travels: Robert Smithson and History*, Yale University Press (New Haven, CT), 2004.

Robert Smithson, Museum of Contemporary Art, Los Angeles (Los Angeles, CA), 2004.

Shapiro, Gary, *Earthwards—Robert Smithson and Art after Babel*, University of California Press (Berkeley, CA), 1995.

Tiberghien, Gilles A., *Land Art*, Princeton Architectural Press (New York, NY), 1995.

PERIODICALS

Architectural Review, June, 2006, Catherine Slessor, "Delight: Robert Smithson's Floating Island Becomes a Reality," p. 98.

Architecture, December, 2002, Abby Bussel, "Spiral Jetty Comes up for Air," p. 15.

Artforum, December, 1967, Robert Smithson, "A Tour of the Monument of Passaic, New Jersey"; November, 1972, Lawrence Alloway, "Robert Smithson's Development"; October, 1973, Moira Roth, "Robert Smithson on Duchamp," p. 47.

Art in America, November-December, 1973, Philip Leider, "For Robert Smithson," pp. 80-82; January, 1992, Holland Cotter, "Robert Smithson Unearthed," p. 113; December, 1998, Suzaan Boettger and Willoughby Sharp, 1969 interview with Smithson, pp. 75-81; January, 2001, Phillip Leider, "Smithson and the American Landscape," pp. 74-79; October, 2005, Carter Ratcliff, "A Heap of Smithson," p. 156; November, 2005, Stephanie Cash, "Smithson's Island Floats at Last," p. 39.

ARTNews, February, 1969, Anthony Robbins, "Smithson's Non-sites Sites," p. 50.

Arts, September, 1976, Ellen Lubell, "Robert Smithson," p. 19; May, 1978, Carl Andre, "Robert Smithson—He Always Reminded Us of the Questions We Ought to Have Asked Ourselves"; October, 1981, Robert Smithson issue; March, 1983, Adam Gopnik, "Basic Stuff: Robert Smithson, Science and Primitivism"; March, 1986, Eugenie Tsai, "The Unknown Smithson."

Avalanche, fall, 1969, Liza Bear and Willoughby Sharp, "Discussion with Heizer, Oppenheim, Smithson"; fall, 1973, "Robert Smithson's 'Amarillo Ramp.'"

Chicago Tribune, April 26, 1981, Alan G. Artner, "With Smithson Sculpture MCA Gets Down to Earth."

Choice, March, 1992, J. Weidman, review of *Robert Smithson Unearthed: Drawings, Collages, Writings*, p. 1066; June, 1996, J. Weidman, review of *Robert Smithson: The Collected Writings*, p. 1632.

Critical Quarterly, autumn, 1990, Marjorie Perloff, "The Demise of 'and': Reflections on Robert Smithson's Mirrors," pp. 81-101.

Desert Morning News, August 7, 2003, Ray Boren, "Time and a Place: Utah's Spiral Jetty," pp. A15-16.

Domus, November, 1972, Bruce Kurtz, "Conversation with Robert Smithson," and Gianni Pettena, "Conversation in Salt Lake City."

Flash Art, November-December, 1990, Dan Cameron, "Incidents of Robert Smithson: Posthumous Dimensions of a Premature Pre-Modern," pp. 103-107.

Life, April 25, 1969, David Bourdon, "What on Earth!"

Los Angeles Times, August 13, 1981, Christopher Knight, "The Very Rich and Complex Work of Robert Smithson."

Nation, September 19, 2005, Arthur C. Danto, "The American Sublime," p. 34.

New York, Thomas B. Hess, "The Condemned Playgrounds of Robert Smithson, pp. 88-89.

New Yorker, September 5, 2005, Peter Schjeldahl, "What on Earth," p. 158.

New York Times, October 6, 1968, Grace Glueck, "Moving Mother Earth"; April 28, 1974, John Russell, "He Dreamed of Floating Islands," p. D19; May 7, 1976, John Russell, "Robert Smithson," p. C12; November 30, 1980, John Russell, "The Fertile Imagination of Robert Smithson," p. D31; December 31, 1993, Charles Hagen, "Smithson's Way of Looking at the Land," p. C3.

New York Times Magazine, October 13, 2002, Michael Kimmelman, "Out of the Deep."

On Site, Number 4, 1973, Alison Sky, "Entropy Made Visible," p. 47.

Res, spring, 2002, Robert Linsley, "Minimalism and the City: Robert Smithson as a Social Critic," pp. 38-55.

Sunset, August, 2005, Peter Fish, "The Spiral Jetty," p. 24.

Village Voice, October 17, 1968, John Perrault, "Long Live Earth"; July, 1973, Fred W. McDarrah, "Robert Smithson," pp. 16-21; January, 1997, Kim Levin, "Robert Smithson—Issues of Entropy."

ONLINE

Official Robert Smithson Home Page, http://www.robertsmithson.com (November 15, 2007).

Robert Smithson.org: A Tribute, http://robertsmithson.org/ (November 15, 2007).

Spiral Jetty Web site, http://www.spiraljetty.org/ (November 15, 2007).

OTHER

Fiori, Robert, *Rundown* (film), 1969.*

Elizabeth George Speare

■ Personal

Born November 21, 1908, in Melrose, MA; died of an aortic aneurysm, November 15, 1994, in Tucson, AZ; daughter of Harry Allan (an engineer) and Demetria George; married Alden Speare (an industrial engineer), September 26, 1936; children: Alden, Jr., Mary Elizabeth. *Education:* Attended Smith College, 1926-27; Boston University, A.B., 1930, M.A., 1932.

■ Career

Writer, 1955-94. Rockland High School, Rockland, MA, teacher of English, 1932-35; Auburn High School, Auburn, MA, teacher of English, 1935-36.

■ Member

Authors Guild, Authors League of America.

■ Awards, Honors

Society of Colonial Wars Award from the State of New York, and Newbery Medal from the American Library Association, both 1959, International Board on Books for Young People (IBBY) Honor List, and selected one of American Institute of Graphic Arts Children's Books, both 1960, and New England Round Table Children's Librarians Award, 1976, all for *The Witch of Blackbird Pond*; Newbery Medal, 1962, and IBBY Honor List, 1964, both for *The Bronze Bow*; one of American Library Association's Best Young Adult Books, Teachers' Choice from the National Council of Teachers of English, one of Child Study Association of America's Children's Book of the Year, one of *School Library Journal*'s Best Books of the Year, a *Booklist* Children's Reviewers Choice, and one of *New York Times* Outstanding Books, all 1983, and Newbery Medal Honor Book, Scott O'Dell Award for Historical Fiction, and Christopher Award, all 1984, all for *The Sign of the Beaver*; Laura Ingalls Wilder Award, 1989, for a distinguished and enduring contribution to children's literature.

■ Writings

HISTORICAL FICTION FOR YOUNG ADULTS

Calico Captive, illustrated by W. Mars, Houghton Mifflin (Boston, MA), 1957.
The Witch of Blackbird Pond, illustrated by Nicholas Angelo, Houghton Mifflin (Boston, MA), 1958.
The Bronze Bow, Houghton Mifflin (Boston, MA), 1961.
The Sign of the Beaver, illustrated by Robert Andrew Parker, Houghton Mifflin (Boston, MA), 1983.

OTHER

Child Life in New England, 1790-1840, Old Sturbridge Village (Sturbridge, MA), 1961.

Life in Colonial America (nonfiction), Random House (New York, NY), 1963.

The Prospering (adult novel), Houghton Mifflin (Boston, MA), 1967.

Contributor of articles to periodicals, including *Better Homes and Gardens, Woman's Day, Parents, American Heritage, Today's Health,* and *Horn Book.* Speare's manuscript collection is at the Mugar Memorial Library at Boston University.

■ Adaptations

Abby, Julia and the Cows (television play; based on an article for *American Heritage*), Southern New England Telephone Company, January 7, 1958; *The Bronze Bow* (record, cassette, filmstrip with cassette), Random House; *The Witch of Blackbird Pond* was optioned for film rights in 1989 by Robert Radnitz, and was adapted for audiocassette, Random House; *The Sign of the Beaver* (cassette, filmstrip with cassette), Random House, and Listening Library, 1998.

■ Sidelights

Elizabeth George Speare's "stories illuminate history through her well-defined characters and fascinating plots," according to an essayist for the *St. James Guide to Young Adult Writers.* Speare's favorite time period to write about was pre-Revolutionary America, although one of her most acclaimed books was set during Jesus's lifetime in Galilee. "The protagonists in Speare's work . . . range in age from thirteen to nineteen, and all struggle with issues of maturity and self-determination," explained the writer for the *St. James Guide to Young Adult Writers.* "Confronted with rigid legalism, bigotry, and injustice, these characters often find themselves acting outside of society's prescribed roles in order to follow their developing convictions." Speare has been especially praised for her ability to merge historical fact with the fiction of her storylines—a skill which came from hours of meticulous research.

Speare's childhood was spent in Massachusetts, and she lived in New England her entire life. In her later writing, Speare reflected that it was easy for her to revisit Colonial times, since many areas of New England look the same now as they did then. Her mother's family would take Speare and her only brother on hikes and picnics in the woods, or to Boston to the theater or concerts. In the summer, they retreated to the shore, where she and her brother often would be the only children around. "I had endless golden days to read and think and dream," Speare wrote in *More Junior Authors.* "It was then that I discovered the absorbing occupation of writing stories."

Childhood Writers

As a child, Speare filled scores of notebooks with stories and poems. She had a large extended family that would meet often for reunions and dinners. At these events, she and a close cousin would greet each other heartily, then sequester themselves in an out-of-the-way place to share the stories each of them had written. Even when adults would shake their heads in dismay over their activity, the girls would not be discouraged. Years later, when the two visited each other at college, they would carry their notebooks with them to share their stories as they had done when they were children.

Speare attended Boston University, earning a master's degree in 1932. She taught high school for a while and married Alden Speare in 1936. The couple moved to Connecticut and had two children. Speare settled into family life, finding that she had little time for writing with her many duties and activities. "Once in a while I would catch a story of my own peeking out of a corner of my mind," she related in *More Junior Authors.* "But before I found time to sit down with a pencil and paper it would have scurried back out of sight."

When her children were both in junior high school, Speare found more time to write. At first, she worked on feature articles about family events like skiing or wrapping Christmas presents. Soon Speare found her niche when she published an article in *American Heritage* about the Smith sisters of Colonial Glastonbury, who refused to pay taxes and had their land confiscated. This article was adapted into a television program.

After reading a history of Connecticut, Speare found a diary written by one Susanna Johnson, dating from 1807. The diary told the intriguing story of her family's kidnapping by Indians, who eventually traded them to the French. From this tragic tale, Speare crafted a full-length novel entitled *Calico Captive.* Speare was haunted not only by the writer of the diary, but also by her sister, Miriam, whose adventures she made up and recorded. Ultimately a well-rounded character emerged. "Speare spins a

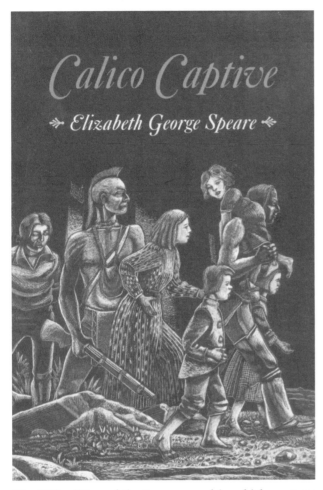

The 2001 edition of the Speare novel in which a young woman and her family are taken captive by Indians.
(Houghton Mifflin, 1985. Jacket art copyright © 2001 by Michael McCurdy. Reproduced by permission of Houghton Mifflin Company.)

fast-moving tale. . . .," admitted an essayist for the *St. James Guide to Young Adult Writers.* "The detailed descriptions and active use of dialogue create a compelling picture of both the geographical terrain and the colonial conflicts of the time." Margaret Sherwood Libby in the *New York Herald Tribune Book Review* praised the work, saying: "It is that rarity in historical novels, one that does not seem to be written to provide 'background' but to tell a good story." Calling the story "superior historical fiction," Jennie D. Lindquist in *Horn Book* predicted that "it will be a favorite."

Colonial Connecticut

For her next book, Speare turned to Wethersfield, Connecticut, the town where she and her husband had resided for twenty years. It was one of the old-est towns in New England, with a rich history. Instead of finding a key event to write about, characters began to form in Speare's mind. "Each of these people began to take on sharper outlines, individual dimensions, and they were already moving and talking and reaching out in relationship to each other, long before I had found a place for them to live or a time in which they could be born. Finally I was compelled to find a home for them,"Speare related in her Laura Ingalls Wilder Award acceptance speech, published in *Horn Book.* The home she found for them was in her book *The Witch of Blackbird Pond,* published in 1958.

The Witch of Blackbird Pond tells of sixteen-year-old Kit Tyler, who travels from the Caribbean island of Barbados to her new home in Connecticut in 1687. Her grandfather, a Barbados plantation owner, has died and Kit, who was living with him, must go to live with her aunt Rachel Wood and her family in the town of Wethersfield. Kit finds companionship with her two cousins: Judith, who is Kit's age, and the slightly older Mercy, who is handicapped. She also makes friends with several young men in town, including Nat Eaton, William Ashley, and John Holbrook. One day in the Great Meadow close to Blackbird Pond outside town, Kit meets the town's outcast, Hannah Tupper, an aged Quaker woman who has been branded a witch because her religious beliefs are different. Although forbidden to go to Hannah's home, Kit secretly visits this kind, understanding woman and finds that Nat Eaton is also a friend of Hannah's. At Hannah's home, she meets Prudence Cruff, a local girl, and begins to teach her how to read and write. When a mysterious disease strikes Wethersfield, many of the young people, including Mercy and Judith, become dangerously ill. The townspeople blame Hannah's witchcraft and try to take her prisoner. Nat and Kit smuggle Hannah safely aboard a ship. But the townspeople turn their attention to Kit, and she is brought to trial for witchcraft. But when Nat explains in court that Kit has been teaching Prudence at Hannah's home, she is released. Nat and Kit end up together at story's end.

Margaret Sherwood Libby in the *New York Herald Tribune Book Review* found *The Witch of Blackbird Pond* to be "even better" than *Calico Captive.* "Rarely has a book taken us back into seventeenth-century life as this does," Libby claimed. "The secret perhaps is that Kit is a fully realized character." The novel, according to Mary Silva Cosgrave in the *Library Journal,* "reveals not only the wisdom, the beliefs and feelings of Elizabeth George Speare, but her imaginative, creative talents and her superb writing abilities." An essayist for the *St. James Guide to Young Adult Writers* found: "In this captivating story, well worthy of its Newbery Medal, the adversity Kit faces serves to mature the strength and exuberance

of her character as she works through disillusion-
ment and alienation to understanding and compassion." "Rarely has a book taken us back into
seventeenth century life as this does," wrote Libby.
Janet Hill, writing in *Signal*, called *The Witch of
Blackbird Pond* "an enjoyable and readable historical
novel." Helen Reeder Cross in *Horn Book* predicted
that the novel may become "an enduring part of
America's artistic heritage."

A Galilee Adventure

Speare stepped out of Connecticut to write her next
novel, *The Bronze Bow*. The story centers on the boy
Daniel, a Jewish boy in first century Galilee who
hates the Romans who have taken over his land. He
runs away from the cruel blacksmith to whom he
was apprenticed and joins the outlaw, Rosh, in
hopes of defeating the Romans. When he returns
home to care for his sister and meets Jesus, he finds
himself torn between his desire for military power
to defeat the Romans and Jesus' message that love
is the way to the kingdom he seeks. He eventually
comes to find peace and acceptance through the
teachings of Jesus. Mary Louise Hector in the *New
York Times Book Review* found *The Bronze Bow* to be
"superbly written" and "alive, adventurous, and
respectful of historical fact and spirit. It offers a
refined understanding of the common man's contemporary reaction to Jesus." Constantine Georgiou,
writing in his study *Children and Their Literature*,
stated: "True to historical fact, this stunning story
. . . is powerful and breathtakingly real. . . . The
portrait of Jesus, particularly, is superbly developed"

In an evaluation of *The Bronze Bow*, an essayist for
the *St. James Guide to Young Adult Writers* wrote:
"Carefully sketched characters such as a fellow Ga-
lilean, Joel, a group of outlaws and a black slave,
Daniel's own mentally ill sister, a roman guard, and
finally Jesus himself, provide the story with a rich
interweaving of personalities and motivations.
Although the novel could be criticized for imposing
a western bias on a middle eastern setting . . . its
predominant themes of hatred and forgiveness,
coming of age, and war and peace are universal
ones with relevance to any society and culture."
"Speare's historical fiction," wrote Francisca Goldsmith in the *School Library Journal*, "is accessible to
both Christians and those wholly unfamiliar with
the personage of Jesus or the New Testament."
Speare wanted to write this novel to show young
children that Jesus could be a real, living character,
and she won a second Newbery for this ambitious
book.

Kit Tyler finds herself at odds with the Puritanical lifestyle of her uncle's family in this 2005 edition of the
Newbery Medal-winning novel. (Thorndike Press, 2005. Cover art
copyright © by Barry Moser. Reproduced by permission of Houghton Mifflin Company.)

Story of a Friendship

In *The Sign of the Beaver*, Speare returned to Colonial
New England to tell a memorable tale about a
young boy whose life is saved by an Indian youth.
Matt Hallowell is left alone in a newly-built cabin
while his father leaves to bring the rest of the family into the wilderness. A wanderer steals his rifle, a
bear steals his flour and molasses, and he is attacked
by bees while collecting honey. The Indian boy Attean saves his life. Matt learns to respect the Native
Americans as they help him and teach him what he
needs to survive. His "thank you" is teaching Attean to read, and the two boys form a close yet tense
bond. When it comes time for the two boys to part
ways, they give each other gifts. Ann Mosley in the
ALAN Review commented: "Attean and Matt make

symbolic gifts of friendship. Attean gives his dog to Matt; in response, Matt rejects his original gift to Attean, the culturally biased *Robinson Crusoe*, in favor of a family heirloom—his father's watch. Each of these gifts represents the culture of its original owner, but even more importantly, each gift is a sign of friendship." "All the characters forcefully emerge as living, breathing humans and as such have striking staying power," wrote Barbara Elleman in *Booklist*. The reviewer for *Junior Bookshelf* summed up: "Speare's novel is a fine one, full of wisdom and practical good sense as well as understanding of human behavior under stress. It is an astonishing achievement for a writer of seventy-five."

An essayist for the *St. James Guide to Young Adult Writers* commented: "Speare's factual depiction of the Indians, so different from *Calico Captive*, shows both respect and sensitivity, and renders the book particularly relevant today." Jean Fritz commented in the *New York Times Book Review* that "as usual in Mrs. Speare's novels, each word rings true."Writing in the *School Library Journal*, Margaret C. Howell praised Speare's "marvelous sense of setting and two memorable characters." Reviewing the sound recording of *The Sign of the Beaver*, a contributor for *Publishers Weekly* called it a "gripping . . . novel about a boy's adventures in the wilderness of 1768." *The Sign of the Beaver* won the Scott O'Dell Award for historical fiction, as well as a Christopher Award.

If you enjoy the works of Elizabeth George Speare, you may also want to check out the following books:

Conrad Richter, *The Light in the Forest*, 1953.
Eric P. Kelly and Janina Domanska, *The Trumpeter of Krakow*, 1966.
Sollace Hotze, *A Circle Unbroken*, 1988.

A Final Award

In 1989, Speare received the Laura Ingalls Wilder Award for her contribution to children's literature. She established her reputation through only a few books, but each one is noted for its quality. In an acceptance speech for one of her Newbery Medals, published in *Horn Book*, Speare asserted her feelings about writing: "I believe that all of us who are concerned with children are committed to the salvaging of Love and Honor and Duty. . . . [Children] look urgently to the adult world for evidence that we have proved our values to be enduring." She challenged other authors and herself by concluding that "those of us who have found love and honor and duty to be a sure foundation must somehow find words which have the ring of truth."

Speare died in 1994, but her works live on, having become classics in the classroom. An acknowledged master of the genre, Speare made history more palatable to young readers without distorting fact for the purposes of fiction. Though her output was small—only four young adult historical novels, two nonfiction books, and one adult novel—Speare made a deep impact on young adult literature as well as on historical fiction. "Speare," Barry X. Miller argued in the *School Library Journal*, "is perhaps the most decorated and honored young adult historical fiction author for the least amount of volumes."

■ Biographical and Critical Sources

BOOKS

American Women Writers, 2nd edition, St. James Press (Detroit, MI), 2000.
Apseloff, Marilyn Fain, *Elizabeth George Speare*, Twayne (New York, NY), 1991.
Authors of Books for Young People, 2nd edition, Scarecrow (Metuchen, NJ), 1971.
Children's Literature Review, Volume 8, Gale (Detroit, MI), 1985.
Georgiou, Constantine, *Children and Their Literature*, Prentice-Hall, 1969.
More Books by More People, Citation (New York, NY), 1974.
St. James Guide to Young Adult Writers, 2nd edition, St. James Press (Detroit, MI), 1999.
Sebesta, Sam Leaton and William J. Iverson, *Literature for Thursday's Child*, Science Research Associates, 1975.
Twentieth Century Children's Writers, 3rd edition, St. James Press (Detroit, MI), 1989.

PERIODICALS

ALAN Review, spring, 1994, Mary Ann Tighe and Charles Avinger, "Teaching Tomorrow's Classics," pp. 9-13; spring, 1995, Ann Moseley, "Signs in Speare's 'The Sign of the Beaver,'" pp. 19-21.

Booklist, April 15, 1983, Barbara Elleman, review of *The Sign of the Beaver*, p. 1098; November 1, 1998, Barbara Baskin, review of *The Sign of the Beaver*, p. 518.

Commonweal, March 22, 1985, p. 178.

English Journal, October, 1985, Mary Helen Thuente, "Beyond Historical Fiction: Speare's 'The Witch of Blackbird Pond,'" pp. 50-55.

Horn Book, October, 1957, Jennie D. Lindquist, review of *Calico Captive*, p. 406; August, 1959, Helen Reeder Cross, review of *The Witch of Blackbird Pond*, pp. 271-274; August, 1962, E.G. Speare, "Report of a Journey: Newbery Award Acceptance"; March-April, 1985, p. 204; March-April, 1988, Elizabeth George Speare, "The Survival Story," pp. 163-172; July-August, 1989, E.G. Speare, "Laura Ingalls Wilder Award Acceptance," pp. 460-464, 465-468.

Junior Bookshelf, June, 1984, review of *The Sign of the Beaver*, p. 145.

Language Arts, November-December, 1983, Ronald A. Jobe, review of *The Sign of the Beaver*, p. 1023.

Library Journal, April 15, 1959, Mary Silva Cosgrave, review of *The Witch of Blackbird Pond*, pp. 1291-1292.

New York Herald Tribune Book Review, November 17, 1957, Margaret Sherwood Libby, review of *Calico Captive*, p. 32; November 2, 1958, Margaret Sherwood Libby, review of *The Witch of Blackbird Pond*, p. 20.

New York Times Book Review, November 12, 1961, Mary Louise Hector, "In the Time of Jesus," p. 20; May 8, 1983, Jean Fritz, review of *The Sign of the Beaver*, p. 37.

Publishers Weekly, March 23, 1959; March 19, 1962; July 13, 1998, review of *The Sign of the Beaver*, p. 19.

School Library Journal, April, 1983, Margaret C. Howell, review of *The Sign of the Beaver*, pp. 118-119; September, 1998, p. 153; September, 2001, Francisca Goldsmith, review of *The Bronze Bow*, p. 76; December, 2001, Barry X. Miller, review of *Calico Captive*, p. 77.

Signal, September, 1972, Janet Hill, "Accepting the Eleanor Farjeon Award," pp. 109-114.

Storyworks, April-May, 2004, Rebecca Hillel, review of *The Sign of the Beaver*, p. 7.

OBITUARIES

PERIODICALS

New York Times, November 16, 1995, p. D24.

School Library Journal, January, 1995, p. 23.*

Frank Stella

(Photograph courtesy of AP Images.)

■ Personal

Born May 12, 1936, in Malden, MA; son of Frank (a gynecologist) and Constance Aida Stella; married Barbara Rose (an art critic), 1961 (divorced 1969); married Harriet McGurk (a pediatrician), 1978; children: (first marriage) Rachel, Michael; (second marriage) Patrick, Peter. *Education:* Princeton University, B.A., 1958.

■ Addresses

Home—New York, NY.

■ Career

Painter, sculptor, and architect. Designer of sets and costumes for Merce Cunningham's dance performance "Scramble," 1967, and Simon Callow's Broadway stage production of *The Pajama Game,* 1999. Charles Eliot Norton lecturer at Harvard University, 1983-84. *Exhibitions:* Work included in exhibitions and permanent collections at Allen Memorial Art Museum, Oberlin College; Museum of Modern Art, New York, NY; Solomon R. Guggenheim Museum, New York, NY; Museum of Fine Arts, Houston, TX; Norton Simon Museum, Pasadena, CA; Art Institute of Chicago, Chicago, IL; Corcoran Gallery of Art, Washington, DC; Wadsworth Atheneum, Hartford, CT; Hirschhorn Museum and Sculpture Garden, Washington, DC; Kunstmuseum, Basel Switzerland; Tate Gallery, London, England; Reina Gallery, Madrid, Spain; and many other institutions and galleries throughout the United States, Europe, and Japan. Sculpture installations include at Prince of Wales Theatre, Toronto, Ontario, Canada, 1992-93; City of Miami, FL, 1991; and National Gallery of Art, Washington, DC, 2001.

■ Writings

Shards, text by Richard Meier, Petersburg Press (New York, NY), 1983.

Frank Stella: Fourteen Prints with Drawings, Collages, and Working Proofs, text by Judith Goldman, Princeton University Art Museum (Princeton, NJ), 1983.

Frank Stella: Paintings, 1958 to 1965: A Catalogue Raisonné, text by Lawrence Rubin, Stewart, Tabor & Chang (New York, NY), 1986.

Working Space, Harvard University Press (Cambridge, MA), 1986.

Contributor to periodicals, including *New York Times Magazine* and *American Heritage.*

Stella at a January, 1982, showing of his work at the Addison Gallery of American Art. (Richard Howard/Time and Life Pictures/Getty Images.)

Images of Stella's work appear in numerous exhibition catalogues, including *Frank Stella: The Black Paintings*, 1976; *Frank Stella: Metallic Reliefs*, 1979; *Frank Stella: The Swan Engravings*, 1984; *Frank Stella: Works and New Graphics*, 1985; *Frank Stella: Moby Dick Series: Engravings, Domes and Deckle Edges*, 1993; and *Frank Stella: Painting into Architecture*, 2007.

■ **Sidelights**

A dominant figure in the world of American art, Frank Stella remains known as an influential minimalist who has revitalized interest in abstract expressionism. Beginning with minimalist black and white paintings in the late 1950s, Stella moved on to create colorful geometric abstract paintings in the 1960s, and then created paintings with multiple surfaces in the 1970s. In more recent years, the prolific artist has moved through mixed-media works into sculptures that, with their organic feel,

incorporate looping, curved elements in an ordered tangle that intrigues and challenges viewers. Throughout his career, Stella, dubbed "a dedicated risk-taker" by *Apollo* contributor David Anfam, also has been a prolific printmaker. His lithographs, paintings, and sculptures are included in numerous museum and corporate collections throughout the world. Saul Ostrow, writing for *Bomb Magazine Online*, called Stella "an artist who, for forty years, has aggressively worked to maintain and reinvigorate abstract painting." "I like to make paintings, and I work at that: it's my job," Stella explained to William Rubin in *Frank Stella: 1970-1987*. "I don't consider myself that different from anybody else."

Born in Malden, Massachusetts, in 1936, Stella attended the prestigious Phillips Academy in Andover before enrolling at Princeton University in 1954. Because Princeton did not offer a degree in art, he majored in history and trained himself as a painter by studying the abstract expressionism of artist such as Jackson Pollock and Jasper Johns and taking every opportunity to visit New York City and roam through its many galleries. Fortunately, during Stella's time at Princeton, art historian William Seitz and painter Stephen Greene were teaching there, and both were willing to mentor the enthusiastic young artist.

Graduating from Princeton in 1958, Stella moved to New York City that summer. In *Working Space,* Stella remembered: "I was convinced that it would only be a temporary stay. After graduation from Princeton in June, I was planning to paint in the city until the following September, at which time I expected to be drafted into the Army in Boston. When I failed the physical examination because of a faulty opposition between the thumb and fingers of my left hand resulting from a childhood accident, I was stunned. . . . I suddenly had to look at my paintings and my ideas about painting with an urgency I had not experienced before." Stella shared a studio with painter Carl Andre and determined to make art his career. He came to New York with very reactionary ideas: interested in creating smooth surfaces unmarred by brush strokes, he also viewed a painting—which he referred to as "a flat surface with paint on it—nothing more"—as an object in and of itself rather than a representation of an object or emotion. His work habits were also unconventional: lines and curves were generated spontaneously, without sketches, and rather than oils, Stella often used house paint. On the strength of his series of works called the "Black Paintings," in which bands of black paint alternate with thin white pinstripes of raw canvas, Stella was given his first solo exhibition at the highly respected Leo Castelli Gallery. They have remained his representative ever since. Stella's "Black Paintings," according to James Panero in the *New Criterion,* "ushered art into the minimalist and—more significantly—conceptualist era." In 1959, the Museum of Modern Art chose four of Stella's "Black Paintings" for inclusion in a group art show called "Sixteen Americans." Eventually, the museum paid 900 dollars for one of the paintings, "The Marriage of Reason and Squalor." In 1993, the Osaka City Museum of Modern Art bought another of the "Black Paintings," titled "Black Stella," for $5 million.

The Geometric Sixties

Stella's career continued to progress during the 1960s, as his work appeared in both national and international group shows, such as those at Brazil's São Paulo Biennial and Harvard University's Fogg Museum of Art, as well as the Solomon R. Guggenheim Museum's "The Shaped Canvas" exhibit in 1964. In works such as his metallic series, Stella focused on the relationship between the shape of a particular canvas and the shape of those objects depicted on that canvas, often using narrow slips of copper or aluminum paint to follow the canvas outline, whether it was a traditional square or rectangle or something irregularly shaped, such as a trapezoid or hexagon. The mid-1960s found Stella moving further away from his minimalist roots and now toying with color, using saturated tones, intersecting shades in decorative fashion, and even incorporating fluorescent colors into his works. In his "Irregular Polygons" series, from 1966, he exchanged narrow stripes for abstract shapes, creating purely pictorial shapes that did not represent any actual object. The following year he produced his "Protractor Series," which featured sweeping, sometimes overlapping arcs of brilliantly hued pigment painted within square borders and arranged to generate circular forms. Constantly innovative, Stella's work was never the same, and in 1970 when his output rated a retrospective exhibition at New York City's Museum of Modern Art, the talent, versatility, and vision of the thirty-three-year-old artist were clearly in evidence.

The Sensuous 'Seventies

During the 1970s Stella continued to experiment with irregularly shaped canvases, which were a feature of his "Polish Village" series. Introduced in 1970, the same year MoMA staged Stella's retrospective, the series incorporated cut pieces of paper, wood, felt, and canvas that were affixed to a stretched canvas, creating a three-dimensional collage effect. The series was inspired by the Jewish synagogues in Poland that were destroyed by the Nazis during World War II. "In making his works," wrote Clifford Chanin in an article posted on the *Legacy Project Web site,* "Stella was not thinking of the synagogues as artifacts of a murdered community. His starting point was the inventive design of these buildings, which happened to be the religious and communal centers of the now-lost Jewish villages of Poland. He was drawn to the builders of the synagogues as distant peers, not as victims, drawn to the singularity of their accomplishment, not the anonymity of their loss."

Stella's "Brazilian" series, begun in 1975, featured honeycomb aluminum and the same vivid colors he had used a decade earlier. Aluminum was also used in his "Exotic Birds" and "Indian Birds" series, in which steel mesh and smeared rather than brushed-on color added another dimensional element. By 1978 he had left straight lines altogether; now his mixed media pictures were animated with French curves and arabesques, as well as distinct brush strokes, giving them an organic look.

Stella standing in front of his painting "The Decanter" at a retrospective showing of his work at the Museum of Modern Art in 1987. (Mario Ruiz/Time and Life Pictures/Getty Images.)

Glittering scraps of metal were incorporated into Stella's artistic mix during the 1980s, beginning with his "Circuit" series and "Shards" series, the latter which featured angular scraps of cut metal applied to a flat aluminum "canvas." In the aptly named "Playskool" metal was joined by wooden dowels and wire mesh. On the strength of his versatility and creativity, Stella was asked to give the Charles Eliot Norton lectures at Harvard University, during the 1983-84 school year. His book *Working Space* is based on those lectures, and proposes that abstraction in art be rejuvenated by achieving the depth and complexity of baroque painting. In 1987 a collection from his work from the 1970s and 1980s was staged as a retrospective at MoMA.

Moves into Sculpture

Following a clear path from flat canvas to three-dimensional collage, Stella moved into wall sculpture in the early 1990s. Using bronze, brass, or stainless steel, he welded found metal and cast unique shapes to create dense, tangled, large-scale abstractions that suggested an overgrown exuberant nature. Other sculptural mediums included Styrofoam blocks, cast plaster, and fiberglass. Both in his sculpture and in his painting, Stella's work became larger in scope. In 1990, for example, he created a mural for Los Angeles' Gas Company Tower that was a full city block long, while another mural was installed at Toronto, Ontario's Prince of Wales Theatre. Other mural installations included the 97-foot-long, three-dimensional fiberglass mural "Loohooloo" that was put on display at New York's Knoedler Gallery. His large-scale sculpture "Prince of Homburg" was installed outside the East Building of the National Gallery of Art in Washington, DC, while in 1995 six metal sculptures were displayed at Manhattan's Gagosian Gallery in 1995, each named for a locale in New York's Hudson River Valley, a region wherein early-twentieth-century industrialization shares space with gracious estates and spectacular vistas. In addition to sculpture, Stella also began to develop an interest in designing public exhibition spaces and other

architecture, and in 1999 he designed an aluminum band shell for Miami, Florida. Many of Stella's architectural designs were included in a 2007 exhibit at the Metropolitan Museum of Art titled "Frank Stella: Painting into Architecture."

As Stella has developed as an artist, he has built on his past rather than discarded techniques and reinvented himself anew. This aspect of his career can be clearly seen in the many retrospectives of his work, which highlight that creative evolution, as well as in works such as "Moby-Dick," which he worked on from 1986 to 1997, to honor the 150th anniversary of Herman Melville's classic novel. With at least one work representing each of the novel's 135 chapters, "Moby-Dick" can be seen as a monumental assemblage of metal sculptures, lithograph prints, and collages, most images incorporating his characteristic vivid colors. Because of the scope of the work, the components of "Moby-Dick" are scattered throughout the world, but images of each piece are collected in Robert K. Wallace's *Moby-Dick: Words and Shapes*.

Speaking to Nancy Wolfson for the *Cigar Aficionado Online*, Stella explained the difference between

Stella's painting "Jasper's Dilemma." (ESM/Art Resource, NY. Reproduced by permission.)

Stella's painting "The Betrothal in Santa Domingo." (Copyright © 2001 Frank Stella/Artists Rights Society (ARS), New York. Art Resource, NY. Reproduced by permission of the publisher and the artist.)

realistic and abstract art: "If you painted a painting with a woman and a red triangle on the canvas, people would be more moved by the woman than by the triangle. On the other hand, it's possible they'd read more into the triangle than the woman. So with the abstract form you have a chance at a more open-ended kind of expression."

If you enjoy the artwork of Frank Stella, you may also want to check out the following artists:

The abstract expressionist painter Barnett Newman, the architect Richard Meier, and the Dada artist Kurt Schwitters.

While Stella continues to break new ground in his art, his earlier abstract minimalist works, such as his "Black Paintings," continue to be the most popular. According to a 2004 report in *ARTNews*, he is grouped, along with Jasper Johns, Cy Twombly, and Robert Rauschenberg, as one of the "Ten Most Expensive Living Artists," based on "the sum paid for a single work of art—regardless of how many works have sold at that level, the production costs involved in creating the work, or how prices for new works measure up." Noting the "brazen physicality" and Baroque quality of many of his more recent sculptures, Karen Wilkin wrote in *New Criterion* that, "in many ways, the brashly articulated, often brilliantly colored recent works Stella is exhibiting . . . are 180 degrees away from the sober, self-contained paintings that first established his reputation, almost fifty years ago." While his output may have changed, much else has not, Wilkin

contended. "Stella's art remains willful, insistent, and notably intelligent. In the best sense, it tests the limit of possibilities and it tests us. That's no small achievement." In *ARTNews*, Carol Diehl also noted Stella's changeability, explaining that, "unlike others of his stature, [he] uses his fame as a platform from which he takes the risk of failing. Even at his worst," Diehl added, "he's interesting, and each new turn provokes speculation as to what he'll do next."

■ Biographical and Critical Sources

BOOKS

Cooper, Harry, and Megan R. Luke, *Frank Stella 1958*, Yale University Press (New Haven, CT), 2006.

Goldberger, Paul, *Frank Stella: Painting into Architecture*, Yale University Press (New Haven, CT), 2007.

Guberman, Sidney, *Frank Stella: An Illustrated Biography*, Rizzoli International (New York, NY), 1995.

Rosenblum, Robert, *Frank Stella*, Penguin (New York, NY), 1970.

Rubin, William, *Frank Stella*, Museum of Modern Art (New York, NY), 1970.

Rubin, William, *Frank Stella, 1970-1987*, New York Graphic Society/Little, Brown (New York, NY), 1987.

Sylvester, David, *Interviews with American Artists*, Yale University Press (New Haven, CT), 2001.

Wallace, Robert K., *Frank Stella's Moby Dick: Words and Shapes*, University of Michigan Press (Ann Arbor, MI), 2000.

PERIODICALS

Apollo, July, 2006, David Anfam, "Eclecticism Is the Mother of Invention," p. 73.

Architectural Digest, September, 1983, Avis Berman, "Artist's Dialogue: A Conversation with Frank Stella," pp. 70, 74, 78; July, 1994, Suzanne Stephens, "Frank Stella: Blurring the Line between Art and Architecture," p. 30.

Art and Auction, February, 1983, Patricia Corbett, "Frank Stella," pp. 59-61.

Artforum (Los Angeles, CA), March, 1965, Robert Rosenblum, "Frank Stella: Five Years of Variations on an Irreducible Theme," pp. 21-25; November, 1966, Michael Fried, "Shape as Form: Frank Stella's New Paintings," pp. 18-27.

Art Forum (New York, NY), December, 1967, Jane Harrison Cone, "Frank Stella's New Paintings," pp. 34-41.

Art in America, January/February, 1972, Irving Sandler, "Stella at Rubin," p. 33; November/December, 1975, Roberta Smith, "Frank Stella's New Paintings: The Thrill Is Back," pp. 86-88; February, 1985, Carter Ratcliff, "Frank Stella: Portrait of the Artist as Image Administrator," pp. 94-107.

Art Monthly, May, 1977, Juliet Steyn, "Frank Stella Talks about His Recent Work," pp. 14-15.

ARTNews, September, 1966, Bruce Glaser, "New Nihilism or New Art?," pp. 55-61; January, 1968, Freerick Castle, "What's That, the '68 Stella? Wow!," pp. 46-47, 68-71; November, 1971, Elizabeth C. Baker, "Frank Stella: Revival and Relief," p. 34; February, 1980, Richard Whelan, "Frank Stella: All Dressed up with No Place to Go," p. 76; January, 1995, Carol Diehl, "Frank Stella," p. 160; May, 1996, George Stolz, "Frank Stella," p. 145; May, 2004, Kelly Devine Thomas, "The Ten Most Expensive Living Artists."

Arts, December, 1969-January, 1970, Nicolas Calas, "Frank Stella, the Theologian," pp. 29-31; December, 1976, Noel Frackman, "Frank Stella's Abstract Expressionist Aerie: A Reading of Stella's New Paintings," pp. 124-126.

Artscribe, July, 1977, Peter Rippon, Terence Maloon, and Ben Jones, "Frank Stella," pp. 13-17.

Atlantic Monthly, October, 1986, Hilton Kramer, review of *Working Space*, pp. 94, 96-98.

Boston Sunday Globe, July 14, 1968, George Kane, "Stripes and Shapes by Stella," pp. 28-32.

Christian Science Monitor, September 23, 1968, Christopher Andreae, "Frank Stella," p. 8.

Cigar Aficionado, autumn, 1995, Nancy Wolfson, "Rings of Art: Frank Stella, One of the Most Renowned Artists of the Late Twentieth Century, Has Been Using Cigar Smoke as an Inspiration."

Economist, June 3, 2000, "Frank Stella's 'Panatellas,'" p. 136.

GEO, March, 1982, Emile de Antonio, "Geo-conversation: Frank Stella—A Passion for Painting," pp. 13-16.

Harvard Magazine, May-June, 1984, Caroline Jones, "Spaces and the Enterprise of Painting," pp. 44-51.

Jerusalem Post Magazine, May 22, 1981, Meir Rommen, "Frank Stella on Making Art," p. 17.

Lugano Review, summer, 1965, Robert Creeley, "Frank Stella: A Way to Go," pp. 189-197.

Nation, March 28, 1966, Max Kozloff, review of Stella's exhibition at the Leo Castelli Gallery, pp. 370-372.

New Criterion, June, 2003, James Panero, "Gallery Chronicle"; June, 2007, Karen Wilkin, "Frank Stella Three Ways," p. 42.

Newsday, July 9, 1986, Celia McGee, "Art Takes Its Chances, and Its Knocks: The *New York Newsday* Interview with Frank Stella."

New York Times, January 19, 1964, Brian O'Doherty, "Frank Stella and a Crisis of Nothingness," Section 2, p. 21; December 10, 1967, Hilton Kramer, "Frank Stella: 'What You See Is What You See,'" Section 2, p. 39; March 25, 1970, Hilton Kramer, "Art: A Retrospective of Frank Stella," p. 34; January 21, 1973, Peter Schjeldahl, "Frank Stella: The Best—and the Last—of His Breed?," Section 2, p. 23; January 19, 1978, John Russell, "Stella Shows His Metal in SoHo," pp. C1, C16; May 14, 1978, Hilton Kramer, "Frank Stella's Vigorous Reaffirmation," p. D27; February 1, 1985, John Russell, "The Power of Frank Stella," pp. C1, C22; December 7, 1986, Douglas C. McGill, "Stella Elucidates Abstract Art's Link to Realism"; May 4, 2007, Roberta Smith, "Beyond Paintbrush Boundaries: Imagining Structures in 3-D."

Time, November 24, 1967, "Painting: Minimal Cartwheels," pp. 64-65.

Times Literary Supplement, March 27, 1987, John Golding, review of *Working Space*, pp. 311-312.

Vanity Fair, November, 1983, "Frank Stella Talks About . . .," p. 94.

Village Voice, March 24, 1966, David Bourdon, "A New Direction," p. 17; May 19, 1975, David Bourdon, "Frank Stella."

Vogue, November 15, 1969, Robert Rosenblum, "Frank Stella," pp. 116-117, 160.

ONLINE

Bomb Magazine Online, http://www.bombsite.com/ (July 24, 2007), Saul Ostrow, "Frank Stella."

Guggenheim Collection Web site, http://www.guggenheimcollection.org/ (June 25, 2007), "Frank Stella."

Legacy Project Web site, http://www.legacy-project.org/ (November 19, 2007), Clifford Chanin, "Frank Stella: The Polish Village Series."*

Caroline Stevermer

(Photograph by Katrina Nesse. Used by permission.)

■ Personal

Surname is pronounced "*Steve*-er-mer"; born January 13, 1955, in Houston, MN; daughter of John Weaver (a farmer) and Carol Jean (a teacher) Stevermer. *Education:* Bryn Mawr College, B.A., 1977.

■ Addresses

Home—Minneapolis, MN. *Office*—Star Tribune, 425 Portland Ave., Minneapolis, MN 55488. *Agent*—Frances Collins Literary Agency, P.O. Box 33, Wayne, PA 19087-0033.

■ Career

Writer. Clerical worker, 1977-84; *Star Tribune* (newspaper), Minneapolis, MN, became editorial assistant, beginning 1984.

■ Member

Newspaper Guild.

■ Writings

NOVELS

(Under name C.J. Stevermer) *The Alchemist: Death of a Borgia* (mystery), Ace Books (New York, NY), 1980.

(Under name C.J. Stevermer) *The Duke and the Veil* (mystery), Ace Books (New York, NY), 1981.

The Serpent's Egg (fantasy), Ace Books (New York, NY), 1988.

(With Patricia C. Wrede) *Sorcery and Cecelia* (fantasy), Ace Books (New York, NY), 1988, revised edition published as *Sorcery and Cecelia; or, The Enchanted Chocolate Pot: Being the Correspondence of Two Young Ladies of Quality Regarding Various Magical Scandals in London and the Country*, Harcourt (Orlando, FL), 2003.

River Rats (science fiction), Harcourt (San Diego, CA), 1992.

A College of Magics (fantasy), Tor (New York, NY), 1994.

When the King Comes Home (fantasy), Tor (New York, NY), 2000.

A Scholar of Magics (fantasy; sequel to *A College of Magics*), Tor (New York, NY), 2004.

(With Patricia C. Wrede) *The Grand Tour; or, The Purloined Coronation Regalia: Being a Revelation of Matters of High Confidentiality and Greatest Importance, Including Extracts from the Intimate Diary of a Noblewoman and the Sworn Testimony of a Lady of Quality* (fantasy), Harcourt (Orlando, FL), 2004.

Scholarly Magics (fantasy; includes *A College of Magics* and *A Scholar of Magics*), 2004.
(With Patricia C. Wrede) *The Mislaid Magician; or, Ten Years After,* Harcourt (Orlando, FL), 2006.

OTHER

Work represented in anthologies, including *Liavek: Wizard's Row,* edited by Will Shetterly and Emma Bull, Ace Books (New York, NY), 1987; *Snow White, Blood Red,* edited by Terri Windling and Ellen Datlow, Morrow (New York, NY), 1993; *The Armless Maiden,* edited by Terri Windling, Tor (New York, NY), 1995; and *The Essential Bordertown,* edited by Terri Windling and Delia Sherman, Tor (New York, NY), 1998.

■ Sidelights

Fantasy novelist Caroline Stevermer has set many of her novels in alternate versions of the past. *The Serpent's Egg* is set in an alternate Elizabethan England that never was; *A College of Magics* and *A Scholar of Magics* are set in a world very much like late 19th-century England, but magic is commonplace; and, in the novels she has written with fellow fantasy novelist Patricia C. Wrede, in a Europe strangely similar to the early twentieth century, but one where magic and sorcery are everyday necessities. Stevermer's novels are often described as a blend of the Regency romance genre with fantasy.

Speaking of her early years, Stevermer once wrote: "I was born on a Minnesota dairy farm within ten miles of the Mississippi River, where an occasional steamboat still churned the muddy waters. I do try not to boast about the one-room country schoolhouse where I acquired four years of education before switching to the 'town school.' After a summer as an exchange student in Sao Paolo, Brazil, I went to Bryn Mawr College in Pennsylvania, where I majored in history of art and the *Million Dollar Movie* on Channel 49.

"After graduation, I tried like hell to live in New York City but found I had no aptitude. As soon as they would let me, I returned to Minnesota. I now speak fluent Minnesotan, take an avid interest in the weather, and spend countless hours every summer at the State Fair."

Mysterious Goings-on During the Renaissance

Stevermer's first novels were mysteries set during the Italian Renaissance and featuring the English alchemist Nicholas Coffin as sleuth. In *The Alchemist:*

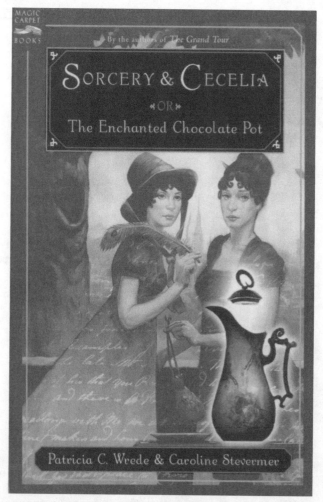

The 2004 edition of the alternate-universe novel in which two friends, Kate and Cecy, exchange letters about the romantic mysteries with which they become involved. (Magic Carpet Books, 2004. Copyright © 2003 by Patricia C. Wrede and Caroline Stevermer. Reproduced by permission of Harcourt, Inc. This material may not be reproduced in any form or by any means without the prior written permission of the publisher.)

Death of a Borgia, murder is committed by using an ingenious poison, one that seeps from a plate's ceramic surface only when touched by hot food. In *The Duke and the Veil,* a murder occurs inside a locked room that was under observation from the outside. When he is not solving such puzzling deaths, Coffin works at the typical alchemist quest of finding the Philosopher's Stone—the means of transforming base lead into pure gold. But Coffin's alchemical furnace keeps blowing up on him.

In Stevermer's next novel, *The Serpent's Egg,* the story moves into pure fantasy. Set in an alternative Elizabethan England where magic in the form of a fabulous crystal called the serpent's egg plays a main role, the story is again a murder mystery. The head of the queen's army is murdered and, while it is known who committed the crime, the killer is so highly-placed in the aristocracy that he is untouchable. Those who wish to see justice done search for the serpent's egg which, while dangerously powerful, can also be used as an effective weapon against the murderer. An essayist for the *St. James Guide to Fantasy Writers* described the story as being full of "engrossing and actionful struggle."

Story of the River Rat

In Stevermer's 1992 sci-fi adventure *River Rats,* she tells the post-apocalyptic story of a group of orphaned teenagers—Tomcat, Esteban and Toby—who ply the polluted Mississippi River in their restored steam-powered paddle-boat, the River Rat. They swap mail, freight, and rock concerts for food, water and clothing. Saving an old man called King from the toxic river breaks their vow to never take on passengers and marks their unplanned involvement with the violent Lester family. According to Ann A. Flowers in a *Horn Book* review, *River Rats* is "an unusual, compelling futuristic novel." Likewise, a *Publishers Weekly* reviewer praised the setting and premise of the story, noting that the author's "unwavering interest in the individuals who live there distinguishes the novel from mere space opera."

Set in an alternate world that resembles historical England of the late nineteenth century, *A College of Magics* revolves around the activities of the teen-aged Duchy of Galazon, Faris Nallaneen. Faris is not yet old enough to claim her throne, so she is sent to the College of Greenlaw while her uncle rules the Duchy for her. Happy to have Faris out of his way, little does Uncle Brinker know that Greenlaw specializes in magic and that Faris will return equipped with the talents and skills she needs to regain her throne. Traveling to Galazon by the Orient Express, she and her best friend Jane encounter assassins and other obstacles before they are able to reach the Duchy. In the words of a *Publishers Weekly* contributor, *A College of Magics* is "clever and witty at its best, this is generally a pleasant read." "To call a book an instant classic is a large hat for a novel to be forced to wear in its publishing infancy," declared Charles De Lint in the Magazine of Science Fiction and Fantasy, "but I don't doubt, all the same, that *A College of Magics* will endure as a favorite of discerning readers for a very long time indeed."

Faris's friend Jane Brailsford returns in *A Scholar of Magics.* Jane is attending England's Glasscastle University when she meets Samuel Lambert, a talented American sharpshooter who has been asked to test a new magical weapon for the university fellows. The pair become involved in a series of wild chases and escapes, attacks and kidnappings, and uncover the secret of a legacy of powerful magic. Michelle West, writing in the *Magazine of Fantasy and Science Fiction,* found that Stevermer's "world is both intelligently and lovingly detailed." "This is the perfect read," the critic for *Publishers Weekly* noted, "for those who enjoy taking ambling walks in orderly alternate worlds where calling cards and starched collars still help make a man."

When the King Comes Home is also a tale of discovery by a young woman with special powers and responsibilities. Hail Rosmer, the young daughter of a rich wool merchant, is apprenticed to an artist.

This 2005 novel is set in a future post-apocalyptic world in which a group of teenagers ply the Mississippi River on a steam-powered riverboat. (Magic Carpet Books, 2005. Copyright © 1992 by Caroline Stevermer. Reprinted by permission of Harcourt, Inc. This material may not be reproduced in any form or by any means without the prior written permission of the publisher.)

This 2006 novel finds Western sharpshooter Samuel Lambert called to Glasscastle University to assist in a secret project. (Starscape, 2006. Reproduced by permission.)

She discovers a medal depicting the legendary King Julian and becomes obsessed with it. Legend says that when needed most, King Julian will reappear and save the kingdom. When Hail believes she has seen King Julian fishing on a riverbank, she befriends him. *Library Journal* reviewer Jackie Cassada praised the "winsome" first-person narration. The novel is "beautifully rendered," concluded a critic for *Kirkus Reviews*. Ginger Armstrong in *Kliatt* found that "the novel is a delight. The plot moves at a brisk pace, and Hail is definitely a strong heroine." Roland Green in *Booklist* called *When the King Comes Home* "a witty tale of what really can happen when legends come to life."

Collaborates with Patricia Wrede

Stevermer has also written three novels with Patricia Wrede. All three novels consist of correspondence between two characters; the two authors took turns writing the letters in character. The first of these novels, *Sorcery and Cecelia*, was revised in 2003 as *Sorcery and Cecelia; or, The Enchanted Chocolate Pot: Being the Correspondence of Two Young Ladies of Quality Regarding Various Magical Scandals in London and the Country*. The novel consists of letters written between two cousins, Katherine (better known as Kate) and Cecelia (nicknamed Cecy), in an alternate-universe, magical, nineteenth-century England. Michele Winship in *Kliatt* called the novel a "charming book told in voices that play off each other in a literary tennis match." When Kate moves to London, Cecy remains in the country, but both quickly find themselves engrossed in romances and mysteries involving poison and sorcery. "Kate and Cecy are witty, intelligent, and venturesome heroines. . . .," according to a *Kirkus Reviews* critic. "This clever romp will appeal to fans of Regency romance and light fantasy."

Kate and Cecy, as well as their new husbands, return in *The Grand Tour; or, The Purloined Coronation Regalia: Being a Revelation of Matters of High Confidentiality and Greatest Importance, Including Extracts from the Intimate Diary of a Noblewoman and the Sworn Testimony of a Lady of Quality*. As the foursome travels through Europe on their honeymoon tours, they come to realize that a group of sorcerers is trying to create an evil empire, so they set out to prevent it. Kay Weisman in *Booklist* described the novel as "a satisfying blend of magic, mystery, adventure, humor, and romance." Writing in *Kliatt*, Claire Rosser found that *The Grand Tour* combines "the formality of the comedy of manners of Austen with magic spells and sorcery. An odd combination, but charming." "It's great fun to watch the authors tweak the tropes of Regency romance into a fantastical mode," commented a *Kirkus Reviews* contributor, and *School Library Journal* reviewer Janet Hilbun noted that "the characters shine as they struggle with their magical legacy and grand adventure."

If you enjoy the works of Caroline Stevermer, you may also want to check out the following books:

Sharon Shimm, *Summers at Castle Auburn*, 2002.
Tamora Pierce, *Will of the Empress*, 2006.
Maria V. Snyder, *Poison Study*, 2007.

The story continues in the 2006 title *The Mislaid Magician; or, Ten Years After*, in which the Duke of Wellington asks Cecy's husband to locate a missing magician. When the couple leave to investigate, they leave their children in the care of Kate and her husband. The correspondence between Cecy, recounting their sleuthing, and Kate, commenting upon it and offering suggestions, is the core of the novel. Jennifer Stubben, writing in the *School Library Journal*, believed that "fans of the first two books will certainly enjoy revisiting these delightful characters." A critic for Kirkus Reviews found that "readers will be captivated by the engaging, headstrong Cecy and reliable (if maladroit) Kate, and charmed by the unexpected twists that a touch of fantasy yields in familiar Regency tropes."

■ Biographical and Critical Sources

BOOKS

St. James Guide to Fantasy Writers, St. James Press (Detroit, MI), 1996.

PERIODICALS

Analog Science Fiction & Fact, September, 1994, Tom Easton, review of *A College of Magics*, pp. 163-164.

Booklist, April 1, 1992, Chris Sherman, review of *River Rats*, p. 1440; October 1, 1992, review of *River Rats*, p. 341; March 15, 1993, review of *River Rats*, p. 1343; March 1, 1994, Roland Green, review of *A College of Magics*, p. 1185; November 15, 2000, Roland Green, review of *When the King Comes Home*, p. 625; April 1, 2004, Frieda Murray, review of *A Scholar of Magics*, p. 1357; September 1, 2004, Kay Weisman, review of *The Grand Tour; or, The Purloined Coronation Regalia: Being a Revelation of Matters of High Confidentiality and Greatest Importance, Including Extracts from the Intimate Diary of a Noblewoman and the Sworn Testimony of a Lady of Quality*, p. 109; January 1, 2007, Carolyn Phelan, review of *The Mislaid Magician; or, Ten Years After*, p. 81.

Book Report, November, 1992, Donna Pool Miller, review of *River Rats*, p. 46.

Bookwatch, June, 1994, review of *A College of Magics*, p. 11.

Bulletin of the Center for Children's Books, July, 1992, review of *River Rats*, p. 306.

Children's Book Review Service, July, 1992, review of *River Rats*, p. 156.

English Journal, January, 1993, John H. Bushman and Kay Parks Bushman, review of *River Rats*, p. 80.

Horn Book, September-October, 1992, Ann A. Flowers, review of *River Rats*, p. 589.

Horn Book Guide, fall, 1992, review of *River Rats*, p. 271.

Journal of Reading, September, 1993, review of *River Rats*, p. 72.

Kirkus Reviews, May 1, 1992, review of *River Rats*, p. 617; February 1, 1994, review of *A College of Magics*, p. 104; October 1, 2000, review of *When the King Comes Home*, p. 1394; April 15, 2003, review of *Sorcery and Cecelia; or, The Enchanted Chocolate Pot: Being the Correspondence of Two Young Ladies of Quality Regarding Various Magical Scandals in London and the Country*, p. 613; February 1, 2004, review of *A Scholar of Magics*, p. 114; September 1, 2004, review of *The Grand Tour*, p. 875; November 1, 2006, review of *The Mislaid Magician*, p. 1125.

Kliatt, January, 1997, review of *River Rats*, p. 16; May, 2002, Ginger Armstrong, review of *When the King Comes Home*, p. 30; May, 2003, Michele Winship, review of *Sorcery and Cecelia*, p. 15; November, 2004, Michele Winship, review of *Sorcery and Cecelia*, p. 26; July, 2006, Claire Rosser, review of *The Grand Tour*, p. 28; November, 2006, Sherry Hoy, review of *A Scholar of Magics*, p. 30.

Library Journal, November 15, 2000, Jackie Cassada, review of *When the King Comes Home*, p. 101; April 15, 2004, Jackie Cassada, review of *A Scholar of Magics*, p. 129.

Locus, April, 1994, review of *A College of Magics*, p. 50; February, 1995, review of *A College of Magics*, p. 39.

Magazine of Fantasy and Science Fiction, August, 1994, Charles de Lint, review of *A College of Magics*, pp. 29-30; October, 2003, Elizabeth Hand, review of *Sorcery and Cecelia*, p. 55; September, 2004, Michelle West, review of *A Scholar of Magics*, p. 34; August, 2006, Charles de Lint, review of *River Rats*, p. 40.

Publishers Weekly, March 16, 1992, review of *River Rats*, p. 81; February 14, 1994, review of *A College of Magics*, p. 84; April 5, 2004, review of *A Scholar of Magics*, p. 46.

School Library Journal, August, 1992, Jack Forman, review of *River Rats*, p. 178; August, 1998, review of *River Rats*, p. 51; November, 2004, Janet Hilbun, review of *The Grand Tour*, p. 156; January, 2007, Jennifer Stubben, review of *The Mislaid Magician*, p. 142.

Voice of Youth Advocates, June, 1992, review of *River Rats*, p. 115; August, 1994, review of *A College of Magics*, p. 160; April, 1998, review of *River Rats*, p. 42.

Washington Post Book World, February 27, 1994, review of *A College of Magics,* p. 11.

Wilson Library Bulletin, December, 1992, Gene La-Faille, review of *River Rats,* pp. 94-95; October, 1994, Fred Lerner, a review of *A College of Magics,* pp. 96-97.

ONLINE

Caroline Stevermer Home Page, http://members.authorsguild.net/carolinestev (November 19, 2007).

Enchanted Chocolate Pot, http://www.tc.umn.edu/~d-lena/Stevermer%20page.html/ (November 19, 2007).*

(Photograph courtesy of AP Images.)

Personal

Born July 2, 1923 in Prowent-Bnin (now Kórnik), Poland; daughter of Wincenty (the steward of Count Wladyslaw Zamoyski's family estate) and Anna Szymborski; married Adam Wlodek, 1948 (divorced, 1954); married Kornel Filipowicz (died, 1990). *Education:* Attended Jagiellonian University, 1945-48.

Addresses

Home—Ul. Krolewska 82/89, 30-079, Kraców, Poland.

Career

Poet and critic. *Zycie literackie* (literary weekly magazine), poetry editor and columnist, 1953-81; *Pismo* (magazine), editor, 1981-83.

Member

Writers' Association (member of general board, 1978-83).

Wislawa Szymborska

Awards, Honors

City of Kraców Literary Prize, 1954; Gold Cross of Merit, 1955; Minister of Culture prize, 1963; Knight's Cross, Order of Polonia Resituta, 1974; Goethe Prize, 1991; Herder Prize, 1995; honorary Ph.D., Adam Mickiewicz University, 1995; Polish PEN Club Award, 1996; Nobel Prize for Literature, Swedish Academy, 1996.

Writings

POETRY

Dlatego zyjemy (title means "That's What We Live For"), [Warsaw, Poland], 1952.

Pytania zadawane sobie (title means "Questions Put to Myself"), [Warsaw, Poland], 1954.

Wolanie do Yeti (title means "Calling out to Yeti"), [Warsaw, Poland], 1957.

Sól (title means "Salt"), Panstwowy Instytut Wydawniczy (Warsaw, Poland), 1962.

Wiersze wybrane (collection), Panstwowy Instytut Wydawniczy (Warsaw, Poland), 1964, reprinted, 2000.

Sto pociech (title means "A Hundred Joys"), Panstwowy Instytut Wydawniczy (Warsaw, Poland), 1967.

Poezje wybrane (title means "Selected Poems"), Ludowa Spoldzielnia Wydawnicza (Warsaw, Poland), 1967.

Poezje, Przedmowa Jerzego Kwiatkowskiego (Warsaw, Poland), 1970.

Wybor poezje (collection), Czytelnik (Warsaw, Poland), 1970.

Wszelki wypadek (title means "There but for the Grace"), Czytelnik (Warsaw, Poland), 1972.

Wybor wierszy (collection), Panstwowy Instytut Wydawniczy (Warsaw, Poland), 1973.

Tarsjusz i inne wiersze (title means "Tarsius and Other Poems"), Krajowa Agencja Wydawnicza (Warsaw, Poland), 1976.

Wielka liczba (title means "A Great Number"), Czytelnik (Warsaw, Poland), 1976.

Sounds, Feelings, Thoughts: Seventy Poems, translation by Magnus J. Krynski and Robert A. Maguire, Princeton University Press (Princeton, NJ), 1981.

Poezje wybrane (II) (title means "Selected Poems II"), Ludowa Spoldzielnia Wydawnicza (Warsaw, Poland), 1983.

Poezje = Poems (bilingual edition), translation by Magnus J. Krynski and Robert A. Maguire, Wydawnictwo Literackie (Kracćw, Poland), 1989.

Ludzie na moscie, Czytelnik (Warsaw, Poland), 1986, translation by Adam Czerniawski published as *People on a Bridge: Poems*, Forest (Boston, MA), 1990.

Wieczor autorski: wiersze (title means "Authors' Evening: Poems"), Anagram (Warsaw, Poland), 1992.

Koniec i poczatek (title means "The End and the Beginning"), Wydawnictwo Literackie (Kracćw, Poland), 1993.

View with a Grain of Sand: Selected Poems, translation by Stanislaw Baranczak and Clare Cavanagh, Harcourt (New York, NY), 1995.

Widok z ziarnkiem piasku: 102 Wiersze, Wydawnictwo Literacki (Kracćw, Poland), 1996.

Nothing Twice: Selected Poems, selected and translated by Stanislaw Baranczak and Clare Cavanagh, Wydawnictwo Literackie (Kracćw, Poland), 1997.

Hundert Gedichte, Hundert Freuden, Wydawnictwo Literackie (Kracćw, Poland), 1997.

O asmierci bez przesady = de la mort sans exagerer, Wydawnictwo Literackie (Kracćw, Poland), 1997.

Nulla e in regalo, Wydawnictwo Literackie (Kracćw, Poland), 1998.

Poems: New and Collected, 1957-1997, translation by Stanislaw Baranczak and Clare Cavanagh, Harcourt Brace (New York, NY), 1998, published as *Poems: New and Collected*, 2000.

Nic darowane = Keyn shum masoneh = Nothing's a gift = Nichts ist geschenkt = Me'um lo nitan be-matanah, Amerykansko-Polsko-Izraelska Fundacja Shalom (Warsaw, Poland), 1999.

Poczta literacka, czyli, Jak zostac (lub nie zostac) pisarzem, Wydawnictwo Literackie (Kracćw, Poland), 2000.

Miracle Fair: Selected Poems of Wislawa Szymborska, translation by Joanna Trzeciak, with a foreword by Czeslaw Milosz, Norton (New York, NY), 2001.

Nowe lektury nadobowiazkowe: 1997-2002, Wydawnictwo Literackie (Kracćw, Poland), 2002.

Nonrequired Reading: Prose Pieces (book reviews), translated from the Polish by Clare Cavanagh, Harcourt (New York, NY), 2002.

Chwila (title means "Moment"), Wydawnictwo Literackie (Kracćw, Poland), 2002, bilingual edition published as *Chwila/Moment*, translation by Clare Cavanagh and Stanislaw Baranczak, 2003.

Wierze, BOSZ (Olszanica, Poland), 2003.

Rymowanki dla duzych dzieci: z wyklejankami autorki (title means "Rhymes for Big Kids"), Wydawnictwo Literackie (Kracćw, Poland), 2003.

Dwukropek (title means "Colon"), 2005.

Monologue of a Dog, translation by Clare Cavanagh and Stanislaw Baranczak, Harcourt (New York, NY), 2006.

OTHER

Lektury nadobowiazkowe (collected book reviews; title means "Non-Compulsory Reading"), Wydawnictwo Literackie (Kracćw, Poland), 1973.

Zycie na poczekaniu: Lekcja literatury z Jerzym Kwiatowskim i Marianem Stala, Wydawnictwo Literackie (Kracćw, Poland), 1996.

Translator of poetry from the French, including works by Agrippa d'Aubigné. Contributor to anthologies, including *Polish Writing Today*, Penguin (New York, NY), 1967; *The New Polish Poetry*, University of Pittsburgh Press (Pittsburgh, PA), 1978; *Anthologie de la poesie polonaise: 1400-1980*, revised edition, Age d'homme, 1981; *The Burning Forest: Modern Polish Poetry*, edited and translated by Adam Czerniawski, Bloodaxe Books, 1988; and *Ariadne's Thread: Polish Women Poets*, edited and translated by Susan Bassnett and Piotr Kuhiwczak, 1988. Contributor of poems to journals, including *Poetry, Triquarterly, Ploughshares*, and *Christian Century*. Contributor, under pseudonym Stanczykówna, to *Arka* (underground publication) and *Kultura* (Paris, France).

Author's work translated into numerous languages, including English, German, Swedish, Italian, Danish, Hebrew, Hungarian, Czech, Slovakian, Serbo-Croatian, Romanian, and Bulgarian.

■ Sidelights

Poet Wislawa Szymborska is one of the most beloved literary figures in her native Poland. Her work has gained a much broader exposure, and a world-wide readership, since Szymborska was honored as the recipient of the Nobel Prize for Literature in 1996. "Like so many Polish poets before her," wrote Lys Anzia in *Moondance,* "Szymborska's wisdom spans numerous wars and changes in politics and national governments. As Poland escaped from the tyranny of military coups, insurgent coalitions, and the ever shifting ends of the political tirade, this is the place where many of the world's best poets were created." "Szymborska is a poet who is read and admired even by people who do not like poetry," Joanna Trzeciak wrote in the *Dictionary of Literary Biography.* "Precise in diction, playful and elegant, her poetry presents few barriers to entry."

A prolific author, Szymborska has seen many of her books translated into English, among them *People on a Bridge, Nonrequired Reading: Prose Pieces,* and *View with a Grain of Sand,* the last of which became a poetry best-seller when it was published in 1995. According to *Los Angeles Times* critic Dean E. Murphy, Szymborska is a master of "seductively simple verse" and in her poems she has successfully "captured the wit and wisdom of everyday life" as it was lived in Poland during the twentieth century. In addition to the Nobel honor, Szymborska was awarded the Goethe Prize in 1991, and the Herder Prize in 1995.

Nobel Prize-winner Szymborska seated at a banquet table. (Copyright © Vander Zwalm Dan/Sygma/CORBIS.)

Szymborska was born in 1923, in Prowent-Bnin (now part of Kórnick), an industrial town in western Poland. At age three her family moved to Torun, and in 1931 they relocated to Kracöw, where they found a home near the railway station and Szymborska attended a convent school. Because her parents were well educated, books and reading were an important part of family life. Prior to his death in 1936, when Szymborska was thirteen years old, her father also encouraged her fledgling efforts at writing poetry. An interest in American films, such as *The Mummy,* starring Boris Karloff, also inspired her interest in history and theatre.

World War and Its Aftermath

Life changed for Szymborska, as it did for people all across Europe, when World War II broke out. German occupation forces entered Poland in 1939, but Szymborska and her family were determined to remain in Kracöw. Despite the suppression of local culture under the Nazis, Szymborska worked as a prompter for an underground theater troupe and found ways to continue her education under the Nazi radar. In 1943, fearing that she would be sent to Germany as a laborer, the twenty-year-old Szymborska got a job as a railroad employee that allowed her to remain in Kracöw. She channeled her creativity into art, illustrating an English-language text, and also began writing short stories and verse.

While attending Jagiellonian University from 1945 to 1948, Szymborska began the study of Polish literature, but her fascination with people and culture soon prompted a switch to sociology. She also published her first poem, "Szukam slowa," in a local daily newspaper while she was still a student. Due to a lack of money, she was unable to complete her degree; in 1948 she left school, found a job as a secretary for an educational magazine, and married poet Adam Wlodek. Although her marriage was

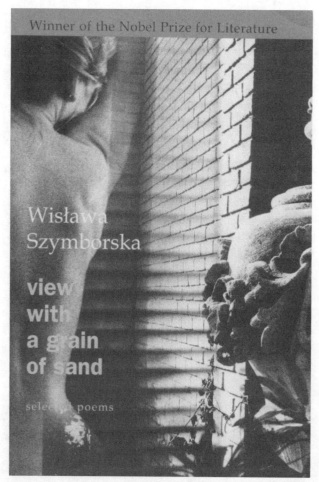

This 1995 collection contains one hundred of Szymborska's poems. (Cover photograph: Moon over Urn by Shelton Walsmith. Harcourt, 1995. English translation by Stanislaw Baranczak and Clare Cavanagh. Copyright © 1998 by Harcourt, Inc. Reprinted by permission of the publisher. This material may not be reproduced in any form or by any means without the prior written permission of the publisher.)

short lived, the couple became involved in Kracóiw's underground literary community, where Szymborska met and was inspired by a young writer named Czeslaw Milosz. Continuing to publish individual poems in local newspapers, she completed her first verse collection the same year she completed her formal education, but could not get her work published due to the dramatic shift in Poland's political climate as communism took hold. With Soviet occupation troops in the country, Poland adopted a Soviet-style constitution. The country's new communist government, working to further entrench itself in the Soviet bloc, was careful to restrict what publishers could print, and Szymborska's poetry was considered too elitist and "bourgeois" to be a benefit to the proletarian masses. Like many Polish intellectuals who had lived during the

Nazi occupation, she at first embraced the socialist ideology of Lenin and Marx, joined the Polish United Workers' party, and willingly revised her poems to suit party officials. Accordingly, in 1952 *Dlatego zyjemy* was printed by a Warsaw publisher.

Growing Disillusionment with Socialism

Although 1954's *Pytania zadawane sobie* shared much with *Dlatego zyjemy*, by the mid-1950s, Szymborska had grow estranged from socialist ideology. Although continuing as a member of the Polish United Party until the mid-1960s, she began to distance herself from her earlier work and developed contact with intellectual dissidents. Although she never became a political activist herself, as a chronicler of the average Polish citizen, she injected her verse with a growing hostility toward the status quo of communist Poland.

In 1953, Szymborska had joined the staff of *Zycie Literackiethe* ("Literary Life"), a literary review in Kracóiw. She served as poetry editor until 1981, when she resigned from her position because of her editor's opposition to Solidarity, the political movement led by Lech Walesa that agitated for economic and political freedoms. She also contributed book reviews through her column "Lektury nadobowiazkowe" beginning in 1968. Her essays and reviews for *Zycie Literackiethe*, collected in book form, include *Nonrequired Reading: Prose Pieces*. Szymborska's "gift for compression" is apparent throughout this work, according to *Library Journal* contributor Nancy R. Ives, the critic going on to praise the "skillful simplicity and lyric quality" of the volume. In each of the prose pieces included, the poet "captures large concepts and brilliantly reduces them to pithy, two-page essays," Ives concluded.

After leaving the *Zycie Literackiethe*, Szymborska spent two years as editor of the monthly magazine *Pismo*, and increasingly worked to oppose the waning power of Poland's communist Prime Minister General Wojciech Jaruzelski, whose efforts to impose martial law following the formation of Solidarity would ultimately fail. Under the pseudonym Stanczykówna, she contributed writing to an underground *samizat* magazine, while continuing to write for *Kultura*, a Paris-based emigré journal edited by her friend, Jerzy Giedroyc.

Signaling a transition, Szymborska's 1957 collection, *Wolanie do Yeti*, expresses her compassion for her fellow Poles and mixes a lighthearted humor with an underlying sense of the tragic. With both *Sól*, published in 1962, and *Sto pociech*, published in

1967, she was seen to mature as a poet. Moving away from the political focus of compatriots Zbiegnew Herbert and Milosz, Szymborska redefined herself as a student of humanity and a chronicler of the everyday. In simple language, she speaks of ordinary things, only to reveal extraordinary truths. In *Publishers Weekly*, Joanna Trzeciak praised "the wit and clarity of Szymborska's turns of phrase. Under her pen, simple language becomes striking. Ever the gentle subversive, she stubbornly refuses to see anything in the world as ordinary. The result is a poetry of elegance and irony, full of surprising turns."

Gains International Stature

More recent collections of verse by Szymborska have continued to cement her literary stature, and

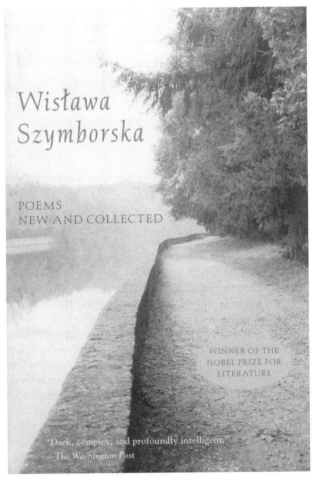

This 2000 collection gathers the best of forty years' worth of Szymborska's poems. (Harcourt, 2000. Copyright © 1993 by Wislawa Szymborsak, English translation by Stanislaw Baranczak and Clare Cavanagh. Copyright © 1998 by Harcourt, Inc. Reprinted by permission of hte publisher. This material may not be reproduced in any form or by any means without the prior written permission of the publisher.)

by the 1990s her work was included in the curriculum in Polish schools. With the translation into English of selected poems as the critically acclaimed *Sounds, Feelings, Thoughts: Seventy Poems*, she began to gain an international readership. Calling her voice "the most elusive as well as the most distinctive" of those post-war Polish writers whose works had been translated, Jaroslaw Anders commented in the *New York Review of Books* that *Sounds, Feelings, Thoughts* "is of interest not only because of Szymborska's importance as a poet, but also because her work demonstrates that the diversity of poetic modes in Poland is much greater than is usually perceived." Alice-Catherine Carls, in a review of the collection for *Library Journal*, praised it as "one of those rare books which put one in a state of 'grace,'" while Robert Hudzik maintained in the same periodical that the volume "reveals a poet of startling originality and deep sympathy."

View with a Grain of Sand provided English-speaking readers a broader view of Szymborska's work. Encompassing the years 1957 through 1993, the collection includes verses from *Koniec i poczatek* that reflect on the poet's long marriage to her husband and her grief following his death in 1990. Published in 1995, *View with a Grain of Sand* became somewhat of a poetry best seller when Szymborska was announced as the recipient of the 1996 Nobel Prize in Literature. Writing in the *New York Review of Books*, Edward Hirsch stated that the work reveals "the full force of [Szymborska's] fierce and unexpected wit," a wit Louis McKee dubbed "wonderfully wicked" in her *Library Journal* review. Lauding Szymborska's directness and her distinctive voice, *Washington Post Book World* critic Stephen Dobyns dubbed *View with a Grain of Sand* "surprising, funny and deeply moving. Szymborska is a world-class poet," Dobyns added, "and this book will go far to make her known in the United States."

A Poetry of Restrained Optimism

The appearance of the translated volumes *Poems: New and Collected, 1957-1997*, *Miracle Fair: Selected Poems of Wislawa Szymborska*, and *Monologue of a Dog* inspired further critical acclaim. "It may seem superfluous to praise a Nobel Laureate in literature, but Szymborska is a splendid writer richly deserving of her recent renown," maintained Graham Christian in a *Library Journal* review of *Poems: New and Collected, 1957-1997*. Noting the poet's "unflinching examination of torture and other wrongs inflicted by repressive regimes," Christian added that Szymborska's verses contain "the exhilarating power of a kind of serious laughter." Despite the sometimes-grim subject matter in the volume, the

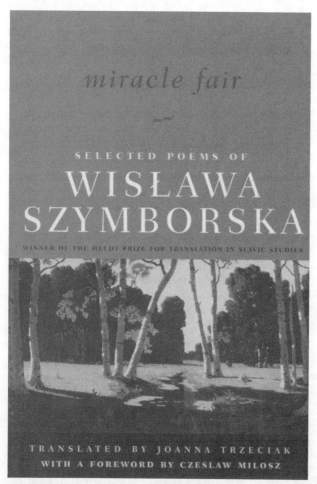

A selective sampling of Szymborska's poetry, covering all of her major themes, is found in this 2002 collection.
(Translated by Joanna Trzeciak. Norton, 2002. Jacket painting, Birch Trees, by Arkhip Kuinji. Used by permission of W.W. Norton & Company, Inc.)

Syzmborska "knows philosophy, literature, and history, but mostly she knows common human experience," explained *Booklist* contributor Ray Olson in describing the poet's oeuvre. "Her work is ultimately wisdom literature, written in a first person that expresses a universal humanity that American poets—lockstep individualists all—haven't dared essay since early in this century. She is like Brecht without hatred, Sandburg without socialist posturing, Dickinson without hermetism, Whitman without illusory optimism: a great poet." According to Stanislaw Baraczak in the *Dictionary of Literary Biography*: "Szymborska is known for her quiet way of life and unwillingness to embrace the status of a celebrity; she shuns public gatherings, rarely travels abroad, hates being photographed or interviewed, and, except for her human rights and democratic reform activities, refuses to be involved in partisan politics."

If you enjoy the works of Wislawa Szymborska, you may also want to check out the following books:

Zbigniew Herbert, *Elegy for the Departure*, 1990.
Seamus Heaney, *Opened Ground: Selected Poems, 1966-1996*, 1999.
Czeslaw Milosz, *New and Collected Poems, 1931-2001*, 2003.

poet's "tough naturalism does allow rays of light to penetrate its bleak landscapes, leaving lasting, sustaining impressions," declared a reviewer for *Publishers Weekly*. Calling Szymborska's work in *Monologue of a Dog* "direct, provocative, and necessary," *Women's Review of Books* contributor Claire Keyes explained the significance of the poet's work: "For Americans," Keyes wrote, "she carries the gravitas of the European who has lived through Hitler's war and Soviet-dominated Poland. . . . Szymborska has survived it all, and she both cherishes that amazing fact and conveys a sense of ruefulness about it." "With characteristically simple language and imagery, wit and irony, she shows us how life can change at any moment," added *Library Journal* contributor Karla Huston. In *Monologue of a Dog*, noted the critic, Szymborska distills "the politics of the everyday" into "little observations on the value of life."

In her Nobel Prize lecture, posted on the Nobel Prize Web site, Szymborska referenced the cultural differences that have shaped her work, but ultimately noted the driving force all poets, everywhere, share. "In more fortunate countries, where human dignity isn't assaulted so readily, poets yearn . . . to be published, read, and understood," she noted, "but they do little, if anything, to set themselves above the common herd and the daily grind. . . . It wasn't so long ago, in this century's first decades, that poets strove to shock us with their extravagant dress and eccentric behavior. But all this was merely for the sake of public display. The moment always came when poets had to close the doors behind them, strip off their mantles, fripperies, and other poetic paraphernalia, and confront—silently, patiently awaiting their own selves—the still white sheet of paper. For this is finally what really counts."

■ Biographical and Critical Sources

BOOKS

Contemporary Literary Criticism, Gale (Detroit, MI), Volume 99: *Yearbook 1996,* 1997, Volume 190, 2004.

Contemporary Women Poets, St. James Press (Detroit, MI), 1998.

Contemporary World Writers, 2nd edition, St. James Press (Detroit, MI), 1993.

Czerniawski, Adam, editor, *The Mature Laurel: Essays on Modern Polish Poetry,* Seren Books, 1991.

Dictionary of Literary Biography, Gale (Detroit, MI), Volume 232: *Twentieth-Century Eastern European Writers, Third Series,* 2001, Volume 332: *Nobel Prize Laureates in Literature, Part 4,* 2007.

Encyclopedia of World Biography Supplement, Volume 25, Gale (Detroit, MI), 2005.

Levine, Madeline, *Contemporary Polish Poetry: 1925-1975,* Twayne (Boston, MA), 1981.

Poetry Criticism, Volume 44, Gale (Detroit, MI), 2003.

Poetry for Students, Volume 15, Gale (Detroit, MI), 2002.

Reference Guide to Holocaust Literature, St. James Press (Detroit, MI), 2002.

Reference Guide to World Literature, 3rd edition, St. James Press (Detroit, MI), 2003.

PERIODICALS

American Poetry Review, July-August, 2000, Stephen Tapscott and Mariusz Przybytek, "Sky, the Sky, a Sky, the Heavens, a Heaven, Heavens: Reading Szymborska Whole," pp. 41-47.

Antioch Review, June 22, 2006, Carol Moldaw, review of *Monologue of a Dog,* p. 580.

Booklist, April 15, 1998, Ray Olson, review of *Poems: New and Collected, 1957-1997;* March 15, 1999, Ray Olson, review of *Poems: New and Collected, 1957-1997,* p. 276; October 15, 2002, Donna Seaman, review of *Nonrequired Reading: Prose Pieces,* p. 364; November 1, 2005, Ray Olson, review of *Monologue of a Dog,* p. 14.

Boston Review, summer, 1998, Frances Padorr Brent, review of *Poems: New and Collected, 1957-1997.*

Cambridge Quarterly, Number 16, 1987.

Chicago Review, Volume 46, numbers 3-4, 2000, Piotr Wilczek, "Polish Nobel Prize Winners in Literature: Are They Really Polish?," pp. 375-377.

Choice, January, 1992, review of *People on a Bridge,* p. 752.

Christian Science Monitor, April 18, 2006, Elizabeth Lund, "A Fascinating Journey with Two Women Poets."

Comparative Literature, winter, 2005, Anastasia Graf, "Representing the Other: A Conversation among Mikhail Bakhtin, Elizabeth Bishop, and Wislawa Szymborska," pp. 84-99.

Encounter, May, 1988.

Humanities Review, spring, 1982, p. 141.

Journal of Literary Semantics, Volume 31, number 2, 2002, Laura Hidalgo Downing, "Creating Things That Are Not: The Role of Negation in the Poetry of Wislawa Szymborska," pp. 113-132.

Kirkus Reviews, August 15, 2002, review of *Nonrequired Reading,* p. 1207.

Kliatt, September, 1995, James Beschta, review of *View with a Grain of Sand,* p. 29.

Library Journal, September 1, 1981, review of *Sounds, Feelings, Thoughts,* p. 1636; July, 1995, Louis McKee, review of *View with a Grain of Sand,* p. 85; April 1, 1998, Graham Christian, review of *Poems: New and Collected, 1957-1997,* p. 92; November 1, 2002, Nancy R. Ives, review of *Nonrequired Reading,* p. 91; October 1, 2005, Karla Huston, review of *Monologue of a Dog,* p. 81.

Literary Imagination: The Review of the Association of Literary Scholars and Critics, fall, 1999, Clare Cavanagh, "Poetry and Ideology: The Example of Wislawa Szymborska," pp. 174-190; fall, 2004, Czeslaw Milosz, "Wislawa Szymborska and the Grand Inquisitor," pp. 328-331.

Los Angeles Times, October 4, 1996, "Winning Words," p. A1; October 13, 1996.

Modern Language Review, January, 2001, John Blazina, "Szymborska's Two Monkeys: The Stammering Poet and the Chain of Signs," pp. 130-139.

New Republic, January 1, 1996, Helen Vendler, review of *View with a Grain of Sand,* p. 36; December 30, 1996, p. 27.

New Yorker, December 14, 1992, p. 94; March 1, 1993, p. 86; October 28, 2002, Dana Goodyear, review of *Nonrequired Reading.*

New York Review of Books, October 21, 1982, Jaroslaw Anders, review of *Sounds, Feelings, Thoughts,* p. 47; November 14, 1996, p. 17; October 21, 1993, p. 42; April 18, 1996, p. 35; November 14, 1996, Czeslaw Milosz, "On Szymborska," p. 17; October 8, 1998, Helen Vendler, review of *Poems: New and Collected, 1957-1997,* p. 37.

New York Times, October 4, 1996, Jane Perlez, "Polish Poet, Observer of Daily Life, Wins Nobel," C13.

New York Times Book Review, October 27, 1996, Stanislaw Baraczak, "The Reluctant Poet," p. 51; October 20, 2002, Natalya Sukhonos, review of *Nonrequired Reading,* p. 24.

New York Times Magazine, December 1, 1996, p. 46.

Observer (London, England), August 18, 1991, p. 51.

Parnassus: Poetry in Review, fall-winter, 1983/spring-summer, 1984, Jonathan Aaron, "'In the Absence of Witnesses': The Poetry of Wislawa Szymborska," pp. 254-264; spring-summer, 2005, Eva Badowska, "'My Poet's Junk': Wislawa Szymborska in Retrospect," pp. 151-168.

People, May 5, 1997, review of *View with a Grain of Sand,* p. 41.

PN Review, May-June, 1994, Felicity Rosslyn, "Miraculously Normal: Wislawa Szymborska," pp. 14-19.

Polish Review, Volume 24, number 3, 1979, Magnus J. Krynski and Robert A. Maguire, "Sounds, Feelings, Thoughts: The Poetry of Wislawa Szymborska," pp. 3-4; Volume 31, numbers 2-3, 1986, John Freedman, "The Possibilities and Limitations of Poetry: Wislawa Szymborska's Wielka liczba," pp. 137-147; Volume 44, number 3, 1999, Charity Scribner, "Parting with a View: Wislawa Szymborska and the Work of Mourning," pp. 311-328; Volume 46, number 4, 2001, Katarzyna Olga Beilin, "Photographing Sky: Time and Beyond in Tokarczuk and Szymborska," pp. 441-460.

Publishers Weekly, April 7, 1997, Joanna Trzeciak, "Wislawa Szymborska: The Enchantment of Everyday Objects," p. 68; March 30, 1998, review of *Poems: New and Collected, 1957-1997,* p. 77; February 19, 2001, review of *Miracle Fair: Selected Poems of Wislawa Szymborska,* p. 87; September 23, 2002, review of *Nonrequired Reading,* p. 69; August 15, 2005, review of *Monologue of a Dog,* p. 34.

Sarmation Review, January, 2006, Mary Ann Furno, "Wislawa Szymborska's 'Conversation with a Stone,'" pp. 1192-1195.

Slavic and East European Journal, summer, 1997, Edyta M. Bojanska, "Wislawa Szymborska: Naturalist and Humanist," pp. 199-223.

Slavonica, November, 2006, Justyna Kostkowska, "'The Sense of Taking Part': Feminist Environmental Ethics in the Poetry of Wislawa Szymborska," pp. 149-166.

Times Literary Supplement, September 17, 1999, Clair Wills, "How Real Is Reality?," p. 25.

Translation Review, Number 55, 1998, Clare Cavanagh, "At the Corner of Maple and Pine: Szymborska in America," pp. 13-16.

U.S. News & World Report, October 14, 1996, "Writing a Résumé for a Nobel Winner," p. 32.

Virginia Quarterly Review, winter, 1996, review of *View with a Grain of Sand,* p. 29.

Washington Post, April 5, 1998, Adam Kirsch, "Laureate of the Metaphysical," p. X8.

Washington Post Book World, July 30, 1995, Stephen Dobyns, review of *View with a Grain of Sand,* p. 8.

Women's Review of Books, May-June, 2006, Claire Keyes, review of *Monologue of a Dog,* p. 22.

World Literature Today, spring, 1982, p. 368; summer, 1991, Alice-Catherine Carls, review of *Poezje = Poems,* p. 519; winter, 1992, Bogdana Carpenter, review of *People on a Bridge,* pp. 163-164; winter, 1997, Bogdana Carpenter, "Wislawa Szymborska and the Importance of the Unimportant," pp. 8-12; May-August, 2006, "A Look Back: Four Polish Nobelists," p. 27.

ONLINE

Books and Writers Web site, http://www./www.kirjasto.sci.fi/ (June 15, 2007), "Wislawa Szymborska."

Moondance, http://moondance.org/ (winter, 2006), Lys Anzia, review of *Monologue of a Dog.*

Nobel Prize Web site, http://www.nobelprize.org/ (June 25, 2007), "Wislawa Szymborska."*

Theodore Taylor

■ Personal

Born June 23, 1921, in Statesville, NC; died of complications from a heart attack, October 26, 2006, in Laguna Beach, CA; son of Edward Riley (a molder) and Elnora Alma (a homemaker) Taylor; married Gweneth Goodwin, October 25, 1946 (divorced, 1979); married Flora Gray Schoenleber (an elementary school librarian and library clerk), April 18, 1981; children: (first marriage) Mark, Wendy, Michael. *Education:* Attended Fork Union Military Academy, VA, 1939-40, U.S. Merchant Marine Academy, Kings Point, NY, 1942, and Columbia University, 1948; studied with American Theatre Wing, 1947-48. *Politics:* Republican. *Religion:* Protestant. *Hobbies and other interests:* Travel, ocean fishing, watching football, listening to classical music, collecting foreign menus.

■ Career

Portsmouth Star, Portsmouth, VA, cub reporter, 1934-39, sports editor, 1941-42; *Daily News,* Washington, DC, copyboy, c. 1942; National Broadcasting Co. (NBC) Radio, New York City, sportswriter, 1942; *Sunset News,* Bluefield, WV, sports editor, 1946-47; New York University, New York City, assistant director of public relations, 1947-48; *Orlando Sentinel Star,* Orlando, FL, reporter, 1949-50; Paramount Pictures, Hollywood, CA, publicist, 1955-56; Perlberg-Seaton Productions, Hollywood, story editor and associate producer, 1956-61; freelance press agent for Hollywood studios, 1961-68; writer, 1961-2006; Twentieth Century-Fox, Hollywood, writer, 1965-69. Producer and director of documentary films. *Military service:* U.S. Merchant Marines, 1942-44; U.S. Naval Reserve, active duty, 1944-46, 1950-55; became lieutenant.

■ Member

Academy of Motion Picture Arts and Sciences, Mystery Guild, Mystery Writers of America, Society of Children's Book Writers and Illustrators, Writers Guild.

■ Awards, Honors

Silver Medal from Commonwealth Club of California, 1969, Jane Addams Children's Book Award, 1970, Women's International League for Peace and Freedom (returned, 1975), Lewis Carroll Shelf Award, Southern California Council on Literature for Children and Young People Notable Book Award, Woodward Park School Annual Book Award, California Literature Medal Award, and Best Book Award from University of California—Irvine, all 1970, all for *The Cay;* Outstanding Book of the Year, *New York Times,* 1976, for *Battle in the Arctic Seas: The Story of Convoy PQ 17;* Spur Award for Best Western for Young People, Western Writers of

America, and Silver Medal for the best juvenile book by a California author, Commonwealth Club of California, both 1977, both for *A Shepherd Watches, A Shepherd Sings*; Mark Twain Award nomination, 1977, for *Teetoncey*, and 1978, for *Teetoncey and Ben O'Neal*; Young Reader's Medal, California Reading Association, and Mark Twain Award nomination, both 1984, both for *The Trouble with Tuck*; Jefferson Cup Honor Book, Virginia Library Association, 1987, for *Walking up a Rainbow*; Best Book Award, American Library Association (ALA), 1989, and Best Middle Grade Book Award, Maryland Reading Association, 1994, both for *Sniper*; Edgar Allan Poe Award and Best Book Award, ALA, both 1992, both for *The Weirdo*; Best Book Award, ALA, 1993, and Mark Twain Award nomination, 1996, both for *Timothy of the Cay*; Mark Twain Award nomination, 1994, for *Tuck Triumphant*; Scott O'Dell Historical Fiction Award, University of Central Florida Libraries, and Children's Literature Council of Southern California Book Award, both 1996, both for *The Bomb*; South Carolina Book Award nomination, 2000, for *A Rogue Wave and Other Red-Blooded Sea Stories*. Taylor has also won three awards for his body of work: the Southern California Council on Literature for Children and Young People Award, 1977, for distinguished contributions to the field of children's literature; the George G. Stone Center for Children's Books Recognition of Merit Award, 1980; and the Kerlan Collection Award, University of Minnesota, 1996.

■ Writings

NOVELS FOR YOUNG ADULTS

The Cay, Doubleday (Garden City, NY), 1969.
The Children's War, Doubleday (New York, NY), 1971.
The Maldonado Miracle, Doubleday (New York, NY), 1973.
Teetoncey, illustrated by Richard Cuffari, Doubleday (New York, NY), 1974.
Teetoncey and Ben O'Neal, illustrated by Cuffari, Doubleday (New York, NY), 1975.
The Odyssey of Ben O'Neal, illustrated by Cuffari, Doubleday (New York, NY), 1977.
The Trouble with Tuck, Doubleday (New York, NY), 1981.
Sweet Friday Island, Scholastic, Inc. (New York, NY), 1984.
Walking up a Rainbow: Being the True Version of the Long and Hazardous Journey of Susan D. Carlisle, Mrs. Myrtle Dessery, Drover Bert Pettit, and Cowboy Clay Carmer and Others, Delacorte (New York, NY), 1986.

The Hostage, illustrated by Darrell Sweet, Delacorte (New York, NY), 1988.
Sniper, Harcourt (San Diego, CA), 1989.
Tuck Triumphant, Doubleday (New York, NY), 1991.
The Weirdo, Harcourt (San Diego, CA), 1992.
Maria, Harcourt (San Diego, CA), 1992.
Timothy of the Cay, Harcourt (San Diego, CA), 1993.
The Bomb, Harcourt (San Diego, CA), 1995.
A Sailor Returns, Blue Sky Press (New York, NY), 2001.
Lord of the Kill (sequel to *Sniper*), Blue Sky Press (New York, NY), 2002.
The Boy Who Could Fly without a Motor (fantasy), Harcourt (San Diego, CA), 2002.
Ice Drift, Harcourt (Orlando, FL), 2004.
Billy the Kid, Harcourt (Orlando, FL), 2005.

NONFICTION FOR YOUNG ADULTS

People Who Make Movies, Doubleday (New York, NY), 1967.
Air Raid—Pearl Harbor! The Story of December 7, 1941, illustrated by W.T. Mars, Crowell (New York, NY), 1971.
Rebellion Town: Williamsburg, 1776, illustrated by R. Cuffari, Crowell (New York, NY), 1973.
Battle in the Arctic Seas: The Story of Convoy PQ 17, illustrated by Robert Andrew Parker, Crowell (New York, NY), 1976.
(With Louis Irigaray) *A Shepherd Watches, a Shepherd Sings*, Doubleday (New York, NY), 1977.
H.M.S. Hood vs. Bismarck: The Battleship Battle, illustrated by A. Glass, Avon (New York, NY), 1982.
The Battle of Midway Island, illustrated by Andrew Glass, Avon (New York, NY), 1983.
Battle in the English Channel, illustrated by A. Glass, Avon (New York, NY), 1983.
Rocket Island, Avon (New York, NY), 1985.

NOVELS FOR ADULTS

The Body Trade, Fawcett (New York, NY), 1968.
The Stalker, D.I. Fine, 1987.
Monocolo, D.I. Fine, 1989.
To Kill the Leopard, Harcourt (San Diego, CA), 1993.

OTHER

The Magnificent Mitscher (biography), Norton (New York, NY), 1954.
Fire on the Beaches, Norton (New York, NY), 1957.
(With Robert A. Houghton) *Special Unit Senator: An Investigation of the Assassination of Senator Robert F. Kennedy*, Random House (New York, NY), 1970.

(With Kreskin) *The Amazing World of Kreskin,* Random House (New York, NY), 1974.

Jule: The Story of Composer Jule Styne, Random House (New York, NY), 1979.

(With Tippi Hedren) *The Cats of Shambala,* Simon & Schuster (New York, NY), 1985.

The Flight of Jesse Leroy Brown (biography), Avon (New York, NY), 1988.

Rogue Wave and Other Red-Blooded Sea Stories (short stories), Harcourt (San Diego, CA), 1996.

Hello, Arctic! (picture book), illustrated by Margaret Chodos-Irvine, Harcourt (San Diego, CA), 2002.

Making Love to Typewriters (autobiography), Pentland Press, 2004.

Author of television plays "Tom Threepersons," *TV Mystery Theater,* 1964, "Sunshine, the Whale," and "The Girl Who Whistled the River Kwai," 1980; author of screenplays *Night without End,* 1959, *The Hold-up* and *Showdown,* both Universal, both 1973, *Diplomatic Immunity,* 1989, and numerous documentary films. Also author of books under the pseudonym T.T. Lang. Contributor of short stories and novelettes to magazines, including *Alfred Hitchcock's Mystery Magazine, Argosy, Ladies' Home Journal, Look, McCall's, New York Times, Redbook,* and *Saturday Evening Post.* Taylor's manuscripts are included in the Kerlan Collection, University of Minnesota.

■ Adaptations

The Cay was adapted as a television film starring James Earl Jones, NBC-TV, 1974, and as a filmstrip, Pied Piper Productions, 1975; *The Trouble with Tuck* was adapted as a filmstrip, Pied Piper Productions, 1986; *Timothy of the Cay* and *The Hostage* have been recorded on audio cassette, Recorded Books, 1996. *The Cay on Stage,* a theatrical production for schools, was created by the California Theatre Center, Sunnyvale, CA. *The Maldonado Miracle* was adapted as a movie directed by actress Salma Hayek.

■ Sidelights

"I believe that a writer should constantly feed his fires by being on the go, doing different things, seeking new experiences," Theodore Taylor once noted. Putting that philosophy into practice in his own life, Taylor worked as a newspaperman, magazine writer, and movie publicist, managed a prize fighter, worked as a merchant seaman, served as a naval officer, and spent time in Hollywood as both a production assistant and a documentary filmmaker. As a writer for the young, Taylor wrote realistic, historical fiction and informational books, most of which he addresses to middle-graders and young adults. His fiction characteristically features young protagonists—preteen or adolescent boys and girls of varying ethnic backgrounds—who cope with challenges that often concern their physical survival. Through their experiences, these characters, who sometimes have lost their senses, such as sight and speech, or have physical disabilities, stand up for their values and learn independence and self-reliance as well as acceptance of other people and cultures.

A Happy Adventure

Taylor was born in the rural town of Statesville, North Carolina, the youngest of six children born to Edward and Elnora Taylor. He described his early childhood in an essay in the *Something about the Author Autobiography Series* (*SAAS*) as "one short happy adventure, knowing and caring little about what was going on in the outside world simply because there was so much going on in my inside world. . . . In terms of material wealth, we had very little, but there was a richness in the surroundings that money could never buy."

As a boy, Taylor was more entranced by the action of World War I than with his studies: "I spent a lot of time drawing Fokkers and Spads and Sopwith Pups and Scouts in aerial battles; looping artillery fire into the Flanders trenches. When I should have been listening to the teacher I filled sheets of paper with war scenes." This fascination, also revealed in many of Taylor's books, would continue throughout his career, making him an acknowledged authority on the U.S. military history of the early twentieth century.

At the age of eight, Taylor got his first library card, although his mother had been reading to him for years. By the time he was nine, Taylor had read Huckleberry Finn, the stories of L. Frank Baum, the "Tom Swift" series, and adult mysteries and detective stories. He noted in *SAAS:* "I read both *Frankenstein* and *Dracula* about then. Heady stuff."

At nine Taylor and his family moved to Johnson City, Tennessee, where his father, a war veteran, entered the Soldier's Home to receive free meals. Taylor and his mother occupied two rooms in a private home. During this period, Taylor and his father went fishing frequently. As he did in Statesville, Taylor explored the countryside in and around

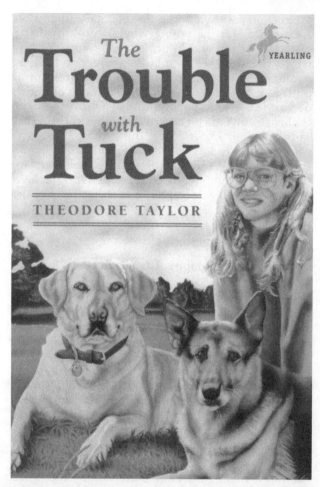

The 2000 edition of the novel telling of a young girl's efforts to help her beloved dog, who is going blind.
(Yearling, 2000. Cover art copyright © 2000 by Charles Collins. Used by permission of Random House Children's Books, a division of Random House, Inc.)

Johnson City. After about a year, Edward Taylor left the Soldier's Home and went off to find part-time work, while Taylor and his mother returned to Statesville. During the Depression, Taylor had a paper route—getting up at four-thirty in the morning to deliver papers—and sold candy by the box; he also picked up scrap metal to sell at the local junkyard. The author commented: "I wasn't alone in these endeavors and I'm not the least sorry that I went through them." At around this time, Taylor acquired Napoleon, a mongrel pup that, the author noted, "began my long love affair with dogs."

In 1933 Taylor and some friends went down the Catawba River on a raft that they had made. "My parents," he told Norma Bagnall in *Language Arts*, "knew I was going and they didn't tell me I couldn't. They depended on me to use my head, not to do anything foolish, not to get myself

drowned." In 1934 Edward Taylor got his first full-time job in years as a molder's helper at the Norfolk Navy Yard in Portsmouth, Virginia. Taylor and his mother took the train to Portsmouth, then traveled a few miles outside of it to make their home in Cradock, a comfortable village built in 1918 to house blue-collar workers during World War I. "I'd never been so excited," Taylor recalled. "Another state; a town near water, near ships." He added: "Somewhere in me is a considerable dollop of salt. . . . I had a hankering for the water long before we moved to Virginia." He wrote on his Web site: "I wanted to be aboard (ships), to be a sailor, go to London and Conakry and Durban and Hong Kong and the Java Sea. With the Second World War, that dream came true."

Becomes a Boy Reporter

Early in 1934 Taylor began his writing career at the age of thirteen as a cub reporter for the Portsmouth *Evening Star.* "Until school began I explored. I highly recommend exploration to young and would-be writers. I followed the Norfolk & Western tracks down to the river, often hopping the slow coaljacks for a ride, to watch the small freighters that chugged down the Elizabeth toward North Carolina on the inland waterway; to see tankers unloading on the South Norfolk side. I followed the streetcar track on foot into Portsmouth and explored the waterfront, spending hours at the Isaac Fass fishing docks watching the boats unload. I watched the side-wheeler ferries, still coal-burners, plying the mile or so across to Norfolk. There was an all-encompassing excitement to this waterfront activity, so different from the flatlands of the Piedmont, and I was caught up in it."

But something happened in the spring of 1935 that would change Taylor's life forever. "I was offered a chance to write a sports column,. . . a typewritten page and a half of copy, for the *Portsmouth Star.* . . . For this, I was to receive fifty cents." The eager Taylor immediately said yes. "I remember studying the sports pages of the *Star* and the larger *Norfolk Virginian-Pilot,* just to see how the stories were written," he recalled of his first days as an honest-to-goodness reporter, "then placing them down by the typewriter for constant referral. . . . After laboring all morning and up to mid-afternoon on the page and a half, I nervously rode the streetcar to Portsmouth clutching my first story, mentally and probably physically crossing fingers that it would be accepted." It was, although the newspaper's editor later commented, "Ted Taylor was the rawest recruit we ever had."

Taylor left his home in Virginia at the age of seventeen and moved north to join the staff of the

Washington *Daily News* as a copyboy. By the age of nineteen he was working as an NBC network sportswriter. During World War II, he joined the United States Merchant Marine, "having no desire to slog around in army mud nor any great desire for navy discipline." He also became a member of the U.S. Naval Reserve and for almost a year and a half served as a seaman aboard a gasoline tanker in the Atlantic and Pacific Oceans and on a freighter plying the seas of Europe before becoming third-mate on two other ships. Returning stateside in 1944, Taylor was called up by the Navy as an ensign aboard the USS *Draco,* a cargo attack vessel in the Pacific. "Following the Japanese surrender, I heard about Operation Crossroads, the nuclear experiment at Bikini to see the bomb go off. Unfortunately, but typically, my ship, the USS *Sumner,* was ordered home before the big blast." Characteristically, his personal experience of this hotly debated military action would continue to haunt Taylor for many years but would ultimately find an outlet in his writing.

Chronicles Military Adventures

In the Korean War, Taylor also saw active duty as a naval officer; during his entire military career, he served a total of five years at sea in both the Atlantic and Pacific Oceans. His experiences at sea during the war form the basis for several of his fiction and nonfiction books. "*Battle in the Arctic Seas: The Story of Convoy PQ 17* (1976) is the result of wartime experience," he explained. "I sailed in convoys, was both fascinated and overwhelmed by them—this great family of ships at sea, moving as a single unit, performing like horses in a drill team. The drama was always incredible: the gathering together, the weighing of anchor, departure and forming-up; the escorts thrashing about; sometimes a U-boat attack, and then another type of drama. I'd always wanted to do a story about the most famous convoy of World War II, and PQ 17 qualified in every way. It is humanly impossible to tell as much as possible by use of a single ship, the *Troubador,* and her unique crew."

In *Battle in the English Channel* (1983) Taylor tells the story of the 1942 episode in the English Channel when a group of German ships were able to successfully elude both British naval and air forces while en route from France to Germany. In the conclusion, Taylor states its central theme: "Operation Fuller failed because of the command structure and not from lack of individual effort on the part of those who had to go out and fight."

While serving as a lieutenant in the navy during the Korean War, Taylor wrote his first book, *The Magnificent Mitscher,* a biography of Admiral "Pete"

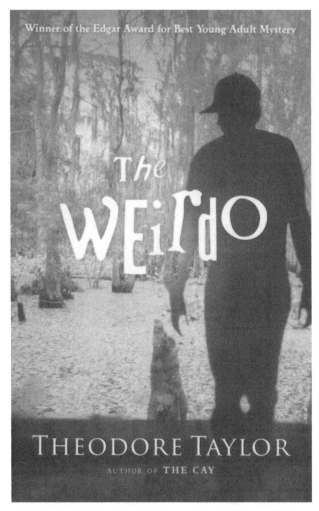

A disfigured Chip Clewt hides in the Powhatan Swamp in this 2006 edition of the Edgar Award-winning novel. (Harcourt, 2006. Cover photographs (figure) copyright © Scott Sinklier/CORBIS, (swamp) copyright © W. Cody/CORBIS. Copyright © 1991 by Theodore Taylor and Flora Taylor 2000 Revocable Community Property Trust. Reprinted by permission of Harcourt, Inc. This material may not be reproduced in any form or by any means without the prior written permission of the publisher.)

Mitscher, a carrier group commander during World War II. A year after its publication, Taylor moved to Hollywood where he worked as a press agent, and later as a story editor and associate producer. He subsequently produced documentary films throughout the world and wrote books.

Using his war experiences, Taylor's second book, *Fire on the Beaches,* told the story of the ships that fled from German submarines along the East Coast during the war, "ships like the Cities Service tanker, SS *Annibal,* the one I'd served on. I stopped off in New York to research *Fire on the Beaches* at the shipping companies and then in Washington at Coast Guard headquarters. One morning at the latter I was reading accounts of ships that were sunk along the Eastern seaboard and down in the Caribbean, over in the Gulf of Mexico, when I came across a paragraph that described the sinking of a small Dutch vessel. An eleven-year-old boy survived the sinking but was eventually lost at sea, alone on a life raft." Taylor was struck by this small drama; its irony would haunt him for several years, until it germinated and grew into the novel *The Cay*.

Life Raft Story for Younger Readers

In 1966, after working for over a year on the film *The Sand Pebbles*, Taylor began work on his first book for younger readers. "My own children were interested in how motion pictures were made," he recalled, "and I thought others might be, too. *People Who Make Movies* was quickly sold to Doubleday and I was astonished some two years later, after the book began circulating in schools, to receive mail from young readers. More than three thousand responded to that book, most seeking Hollywood careers. . . . In writing for adults, I'd probably received a dozen letters.

"Two years later, I decided to go ahead with the long-brewing story of the boy on the life raft in the Caribbean. A few days after returning home from Florida, I rolled fresh paper into the typewriter. Three weeks later *The Cay* was completed and the printed version is little different from the first draft." Although Taylor would note that *The Cay* was "the quickest and easiest book I've ever written," he also acknowledged that over ten years of thought and reflection also greatly contributed to the ease with which the work was written.

The Cay is a two-character story about an eleven-year-old boy, Phillip, and a seventy-year-old black Caribbean seaman named Timothy who are stranded on a raft after their boat is torpedoed by German submarines in 1942. The two eventually land on a cay, or coral island. There, the boy, who was raised with a racist outlook and who has lost his sight, learns to trust the old man; knowing he is ailing, Timothy trains the lad to fend for himself, thus ensuring his survival and rescue after the old man's death. Taylor dedicated the book to the dream of Dr. Martin Luther King, "which can only come true if the very young know, and understand."

After its publication in 1969, *The Cay* received numerous awards, was translated into nine languages, and was adapted into a successful film for television. It also received a great deal of critical praise: the relationship between Timothy and Phillip was described by Marilyn Singer in *School Library Journal* as "a hauntingly deep love, the poignancy of which is rarely achieved in children's literature"; while Charles W. Dorsey, writing in the *New York Times Book Review*, declared that Taylor "skillfully developed the perenially popular castaway plot into a good adventure story . . . ." However, it also attracted hostile criticism from some reviewers, such as Albert V. Schwartz who called it "an adventure story for white colonists—however enlightened—to add to their racist mythology," in a 1971 article in *Interracial Books for Children*. Attacks also came from representatives of the Interracial Council on Children's Books, who exerted enough pressure to ban the novel in several libraries. Five years after Taylor received the esteemed Jane Addams Book Award, he was requested to return it.

For his own part, the author noted that the charges of racism levelled at his novel were largely supported by isolated passages in *The Cay*, "usually descriptive of the black character, Timothy; then the broader contention that the white character, the boy Phillip, was not changed by his experience with the 70-year-old West Indian. Needless to say," Taylor contends in a letter to the editor he submitted to *Top of the News*, "passages in any book can be underlined and utilized for whatever purpose the reader chooses. That purpose does not always coincide with what the writer had in mind; nor always with the total meaning; nor always with the majority of the readers. In my own mind, I did not set out to write a 'racist' novel, vintage 1942; harm any human being, black or white; damage the black struggle for human equality. Further, I am not at all convinced that I did write a 'racist' novel. The goal was to the contrary. Directed primarily toward the white child (thinking that the black child did not need to be told much about prejudice), I hoped to achieve a subtle plea for better race relations and more understanding. I have reason to believe that I partially achieved that goal, despite acknowledged omissions and . . . flaws."

Like the "Teetoncey Trilogy"and *The Cay*, the majority of Taylor's stories for young readers are tales of adventure whose survival heroes are young people challenged by the intrusion of the unfamiliar. He alternates between nonfiction and fiction, with one book very often leading to another. "In the early seventies I'd come across a clipping from the *Fresno Bee* about a Basque shepherd who sang to his sheep," Taylor recalled in *SAAS*. "I sensed a story in this San Joaquin Valley man and after rereading the clipping in 1975, made contact with him. *A Shepherd Watches, a Shepherd Sings*, for Doubleday, resulted. In addition to extensive use of taped interviews for a book of this type I also independently do extensive research. That time, on sheep.

Two Inuit brothers find themselves adrift on an ice floe, facing the dangers of the Arctic North alone, in this 2006 edition of the adventure novel. (Harcourt, 2006. Cover illustration copyright © 2006 by James Bernardin. Copyright © 2005 by Theodore Taylor and Flora Taylor 2000 Revocable Community Property Trust. This material may not be reproduced in any form or by any means without the prior written permission of the publisher.)

Much to my surprise I learned that sheep were being driven across the United States from as far away as Vermont in the early 1850s to feed the gold miners of California. That bit of information became a novel, *Walking up a Rainbow*, published in 1986 by Delacorte."

One night in 1974, Taylor was dining with a friend and his stepson, a lawyer from San Francisco. "During the course of the meal, said, 'Okay, you wrote a story about a blind boy in *The Cay*; now let me tell you a story about our blind dog.' Whenever someone says, 'Let me tell you a story,' I listen but ninety-nine times out of a hundred the listening is for naught. This time Tony Orser's story became a short story for *Ladies' Home Journal*, published in 1977,

then a teleplay, . . .; finally, *The Trouble with Tuck* was published by Doubleday in 1981." The story of a blind Labrador retriever who eventually learns to maneuver with the help of a guide dog named Daisy, *The Trouble with Tuck* was popular with many young animal lovers.

"I often work on three [books] at once, switching from number one to number two if I write myself into a hole. An adult suspense novel, *The Stalker*, sprang from an episode of CBS's *60 Minutes*." In similar fashion, Taylor's 1987 young adult novel *The Hostage* was inspired by a front-page article he read in the *Los Angeles Times* and imaginatively transformed into a fourteen-year-old boy's predicament as he is forced to weigh environmental and personal moral concerns against his family's economic well-being after he and his father capture a killer whale and contemplate selling the animal to a California marine park.

In later years, Taylor built upon his characteristic themes of survival and maturation through both sequels to earlier novels and new works of young adult fiction. Through such works as *Timothy of the Cay*, a continuation of his controversial 1969 novel *The Cay*, historically grounded fictions like *The Bomb*, and the popular action novel *Sniper*, elements of suspense intermingle with Taylor's young protagonists' attempts to make mature choices in order to survive life-and-death predicaments. These later novels continue to show Taylor to be a talented spinner of edge-of-your-seat adventure yarns.

Placing *The Cay* in Time and History

In 1993's *Timothy of the Cay*, Taylor links past with future, juxtaposing the attempts of Phillip Enright, the blind protagonist of the earlier novel, to regain his sight with the Caribbean-born sailor Timothy's early years as a cabin boy. Following each character in alternating chapters—Phillip's story is narrated in the first person while Timothy's reads as a laudatory historical account—*Timothy of the Cay* answers many questions left in the minds of readers of the previous novel by covering two time periods: the years before the two find themselves shipwrecked on the tiny island, and the months immediately after Phillip's rescue. Taylor explores the same social and racial prejudices that characterized his earlier novel, while also highlighting the similarities between Phillip's brave decision to endure a high-risk operation that may restore his sight and young Timothy's struggle against both prejudice and poverty in his determination to captain a ship of his own. Although noting that the novel's attempt to deal with the subject of racial prejudice tends to cause gaps and imbalances in the story line, Stephanie Zvirin noted in *Booklist* that Taylor "also manages some moving moments of introspection and quiet heroism as well as an occasional snatch of the same wild drama that fired *The Cay.*"

In another sequel, *Tuck Triumphant,* published in 1991, the tail-wagging Labrador hero of *The Trouble with Tuck* returns with lead dog Daisy in tow to help fourteen-year-old Helen cope with the arrival of an adopted brother. Her new sibling sends Helen on a roller-coaster of emotions as she shifts from disappointment over the young Chok-Do's being a rambunctious six-year-old rather than a cuddly baby, confusion over the orphaned boy's deafness, and finally, love and sadness when she realizes that he may be sent to a private boarding school. Praised by *Voice of Youth Advocates* reviewer Donna Houser as "a beautiful, poignant story of two special dogs and a lonely, deaf little boy," *Tuck Triumphant* echoed Taylor's earlier efforts as a children's author.

Imaginative Fiction of High Adventure

Taylor's abilities as a writer have continued to transcend genres; while *Tuck Triumphant* and *Timothy of the Cay* were primarily character studies, other novels have combined equally realistically drawn characters with much more highly imaginative, suspense-filled storylines. 1989's *Sniper* features Ben Jepson, a young man who faces down danger in an effort to save the animals held in his family's privately held zoological preservation. Located in the California landscape familiar to readers of Taylor's work, the Los Coyotes Preserve where Ben and several animal handlers live contains such exotic animals as lions and tigers. When Alfredo, whom Ben's parents have left in charge of the preserve while they are away covering an assignment for *National Geographic,* becomes seriously injured in a car accident, fourteen-year-old Ben finds himself in charge. Unfortunately, his increased duties at the preserve soon include fighting for his life as a mysterious sniper armed with a night-scoped rifle begins a guerrilla-like attack on all the inhabitants of the preserve. Aided by an African veterinarian, a pair of Spanish-speaking animal handlers, and his girlfriend, Ben must make decisions that will decide the fate of both the animals and his family's life work.

Published in 1992, Taylor's *The Weirdo* went on to win that year's Edgar Allan Poe Award for best young adult mystery. In this action novel, seventeen-year-old Chip Clewt, a survivor of an airplane ac-

cident that occurred when he was seven and left the left side of his body disfigured, has fled with his recovering-alcoholic father to a small cabin deep in the wilderness of North Carolina's Powhatan Swamp wildlife refuge. Encountering Tom Telford and his assistant, Samantha Sanders, two students doing field work on the native black bear population, he decides to help them in their efforts to track and tag the bears. The tagging project—intended to help influence state authorities to extend the ban on hunting that has protected the bears for the past four years—runs afoul of the desire of several local hunters, who decide to hunt the young people down. Telford mysteriously disappears. In addition to portraying Chip's maturation and realization that he can transcend his physical handicap, Taylor highlights environmental issues through Samantha's mixed feelings about her own beliefs and her respect for her father, who is a devout hunter. "Murder, suspense, and intrigue abound, as does a hint of romance, but the environmental message is a clear and realistic one," explains Frances Bradburn in *Wilson Library Bulletin.* While noting that the author ultimately sides with wildlife preservationists, "Taylor is also careful to present the native population's desire—even need—to preserve a way of life that has been a part of the eastern North Carolina/Virginia heritage for generations. Pitting 'bad' hunters against 'good' environmentalists is a trap that Taylor will not allow himself to spring."

To Kill the Leopard, an action novel for adults published by Taylor in 1993 that has its roots in his experiences during World War II, was followed a year later by *Sweet Friday Island.* Taking place on the Sea of Cortez, which separates Baja California from Mexico, this adventure novel finds spunky fifteen-year-old Peg and her father vacationing on what they believe to be the uninhabited island of Viernes Dulce—Sweet Friday Island. Expecting to spend their annual "father and daughter only" vacation swimming, loafing, and exploring the craggy island terrain, and undeterred by the hostile reception they received at the Mexican border, the two campers suddenly find their tenting holiday transformed into a fight for their lives after docking on the remote island brings them face to face with a hostile but invisible enemy who punctures their raft, drains their supply of drinking water, and makes off with Peg's father's medical kit. Without insulin, he soon lapses into a diabetic coma and Peg is left to match wits with the enemy, knowing the lives of both she and her father hang in the balance.

Reaping the Bitter Harvest of Technology

Taylor earned resounding critical praise for still another award-winning effort, 1995's *The Bomb.* Set against the backdrop of the 1945 U.S. liberation of

Japanese-occupied Bikini Atoll—a coral island in the Western Pacific located 2,200 miles from Hawaii—this poignant story of human perseverance and, ultimately, tragedy finds an echo in the current debate over nuclear weapons testing around the globe. Like his neighbors, *The Bomb*'s fourteen-year-old protagonist Sorry Rinamu is grateful to the United States after the departure of their liberating forces, and feels a sense of security as life on his tropical island returns to normal. However, when the "helpful" U.S. Army forces return to his home a year later and announce that they will be "temporarily" relocating island residents in order to conduct tests of their latest atomic bomb in the Bikini lagoon, Sorry and his Uncle Abram are convinced, rightly, that such a weapon will certainly destroy their home; the residents of this quiet island will be left without a home. Their efforts to convince their neighbors that all the plants and animals on their homeland will be destroyed fall on deaf ears, and Uncle Abram dies in the process. Left alone with the realization of impending disaster, Sorry attempts to fight for his native homeland on his own, realizing too late that one person from an insignificant country cannot influence the actions of a superpower.

Taylor ends his moving fiction with an epilogue documenting the actual results of the U.S. government's destruction of Bikini Atoll and its impact on the lives of the villagers. Much of this information was based on the author's personal experiences in the mid-1940s, when he served as a U.S. Navy ensign during Operation Crossroads; while aboard the *USS Sumner* Taylor was involved with relocating the inhabitants of a similar small island in preparation for nuclear weapons testing. He described the navy's plan in an article accompanying his novel: "Almost one hundred unmanned warships would gather in the atoll's lagoon for two 'shots' —one aerial, one undersea. Navy officials wanted to know if the ships would survive the cataclysmic force of nuclear explosions. Animals would take the place of human crews on the target ships. Goats would be tethered on the open decks; guinea pigs and five thousand rats would be inside the ships, along with cancer-prone white mice. . . . All would be exposed to radiation." More than fifty years later, the once-beautiful Bikini Atoll is still poisoned by radioactive fallout from Operation Crossroads.

The Boy Who Could Fly without a Motor is "a wry, small fantasy that a grandfather might spin from his own youth," observed GraceAnne A. DeCandido in *Booklist*. Nine-year-old Jon Jeffers lives with his family on Clementine Rock, a lonely island nineteen miles off the coast of California, where his father tends a lighthouse and the ghosts of ship-

This 2007 edition of the novel tells the background stories of both Timothy and Phillip in alternating chapters. (Harcourt, 2007. Cover photographs (face) copyright © Jupiterimages/ Roxann Arwen Mills, (palm tree) copyright © Photodisc/Veer. Reproduced by permission of Harcourt.)

wrecked sailors are said to still linger. There is little for Jon to do there, and he fills his solitary days with stories and activities drawn from his own imagination. Mostly he wishes he could leave the island; if he could fly, he could do just that. After reading a magazine article on parapsychology, Jon becomes obsessed with the subject, practicing telepathy and reaching out to anyone who can hear him. Unexpectedly, he contacts Ling Wu, and ancient Chinese magician who agrees to teach the boy how to fly. Ling Wu sets down some very strict rules designed to ensure that Jon does not get caught displaying his newfound skill. Though the boy readily agrees, and begins practicing in the solitude of his room, he is soon unable to resist temptation and flies out over the ocean. A series of events, including Jon's sighting by the crew of a fishing trawler and a UFO investigation brought on by his flight, leads to him demonstrating his flying skills for President Roosevelt himself. Soon, Jon's levitating skill becomes a burden, and he finds he suddenly cannot turn it off. He is even more securely trapped on the island as the Coast Guard constantly patrols the area to keep away potential kidnappers. Eventually, Jon tires of his gift and asks Ling Wu to help him return to normal. Reviewer Ellen Fader, writing in the *School Library Journal*, observed that the book's "plot, the large-size font, and the many references to the paranormal will appeal to many children." A *Publishers Weekly* contributor thought that the story ended too abruptly, but noted: "Taylor's tight writing and flair for the fanciful otherwise keeps this caper agreeably airborne."

Ice Drift is a tale of survival that pits two Inuit boys against the harsh and unforgiving landscape of the far north. Fourteen-year-old Alika and his younger brother Sulu are enjoying a day of ice fishing when the floe they are standing on breaks free of the larger ice mass and begins a slow, inexorable drift southward. Quick-thinking Alika releases all the sled dogs but one, hoping that the canines will swim back to shore and somehow alert the boys' parents to their dangerous predicament. Though the ice-ship they are floating on is quite large, the warmer southern waters will quickly melt it away. Worse, as the ice floe shrinks, any animals also trapped upon it will be forced into close proximity with the boys. As the months pass, Alika and Sulu learn to survive in a perilous and austere environment by fishing, hunting for seals, and deriving fresh water from the ice. Challenged by encounters with polar bears and the need to stay warm, Alika also serves as stolid caretaker for his frightened younger brother, reassuring him that they will survive and make their way back to their worried parents. *Booklist* reviewer Jennifer Mattson commented that readers "will enjoy both the intense survival detail and the gratifying conclusion." Coop Renner, writing in the *School Library Journal*, called *Ice Drift* "a masterful and detailed look into a culture unfamiliar to most Americans, a gripping adventure, and a moving depiction of brotherly love."

The Maldonado Miracle, which was made into a major motion picture directed by actress Salma Hayek, is a "pleasant but uneventful family story about human faith and spiritual crisis," according to Marilyn Moss in *Hollywood Reporter*. Twelve-year-old Jose risks an illegal border crossing in order to be with his father, who is employed as a worker among the farmlands of California. Injured during his trip to San Ramos, Jose avoids detection and hides in a small church, where his blood drips onto a statue of Christ. A woman who visits the church sees the blood on the statue and is convinced a miracle has

occurred. Word of the "miracle" quickly spreads through town and beyond, bringing in reporters, miracle-seekers, and the curious from all over the country. The priest of the church, Father Russell, knows that no such miracle has occurred, but he opts to help Jose rather than reveal the true source of the Maldonado Miracle. In the process, others in town are helped through times of crisis or stagnation in response to the miracle.

Billy the Kid provides a fictionalized account of the life of notorious western outlaw, William Bonney—Billy the Kid. Life in Arizona is not profitable for Billy the Kid. Down on his luck and with only eight dollars between himself and starvation, Billy looks to improve his fortunes by taking part in a daring train robbery near his hometown. But the robbery only makes things worse for Billy. The Smiths, who invited Billy to participate in the robbery, are known criminals who cheat him without a second thought. He is recognized by a local during the robbery. He has been forced to kill one of his criminal comrades in self-defense, and even though he ends up with all the money from the heist, he rouses the ire of the gang leader, who begins a relentless search for Billy, the money, and revenge. Perhaps worst of all, the lawman responsible for bringing him to justice is his cousin and best friend, Willie. Even when Billy agrees to go peacefully with Willie for a trial, there seems to be nothing he can do to escape his fate, and his ultimate doom. "Taylor's colorful descriptions and authentic language solidly anchor the setting in the Southwest," commented Catherine Callegari in the *School Library Journal*. "Taylor smoothly fuses solid storytelling with the stuff of legend," commented a reviewer in *Publishers Weekly*.

If you enjoy the works of Theodore Taylor, you may also want to check out the following books:

Gary Paulsen, *The Voyage of the Frog*, 1989.
Jean Craighead George, *On the Far Side of the Mountain*, 1990.
Joel Matus, *Leroy and the Caveman*, 1993.

As a literary stylist, Taylor favored fast-paced narratives written in spare but descriptive language. The author included various techniques in his works, such as alternating chapters, interior monologues, flashbacks, epilogues, use of present tense and third person, and inclusion of dialect and words in other languages. Thematically, Taylor's works reflected his environmental, political, and social consciousness as well as his interest in nature lore, dogs, islands, and, especially, the sea. Acknowledged for his respect for and understanding of both people and animals, he blended history, psychology, and suspense to promote tolerance, freedom, independence, respect for the natural world, and connections among people of all ages and races.

Promoting Models of Self-Reliance

Throughout his long career as a writer, Taylor shared his wide-ranging life experience and interests with young readers, making them both entertaining and insightful. "Every story I have written is about real people and stems from real-life events," he told Norma Bagnall in an interview in *Language Arts.* "They include kids who have figured out things for themselves because kids like that really exist. I think they serve as models; I *hope* they serve as models, models of self-sufficiency and self-reliance." As an author, Taylor also served as a model. "Long ago I learned about discipline and have no trouble going to my office about eight-thirty each morning,"he noted in his *SAAS* essay, describing the personal writing regimen that allowed him this success. "With a half-hour off for lunch, I work until four-thirty; sometimes five. I do this seven days a week except during football season. September to Super Bowl Sunday. During this grunt-grind period on the gridiron, I work only five days weekly—*without guilt.* Otherwise, I feel enormous guilt if I don't work. Precious hours going to waste."

■ Biographical and Critical Sources

BOOKS

Children's Literature in the Elementary School, 3rd edition, Holt (New York, NY), 1979.

Children's Literature Review, Volume 30, Gale (Detroit, MI), 1993.

Drew, Bernard A., *The One Hundred Most Popular Young Adult Authors,* Libraries Unlimited, 1996.

Hipple, Ted, editor, *Writers for Young Adults,* Scribner's (New York, NY), 1997.

St. James Guide to Young Adult Writers, 2nd edition, St. James Press (Detroit, MI), 1999.

Silvey, Anita, editor, *Children's Books and Their Creators,* Houghton (Boston, MA), 1995.

Something about the Author Autobiography Series, Volume 4, Gale (Detroit, MI), 1987.

Speaking for Ourselves, Too: More Autobiographical Sketches by Notable Authors of Books for Young Adults, National Council of Teachers of English (Urbana, IL), 1993.

Twentieth-Century Children's Writers, 3rd edition, St. James Press (Detroit, MI), 1989.

PERIODICALS

Black Issues in Higher Education, February 4, 1999, Willie L. Hensley, review of *The Flight of Jesse Leroy Brown,* p. 45.

Booklist, September 15, 1992, Chris Sherman, review of *Maria: A Christmas Story,* p. 104; September 15, 1993, Stephanie Zvirin, review of *Timothy of the Cay,* p. 153; October 1, 1995, Susan Dove Lempke, review of *The Bomb,* p. 309; June 1, 1996, Jeanette Larson, review of *The Weirdo,* p. 1749; November 1, 1996, Susan Dove Lempke, review of *Rogue Wave: And Other Red-Blooded Sea Stories,* p. 491; November 15, 1996, Jeanette Larson, review of *The Bomb,* p. 604; October 15, 1998, Roland Green, review of *The Flight of Jesse Leroy Brown,* p. 378; May 1, 2001, Carolyn Phelan, review of *A Sailor Returns,* p. 1684; June 1, 2002, GraceAnne A. DeCandido, review of *The Boy Who Could Fly without a Motor,* p. 1726; October 1, 2002, GraceAnne A. DeCandido, review of *Hello, Arctic!,* p. 339; January 1, 2003, Frances Bradburn, review of *Lord of the Kill,* p. 872; February 1, 2005, Jennifer Mattson, review of *Ice Drift,* p. 962; May 15, 2005, Kathleen Odean, review of *Billy the Kid,* p. 1671.

Book World, May 4, 1969, Polly Goodwin, review of *The Cay,* p. 36.

Children's Bookwatch, May, 2005, review of *Ice Drift.*

Growing Point, January, 1971, Margery Fisher, author interview, p. 1669.

Hollywood Reporter, October 10, 2003, Marilyn Moss, "The Maldonado Miracle," p. 14.

Horn Book, April, 1982, review of *The Trouble with Tuck,* p. 170; January-February, 1990, Nancy Vasilakis, review of *Sniper,* p. 72; March-April, 1992, Margaret A. Bush, review of *The Weirdo,* p. 211; May-June, 1995, Kristi Beavin, review of *Timothy of the Cay,* p. 318.

Journal of Adolescent & Adult Literacy, November, 2005, Liza Kiesell, review of *Billy the Kid,* p. 247.

Kirkus Reviews, April 15, 2002, review of *The Boy Who Could Fly without a Motor,* p. 580; July 15, 2002, review of *Hello, Arctic!,* p. 1045; November 1, 2002, review of *Lord of the Kill,* p. 1614; December 15, 2004, review of *Ice Drift,* p. 1209.

Kliatt, September, 2004, Michele Winship, review of *Lord of the Kill,* p. 26; May, 2005, Paula Rohrlick, review of *Billy the Kid,* p. 18; September, 2006, Paula Rohrlick, review of *Billy the Kid,* p. 28.

Language Arts, January, 1980, Norma Bagnall, "Theodore Taylor: His Models of Self-Reliance," pp. 86-91.

Library Journal, August, 1985, review of *The Cats of Shambala*, p. 106.

New York Times Book Review, January 29, 1995, review of *Walking up a Rainbow*, p. 20.

People Weekly, May 3, 1993, review of *To Kill the Leopard*, p. 294; December 20, 1993, Kim Hubbard, "Return to the Cay: Theodore Taylor Reprises His Controversial Classic," p. 105.

Publishers Weekly, July 16, 1982, review of *.M.S. Hood vs. Bismarck: The Battleship Battle*, p. 79; June 7, 1985, review of *The Cats of Shambala*, p. 72; April 25, 1986, Diane Roback, review of *Walking up a Rainbow*, p. 84; April 10, 1987, Sybil Steinberg, review of *The Stalker*, p. 85; December 11, 1987, Diane Roback, review of *The Hostage*, p. 66; August 11, 1989, Sybil Steinberg, review of *Give My Heart Ease*, p. 441; December 14, 1990, Diane Roback and Richard Donahue, review of *Tuck Triumphant*, p. 67; November 22, 1991, review of *The Weirdo*, p. 57; September 7, 1992, Elizabeth Devereaux, review of *Maria*, p. 69; May 3, 1993, review of *To Kill the Leopard*, p. 294; September 6, 1993, review of *Timothy of the Cay*, p. 98; September 18, 1995, review of *The Bomb*, p. 133; October 12, 1998, review of *The Flight of Jesse Leroy Brown*, p. 65; May 21, 2001, review of *A Sailor Returns*, p. 108; May 13, 2002, review of *The Boy Who Could Fly without a Motor*, p. 71; July 29, 2002, review of *Hello, Arctic!*, p. 70; June 27, 2005, review of *Billy the Kid*, p. 65.

School Library Journal, September, 1969, Marilyn Singer, review of *The Cay*, p. 162; January, 1982, review of *The Trouble with Tuck*, p. 82; May, 1982, review of *The Battle off Midway Island*, p. 75; April, 1984, Civia M. Tuteur, review of *Battle in the English Channel*, p. 127; August, 1986, Dorcas Hand, review of *Walking up a Rainbow*, p. 107; March, 1988, Patricia Manning, review of *The Hostage*, p. 200; November, 1989, Susan Schuller, review of *Sniper*, p. 115; March, 1991, Ellen Ramsay, review of *Tuck Triumphant*, p. 196; December, 1991, Eldon Younce, review of *Air Raid—Pearl Harbor: The Story of December 7, 1941*, p. 130; January, 1992, Yvonne Frey, review of *The Weirdo*, p. 137; January, 1993, Ruth Semrau, review of *Maria*, p. 104; October, 1993, Susan Knorr, review of *Timothy of the Cay*, p. 132; May, 1994, Susan Knorr, review of *Sweet Friday Island*, p. 135; July, 1996, Stephanie Gall Miller, review of *The Hostage*, p. 51; August, 1996, Pat Griffith, review of *The Weirdo*, p. 64; April, 1997, Melissa Hudak, review of *Rogue Wave*, p. 142; April, 1999, Carol Clark, review of *The Flight of Jesse Leroy Brown*, p. 166; April, 2001, Tim Rausch, review of *A Sailor Returns*, p. 150; May, 2002, Ellen Fader, review of *The Boy Who Could Fly without a Motor*, p. 161; November, 2002, Sally R. Dove, review of *Hello, Arctic!*, p. 138; January, 2003, Ellen Fader, review of *Lord of the Kill*, p. 144; August, 2003, Kathy Piehl, review of *The Weirdo*, p. 117; January, 2005, Coop Renner, review of *Ice Drift*, p. 137; July, 2005, Coop Renner, review of *The Maldonado Miracle*, p. 45; July, 2005, Catherine Callegari, review of *Billy the Kid*, p. 109.

Top of the News, April, 1975, Theodore Taylor, letter to the editor, pp. 284-288.

Wilson Library Bulletin, March, 1990, Lesley S.J. Farmer, review of *Sniper*, p. S13; September, 1992, Frances Bradburn, review of *The Weirdo*, p. 93.

ONLINE

ALAN Review Online, http:// scholar.lib.vt.edu/ (November 18, 2001), Theodore Taylor, "Exploding the Literary Canon."

For the Middle Grades Only Web site, http://www. kidstrek.com/ (November 18, 2001), Theodore Taylor, "On Writing *Timothy of the Cay*."

KidsReads.com, http:// www.kidsreads.com/ (December 6, 2005), Tamara Penny, review of *A Sailor Returns*.

Scoop Web site, http:// www.friend.ly.net/ (November 18, 2001), Theodore Taylor, "On Writing *The Bomb*."

TeenReads.com, http:// www.teenreads.com/ (December 6, 2005), Sally M. Tibbetts, review of *Billy the Kid*.*

Amos Tutuola

(Photograph courtesy of Harry Ransom Humanities Research Center, The University of Texas at Austin. Reproduced by permission.)

■ Personal

Born 1920, in Abeokuta, Nigeria; died from hypertension and diabetes, June 8, 1997, in Ibadan, Nigeria; son of Charles (a cocoa farmer) and Esther Tutuola; married Alake Victoria, 1947; children: Olubunmi, Oluyinka, Erinola, five others. *Education:* Attended schools in Nigeria. *Religion:* Christian.

■ Career

Worked on father's farm; trained as a coppersmith; employed by Nigerian Government Labor Department, Lagos, and by Nigerian Broadcasting Corp., Ibadan, Nigeria. Freelance writer. Visiting research fellow, University of Ife, 1979; associate, international writing program at University of Iowa, 1983. *Military service:* Royal Air Force, 1943-45; served as metal worker in Nigeria.

■ Member

Modern Language Association of America, Mbari Club (Nigerian authors; founder).

■ Awards, Honors

Named honorary citizen of New Orleans, 1983; *The Palm-Wine Drinkard and His Dead Palm-Wine Tapster in the Dead's Town* and *My Life in the Bush of Ghosts* received second place awards in a contest held in Turin, Italy, 1985; Noble Patron of Arts, Pan African Writers Association, 1992.

■ Writings

The Palm-Wine Drinkard and His Dead Palm-Wine Tapster in the Dead's Town, Faber, 1952, Grove, 1953.

My Life in the Bush of Ghosts, Grove, 1954, reprinted, Faber, 1978.

Simbi and the Satyr of the Dark Jungle, Faber, 1955.

The Brave African Huntress, illustrated by Ben Enwonwu, Grove, 1958.

The Feather Woman of the Jungle, Faber, 1962.

Ajaiyi and His Inherited Poverty, Faber, 1967.

(Contributor) *Winds of Change: Modern Short Stories from Black Africa,* Longman, 1977.

The Witch-Herbalist of the Remote Town, Faber, 1981.

The Wild Hunter in the Bush of the Ghosts (facsimile of manuscript), edited with an introduction and a postscript by Bernth Lindfors, Three Continents Press, 1982, 2nd edition, 1989.

Pauper, Brawler, and Slanderer, Faber, 1987.

The Village Witch Doctor and Other Stories, Faber, 1990.

The Palm-Wine Drinkard [and] *My Life in the Bush of
  Ghosts,* Grove Press, 1993.
*Tutuola at the University: The Italian Voice of a Yoruba
  Ancestor,* Bulzoni (Rome, Italy), 2000.

■ **Adaptations**

Kola Ogunmola has written a play in Yoruba
entitled *Omuti,* based on *The Palm-Wine Drinkard,*
published by West African Book Publishers.

■ **Sidelights**

Amos Tutuola became the first internationally
recognized Nigerian writer following the publication of his novel *The Palm-Wine Drinkard and His
Dead Palm-Wine Tapster in the Dead's Town* in 1952.
Drawn from traditional Yoruba folktales he had
heard as a child, Tutuola's story is told in the style
of the tribe's oral storytellers. *The Palm-Wine
Drinkard* was praised by European critics for its
unconventional use of the English language, its
adherence to the Nigerian oral tradition, and its
unique, fantastical characters and plot. In Nigeria,
however, the reception was less than enthusiastic;
though he was his country's first internationally
recognized writer, his works were derided as
ungrammatical and poor examples of Nigerian
culture.

Tutuola was born in 1920 in Ipose-Ake, Abeokuta, a
Yoruba area of Nigeria that was situated some fifty
miles from the capital city of Lagos. The Yoruba are
one of Nigeria's main ethnic groups, along with the
Hausa, Ibo, Fulani, and several others. At the time
of Tutuola's birth, the country was a British protec-
torate, and it remained so for the following forty
years.

A Childhood of Stories

As a child, Tutuola heard Yoruba folk tales told by
his mother and aunt and soon began to enjoy telling them to others himself. His father was a cocoa
farmer, and for a time Tutuola was able to attend a
school run by Salvation Army missionaries. When
his father could no longer afford the tuition, Tutuola learned how to farm; he later took a job as a
houseboy to a local government clerk, who then
paid for Tutuola to continue his education. The man
was transferred to Lagos, and Tutuola went with
him, where he enrolled in high school.

the **palm-wine**
drinkard
AMOS TUTUOLA
and
my life in the
bush of **ghosts**

This 1993 collection contains Tutuola's first two novels.
(Grove Press, 1994. My Life in the Bush of Ghosts © 1954 by Grove Press. The Palm-
Wine Drinkard © 1953 by George Braziller. Used by permission of Grove/Atlantic,
Inc.)

As a young man, Tutuola learned the coppersmith
trade and served in Britain's Royal Air Force during
World War II as a blacksmith. He married Victoria
Alake in 1947, with whom he had eight children.
An attempt to begin his own blacksmith business
failed, and so Tutuola took a job instead as a mes-
senger and storeroom clerk for Nigeria's Labour
Department. To while away the idle hours at his
desk, he began jotting down Yoruba tales.

Tutuola never intended to publish his stories, but
one day he contacted an English photography-book
firm and inquired as to whether they would be
interested in a book about Nigerian bush tales—
illustrated with actual photographs of the spirits
said to inhabit the forest. An amused editor replied
in the affirmative and soon received a 76-page
manuscript, in Tutuola's hand, with photographic
negatives that were snapshots taken of artistic

renderings of the spirits. That work, *The Wild Hunter in the Bush of the Ghosts* did not appear until 1982, well into Tutuola's career, but it contained all the hallmarks of his fiction: its hero sets out on an epic journey fraught with peril, witnesses many ghastly events, and survives through his own intelligence or, failing that, through the intervention of a protective spirit.

Nigerian Folktales Published

In the early 1950s Tutuola came across an advertisement in a Nigerian magazine from the United Society for Christian Literature that listed some titles by African authors. He sent another manuscript to them, and while the editors there passed on publishing it themselves, they believed it to be imaginative enough to send to professional colleagues elsewhere. London's publishing house of Faber and Faber bought *The Palm-Wine Drinkard and His Dead Palm-Wine Tapster in the Dead's Town,* and upon publication in 1952 it became a minor sensation in Britain. A review by notable Welsh poet Dylan Thomas in the *Observer* newspaper did much to publicize the book, which went on to American and French editions soon afterward. Thomas termed it a "brief, thronged, grisly and bewitching story," and he concluded that here Tutuola's "writing is nearly always terse and direct, strong, wry, flat and savoury. . . . Nothing is too prodigious or too trivial to put down in this tall, devilish story."

Tutuola's genius is described by reviewers as an ability to refashion the traditional Yoruba myths and folktales that are the foundation of his work. Eustace Palmer noted, for instance, in *The Growth of the African Novel:* "Taking his stories direct from his people's traditional lore, he uses his inexhaustible imagination and inventive power to embellish them, to add to them or alter them, and generally transform them into his own stories conveying his own message." O.R. Dathorne commented in an essay published in *Introduction to Nigerian Literature:* "Tutuola is a literary paradox; he is completely part of the folklore traditions of the Yorubas and yet he is able to modernize these traditions in an imaginative way. It is on this level that his books can best be approached. . . . Tutuola deserves to be considered seriously because his work represents an intentional attempt to fuse folklore with modern life."

In *The Palm-Wine Drinkard,* for example, the Drinkard's quest for his tapster leads him into many perilous situations, including an encounter with the Red Fish, a monster Tutuola describes as having thirty horns "spread out as an umbrella," and

numerous eyes that "were closing and opening at the same time as if a man was pressing a switch on and off." Tutuola also amends a traditional tale concerning a Skull who borrows appendages belonging to other persons in order to look like a "complete gentleman" to include references to modern warfare. Tutuola writes: "If this gentleman went to the battle field, surely, enemy would not kill him or capture him and if bombers saw him in a town which was to be bombed, they would not throw bombs on his presence, and if they did throw it, the bomb itself would not explode until this gentleman would leave that town, because of his beauty." Gerald Moore observes in *Seven African Writers* that these descriptions are evidence "of Tutuola's easy use of the paraphernalia of modern life to give sharpness and immediacy to his imagery."

The Palm-Wine Drinkard was hailed by critics such as V.S. Pritchett. The work also has been favorably compared to such classics as *The Odyssey, Pilgrim's Progress,* and *Gulliver's Travels.* Some critics, however, expressed reservations about Tutuola's ability to repeat his success. According to Charles R. Larson's *The Emergence of African Fiction,* critic Anthony West stated: "*The Palm-Wine Drinkard* must be valued for its own freakish sake, and as an unrepeatable happy hit."

Continues to Draw on His Native Stories

Despite the reservations of critics like West, Tutuola went on to publish additional works, and while critics were, as Larson observed in *The Emergence of African Fiction,* "a little less awed now than they were in the early 1950's," Tutuola's works continue to merit critical attention. Among the more widely reviewed of these books is *The Witch-Herbalist of the Remote Town.* Published thirty years after *The Palm-Wine Drinkard,* this book involves a quest initiated by the protagonist, a hunter, to find a cure for his wife's barrenness. The journey to the Remote Town takes six years; along the way the hunter encounters bizarre and sometimes frightening places and people, including the Town of the Born-and-Die Baby and the Abnormal Squatting Man of the Jungle, who can paralyze opponents with a gust of frigid air by piercing his abdomen. The hunter eventually reaches the Remote Town, and the witch-herbalist gives him a broth guaranteed to make his wife fertile. The plot is complicated though, when the hunter, weak from hunger, sips some of the broth.

As with *The Palm-Wine Drinkard,* critical commentary of *The Witch-Herbalist of the Remote Town* focuses in particular on Tutuola's use of the English language. Edward Blishen, for instance, commented in the *Times Educational Supplement:* "The language is wonderfully stirring and odd: a mixture of straight translation from Yoruba, and everyday modern Nigerian idiom, and grand epical English. The imagination at work is always astonishing. . . . And this, not the bargain, is folklore not resurrected, but being created fresh and true in the white heat of a tradition still undestroyed." *Voice Literary Supplement* critic Jon Parales wrote: "His direct, apparently simple language creates an anything-can-happen universe, more whacky and amoral than the most determinedly modern lit." *Washington Post Book World* contributor Judith Chettle offered this view: "Tutuola writes with an appealing vigor and his idiosyncratic use of the English idiom gives the story a fresh and African perspective, though at times the clumsiness of some phrasing does detract from the thrust of the narrative. No eye-dabbing sentimentalist, Tutuola's commentary is clear-eyed if not acerbic, but underlying the tale is a quiet and persistent lament for the simpler, unsophisticated and happier past of his people."

An *Africa Today* contributor, Nancy J. Schmidt, observed that Tutuola's language became increasingly more like that of standard English over the years. She cited other differences between this work and earlier ones as well. "Tutuola's presence is very evident in *Witch-Herbalist,* but the strength of his presence and his imagination are not as strong as they once were," wrote Schmidt, who added that "neither Tutuola nor his hero seem to be able to take a consistent moral stand, a characteristic that is distinctly different from Tutuola's other narratives." Commenting on the reasons for these differences, Schmidt wrote: "They may reflect contemporary Yoruba culture, Tutuola's changing attitude toward Yoruba and Nigerian cultures as well as his changing position in Yoruba and Nigerian cultures, the difficulties of writing an oral narrative for an audience to whom oral narratives are becoming less familiar and less related to daily behavior, and the editorial policies for publishing African fictional narratives in the 1980s."

In the *New York Times Book Review* Charles Larson likewise noted Tutuola's use of standard English, but maintained that "the outstanding quality of Mr. Tutuola's work—the brilliance of the oral tradition—still remains." Larson concluded: "*The Witch-Herbalist of the Remote Town* is Mr. Tutuola at his imaginative best. Every incident in the narrative breathes with the life of the oral tradition; every episode in the journey startles with a kind of indigenous surrealism. Amos Tutuola is still his continent's most fantastic storyteller."

Tutuola's 1990 story collection, *The Village Witch Doctor and Other Stories,* contains eighteen stories based on traditional Yoruba fables. Like most of his previous work, the stories in this collection deal with greed, betrayal, and tricksterism. In the title story, for instance, a village witch doctor tricks others again and again before getting a dose of his own medicine. *Dictionary of Literary Biography* essayist Bernth Lindfors remarked that "the same buoyant imagination [found in his earlier work] is in evidence, the same fascination with comically grotesque fantasy worlds. Tutuola, after more than forty years of writing, remains a very resourceful raconteur."

If you enjoy the works of Amos Tutuola, you may also want to check out the following books:

Wole Soyinka, *Ake: The Years of Childhood,* 1989.
Ben Okri, *The Famished Road,* 1993.
Chinua Achebe, *Anthills of the Savannah,* 1997.

An essayist for *Contemporary Novelists* pointed out the commonalities that Tutuola's stories have, not only between themselves, but with the folklore and legends of other peoples from around the world. Tutuola' "books follow the same basic narrative pattern. A hero (or heroine) with supernatural powers or access to supernatural assistance sets out on a journey in quest of something important and suffers incredible hardships before successfully accomplishing his mission. He ventures into unearthly realms, performs arduous tasks, fights with fearsome monsters, endures cruel tortures, and narrowly escapes death. Sometimes he is accompanied by a relative or by loyal companions; sometimes he wanders alone. But he always survives his ordeals, attains his objective, and usually emerges from his nightmarish experiences a wiser, wealthier man. The cycle of his adventures—involving a Departure, Initiation, and Return—resembles that found in myths and folktales the world over."

Arguing for the importance of Tutuola's writings, Lindfors concluded that his "works unite oral and written art, bridging folk narratives on the one hand with precursors of the novel (such as The Pilgrim's Progress) on the other. Tutuola could be called the link between preliterate and literate man, for his creativity is firmly rooted in the cultural heritage of both. One sees in his works how two disparate systems of expressive conventions can be joined in a productive synthesis. Tutuola's writings will no doubt continue to interest readers for some time to come because they are a fascinating amalgam of old and new, indigenous and foreign, and oral and written materials."

Tutuola died in Ibadan, Nigeria, in June of 1997. He was seventy–seven years old. Robert Elliot Fox, who shared an office with him at the University of Ife in the late 1970s, recalled his memories of Tutuola in an article for *Research in African Literatures,* and concluded by firmly placing him in the canon of twentieth-century African literary icons. "Whatever else may be said about his work, it undeniably is part of the foundation of African writing—that part which is sunk most deeply in the substratum and psyche of African culture and imagination," asserted Fox. "However high and wide the African literary edifice grows, we'll keep coming back to Tutuola, not just as an historically important entity, but as a necessary counterpoint to other developments."

■ Biographical and Critical Sources

BOOKS

Amos Tutuola, Scribner, 1997.

Black Literature Criticism, Gale (Detroit, MI), 1992.

Collins, Harold R., *Amos Tutuola,* Twayne, 1969.

Contemporary Literary Criticism, Gale (Detroit, MI), Volume 5, 1976, Volume 14, 1980, Volume 29, 1984.

Contemporary Novelists, 6th edition, St. James Press (Detroit, MI), 1996.

Dictionary of Literary Biography, Volume 125: *Twentieth-Century Caribbean and Black African Writers,* second series, Gale (Detroit, MI), 1993.

Herskovits, Melville J. and Francis S. Herskovits, *Dahomean Narrative: A Cross-Cultural Analysis,* Northwestern University Press, 1958.

Irele, Abiola, *The African Experience in Literature and Ideology,* Heinemann, 1981.

King, Bruce, editor, *Introduction to Nigerian Literature,* Evans Brothers, 1971.

Larson, Charles R., *The Emergence of African Fiction,* revised edition, Indiana University Press, 1972.

Laurence, Margaret, *Long Drums and Cannons: Nigerian Dramatists,* Praeger, 1969.

Lindfors, Bernth, editor, *Critical Perspectives on Amos Tutuola,* Three Continents Press, 1975.

Lindfors, Bernth, *Early Nigerian Literature,* Africana Publishing, 1982.

Moore, Gerald, *Seven African Writers,* Oxford University Press, 1962.

Osofisan, Femi, *The Orality of Prose: A Comparatist Look at the Works of Rabelais, Joyce, and Tutuola,* Ife Monographs on African Literature, 1986.

Palmer, Eustace, *The Growth of the African Novel,* Heinemann, 1979.

Quayson, Ato, *Strategic Transformations in Nigerian Writing: Orality and History in the Work of Rev. Samuel Johnson, Amos Tutuola, Wole Soyinka and Ben Okri,* Edinburgh University Press (Edinburgh, Scotland), 1999.

Tucker, Martin, *Africa in Modern Literature: A Survey of Contemporary Writing in English,* Ungar, 1967.

Tutuola, Amos, *The Palm-Wine Drinkard and His Dead Palm-Wine Tapster in the Dead's Town,* Faber, 1952, Grove, 1953.

PERIODICALS

Africa Today, Volume 29, number 3, 1982.

Ariel, April, 1977.

Books Abroad, summer, 1968.

Critique, fall/winter, 1960-61; fall/winter, 1967-68.

Journal of Canadian Fiction, volume 3, number 4, 1975.

Journal of Commonwealth Literature, August, 1974; August, 1981; volume 17, number 1, 1982.

Listener, December 14, 1967.

London Review of Books, April 2, 1987.

Los Angeles Times Book Review, August 15, 1982.

Nation, September 25, 1954.

New Statesman, December 8, 1967.

New Yorker, April 23, 1984.

New York Times Book Review, July 4, 1982.

Observer, July 6, 1952; November 22, 1981.

Okike, September, 1978.

Presence Africaine, third trimester, 1967.

Spectator, October 24, 1981.

Times Educational Supplement, February 26, 1982.

Times Literary Supplement, January 18, 1968; February 26, 1982; August 28, 1987; May 18, 1990, p. 534.

Voice Literary Supplement, June, 1982.

Washington Post, July 13, 1987.

Washington Post Book World, August 15, 1982.

World Literature Today, summer, 1991, p. 539.

OBITUARIES

PERIODICALS

New York Times, June 15, 1997.

Washington Post, June 22, 1997.*

Jack Williamson

■ Personal

Full name John Stewart Williamson; born April 29, 1908, in Bisbee, Arizona Territory (now the state of Arizona); died November 10, 2006, in Portales, NM; son of Asa Lee (a rancher and teacher) and Lucy Betty (a teacher) Williamson; married Blanche Slaten Harp (a merchant), August 15, 1947 (died January 5, 1985, in a car accident); children: (stepchildren) Keigm Harp, Adele Harp Lovorn. *Education:* Home schooled until he was twelve, then attended high school in Richland, NM; attended West Texas State Teachers College (now West Texas State University), 1928-30, and University of New Mexico, 1932-33; Eastern New Mexico University, B.A. (summa cum laude) and M.A., 1957; University of Colorado at Boulder, Ph.D., 1964. *Politics:* Democrat. *Religion:* Methodist.

■ Career

Fantasy and science fiction writer, beginning 1928; *News Tribune,* Portales, NM, wire editor, 1947; creator of comic strip "Beyond Mars" for New York *Sunday News,* 1953-56; New Mexico Military Institute, Roswell, instructor in English, 1957-59; University of Colorado at Boulder, instructor in English, 1960; Eastern New Mexico University, Portales, associate professor, 1960-69, professor, 1969-77, became Distinguished Research Professor in English.

■ Member

Science Fiction Writers of America (president, 1978-80), National Council of Teachers of English, Masons, Rotary Club.

■ Awards, Honors

First Fandom Science Fiction Hall of Fame Award, 1968; Pilgrim Award, Science Fiction Research Association, 1973; Grand Master Award for lifetime achievement, Science Fiction Writers of America, 1976; Guest of honor, Thirty-fifth World Science Fiction Convention, Miami, 1977, and at numerous regional conventions; Hugo Award, 1985, for *Wonder's Child: My Life in Science Fiction;* World Fantasy Award for life achievement, World Fantasy Convention, 1994; Hugo Award for Best Novella, World Science Fiction Society, and Nebula Award in novella category, both 2001, both for *The Ultimate Earth;* John W. Campbell Memorial Award for best science fiction novel of the year, University of Kansas, 2001, for *Terraforming Earth;* Bram Stoker Award, Horror Writers Association, for lifetime achievement.

■ Writings

SCIENCE FICTION NOVELS

(With Miles J. Breuer) *The Girl from Mars,* Stellar (New York, NY), 1929.

The Legion of Space (also see below), illustrated by A.J. Donnell, Fantasy Press (Reading, PA), 1947.

Darker than You Think, Fantasy Press (Reading, PA), 1948, reprinted, Orb (New York, NY), 1999.

The Humanoids (originally published in *Astounding* as *And Searching Mind*), Simon & Schuster (New York, NY), 1949.

One against the Legion (also see below), Fantasy Press (Reading, PA), 1950, published with novella *Nowhere Near,* Pyramid (New York, NY), 1967.

The Green Girl, Avon (New York, NY), 1950.

The Cometeers (also see below), illustrated by Ed Cartier, Fantasy Press (Reading, PA), 1950.

Dragon's Island, Simon & Schuster (New York, NY), 1951, published as *The Not-Men,* Belmont (New York, NY), 1968.

The Legend of Time, Fantasy Press (Reading, PA), 1952, published as *The Legion of Time* and *After Worlds End,* two volumes, Digit, 1961.

Dome around America, Ace (New York, NY), 1955.

(With James E. Gunn) *Star Bridge,* Gnome Press (New York, NY), 1955.

The Trial of Terra, Ace (New York, NY), 1962.

Golden Blood, Lancer (New York, NY), 1964.

The Reign of Wizardry, Lancer (New York, NY), 1964.

Bright New Universe, Ace (New York, NY), 1967.

Trapped in Space (juvenile), illustrated by Robert Amundsen, Doubleday (Garden City, NY), 1968.

The Moon Children, Putnam (New York, NY), 1972.

The Power of Blackness, Berkley (New York, NY), 1976.

Brother to Demons, Brother to Gods, Bobbs-Merrill (Indianapolis, IN), 1979.

The Humanoid Touch (sequel to *The Humanoids*), Holt (New York, NY), 1980.

Three from the Legion (contains *The Legion of Space, The Cometeers,* and *One against the Legion*), Doubleday (Garden City, NY), 1981.

(With Miles J. Breuer) *The Birth of a New Republic: Jack Williamson—The Collector's Edition,* Volume II, P.D.A. Enterprises (New Orleans, LA), 1981.

Manseed, Ballantine (New York, NY), 1982.

The Queen of the Legion, Pocket Books (New York, NY), 1983.

Lifeburst, Ballantine (New York, NY), 1984.

Firebird, Bluejay (New York, NY), 1986.

Firechild, Bluejay (New York, NY), 1986.

(With Frederik Pohl) *Land's End,* T. Doherty (New York, NY), 1988.

Mazeway, Ballantine (New York, NY), 1990.

(With Frederik Pohl) *The Singers of Time,* Doubleday (New York, NY), 1991.

Beachhead, Tor (New York, NY), 1992.

Demon Moon, Tor (New York, NY), 1994.

The Black Sun, Tor (New York, NY), 1997.

The Silicon Dagger, Tor (New York, NY), 1999.

Terraforming Earth, Tor (New York, NY), 2001.

The Stonehenge Gate, Tor (New York, NY), 2005.

"JIM EDEN" SERIES; WITH FREDERIK POHL

Undersea Quest, Gnome Press (New York, NY), 1954.

Undersea Fleet, Gnome Press (New York, NY), 1956.

Undersea City, Gnome Press (New York, NY), 1958.

"STARCHILD" TRILOGY; WITH FREDERIK POHL

The Reefs of Space (also see below), Ballantine (New York, NY), 1964.

Starchild (also see below), Ballantine (New York, NY), 1965.

Rogue Star (also see below), Ballantine (New York, NY), 1969.

The Starchild Trilogy (contains *The Reefs of Space, Starchild,* and *Rogue Star*), Doubleday (Garden City, NY), 1977.

"CUCKOO'S SAGA"; WITH FREDERIK POHL

Farthest Star (also see below), Ballantine (New York, NY), 1975.

Wall Around a Star (also see below), Ballantine (New York, NY), 1983.

The Saga of Cuckoo (contains *Farthest Star* and *Wall Around a Star*), Doubleday (Garden City, NY), 1983.

SHORT STORY COLLECTIONS

Lady in Danger, Utopian (New York, NY), 1945.

(With Murray Leinster and John Wyndham) *Three Stories,* Doubleday (Garden City, NY), 1967, published as *A Sense of Wonder: Three Science Fiction Stories,* edited by Sam Moskowitz, Sidgwick & Jackson (London, England), 1967.

The Pandora Effect, Ace (New York, NY), 1969.

People Machines, Ace (New York, NY), 1971.

The Early Williamson, Doubleday (Garden City, NY), 1975.

Dreadful Sleep, Weinberg (Chicago, IL), 1977.

The Best of Jack Williamson, introduction by Frederik Pohl, Ballantine (New York, NY), 1978.

The Alien Intelligence: Jack Williamson—The Collector's Edition, Volume I, P.D.A. Enterprises (New Orleans, LA), 1980.

(With others) *Medea: Harlan's World,* edited by Harlan Ellison, illustrated by Kelly Freas, cartography by Diane Duane, Bantam (New York, NY), 1985.

The Metal Man and Others, foreword by Hal Clement, Haffner Press (Royal Oak, MI), 1999.

Wolves of Darkness, foreword by Harlan Ellison, Haffner Press (Royal Oak, MI), 1999.

Spider Island: The Collected Stories of Jack Williamson, Volume Four, Haffner Press (Royal Oak, MI), 2001.

Dragon's Island and Other Stories, Five Star (Waterville, ME), 2002.

OTHER

Teaching Science Fiction (nonfiction), privately printed, 1973.

(Editor) *Teaching Science Fiction: Education for Tomorrow* (essays), Owlswick (Philadelphia, PA), 1980.

Wonder's Child: My Life in Science Fiction (autobiography), Bluejay (New York, NY), 1985, reprinted, BenBella Books (Dallas, TX), 2005.

Seventy-five: The Diamond Anniversary of a Science Fiction Pioneer (collection), Haffner Press (Royal Oak, MI), 2003.

Also author of the novella *The Ultimate Earth.* Contributor of stories to science-fiction anthologies, including *Of Worlds Beyond,* edited by Lloyd Arthur Eshbach, Fantasy Press (Reading, PA), 1947; *The Mirror of Infinity,* edited by Robert Silverberg, Harper (New York, NY), 1970; *The Science Fiction Hall of Fame,* edited by Ben Bova, Doubleday (Garden City, NY), 1973; *Before the Golden Age,* edited by Isaac Asimov, Doubleday (Garden City, NY), 1974; *Science Fiction: Today and Tomorrow,* edited by Reginald Bretnor, Harper (New York, NY), 1974; and *Number Six,* edited by Terry Carr, Holt (New York, NY), 1977. Contributor of short stories to periodicals, including *Amazing Stories, Science Wonder Stories, Air Wonder Stories, Astounding Stories, Wonder Stories, Weird Tales, Astounding Science Fiction,* and *Argosy.* Williamson's work has been translated into numerous languages. A collection of his work can be found at Eastern New Mexico University in Portales, New Mexico.

SCIENCE-FICTION NOVELS; UNDER PSEUDONYM WILL STEWART

Seetee Shock (originally published serially), Simon & Schuster (New York, NY), 1950, reprinted under name Jack Williamson, Lancer (New York, NY), 1968.

Seetee Ship (originally published serially), Gnome Press (New York, NY), 1951, reprinted under name Jack Williamson, Lancer (New York, NY), 1968.

■ Sidelights

Jack Williamson, "a distinguished writer of science fiction," as Margalit Fox described him in the *New York Times,* was one of the pioneers of serious sci-

ence fiction during that genre's Golden Age of the 1930s. In a career spanning some eighty years, Williamson helped to define the science fiction field. A writer for the *Daily Telegraph* noted that Williamson "began publishing before the term science fiction had even been coined" and credited the author with having "introduced android and terraforming to the lexicon." "Williamson was perhaps the greatest, and certainly the longest lived, of the writers who became prominent in the mass-market magazines of prewar days," wrote Christopher Priest in the London *Guardian.* "Williamson's skills as a writer enabled him to outgrow that past, and for most of his later career he was recognised for his varied and subtle books, many of them written for young readers." Williamson's recurring theme was the relationship between man and machine. Many of his works warn of the dangers of having machines deprive us of our humanity by taking away the most fundamental tasks of human beings. Ironically, for a man

Williamson and fellow science fiction writer James E. Gunn at the Science Fiction and Fantasy Hall of Fame at the University of Kansas. (Reproduced by permission of William Tienken.)

best known for his visions of the technological future, Williamson was born in a time and place far removed from modern civilization.

Born in the Desert

Williamson was born April 29, 1908, in the Arizona Territory, now the state of Arizona. The family soon journeyed by covered wagon to New Mexico, where they established a ranch. The family's finances were never stable and Williamson was not able to finish college. While living in the desert land of New Mexico, Williamson discovered Hugo Gernsback's magazine, *Amazing Stories.* Williamson decided to take a chance writing in the genre and sold his first story, "The Metal Man," to *Amazing Stories* in 1928. Thirteen of his first twenty-one published stories were spectacular enough to gain covers in the early science-fiction magazines, often appearing in installments. Williamson said he once earned his living writing for these magazines for as little as a half-cent per word.

During World War II, Williamson served in the Army as a weather forecaster in the Pacific. Returning from the war, he worked for the *News Tribune* in Portales, New Mexico, and wrote a comic strip, "Beyond Mars," for the New York *Sunday News.* In 1957, Williamson finally was able to finish college and began a teaching career. In 1960 he began teaching at Eastern New Mexico University, where he stayed until retirement.

"If science-fiction writing is an art that can be taught, there is probably no one in the world better qualified to teach it than Jack Williamson," remarked Sam Moskowitz in *Seekers of Tomorrow: Masters of Science Fiction.* "[Williamson is] an author who pioneered superior characterization in a field almost barren of it, realism in the presentation of human motivation previously unknown, scientific rationalization of supernatural concepts for story purposes, and exploitation of the untapped story potentials of antimatter." As an academic, Williamson also legitimized science fiction as a field deserving of literary attention. In recognition of his contributions, he received the Grand Master Award for lifetime achievement from the Science Fiction Writers of America in 1976.

Gains a Following

Williamson's output during the 1930s was phenomenal. "His early prolificness was indeed almost manic," wrote John Clute in the *Independent.*

A small-town reporter, investigating a string of grisly deaths, finds that something savagely supernatural is afoot in this 1999 novel. (Orb, 1999. Reproduced by permission.)

"Almost everything contained in the first six large volumes of his complete short stories . . . was published before writers like Isaac Asimov and Robert A. Heinlein entered the field in 1939 and began to transform it; in their dozens, these stories exhibit an inner agitation that he never wholly escaped." Williamson initially attracted attention in the science fiction genre as a master of the space opera, a subgenre of science fiction so-called because of their over-sized, operatic plots set in deep space. Fans voted his character Giles Habibula to be their favorite character in science fiction. "He was a star in the young and growing field of science fiction almost from the first," noted Frederik Pohl in his introduction to *The Best of Jack Williamson,* "proved by the response of the fans, the imitation of younger writers, and the eagerness with which editors sought his work."

The Legion of Space, the first book of what was to become a series, put Williamson on equal ground with such science fiction writers as John W. Campbell and Edward E. "Doc" Smith. Set in the thirtieth century, the work's authenticity rests on the development of the memorable comic figure Giles Habibula. Alfred D. Stewart wrote in the *Dictionary of Literary Biography*: "Developed in Dickensian fashion through distinctive traits of speech and character, [Habibula] is modeled on Shakespeare's Falstaff; he is a born thief who whines about his ills and threats to his personal safety throughout the series." The second book in the series, *The Cometeers*, introduces another interesting character, Orco. During the course of the story, Orco discovers, to his distress, that he is not a true human. While the characterization in these early stories was found to be rather striking by reviewers, Moskowitz claimed that Williamson's true expertise at characterization came in the stories that followed. "Realism was present in the characterization as well as in the plotting of [his later] stories. Giles Habibula had been a milestone, but Garth Hammond, aptly labeled 'a hero whose heart is purest brass,' in [the short story 'Crucible of Power'], was a giant step towards believability in science fiction. Hammond was the man who made the first trip to Mars and built a power station near the sun for sheer selfish, self-seeking gain. . . . There had never been anything as blunt as this in science fiction before. . . . After [Williamson] showed the way, not-completely-sympathetic and more three-dimensional people began to appear" in science fiction.

Reviewers labeled Williamson's early writing, such as the "Legion of Space" novels, fantasy literature. Stewart stressed that such novels were "vehicles for cosmic plotting and pseudo-scientific devices, not for the examination of man's possibilities. Williamson's [eventual] fascination with [Charles] Darwin, H.G. Wells, and evolution led him, in his best thought-out and best written books, to deal with real possibilities for man, not exaggerated romantic vagaries." Williamson's writing, beginning in the forties, became more grounded in logical scientific explanations. He wrote his "Seetee" series in the early part of the decade under the pseudonym Will Stewart; to some they are considered the best expositions on the subject of antimatter ever written. (The concept of antimatter, or contra-terrene, is the condition in which positive and negative charges are reversed from that typical on earth.) In *Seetee Ship*, the earth has become morally and politically stagnant, and scientists, known as "asterites," strive to legalize the use of antimatter as a means of reestablishing freedom and progress for mankind. But the asterites and the Establishment are at odds. In the sequel, *Seetee Shock*, the conflict has expanded—the asterites are convinced the power of

antimatter should be available to all inhabitants on all planets. When the novel's hero, Nick Jenkins, manages to turn on a special transmitter, the Fifth Freedom results, destroying governments and establishing freedom for all in the universe.

Williamson's most famous novel, *The Humanoids*, also concerns the struggle for human freedom, but the outcome is disastrous. The humanoids are small robots who have as their goal the protection and happiness of man. However, Stewart pointed out: "As Williamson remarked in a talk at the 1977 World Science Fiction Convention, 'Their built-in benevolence goes too far. Alert to the potential harm in nearly every human activity, they don't let people drive cars, ride bicycles, smoke, drink, or engage in unsupervised sex. Doing everything for everybody,

After the Earth is destroyed in a meteor crash, the few human survivors must rebuild civilization in this 2003 novel. (Tor, 2003. Reproduced by permission.)

they forbid all free action. Their world becomes a luxurious but nightmarish prison of total frustration.'" Eventually man must regain his freedom and does so by developing psychic powers. A contributor to the *New York Herald Tribune Book Review* thought that *The Humanoids* "deals, essentially, with the conflict that began when the wheel and the lever were invented: the battle between men and machines." Thirty years later Williamson wrote the sequel to *The Humanoids*, titled *The Humanoid Touch*.

Several of Williamson's other works focus on genetic engineering, advanced human evolution, and a number of additional evolutionary possibilities. Four distinct species of man exist in *Brother to Demons, Brother to Gods*: premen, trumen, mumen, and stargods. Because of the varying abilities and moralities of these four species, a power struggle arises and the only hope for universal peace is the evolution of "ultiman," a being of perfect love and power. According to Stewart, "*Brother to Demons, Brother to Gods* focuses in the end on humanity's stupendous potential." *Fireways*, set in the contemporary world, also explores the positive and negative possibilities inherent in genetic engineering. Scientists at a top-secret lab create a completely new life form, a tiny pink "worm" that is capable of communicating telepathically with humans. However, in the course of their experimentation, they also manage to unleash a genetic plague that destroys an entire town. Along the way the CIA, the KGB, the Pentagon, and religious fanatics all get into the act.

Writing Late in Life

Throughout his eighties, Williamson continued to produce a variety of critically-praised science-fiction novels at a steady pace. In *Mazeway*, set against a far-future interstellar backdrop, young Ben Dain attempts to save a dying Earth by convincing the El-dren, an ancient and powerful alien race, that humans are worthy of their attention. A reviewer for *Kliatt* called it a "well-done tale" with "unusual and wonderfully depicted aliens, subverted robots, death, and mystery." Joel Singer in *Voice of Youth Advocates* felt that the book is "well thought out and plotted," but suffers from a disjointed writing style from one chapter to the next.

Beachhead returns to the near-future by focusing on the human exploration and colonization of Mars. The adversities the pioneers must confront—a deadly virus, a mutiny, a crash landing—are played against a parallel plot involving the financial machinations and intrigues within the multinational

Williamson tells the story of his own life, and of the rise and development of the science fiction field, in this 2005 autobiography. (BenBella Books, 2005. Reproduced by permission.)

consortium backing the mission. Dan Chow, writing in *Locus*, remarked that "*Beachhead* shows a freshness and vigor which would be remarkable in a writer generations younger."

Demon Moon, harkens back to Williamson's pulp origins with a tale of a world infested by wolves, wyverns, and dragons that is reminiscent of his classic *Darker than You Think*. According to Russell Letson in *Locus*, the book "creates a surface of high-fantasy motifs whose rationalizations turn out to be science fictional." Letson felt that the book's world is both "fantastic and real enough to push back when poked." Tom Easton in *Analog Science Fiction & Fact* credited *Demon Moon* as a successful thriller, but found it lacking in originality and too derivative of other work in the field.

In *The Black Sun*, a ravaged Earth sends out ninety-nine star ships in an attempt to seed the galaxy with humanity and ensure the survival of the species. The book deals with the travails of the last ship to leave Earth: its landing on a frozen planet, its incompetent and crazed captain, and the strange discoveries of past habitation on the planet as the crew members attempt to explore their new world and survive. "Master craftsman Williamson . . . evokes terror and uncertainty on the frozen planet in this highly recommended adventure," wrote Susan Hamburger in the *Library Journal*. A critic for *Publishers Weekly* believed that the novel possessed "that essential SF attribute, the sense of wonder, which Williamson once again generates in spades by skillfully evoking an unknown, alien planet and the inhuman intelligences who once populated it."

Speaking of the 1999 novel *The Silicon Dagger, Magazine of Fantasy and Science Fiction* reviewer Charles de Lint observed: "Williamson proves with his latest novel that he still has what it takes to tell an engaging story." Clay Barstow travels to Kentucky to investigate the murder of his brother, Alden Kirk, and stumbles upon a top-secret technology with the potential to cause a civil war within the United States. De Lint observed that much of the book contains discussions about the ease with which information is distributed today and how new technologies will change the way the United States defends itself. The reviewer noted that rather than overwhelming the story, "these discussions are the story, and a riveting one at that." De Lint went on to call *The Silicon Dagger* "a novel of ideas" and "a fascinating read." In *Booklist*, Roland Green stated: "Williamson's understated prose heightens dramatic impact, and his characterizations are as solid as ever."

In Williamson's next book, *Terraforming Earth*, an asteroid collides with Earth, leaving the planet devoid of life save for a small group of clones who managed to escape to a colony on the moon. From the moon, generation after generation of clones gaze upon Earth and wait for the time to return and terraform—ready the planet for human life—the Earth. Jackie Cassada of *Library Journal* termed *Terraforming Earth* a "vividly imagined tale of life at the far end of time," while *Booklist* reviewer Green remarked: "This is indeed the work of a grand master of [science fiction.]" Similarly, a *Publishers Weekly* critic called it a "masterful work by a superb chronicler of the cosmic."

The Stonehenge Gate, Williamson's 2005 effort, centers on a group of four poker-playing academics who discover what appears to be a Stonehenge-like structure buried beneath the Sahara Desert. After unearthing the structure, the group determines that it is actually a portal to another planet with inhabit-

This 2006 novel tells of four friends who uncover an ancient gateway between worlds. (Tor, 2006. Reproduced by permission.)

ants who may be connected to the origins of life on Earth. Regina Schroeder of *Booklist* described the book as a "surprisingly successful" mix of "technological inventiveness and heroic quest" that offers "a neat origin story for humanity." In the *Library Journal*, Cassada reported that *The Stonehenge Gate* "challenges the imagination at every turn."

Williamson's shorter works appear in *Spider Island: The Collected Stories of Jack Williamson, Dragon's Island and Other Stories*, and *Seventy-five: The Diamond Anniversary of a Science Fiction Pioneer*. Commenting on the works included in *Dragon's Island and Other Stories, Booklist* contributor Green noted: "Williamson's spare prose keeps the melodrama in hand and makes it consistently readable." In reviews for *Library Journal*, Michael J. Rogers called the stories in

Spider Island "vintage sf at its best," and defined *Seventy-five* as a "glorious tribute" to Williamson and his work.

Stewart felt that "the future of science fiction is now as unlimited as the future of science itself, and Jack Williamson is one of the pioneer writers who made it so." Yet more than a pioneer, Williamson remained a significant voice in the field. Before Williamson's death in 2006 at the age of ninety-eight, Moskowitz credited him as "one of the most adaptable science-fiction writers alive." Chow noted: "This man simply cannot be underestimated or dismissed as a relic of prehistory. Many are the authors, decades younger, who have fallen by the wayside. Yet Williamson goes on, by the evidence, as fresh as ever."

If you enjoy the works of Jack Williamson, you may also want to check out the following books:

John Varley, *Mammoth*, 2004.
Leigh Brackett, *Sea Kings of Mars and Otherworldly Stories*, 2005.
Larry Niven, *The Draco Tavern*, 2006.

Speaking to Jayme Lynn Blaschke in *Interzone*, Williamson stated: "I've never written bestsellers or made a great deal of money at it, but when I look back, I've been able to spend most of my life doing something I enjoyed. When I look at people around me, many of them are working at dollar jobs, at jobs they hate, jobs that bore them. For me it's been largely rewarding. Of course, writing is hard work, sitting at the typewriter or computer and pounding the keys. For many years as a pulp writer trying desperately to make a living, I worked on stories that were ill-conceived or failed to say something I wanted to say and came to no good end. In recent years I've had more freedom to write only what I wanted to write. A story doesn't work unless it's something you really believe. The reader won't believe it if you don't; won't be interested if you're not interested."

Late in life, Williamson looked back on his career: "Since I discovered science fiction—back in 1926, before it had been named science fiction—it has been half my life. For the first twenty years and more; writing it paid barely enough to let me keep writing it, but in recent decades the rewards in recognition as well as in royalties have been more generous than I had ever dared expect. Looking back on a life of being reasonably well rewarded for doing exactly what I wanted to do, I feel pretty lucky. Pretty optimistic, too, about the ability of homo sapiens to keep on surviving crises as it has always survived them, and about my own ability to survive a little longer as a science-fiction writer."

■ **Biographical and Critical Sources**

BOOKS

Clareson, Thomas D., editor, *Voices for the Future: Essays on Major Science-Fiction Writers*, Volume 1, Bowling Green University (Bowling Green, OH), 1976.
Contemporary Literary Criticism, Volume 29, Gale (Detroit, MI), 1984.
Dictionary of Literary Biography, Volume 8: *Twentieth-Century American Science-Fiction Writers*, Gale (Detroit, MI), 1981.
Haffner, Stephen, editor, *In Memory of Wonder's Child: Jack Williamson, April 29, 1908-November 10, 2006*, Haffner Press (Royal Oak, MI), 2007.
Hauptmann, Richard A., *The Work of Jack Williamson: An Annotated Bibliography and Literary Guide*, edited by Boden Clark, Borgo Press (San Bernardino, CA), 1997.
McCaffrey, Larry, *Jack Williamson: An Interview*, Northhouse & Northhouse (Dallas, TX), 1988.
Meyers, Robert E., editor, *Jack Williamson: A Primary and Secondary Bibliography*, G.K. Hall (Boston, MA), 1980.
Moskowitz, Sam, *Seekers of Tomorrow: Masters of Science Fiction*, World Publishing (Cleveland, OH), 1966.
St. James Guide to Science Fiction Writers, 4th edition, St. James Press (Detroit, MI), 1996.
Williamson, Jack, *Wonder's Child: My Life in Science Fiction* (autobiography), Bluejay (New York, NY), 1985.
Zelany, Roger, editor, *The Williamson Effect*, Tor (New York, NY), 1996.

PERIODICALS

Analog Science Fiction & Fact, February, 1987, review of *Firechild*, p. 180; February, 1991, review of *Mazeway*, p. 176; December 15, 1994, Tom Easton, review of *Demon Moon*, p. 165; June, 2000, review of story "The Stone from the Green Star" from *Wolves of Darkness*, p. 130.

Booklist, April 15, 1999, Roland Green, review of *The Silicon Dagger,* p. 1518; May 15, 2001, Roland Green, review of *Terraforming Earth,* p. 1739; September 15, 2002, Roland Green, review of *Dragon's Island and Other Stories,* p. 212; August, 2005, Regina Schroeder, review of *The Stonehenge Gate,* p. 2010.

Book World, March 30, 1997, review of *The Black Sun,* p. 8.

Chronicle, December, 1992, review of *Beachhead,* p. 37; September, 1994, review of *Demon Moon,* p. 37; June, 1997, review of *The Black Sun,* p. 41; September, 2005, Don D'Ammassa, review of *The Stonehenge Gate,* p. 28.

Emergency Librarian, January, 1988, review of *The Humaniods,* p. 26.

Extrapolation, fall, 1989, review of *Darker Than You Think,* p. 205.

Guardian Weekly, June 26, 1988, review of *Firechild,* p. 28.

Interzone, January, 1999, Jayme Lynn Blaschke, "A Conversation with Jack Williamson."

Kirkus Reviews, June 15, 1992, review of *Beachhead,* p. 754; June 15, 2005, review of *The Stonehenge Gate,* p. 668.

Kliatt, fall, 1978, review of *The Best Of Jack Williamson,* p. 19; spring, 1981, review of *Brother To Demons, Brother To Gods,* p. 20; fall, 1981, review of *The Humanoid Touch,* p. 24; spring, 1986, review of *The Legion of Time,* p. 26, and review of *Wonder's Child,* p. 29; January, 1991, review of *Mazeway,* p. 25; September, 2004, Janet Julian, review of *The Humanoids [and] With Folded Hands* audio edition, p. 61; September, 2006, Sherry Hoy, review of *The Stonehenge Gate,* p. 35.

Library Journal, July, 1972, review of *The Moon Children,* p. 2438; September 15, 1972, review of *The Moon Children,* p. 2971; January 15, 1976, review of *The Power of Blackness,* p. 362; July, 1980, Susan L. Nickerson, review of *Teaching Science Fiction,* p. 1510; October 15, 1982, review of *Manseed,* p. 2007; January 15, 1983, review of *The Queen of the Legion,* p. 148; December, 1984, Jackie Cassada, review of *Lifeburst,* p. 2301; September 15, 1986, Jackie Cassada, review of *Firechild,* p. 103; November 15, 1988, review of *The Humanoids,* p. 31; February 15, 1997, Susan Hamburger, review of *The Black Sun,* p. 164; April 15, 1999, Jackie Cassada, review of *The Silicon Dagger,* p. 149; July, 2001, Jackie Cassada, review of *Terraforming Earth,* p. 131; May 15, 2002, Michael J. Rogers, review of *Spider Island: The Collected Stories of Jack Williamson,* p. 131; December 1, 2004, Michael J. Rogers, review of *Seventy-five: The Diamond Anniversary of a Science Fiction Pioneer,* p. 184; August 1, 2005, Jackie Cassada, review of *The Stonehenge Gate,* p. 76.

Library Media Connection, March, 1987, review of *Firechild,* p. 34.

Locus, July, 1992, Dan Chow, review of *Beachhead,* p. 29; May, 1994, Russell Letson, review of *Demon Moon,* p. 27; June, 1994, review of *Demon Moon,* p. 60; October, 1994, review of *Demon Moon,* p. 56.

Magazine of Fantasy and Science Fiction, March, 1974, review of *H.G. Wells,* p. 45; February, 1976, review of *The Early Williamson,* p. 46; April, 1985, Algis Budrys, review of *Wonder's Child,* p. 31; May, 1985, Algis Budrys, review of *Lifeburst,* p. 38; August, 1999, Charles de Lint, review of *The Silicon Dagger,* p. 43.

New York Herald Tribune Book Review, October 9, 1949, review of *The Humanoids.*

Publishers Weekly, May 1, 1972, review of *The Moon Children,* p. 49; June 16, 1975, review of *The Early Williamson,* p. 75; December 15, 1975, review of *The Power of Blackness,* p. 47; January 22, 1979, review of *Brother to Demons, Brother to Gods,* p. 367; July 30, 1979, review of *The Reign of Wizardry,* p. 53; June 6, 1980, review of *Golden Blood,* p. 76; September 12, 1980, Barbara A. Bannon, review of *The Humanoid Touch,* p. 60; August 27, 1982, review of *Manseed,* p. 349; December 3, 1982, review of *The Queen of the Legion,* p. 58; December 24, 1982, review of *Wall around a Star,* p. 62; April 22, 1983, review of *New Earths,* p. 102; March 23, 1984, review of *Wonder's Child,* p. 64; November 2, 1984, review of *Lifeburst,* p. 69; August 23, 1985, review of *Wonder's Child,* p. 70; July 18, 1986, Sybil Steinberg, review of *Firechild,* p. 83; July 10, 1987, review of *Firechild,* p. 65; February 16, 1990, Sybil Steinberg, review of *Mazeway,* p. 70; January 20, 1997, review of *The Black Sun,* p. 399; March 29, 1999, review of *The Silicon Dagger,* p. 96; June 25, 2001, review of *Terraforming Earth,* p. 55; August 12, 2002, review of *Dragon's Island and Other Stories,* p. 282; July 18, 2005, review of *The Stonehenge Gate,* p. 189.

Tribune Books (Chicago, IL), January 18, 1987, review of *Firechild,* p. 6; August 30, 1992, review of *Beachhead,* p. 6.

Voice of Youth Advocates, December, 1986, review of *Firechild,* p. 242; February, 1991, Joel Singer, review of *Mazeway,* p. 389; April, 1993, review of *Beachhead,* p. 23; December, 1994, review of *Demon Moon,* p. 291; August, 1999, review of *The Black Sun,* p. 197.

ONLINE

Science Fiction Weekly Web site, http://www.scifi.com/ (September 30, 2002), Kathie Huddleston, "After 75 Years of Publishing, Jack Williamson Is SF's Grand Master."

OBITUARIES

PERIODICALS

Daily Telegraph (London, England), November 15, 2006, "Obituary of Jack Williamson: Doyen of Science Fiction Whose First Stories Appeared before the Term Was Coined."

Grand Rapids Press (Grand Rapids, MI), November 15, 2006, p. B7.

Guardian (London, England), December 5, 2006, Christopher Priest, "Jack Williamson: Last of the Pulp SF Novelists, He Overcame Chronic Writer's Block," p. 33.

Independent, November 13, 2006, John Clute, "Jack Williamson: Father of Science Fiction."

Los Angeles Times, November 14, 2006, Dennis McLellan, "Jack Williamson, Pioneering Science Fiction Writer, Dies at 98."

New York Times, November 14, 2006, Margalit Fox, "Jack Williamson, 98, an Author Revered in Science Fiction Field," p. C15.

Portales News-Tribune (Portales, NM), November 11, 2006, Karl Terry, "Sci-fi Legend Williamson Dies"; November 17, 2006, Karl Terry, "Local Writer Remembered."*

Robert Wise

(The Kobal Collection/The Picture Desk, Inc.)

■ Personal

Born September 10, 1914, in Winchester, IN; died of heart failure, September 14, 2005, in Los Angeles, CA; married Patricia Doyle, 1942; married Millicent Franklin, 1977; children: (first marriage) Robert E.; (stepdaughter) Pamela. *Education:* Studied journalism at Franklin College.

■ Career

RKO Studios, Hollywood, CA, assistant editor, 1933, editor, beginning 1939; took over direction of *The Curse of the Cat People,* 1944; independent producer for Mirisch Corporation, 1959, and for Fox, 1963. Director of films, including: *The Body Snatcher,* 1945, *Born to Kill,* 1947, *Blood on the Moon,* 1948, *The Day the Earth Stood Still,* 1951, *Executive Suite,* 1954, *Run Silent, Run Deep,* 1958, *I Want to Live,* 1958, *West Side Story,* 1961, *The Haunting,* 1963, *The Sound of Music,* 1965, *The Sand Pebbles,* 1966, *The Andromeda Strain,* 1970, *The Hindenburg,* 1975, and *Star Trek: The Motion Picture,* 1979.

■ Awards, Honors

Academy Award nomination, 1941, for best editing; Academy Award for best direction (with Jerome Robbins), for *West Side Story,* 1961; Academy Award for best direction, and Directors Award, Directors Guild of America, both 1965, both for *The Sound of Music;* Irving G. Thalberg Memorial Academy Award, 1966; D.W. Griffith Award, Directors Guild of America, 1988.

■ Writings

(With Richard L. Bare) *The Film Director: A Practical Guide to Motion Picture and Television Techniques,* IDG Worldwide Books, 1973.

(With Sergio Leemann) *Robert Wise on His Films: From Editing Room to Director's Chair* (interviews), Silman-James Press (Los Angeles, CA), 1995.

■ Adaptations

All of Wise's films are available on DVD.

■ Sidelights

Best known as the director of the musical smash hits *West Side Story* and *The Sound of Music* in the 1960s, director Robert Wise was also known for directing a number of classic science fiction and

A film still from Wise's 1951 science fiction classic *The Day the Earth Stood Still,* **showing the alien visitor.** (CORBIS.)

horror films, including *The Curse of the Cat People, The Day the Earth Stood Still, The Haunting* (based on Shirley Jackson's novel *The Haunting of Hill House*), and *Star Trek: The Motion Picture.* Early in his career, he also served as editor on the landmark film *Citizen Kane.* Writing in *Robert Wise on His Films: From Editing Room to Director's Chair,* Sergio Leemann summed up Wise with these words: "He is a film storyteller par excellence." "Wise," according to Jonathan Stryker in an article for *The Horror Express,* "is one of the best directors this country has ever produced."

An Accidental Film Career

Wise was born September 10, 1914, in Winchester, Indiana, and grew up in the town of Connersville, in the east-central part of the state. His father was a meatpacker. As a youth Wise went to the movies as often as four times a week, but his first dream was to become a sportswriter. After graduating from high school in 1929 he enrolled at Indiana's Franklin College to study journalism, but the family funds ran out during the Great Depression of the early 1930s. Unable to find a job at home, he took advantage of a family connection in one of the few industries that was hiring: his brother was an accountant at RKO Studios in Hollywood, so he went to work there in 1933 as a porter, carrying cans of film from one part of the building to another.

By spending plenty of time in RKO's cutting rooms, Wise got a practical course in film editing. He eventually found a place in the growing industry for his talents. His first film credit was as assistant editor on the film *Stage Door* in 1937, and by 1939 he was serving as editor on such major productions as a remake of *The Hunchback of Notre Dame,* starring Charles Laughton as the unfortunate Quasimodo. He was still considered a fresh face, however, when he met Orson Welles in 1941, as Welles was laying plans for *Citizen Kane,* his ambitious, lightly fictionalized biography of muckraking newspaper publisher William Randolph Hearst.

Works with Orson Welles

Wise's inexperience attracted Welles; he wanted someone "young and uninfluenced by tradition," according to a writer in the *Independent.* Wise was hired as editor, and the relationship was mutually beneficial. The clarity and intensity of *Citizen Kane* shaped Wise's approach to filmmaking. "There are a few things I'm sure I learned from him," Wise was quoted as saying in the *Independent.* "One was

to try and keep the energy level high, the movement forward in the telling of the story. Another was the use of deep-focus photography. I've shot many of my films, particularly in black-and-white, with wide-angle lenses, so we could have somebody close in the foreground and still have things in the background in focus." As for Welles, although he later tried to claim credit for much of the editing himself, he benefited from a superb job by Wise; others on the set confirmed Wise's key role. Wise earned a 1941 Academy Award nomination for best editing.

Wise and Welles reunited for Welles's next film, *The Magnificent Ambersons,* but this time the collaboration ended less happily. Set in Indianapolis, the film was a complex family drama with an unsympathetic central character, and it tested badly among preview audiences. Executives at the financially troubled RKO panicked. They demanded that the original 148-minute film be cut by about an hour. Since Welles was in South America on another film project, they brought in Wise to cut the film and direct several new scenes that clarified the abbreviated story. An outraged Welles felt that Wise had butchered the film, but Wise maintained that he had done the best he could under the circumstances.

Robert Wise directing the 1961 musical *West Side Story*.
(The Kobal Collection/The Picture Desk, Inc.)

Natalie Wood and Richard Beymer in a scene from the 1961 musical *West Side Story,* **directed by Wise.** (The Kobal Collection/ The Picture Desk, Inc.)

He was partially vindicated by the later reputation of *The Magnificent Ambersons* as one of the greatest of all American films, even in its shortened state. "In terms of a work of art, I grant you Orson's original film was better," Wise conceded years later, according to the *Times* of London. "But we were faced with the realities of what the studio was demanding."

Helms a Horror Film

Studio executives next called on Wise to salvage *The Curse of the Cat People* after the project's original director, Gunther von Fritsch, was fired and the film was behind schedule. A sequel to the successful horror film *The Cat People*, produced by Val Lewton, *The Curse of the Cat People* is an atmospheric film with little violence but with a strong sense of psychological unease. Lonely six-year-old Amy begins to see a ghostly friend, a lovely woman, in the family's garden. Her parents are distraught and try to convince her that she is only imagining her friend. But the girl insists that the woman looks like her father's first wife, whom she has seen in a photograph. Whether Amy is seeing a real ghost or only imagining is never completely answered. A reviewer for *Moria: The Science Fiction, Horror & Fantasy Film Review* found that the film is directed with "great subtlety and finesse."

Val Lewton called on Wise to direct 1945's *The Body Snatcher*, starring Boris Karloff as a grave robber in 1830s Scotland. Karloff supplies corpses to a doctor who is conducting medical research. The laws of the time forbid the use of corpses for such purposes, no matter how beneficial such research may be for medical science. When it becomes difficult to continue robbing graves for the corpses, the unscrupulous Karloff turns to murder to get the bodies. He drags the doctor into the scheme, knowing that he will keep his silence. The film also starred Bela Lugosi as the doctor's porter. It would be the last film in which Karloff and Lugosi would costar. According to a critic of *The Body Snatcher* in *Moria: The Science Fiction, Horror, and Fantasy Film Review*: "Wise demonstrates a considerable mastery of the trademark Lewtonian effect of suggested horror." Writing in *Robert Wise on His Films*, Wise remembered working with producer Val Lewton: "Val was tremendously supportive to those of us who were just starting as directors. He never interfered with you on the set, he was only helpful."

Wise continued to direct a variety of films over the next few years, but most of his films were "B-movies," low-budget productions designed for quick consumption at neighborhood cinemas in the days before television. In 1950, he was fired from RKO Studios after Howard Hughes bought the company. He moved on to 20th Century Fox where, in 1951, he directed one of his most highly regarded films, the science-fiction thriller *The Day the Earth Stood Still*. The film tells of an alien visitor named Klaatu who arrives in a flying saucer and warns humans of the dangers of war. Paradoxically, he threatens to destroy Earth unless humans stop their violence. Accompanied by an indestructible robot named Gort, and able to come back from the dead by using advanced technology, the alien is unable to change the opinions of the people he confronts. The film has been taken as everything from a commentary on the Cold War to a religious allegory. Wise himself was ambiguous about the significance of the alien, but enjoyed the film's message. He explained: "The whole purpose of it was for Klaatu to deliver that warning at the end. I feel very strongly in favor of what the movie says. It's very much of a forerunner in its warning about atomic warfare, and it shows that we must all learn to get along together." David Litton, writing for *Movie Eye,* called the film "an above-average science fiction escapade that achieves greatness through its storytelling and broad canvas of thought." In a review posted on the *Edinburgh University Film Society Web site,* David Kuhne called *The Day the Earth Stood Still* "an intelligent movie that makes you think not only about the nuclear industry, but also about xenophobia and the abuse of science. . . . Robert Wise directed this film with spirit."

With *Run Silent, Run Deep,* Wise told the story of an American submarine in the South Pacific during World War II. Based on a novel written by Captain Edward Beach, President Dwight Eisenhower's Navy aide, the film stars Clark Gable as commander of the submarine *U.S.S. Nerka* and Burt Lancaster as his lieutenant. The *Nerka* has been sent out after a Japanese destroyer that has been sinking U.S. submarines, including one previously commanded by Gable. When an obsessed Gable takes what Lancaster and other crew members deem to be risky steps to sink their target, conflict develops. The U.S. Navy supplied an actual submarine for the film's interior scenes. A critic for *Channel 4.com* noted that "50s classic *Run Silent, Run Deep* set the standard for all underwater films to follow." Bosley Crowther, writing in the *New York Times,* concluded that *Run Silent, Run Deep* "has more than drama. It has the hard, cold ring of truth."

Creates a Musical Milestone

In the early 1960s, Wise was to achieve lasting fame for directing two of cinema history's most popular musicals. Wise was selected, along with choreographer Jerome Robbins, to direct the big-budget film adaptation of the Broadway musical *West Side Story* in 1961. The two directors worked through the kinks of the difficult dual-helm arrangement, with Wise supervising the dramatic scenes and Robbins directing the musical numbers. When the film fell behind schedule, though, Robbins was removed in what Wise called "a very uncomfortable, emotional, and difficult time for everybody." Wise, working with Robbins's assistants, succeeded in bringing the film together, and it became a major commercial success.

Claire Bloom and Julie Harris in a scene from Wise's 1963 horror film *The Haunting*. (MGM/The Kobal Collection/The Picture Desk, Inc.)

Julie Andrews and Robert Wise on set of the film *The Sound of Music*. (20th Century Fox/The Kobal Collection/The Picture Desk, Inc.)

Wise found that adapting a play to film has its own unique problems: "Putting a stage musical on the screen represents challenges. When you're in the live theater, . . . you're once-removed from reality. The screen is a very real medium and doesn't take kindly to stylization. One of the things we struggled with most in *West Side Story* was how to take all the highly stylized aspects of it and deal with them effectively in the reality of the screen. On the stage, you can have characters break out of a dialogue scene and go right into song and dance and you don't feel a twinge of embarassment, but you can feel that on the screen. On the stage, the turf that the kids fight over were stylized sets. There was no way I could realistically open the film without opening it in the real New York streets."

West Side Story adapts William Shakespeare's *Romeo and Juliet* as a love story between a boy and a girl who are members of rival street gangs in New York City. The Jets and the Sharks face off in a fight over turf on the city's west side. Although the gangs agree to a fist fight between two of their members to settle their differences, rather than engage in widespread war, the proposed fight ends in a knifing that leaves a boy dead. Amid the violence, the doomed love story between Maria, a member of the Sharks, and Tony, a member of the Jets, plays itself out. The fight scenes are choreographed as elaborate dances. Writing in *Entertainment Weekly Online*, Scott Brown claimed that the film's dances—"the jagged formations, the impassioned high-kick detonations, the off-balance acrobatics ricocheting off hard urban angles—set an exhilarating sensory tempo we've been dancing and fighting and bullet-dodging to ever since." "From start to end," wrote a critic for the *Montreal Film Journal*, "I was dazzled by *West*

Side Story, which blends somber social drama, flashy musical numbers and the most timeless of love stories." In the *Chicago Sun-Times Online,* Roger Ebert concluded: "*West Side Story* remains a landmark of musical history."

Films a Family Classic

Wise won an Academy Award for *West Side Story,* sharing the Best Director honor with choreographer Robbins. The film also won for Best Picture. That track record made him an obvious choice to helm another musical adaptation, *The Sound of Music,* the 1965 Julie Andrews vehicle that became one of the top-grossing films of all time. Even today, the film ranks among the top five moneymakers in cinema history. *The Sound of Music* is loosely based on a real-life story. It was originally a nonfiction book, then a German-language film, and then a Broadway play written by Rodgers and Hammerstein. The film follows the Broadway version closely, although

removing a few songs and adding a few new ones. Set in Austria just before the outbreak of World War II, the story centers on Maria, played by Andrews, who leaves a nunnery to serve as governess to a widowed naval officer's seven children. Maria transforms the children's harsh environment into one of carefree fun, something that initially leads to conflict with their father, Captain von Trapp. In the end, Maria marries the Captain and the family flees Austria after it has been taken over by the Nazis. "We thought we had a good chance at a successful film," Wise later recalled. "but I don't think any of us anticipated that *The Sound of Music* was going to go through the roof like it did. It's a story about love, family, and togetherness. If there's one thing that people have in common in this world, it is the love for one another in terms of the family. That's the enduring quality of this story." "Wise's direction is both playful and gracious," wrote a critic for the *Montreal Film Journal,* "and the movie hardly ever loses its grip on the audience. . . . The 174 minute running time worried me, but this wasn't an issue,

A scene in the Austrian mountains with Julie Andrews and the von Trapp children from the 1965 Wise film *The Sound of Music.* (The Kobal Collection/The Picture Desk, Inc.)

the movie just flew by." "Be prepared to be entertained from beginning to end," wrote Liz Burroughs of the *Edinburgh University Film Society Web site*, "by the unique combination of a strong and moving story, great acting and direction and a particularly impressive score." Wise won an Academy Award for best direction, and the Directors Award of the Directors Guild of America, both for his work on *The Sound of Music.*

A Most Haunted House

In between filming *West Side Story* and *The Sound of Music,* Wise directed an adaptation of the Shirley Jackson novel *The Haunting of Hill House.* Best known for her short story "The Lottery," a staple in anthologies for some fifty years, Jackson wrote a deeply disturbing ghost story with *The Haunting of Hill House.* Adapted as *The Haunting,* the story tells of a group of paranormal investigators who move into an abandoned mansion, Hill House, that has been the scene of mysterious happenings and even deaths. Led by Dr. John Markway, a college professor, the group includes a psychic, a member of the family that owns the house, and Eleanor, who has experienced poltergeist activities. From the beginning, Eleanor displays a strange affinity for Hill House. A mousy woman who has spent much of her life caring for her sickly mother, she feels that she belongs there. Eerie messages written on a wall, mysterious cold spots, and nocturnal bangings convince the team that the house is haunted. In the end, Eleanor's inability to leave Hill House leads to tragedy. According to the critic for *Moria: The Science Fiction, Horror & Fantasy Film Review:* "The shocks that Robert Wise crafts in *The Haunting* are some of the most sophisticated and finely constructed ever placed on film." Speaking to Stryker, Wise explained why he wanted to direct the film: "It was a desire to go back to my beginnings, actually, back to the days of *The Curse of the Cat People* and the Val Lewton period and so forth." He also admitted: "I've always been rather intrigued by the supernatural, or rather the possibility of the supernatural. I've never had a psychic experience, although I have to believe that there is something out there beyond what we can just see, feel, touch, and smell. So, that's what really made me interested in it."

Returns to Science Fiction

Wise's later projects included the 1971 virus-peril thriller *The Andromeda Strain.* Based on the Michael Crichton thriller, the story begins when the residents of a little desert town in the Southwest begin dying after a NASA space satellite crashes nearby. A team of scientists is rushed in to investigate. They discover that the satellite, which has been on an interplanetary mission, has brought back an unknown, deadly virus that seems unstoppable. The scientists have a limited amount of time to discover a way to control the virus before it wipes out mankind. "I liked the today-ness of the story," Wise remarked, "the fact that it dealt with technology and space." Tony Mastroianni of the *Cleveland Press* agreed with the film's contemporary feel: "The story sounds as if it could happen." Graeme Clark, in a review for *The Spinning Image,* wrote: "Cleverly assembled, the film builds towards two revelations, both pointing the finger at humanity being the biggest threat to itself. . . . With its cold, businesslike look and a nice line in irony, *The Andromeda Strain* will satisfy you if you're after an original twist on a familiar story."

Wise directed another popular thriller in 1975, *The Hindenburg,* a story based on the real-life crash of a German zeppelin in New Jersey in 1937. The tragedy effectively ended the use of zeppelins as transportation vehicles. In the film, Nazi agents are worried about a rumor that an underground resistance movement has planted a bomb on board the giant airship. George C. Scott plays the military intelligence officer assigned to oversee the investigation. The many suspicious passengers aboard the Hindenburg keep Scott busy throughout the Transatlantic flight from Germany to America. "The film is stylishly directed by Robert Wise . . ., with a keen eye to accuracy of detail," according to Pablo Vargas in a review for the *Spinning Image.* "He has also made the decision to overcome the predictability of the story by filming it as a 'whodunnit' mystery." Vargas concluded: "*The Hindenburg* is probably the most beautiful, elegant and ambitious disaster movie ever made."

In 1979 Wise was tasked with bringing the popular *Star Trek* television series to the big screen. Few television series adapt well to film. Wise knew that he faced a challenge. In addition, the show's creator, Gene Roddenberry, and several of the actors, had their own ideas about how the film should be made. Wise explained: "Gene Roddenberry always had his own versions; and the actors, especially Leonard Nimoy and William Shatner, had their own concepts about what the scenes should be like as related to their established characters. It was a three-ring circus in some ways. At the last few days of shooting, the scenes were being rewritten so much that I was getting three sets of changes a day." The resulting film, *Star Trek: The Motion Picture,* successfully brought the television program to the big screen and was a popular hit with fans and critics alike.

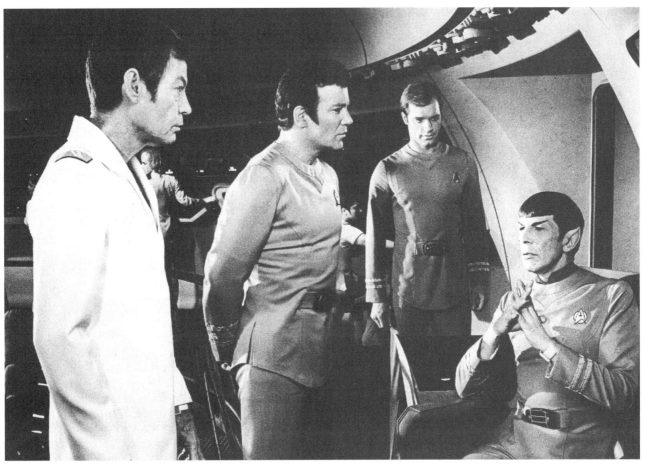

The first of the "Star Trek" films, 1979's *Star Trek: The Motion Picture* starred Deforest Kelley, William Shatner, and Leonard Nimoy. (The Kobal Collection / Paramount / The Picture Desk, Inc.)

If you enjoy the films of Robert Wise, you may also want to check out the following films:

Forbidden Planet, directed by Fred M. Wilcox; *The King and I,* directed by Walter Lang; *The Innocents,* directed by Jack Clayton; and *Fiddler on the Roof,* directed by Norman Jewison.

"The film's chief virtue for fans of the series," according to Mastroianni, "is its reunion of the original cast after a decade, picking up the old relationships and rivalries, repeating lines of dialog that have become permanently associated with some of the characters." Garth Franklin, writing in *Strange Horizons,* argued that Wise's effort was unlike the television program, and more serious than later films in the series. "The first Trek film adventure is unlike anything that came before or since for the franchise. The original series before was a low budget, high adventure camp western in space. The movies and spin-off series afterward are more tightly written adventure/dramas combining action, humour and stories with meaning—though not too much. *The Motion Picture,* on the other hand, is the most expensive, epic, deep and overall pure sci-fi effort the franchise ever did."

Wise celebrated his ninety-first birthday in the late summer of 2005, but had a heart attack later that week. He died of heart failure at the University of California—Los Angeles Medical Center on September 14, 2005. Wise will be remembered for the sheer variety of his films—from science fiction to musicals, and from horror to drama—and for his ability to create crowd-pleasing works that continue to entertain audiences. "Through the wide range of his work," wrote an essayist for the *International Dictionary of Films and Filmmakers,* "Wise proved himself to be a highly versatile director." In nearly all of his projects, "Wise invariably gave audiences strong, intelligent stories with fine casts, made in a style that was flawlessly lucid," wrote Michael Wilmington in the *Chicago Tribune.*

■ Biographical and Critical Sources

BOOKS

Carr, Charmian, *Forever Lies!: A Memoir of "The Sound of Music,"* Penguin (New York, NY), 2001.

Hirsch, Julia Antopol, *The Sound of Music: The Making of America's Favorite Movie,* foreword by Robert Wise, Contemporary Books(Chicago, IL), 1995.

International Dictionary of Films and Filmmakers, 4th edition, St. James Press (Detroit, MI), 2000.

Kantor, Bernard and others, editors, *Directors at Work,* [New York, NY], 1970.

Keenan, Richard, *The Films of Robert Wise,* Scarecrow Press, 2007.

Wise, Robert, and Sergio Leemann, *Robert Wise on His Films: From Editing Room to Director's Chair* (interviews), Silman-James Press (Los Angeles, CA), 1995.

PERIODICALS

Action, July/August, 1971, "Impressions of Russia."

American Cinematographer, January, 1976, "The Production of 'The Hindenburg'"; July, 1976, "Robert Wise Talks about 'The New Hollywood'"; March, 1980, "An AFI Seminar with Robert Wise and Milton Krasner ASC."

Bright Lights, July, 1993, C.J. Kutner, "Robert Wise. Part One: The Noir Years"; fall, 1993, C.J.Kutner, "Robert Wise. Part Two: Life at the Top"; August, 2003, Robert von Dassanowsky, "An Unclaimed Country: The Austrian Image in American Film and the Sociopolitics of *The Sound of Music.*"

Cinefantastique, Numbers 4-5, 1997, F.C. Szebin, "The Sound of Screaming."

Cleveland Press, March 25, 1965, Toni Mastroianni, "*Sound of Music* Is Great Family Fare"; May 15, 1971, Toni Mastroianni, "*The Andromeda Strain* Is Superior Science Fiction"; December 22, 1979, Toni Mastroianni, "*Star Trek*—Motion Picture Is Bigger, Not Better."

Dialogue on Film, Volume 2, number 1, 1972, special Robert Wise issue.

Filmnews, July, 1995, "The Past Pays Off" (interview).

Films and Filming, November, 1977, R. Appelbaum, "Audrey Rose: In Search of a Soul."

Films in Review, January, 1963, Samuel Stark, "Robert Wise."

Focus on Film, winter, 1972, Ruy Nogueira, "Robert Wise at RKO"; spring, 1973, Ruy Nogueira, "Robert Wise at Fox"; autumn, 1973, Ruy Nogueira and Allen Eyles, "Robert Wise Continued"; autumn, 1974, Ruy Nogueira, "Robert Wise to Date."

Millimeter, November, 1975, P. Stamelman, "Robert Wise and *The Hindenburg*"; March, 1989, L. Vinecnzi, "Robert Wise" (interview).

Monthly Film Bulletin, November, 1979, "Time and Again" (interview).

New York Times, March 28, 1958, Bosley Crowther, review of *Run SIlent, Run Deep.*

Scarlet Street, Number 25, 1997, K.G. Shinnick, interview with Wise.

Tucson Weekly, July 11, 1996, Stacey Richter, review of *The Day the Earth Stood Still.*

ONLINE

Channel 4.com, http://www.channel4.com/ (November 7, 2007), review of *Run Silent, Run Deep.*

Chicago Sun-Times Online, http://rogerebert.suntimes.com/ (April 9, 1971), Roger Ebert, review of *The Andromeda Strain;* (February 15, 2004), Roger Ebert, review of *West Side Story.*

Classic Horror, http://www.classic-horror.com/ (January 6, 2001), Brandt Sponseller, review of *The Haunting.*

Dark Horizons, http://www.darkhorizons.com/ (May 8, 2007), Garth Franklin, review of *Star Trek: The Motion Picture.*

Edinburgh University Film Society Web site, http://www.eufs.org.uk/ (March 5, 2001), David Kuhne, review of *The Day the Earth Stood Still;* (May 8, 2007), Liz Burroughs, review of *The Sound of Music;* (May 8, 2007), Keith H Brown, review of *Curse of the Cat People.*

Entertainment Weekly Online, http://www.ew.com/ (March 31, 2003), Scott Brown, review of *West Side Story.*

Horror Express, http://www.horrorexpress.com/ (May 8, 2007), review of *The Haunting,* and Jonathan Stryker, "Robert Wise: The Protean Director," interview.

Montreal Film Journal, http://www.montrealfilmjournal.com/ (May 8, 2007), reviews of *West Side Story* and *The Sound of Music.*

Moria: The Science Fiction, Horror & Fantasy Film Review, http://www.moria.co.nz/ (May 8, 2007), reviews of *The Haunting, The Body Snatcher,* and *Curse of the Cat People.*

Movie Eye, http://www.movieeye.com/ (March 26, 2003), David Litton, review of *The Day the Earth Stood Still.*

Spinning Image, http://www.thespinningimage.co.uk/ (May 8, 2007), Graeme Clark, review of *The Andromeda Strain;* (November 7, 2007), Mario Vargas, review of *The Hindenburg.*

OBITUARIES

PERIODICALS

Chicago Tribune, September 16, 2005, Michael Wilmington, obituary, Section 3, p. 9.

Daily Telegraph (London, England), September 16, 2005.

Daily Variety, September 16, 2005.

Entertainment Weekly, September 30, 2005, p. 21.

Herald (Glasgow, Scotland), September 17, 2005.

Independent (London, England), September 16, 2005.

Los Angeles Times, September 15, 2005, p. B10.

New York Times, September 16, 2005, p. A25.

Times (London, England), September 16, 2005, p. 74.

Washington Post, September 16, 2005, p. B7.*

Author/Artist Index

The following index gives the number of the volume in
which an author/artist's biographical sketch appears: